The Sound Handbook

Today we inhabit a media world of sound that is truly interdisciplinary, in which the old boundaries no longer apply. The emerging practitioners of today and tomorrow face a multimedia environment in which their skills and understanding must be equal to the test of emerging platforms, technologies and genres. Be it radio, film, theatre, games, the internet – or, indeed, increasingly the world of the gallery and museum – the common denominator will always be sound. The challenge is to retain, through the dazzling technical opportunities, a sense of understanding for the role sound plays in the content itself. For students and their teachers alike, there has never been a more significant moment to grasp the opportunities afforded by these exciting changes and, crucially, to apply the theories underpinning the practice across the various fields. Tim Crook has written an important and much-needed book, and its arrival on our shelves has come at a highly appropriate time.

Professor Seán Street
Bournemouth University

The Sound Handbook maps theoretical and practical connections between the creation and study of sound across the multimedia spectrum of film, radio, music, sound art, websites, animation and computer games entertainment, and stage theatre.

Using an interdisciplinary approach, Tim Crook explores the technologies, philosophies and cultural issues involved in making and experiencing sound, investigating soundscape debates and providing both intellectual and creative production information. The book covers the history, theory and practice of sound and includes practical production projects and a glossary of key terms.

The Sound Handbook is supported by a companion website, www.routledge.com/textbooks/crook, signposted throughout the book, with further practical and theoretical resources dedicated to bridging the creation and study of sound across professional platforms and academic disciplines.

Tim Crook is Senior Lecturer and Head of Radio at Goldsmiths, University of London. He has worked professionally in radio, theatre, television and film as a journalist, producer, director and sound designer for more than 30 years. He is the author of *Comparative Media Law and Ethics* (2009), *Radio Drama: Theory and Practice* (1999) and *International Radio Journalism: History, Theory and Practice* (1997).

Media Practice

Edited by James Curran, Goldsmiths College, University of London

The *Media Practice* handbooks are comprehensive resource books for students of media and journalism, and for anyone planning a career as a media professional. Each handbook combines a clear introduction to understanding how the media works with practical information about the structure, processes and skills involved in working in today's media industries, providing not only a guide on 'how to do it' but also a critical reflection on contemporary media practice.

The Advertising Handbook
3rd edition
Helen Powell, Jonathan Hardy, Sarah Hawkin and Iain MacRury

The Alternative Media Handbook
Kate Coyer, Tony Dowmunt and Alan Fountain

The Cyberspace Handbook
Jason Whittaker

The Documentary Handbook
Peter Lee-Wright

The Fashion Handbook
Tim Jackson and David Shaw

The Graphic Communication Handbook
Simon Downs

The Magazines Handbook
2nd edition
Jenny McKay

The Music Industry Handbook
Paul Rutter

The New Media Handbook
Andrew Dewdney and Peter Ride

The Newspapers Handbook
4th edition
Richard Keeble

The Photography Handbook
2nd edition
Terence Wright

The Public Relations Handbook
4th edition
Alison Theaker

The Radio Handbook
3rd edition
Carole Fleming

The Sound Handbook
Tim Crook

The Television Handbook
4th edition
Jeremy Orlebar

The Sound Handbook

Tim Crook

Routledge
Taylor & Francis Group

LONDON AND NEW YORK

First published 2012
by Routledge
2 Park Square, Milton Park, Abingdon, Oxon OX14 4RN

Simultaneously published in the USA and Canada
by Routledge
711 Third Avenue, New York, NY 10017

Routledge is an imprint of the Taylor & Francis Group, an informa business

British Library Cataloguing in Publication Data
A catalogue record for this book is available from the British Library

Library of Congress Cataloging in Publication Data
Crook, Tim, 1959–
  The sound handbook / Tim Crook.
    p. cm. — (Media practice)
  Includes bibliographical references and index.
  1. Sound—Recording and reproducing. 2. Radio broadcasting—
  Sound effects. 3. Motion pictures—Sound effects. 4. Television
  broadcasting—Sound effects. I. Title.
  TK7881.4.C7455 2012
  621.389'3—dc23   2011023599

ISBN: 978–0–415–55150–2 (hbk)
ISBN: 978–0–415–55152–6 (pbk)
ISBN: 978–0–203–15320–8 (ebk)

Typeset in Helvetica and Avant Garde
by Florence Production Ltd, Stoodleigh, Devon

Printed and bound in Great Britain by
TJ International Ltd, Padstow, Cornwall

Contents

List of figures   vi
List of tables   ix
Preface   xi
Acknowledgements   xiii

1 Sound philosophies   1

2 Sound technologies   90

3 Sound practice and theory in radio   120

4 Sound practice and theory in stage theatre   158

5 Sound practice and theory in music   165

6 Sound practice and theory in film   171

7 Sound practice and theory in animation and games   176

8 Sound practice and theory in art exhibition and
   installation   181

9 Sound practice and theory in Internet broadcasting
   and podcasting   186

Glossary   193
Bibliography   220
Index   239

Figures

While every effort has been made to trace copyright holders and obtain permission, this has not always been possible in all cases. If any proper acknowledgement has not been made, we would invite copyright holders to inform us of the oversight.

1.1   'Grand opera by radio inaugurated as regular program of Chicago company. Mary Garden . . . listening as Miss Edith Mason . . . sings into the radio transmitter for the first regular radio program of operas' (*c*14 November 1921, Underwood & Underwood. Repository: Library of Congress Prints and Photographs Division (LoC P&P). Reproduction Number: LC-USZ62-73232 (b&w film copy neg.). Images submitted for US Library of Congress copyright by Underwood & Underwood are in the public domain). From singing birds to singing opera singers in Chicago 1921. Musical theatre proved to be commercially viable and very popular in the early years of US radio   3

1.2   'Tommy Dorsey (top right) interviews the English pigeon, Beryl Davis, for his first disc jockey stint, with such names as Georgie Auld, Ray McKinley, Mary Lou Williams, Josh White and others visible in the background' (William P. Gottlieb 1947, 'Picture views of music world personalities', *Down Beat*, 14(21): 20. Repository: LoC P&P, William P. Gottlieb Collection (DLC) 99-401005. In accordance with the wishes of William Gottlieb, the photographs in this collection entered into the public domain on 16 February 2010). Dorsey interviews Beryl Davis at WMCA in America in 1947. This sophisticated on-air broadcast studio features close microphone interviewing between presenter/DJ and celebrity guest in terms of foreground sound and background sound

and potential focus on the performance of singers and other guests
to the rear. Sound absorbent panels and clear glass panelling for the
producer and studio manager's control room are also visible. The
general rule in sound production is that the more busy and
over-populated soundtracks tend to generate a greater intensity of
dramatic effect through silence   13

1.3   'Cripplld [*sic*] by fall while putting up aerial this radio fan still "listens
       in"' (18 April 1922, Underwood & Underwood. Repository: LoC
       P&P. Reproduction Number: LC-USZ62-134576 (b&w film copy neg.).
       Images submitted for US Library of Congress copyright by
       Underwood & Underwood are in the public domain). Sound
       entertainment was so alluring that in the early days of radio people
       would risk their lives to achieve a decent signal. This is 1922 and
       Lester Picker is lying in bed wearing earphones connected to a
       shortwave radio; he is convalescing after breaking his back when
       he fell 55 feet while erecting an aerial for his radio   15

1.4   'Radio in a Straw Hat' (Source: Nationaal Archief/Spaarnestad
       Photo/Het Leven/Fotograaf onbekend, SFA022812804). Radio in
       a straw hat in the 1920s – an anticipation of the possibilities of
       portable listening   23

1.5   'The shut-in's Sunday service' (*c*28 March 1923, Clark Music Co.
       Repository: LoC P&P. Reproduction Number: LC-USZ62-134575
       (b&w film copy neg.)). In the early days of sound broadcasting radio
       was about young people enjoying storytelling across the airwaves,
       and this elegant American woman is listening on headphones to live
       radio in the splendour of her Art Deco drawing room in 1923   78

2.1   Historical artefacts in the storage of sound (Photo: copyright
       Marja Giejgo). Reel to reel tape, cassette, 5 and a quarter inch
       'floppy disk', mini-disc, hard disk for laptop computer, SD card
       and mini-SD card   91

2.2   Two condenser lapel microphones from American Audio Pocket
       Record on stereo boom (Photo: copyright Marja Giejgo). How budget
       equipment can be adapted to generate stereo sound fields: in this
       case the two omnidirectional microphones are positioned similarly to
       the position of somebody's ears and the pick-up field is more like
       the experience of hearing in the sense that sound is being received
       from all directions stereophonically   98

2.3   Zoom H1 Handy Stereo digital recorder on tripod (Photo: copyright
       Marja Giejgo). An example of a budget digital sound recorder.
       Its 2 gigabyte micro SD card can record more than thirty-three hours
       of broadcastable MP3 sound files, and it is the size of a small
       fingernail   102

2.4   Edirol R-OH9 digital sound recorder by Roland (Photo: copyright
       Marja Giejgo). The Edirol R-OH9 digital sound recorder, hand-sized,

with two inbuilt qualitative microphone capsules arranged for
coincidental stereo recording. Versatile and flexible with professional
standard recordings achieved through pressing of buttons and
simple positioning   103

3.1   Broadcasting House in Portland Place, Headquarters of the BBC,
completed in 1932 (Photo: copyright Tim Crook)   129

3.2   Mr J.C.W. Reith, Managing Director of the British Broadcasting
Company (C.A. Lewis 1924, *Broadcasting from Within*, London:
George Newnes, opposite p. 21). Reith, Managing Director of the
BBC from 1922–29, was then Director General until he left in 1937.
He is said to have founded the ethos of public service broadcasting
and advocated the 'brute force of monopoly'   146

4.1   The Three Witches in a rehearsal of *Macbeth* (Rudolf Arnheim 1936,
Radio, London: Faber & Faber, facing p. 145). Radio drama in
performance from the 1930s. The three witches of Shakespeare's
Macbeth, arms outstretched, scripts in the air seen from the
perspective of the microphone   159

4.2   Flight of steps in a new dramatic radio studio in Berlin in the 1930s
(Rudolf Arnheim 1936, *Radio*, London: Faber & Faber, facing p. 48).
Live radio drama needed to operate in spatiality and generate realistic
acoustics; not unlike the sound in modern stage theatre   162

6.1   Film crew for *Beyond the Forest* on location with the sound
recordist holding microphone suspended from boom, August 2010
(Photo: copyright Tim Crook)   173

8.1   'Circle of Sound Sculpture' by Dr Julian Henriques 2011
(Photo: copyright Tim Crook). The sound design is controlled by
complex logarithmic and geometrical computer digital design in
surround and transmitted through eight different speakers to
immerse visitors to the building who wander around for lectures
and meetings   182

Tables

1.1 A proposed critical matrix for an academic textual analysis of
sound   16

1.2 A comparison along with the functions and story moves that
underpin Propp's theory   48

1.3 An interface of the cross-disciplinary nature of this book's enquiry
into the practice as well as the theory of sound   82

2.1 The creative aims and objectives of the essential sound designers'
technological skill set   92

2.2 A practical guide to the operational possibilities of a competitively
priced digital audio recorder   99

2.3 Formats for reading sound   102

2.4 A summary of the standard technology and varieties of microphone
used in professional applications with an explanation of the
meaning of the technical specifications   106

2.5 Standard sound processing and editing tools (these are also
demonstrated by sound and video sequences on the book's
companion website)   112

3.1 A selection of audio programme-making sites where there is a
creative aesthetic and commitment to idealist and ideological
aspirations for communicating storytelling through sound   122

3.2 A variety of modern legal, quasi-legal and voluntary journalistic
codes   125

3.3 Recommended reading for the broad categories of skills acquisition
in radio/sound journalism, creative feature/documentary and radio
drama   135

3.4   *Talk Radio* and the cultural phenomenon of the 'Shock Jock':
       The intermedia connections and contestation about US talk radio
       representation, First Amendment freedom of expression, and
       irresponsible and violence-provoking propaganda   139
3.5   Some issues arising from the intersection between powerful
       individuality and institutional and cultural context   147
3.6   A profile of issues arising out of Radio Four's role as a media
       institution   148
3.7   Some of the issues arising out of BBC Radio Two's role as a
       media institution exercising considerable influence and
       communicational power   156

Preface

This book is intended to be a bridging and gateway text for the theory and practice of sound. It seeks to map recommended methods of producing sound for the ever-expanding and rich spheres of multimedia publication. I have also tried to write a guide for studying the academic theories that underpin the history and analysis of sound expression.

My intention is to report and celebrate existing publications, discourses and productions, primarily in English, and my analysis seeks to identify connections, synergies and meeting points. In a way I have been trying to mediate across an interdisciplinary and multidisciplinary dimension of discussion, debate and practice. The theoretical and practical passport is, simply, sound. I apologise unreservedly for any omission and unfamiliarity in respect of books, papers, articles and practices not mentioned. As Socrates once boldly admitted, I start by stating that I know nothing, and this means that I can never stop learning.

This handbook could be the beginning of your journey of discovery to find out how to produce qualitative sound for drama, documentary, journalism in radio, theatrical stage production, television and film, musical performance and recording, online Internet broadcasting and podcasting, animation, computer games and/or sound art installation.

I cannot claim to be comprehensive, but I can admit to being eclectic and enthusiastic. I hope that by the end of the book you may feel confident and interested in talking about the practical and theoretical common ground in the production and expression of sound in what had been seen previously as discrete media practice and academic disciplines. The attention and focus is not evenly distributed in the published book form as I felt there was a risk of producing a journey akin to wading across the River Plate, when sometimes there is greater merit in doing the rapids in the Colorado. Where some practice-theory combinations might appear thin in their treatment I have endeavoured to compensate with the companion website, which is becoming something of a trend in academic publishing and of which I am a great enthusiast. This means that the book intersects with a dynamic companion parallel of multimedia that is open access and strives to keep you as up-to-date as I can be. In the end I hope you will have been inspired to have a go at producing sound yourself in any of the media investigated.

Acknowledgements

There are hundreds of people who have provided invaluable advice, encouragement and help with this project and I express my eternal gratitude. They include the people I have worked with professionally and all the students I have had the privilege of teaching.

I would like to emphasise those responsible for the commissioning of, and encouragement and help with the writing of the book and the development of its companion resources. At Routledge they include Aileen Storry and Eileen Srebernik. At Goldsmiths they include James Curran, Neil Bull, Keith Waghorn and colleagues in the Department of Media and Communications, and my partner, Marja Giejgo, who is the web designer and manager of the cyberspace dimension of my educational publishing.

Also included are associate lecturers at Goldsmiths, Nikki Townley, Richard Shannon and Heather Bond, and sound teaching colleagues elsewhere in the British university world, including Seán Street, Rhys Davies, Richard Rudin, Richard Hand, Mary Traynor, Diane Kemp and Heather Purdey.

I also want to express enormous gratitude and respect for all of the artists, writers, producers, academics, poets and sound auteurs quoted and referred to in the text for the purposes of review, scholarship and academic analysis. Teaching and learning is an infinite journey of collaboration and inspiration and is a creation of ongoing past, present and future discussion and debate.

TEXT ACKNOWLEDGEMENTS

Excerpts from *Blue* © Derek Jarman 1993. Reproduced with kind permission.

CHAPTER 1

Sound philosophies

ROMANCING THE SOUND

I find that one of the most romantic expressions of sound in cinema takes place during the 1994 film *Shawshank Redemption*, about a banker sent to a brutal US penitentiary for a double murder he did not commit. The central character, Andrew 'Andy' Dufresne, being an educated man, achieves some redress from the horrors of his prison environment through a friendship with a black 'lifer' called Ellis 'Red' Redding, played by Morgan Freeman. He is also allowed to work in and develop the inmates' library while plying his banker's skills to money launder the personal fortunes of the corrupt Governor and his guards. Classical records and a gramophone player are donated along with thousands of new books.

One afternoon Andy locks a friendly guard in the toilet so he can hook up the gramophone to the prison's public address system and play the entire 'Duettino sull'aria' from Wolfgang Amadeus Mozart's *Marriage of Figaro*. One of the most beautiful duets from classical opera fills the ghastly chambers and yards of carceral existence to underline the maxim on the film's promotional poster 'Fear can hold you prisoner. Hope can set you free'. Sound symbolically fills the world of this film with the values of integrity, love, freedom and self-worth through melody and the harmonies of the human voice. The experience for the characters in the film (diegetic) and the audience outside of it (non-diegetic) is spatial.

The writer and director, Frank Darabont, enhances the poetics of this expression of combined sound and film art with a narrative speech from Red that has the quality of fine literature:

I have no idea to this day what those two Italian ladies were singing about. The truth is, I don't want to know. Some things are best left unsaid. I like to think they were singing about something so beautiful it can't be expressed in words, and makes your heart ache because of it. I tell you those voices soared higher and farther than anybody in a grey place dares to dream. It was like some beautiful bird flapped into our drab little cage and made those walls dissolve away. And for the briefest of moments every last man at Shawshank felt free.

(Darabont 1994)

It struck me when working as a drama workshop leader in prison environments how the interior acoustics appeared deliberately or culturally architectured to ensure a harsh and hard resonance. The lack of carpets, curtains and soft panelling battered human speech and sonic existence. It seemed that the existential being of imprisonment was as much an issue of sound as visual ugliness and brutality and a confinement from nature and the rest of society. The early regime in Canada's most notorious penitentiary, the Oakalla Prison Farm in British Columbia, deprived its inmates of music, media and the basic human right to communicate with each other: 'Strict silence must be observed in all parts of the Gaol. No conversation between prisoners will be allowed except by special permission of the Gaoler under whose charge they are' (quoted in Andersen 1994:19).

The sequence from *Shawshank Redemption* offers many opportunities for critical discussion and argument about the function and significance of the sound. Music theory is engaged with respect to the aesthetic and social development of live opera music to recorded and played-back interaction with audiences. Film theory is engaged in respect of the symbolic use of sound with visual narrative, and the discipline of film studies is interested in the balance and place of this classical recording played back diegetically within the fictional environment of the film and the overlapping multi-tracking of the composed and Oscar-nominated soundtrack by Thomas Newman, heard non-diegetically by the audience.

The sound sequence might be effective as audio drama were it stripped of its moving visual association. Furthermore, the partnership, symbiosis and tension between film production and narrative in the history of radio drama is a matter of extensive cultural studies debate. *Lux Hollywood Radio Theatre* promoted the film industry, and the film industry in partnership with a soap manufacturer funded and promoted the radio industry. The use of sound by Orson Welles in his 1940 film *Citizen Kane* was informed by the development of his art of sound narrative in the *Mercury Theatre on the Air* radio drama series broadcast by CBS from 1938.

The social and political symbolism inherent in the *Shawshank Redemption* 'Duettino' metaphor and articulated commentary by the character Red raises debates central to sociology and criminology. My brief discussion of how Jeremy Bentham's idea of the surveillant penal panopticon can encompass the dimension of sound and silence chimes with the content of Michel Foucault's seminal text *Discipline and*

Punish. The hard interior acoustics of prison buildings attack the inmates with 360° spatiality. The imposition of silence and disembodying of the voices of the prisoners is equally all-enveloping in terms of sensation and perception. Critical analysis of sound discourse interrogates silence and noise in terms of aesthetics and social, cultural and symbolic communication.

I would venture to suggest that at the time of writing, the role, significance and meaning of sound is gaining in prominence and attention across popular culture as well as academia. Michael Wood in his BBC television and documentary series *The Story of India* and the accompanying book argued that the mysterious chanting of mantras in the performing ritual rites to the god of fire by Nambudiri brahmins had its roots in the sounds of prehistory:

> When experts analysed recordings of the mantras they were mystified. The patterns had no analogue in human culture. Not even music in the end was helpful, although mantras do have refrains, cycles and triplets. The breakthrough was only made possible by the development of computer technology. Patterns of mantras from the twelve-day Agni ritual recorded in 1975 were put on to a computer, and computer analysis showed that the nearest analogue of these sound sequences was birdsong. An astonishing conclusion might follow: the possibility that the performance of such patterns of sounds is older than human language, a remnant of a pre-linguistic stage when sound was used in a purely syntactical or ritual manner. *Homo sapiens*, it is now suspected, developed speech only in the last 50,000 years, since the migration from Africa, and perhaps much more recently. But we know from the animal kingdom that there

FIGURE 1.1
'Grand opera by radio inaugurated as regular program of Chicago company. Mary Garden . . . listening as Miss Edith Mason . . . sings into the radio transmitter for the first regular radio program of operas' (Repository: LoC P&P). From singing birds to singing opera singers in Chicago 1921. Musical theatre proved to be commercially viable and very popular in the early years of US radio.

was ritual before there was speech – when sound and gesture are combined in 'ritual behaviour'. If so, the combination of ritual with pre-speech sounds perhaps takes us to the dawn of humanity, the beginning of ritual and religion and science.

(Wood 2007:19)

Michael Wood is therefore analysing and critically evaluating sound through human history, anthropology, geography and the relationship between human existence and the sonic environment. He is engaged with understanding what Canadian composer R. Murray Schafer described as 'The Soundscape: the Tuning of the World' (Schafer 1977:i). In his first chapter, 'The Natural Soundscape', Schafer seeks to answer the question, what was the first sound heard?

It was the caress of the waters. Proust calls the sea 'the plaintive ancestress of the earth pursuing, as in the days when no living creature existed, its lunatic immemorial agitation.' The Greek myths tell how man arose from the sea: 'Some say that all gods and all living creatures originated in the stream of Oceanus which girdles the world, and that Tethys was the mother of all his children.'

The ocean of our ancestors is reproduced in the watery womb of our mother and is chemically related to it. Ocean and Mother. In the dark liquid of ocean the relentless masses of water pushed past the first sonar ear. As the ear of the fetus turns in its amniotic fluid, it too is tuned to the lap and gurgle of water.

(1977:15)

THE IMPORTANCE OF BEING CRITICAL

The academic analysis of sound in the early twenty-first century involves the research and expression of a coherent expression of critical thinking. The methodology requires intellectual reference points and usually a dialectical tradition of thesis and anti-thesis or Socratic testing of propositions and assertions through the asking of questions and rational debate. This activity has a tendency to apply and juxtapose contemporary and near contemporary thinkers rather than those of the distant past. The critical debate generally centres on the meaning of existence in terms of personal being and consciousness. This is often described as ontology though traditional philosophers normally see the word relating to a study of whether God exists and the nature of the understanding of God. Another focus concentrates on how and from what knowledge is acquired and developed. This is known as epistemology. Putting it simply, one of the key debates in the twentieth century was preoccupied with the question of whether human beings were objects or subjects in their social and cultural environment. Sound, vision, touch, taste, emotions and the human imagination all perform a vital role in this negotiation, which can of course be embraced by the idea of communication and media.

CRITICAL TRADITIONS

'Pure' philosophy has several critical traditions that are available to the study and practice of sound:

- Aesthetics and the philosophy of art
- Metaphysics and the philosophy of science
- Epistemology and the philosophy of knowledge
- Ontology and the philosophy of religion
- Logic and the philosophy of analysis and argument
- Ethics and the philosophy of morality
- Politics and the philosophy of ideology.

But a basic intellectual courtesy needs to be accorded the current disciplines of History, English Literature, and Media and Communications studies that in recent decades have framed a doctrinal approach to textual and contextual analysis of what have become defined as media texts. These include any production and expression using sound. These academic subjects provide the essential crossroads for theoretical engagement with sound expression but there is no reason why the student of sound should be prevented from taking any turn and pursuing any journey of academic aesthetic and intellectual analysis.

KEY CONCEPTS AND THEORETICAL CONCERNS FROM MEDIA STUDIES

There has already been a background and significant foundation of academic writing about sound in the context of media and communication studies. Distinguished academics such as Andrew Crisell, David Hendy, Guy Starkey and Hugh Chignell have explored in some depth a framework of critical vocabulary in books such as *Understanding Radio, Radio in the Global Age, Radio in Context* and *Key Concepts in Radio Studies*. Sound communication, primarily in the context of radio content, production and reception has been analysed in terms of genres, audiences, media institutions within the 'radio industry', and politics and public sphere. Professor Seàn Street has completed an important monograph *Radio and the Poetic Imagination: The Colour of Sound* that explores the idea of the poetic in radio and sound and the concept of sound as poetry both historically and within a contemporary perspective.

Professor Andrew Crisell pioneered a consideration of the semiotics of radio in the chapter entitled 'Radio Signs and Codes' that appeared in the first edition of *Understanding Radio* in 1986:

> In radio all the signs are auditory: they consist simply of noises and silence, and therefore use, *time*, not space, as their major structure agent. [. . .] The noises of radio can be subdivided into words, sounds and music, and we will look at each of these in turn and also at the nature and functions of silence before attempting some general observations about the codes of radio. [. . .]
>
> Unlike words, which are a human invention, sound is 'natural' – a form of signification which exists 'out there' in the real world. It seems never to exist as an isolated phenomenon, always to manifest the presence of something else. Consequently we can say that sounds, whether in the world or on the radio, are generally indexical. We could of course say that recorded sound on the radio is iconic in the elementary sense that it is an icon or image of the original sound or that a sound in a radio play is an icon of a sound in the real world, but if we do we are still faced with the question of what the sound *signifies*, what it is that is *making* the sound. Thus sounds such as the ringing of a door-bell or the grating of a key in a lock are indexical in signifying someone's presence.
>
> (Crisell 1996:43–4)

David Hendy offered a progressive advancement on Andrew Crisell's *Understanding Radio* by focusing on radio in the social landscape, industry in terms of global structures, commercialisation, and the interaction of technology, production in terms of producers, formats and creativity, audiences as an act of listening, the concept of the radio audience and the extent to which it was active or not, the meanings of radio texts, the relationship between radio and modernity and radio's place in culture in terms of democracy, identity, music and cultural change. This was ground-breaking work. His recent theoretical work includes a much-celebrated history of the national BBC radio channel Radio Four in 2007. The work represents a canonisation of an establishment media institution in radio by Oxford University Press, which could be described as an elite brand in academic literature, and was accompanied by endorsements on the book's dust jacket asserting that Radio Four is 'The greatest broadcasting channel in the world', 'The heartbeat of the BBC' and 'A cultural icon of Britishness' (Hendy 2007:dust jacket). With added endorsements from the *Daily Telegraph*'s radio critic Gillian Reynolds, who was awarded a Member of the British Empire honour for her services to radio, and the statement of the BBC's official historian Professor Jean Seaton: 'a tremendous read: impeccable research used with wit and insight about a national treasure', we are presented with evidence of a canonisation of higher educational, political and media institutional power.

David Hendy has recently broadcast a series of talks on the relationship between radio and modernity entitled *Rewiring the Mind*, and broadcast in 2011 on the BBC Radio Three strand *Essay*: 'The Ethereal Mind', 'The Cultivated Mind', 'The Anxious Mind', 'The Fallible Mind' and 'The Superficial Mind', but they are not available on listen-again archive resources. The exercise of limited access through seven-day 'listen again' can be seen as an exercise of intellectual property ownership where the public sector broadcasting (PSB) culture is effectively rationing intellectual and educational communication. This is a commodification of culture in the global capitalist market. The programmes could be available online at any time and on free access, but the buying and selling of rights means that radio drama retains some of its original ephemeral and linear-time framed parameters.

Guy Starkey engages a stimulating practice and theory dynamic through chapters in his book *Radio in Context* that concentrate on radio programme genres such as speech packages, live sequences and phone-ins, music scheduling, formats and branding, magazine programmes, advertisements and trails, light entertainment, drama and documentaries. I endeavoured to analyse the cross-disciplinary and historical investigation of critical terms in *Radio Drama: Theory and Practice* (Crook 1999:70–89) and engaged the theoretical writing of Andrew Crisell, Lance Sieveking, Hilda Matheson, Martin Esslin and Michel Chion.

Chion's treatise about sound on screen, *Audio-Vision* is regarded as a seminal text on the critical evaluation of sound construction and expression across the academic disciplines and more recently inspired an enlightening and stimulating discourse by Louis Niebur in *Special Sound*, where his study of the sound in BBC radio drama productions in the 1950s and 1960s led him to find an evolution of Chion's cinematic sound language. In his effort to define audio dramatic grammar Niebur writes: 'For those situations where created sounds exist as representations of a fictional technology, I will refer to "synchretic acousmêtre," since they embody elements of both terms at the same time' (Niebur 2010:12). In his study of Donald McWinnie's 1957 production and direction of Samuel Beckett's first play for radio *All That Fall* Niebur develops Chion's discourse on *acousmêtre* in relation to the radio play's stylised use of echo and actors' non-verbal rendering of effects:

> Again, I think Chion's terms are useful for describing exactly why these sounds are such 'nightmare realizations.' Although we as listeners can recognize the source of the sound (e.g. 'rain', 'bicycle', 'train', 'people'), these elements don't sound the way they are meant to sound. They have been rendered virtual *acousmêtre* by the nature of the change they have undergone. And it is precisely the mystery of the cause of the change that results in our tension, our feeling of bewilderment. In terms of the necessary combination of synthesis and synchronization, the sounds lack the proper synthesis to achieve synchresis; they don't contain the expected elements of the anticipated sounds. Instead we are offered a replacement, an alternate that doesn't exist in any real word. The world is possibly the world inside Rooney's head, the sound effects perhaps

an example of 'internal sound' (e.g. diegetic sound that corresponds to the physical and/or mental interior of a character).

(Niebur 2010:23–4)

Nutshell definitions of the critical terms *acousmêtre*, semiotic, synchresis, diegesis and non-diegesis can be found in the glossary.

A significant engagement with cross-disciplinary bridging in the semiotic analysis of sound expression was achieved with great elegance and intellectual accomplishment by Professor Theo Van Leeuwen in his 1999 publication *Speech, Music, Sound*:

> Recording technology has brought music back into everyday life – through muzak, the transistor radio, the car stereo, the Walkman. The boundaries between speech, music and other sound have weakened. Composers have experimented with combinations of musical instruments, singing and speaking voices, and non-musical sounds. Satie added a typewriter to the orchestra, Gershwin a taxi-horn, Antheil a propeller, Zappa a cash register, Reich car alarms. Schoenberg, Berio and others wrote Sprechgesänge ('speech songs') – and so, in a different way, do contemporary Rap artists. The Futurist composer Russolo created a noise orchestra consisting of noise makers, boxes cranked by a handle: buzzers, bursters, a thunderer, whistlers, rustlers, gurglers, a shatterer, a shriller and a snorter. And, most significantly, he redefined noise as music.

(Van Leeuwen 1999:2)

Van Leeuwen discussed the relationship between speech, music and sound in terms of six key domains: 'sound perspective, sound time and rhythm, the interaction of "voices" (for instance by taking turns or speaking, singing, playing or sounding together in different ways), melody, voice quality and timbre and modality' (1999:9). Van Leeuwen's semiotic analysis is both sociological and culturalist and raises thought-provoking debates that invite exciting developments in sound scholarship:

> The trend in communication is now towards immersion rather than detachment, towards the interactive and the participatory rather than towards solitary enjoyments, towards ever-changing dynamic experiences rather than towards the fixing of meanings as objects to be collected. Even though sound is at present still very much undervalued and underused in the new media, and often treated as little more than a kind of optional extra, there is every chance that it will have a much increased role to play in the very near future.

(1999:197)

What Van Leeuwen has described as the issue of immersion has developed into an interesting debate about media saturation. The individual in twenty-first-century society in both urban and rural communities experiences a soundscape that is punctuated and immersed with synthesised sound growing and intensifying to the point where there is evidence of a resistance, protest and challenge concerning audio *saturation*. This emerges in politicking about noise pollution. Regulatory broadcasting bodies in many countries frequently have to negotiate complaints about sonic enhancement of commercials or advertisements (Ofcom n.d.). An attempt was also made to introduce US federal legislation in 2008 to mitigate the loudness of broadcast advertisements ('Commercial Advertisement Loudness Mitigation Act' 2008).

It is sometimes argued that broadcasters covertly conspire with advertisers to increase the decibel level of adverts compared to the musical and speech programming being sponsored or funded. Where 'noise level' regulatory limits are imposed, broadcasters and the producers of commercial spots promoting services and products can simulate enhanced listening by an electronic sound processing technique of middle and lower frequency compression. The listener and viewer's perception is one of loudness, particularly in older viewers who have lost higher frequency hearing ability, whereas the actual physical measurement does not indicate that the advertisement is 'louder' than the programming around it (BBC News 2008).

A complaint was raised in 2011 about sonic saturation in the mixing of contemporary rock music in order to make a series of documentaries on science more attractive to a younger audience. More than one hundred viewers complained that the narrative of Professor Brian Cox (a former rock musician) had been smothered into a whisper by the high level of excessively loud background music mixed in a digital surround sound field in the series *Wonders of the Universe*. In the home cinema environment surround sound mixing can sometimes create the effect of music 'crashing' in with power into the rear speakers and when encoded into stereo or mono reception there is sometimes a perceptive effect of 'drowning out' the narrative voice of the presenter.

In 2010, BBC Vision carried out two separate online surveys among a 20,000 strong panel to identify specific audibility issues. Based on these findings, the BBC and the Voice of the Listener and Viewer (VLV) sound engineers carried out an enquiry to establish the underlying causes of complaints about listening discomfort and inaudibility. A further research study devised a test of different sound mixes with different audience groups. In 2011 the conclusions of the television audibility research project were set out as a basis for best practice in future production:

> Audibility issues can rarely be attributed to one factor; it is usually a combination of factors. For example, a strong regional accent recorded in a noisy location; a softly spoken contributor looking away from the camera; background music or people talking over each other.

> The vast majority of audibility problems can be eliminated before any material is shot, eg location choice, sound set up, sound rehearsal time, briefing presenters and contributors.

> Audibility issues can be compounded with the addition of background music; a slight reduction in music levels (4DB) make a considerable difference to the audibility of programmes.
>
> (BBC Press Office 2011)

The BBC's online College of Production (part of the BBC Academy) uploaded a series of best practice resources and acknowledged that this resource, in finding that 60 per cent of television viewers had difficulties with sound immersion, saturation or distortion, needed to alert producers to the risks of: 'Background noise: locations with heavy traffic, bubbling streams, farmyard animals; Background music: particularly spiky, heavily percussive music or lyrics that cut across dialogue'.

In 2003 Lars Nyre presented a doctoral thesis to the Department of Media Studies, University of Bergen in Norway on *Fidelity Matters: Sound Media and Realism in the 20th Century*. In essence it was a history of cultural perception in sound and Nyre further developed this cross-disciplinary discourse into the academic publication in 2008, *Sound Media: From Live Journalism to Music Recording*. It might be argued that Nyre was extending Van Leeuwen's work in studying 'how music recording, radio broadcasting, and muzak influence people's daily lives' (Nyre 2008:i). In 'Sound and Listening' Nyre analyses natural sound, mediated sound and medium is the message theory with a focus on 'materiality up front', 'documentary realism', 'the history of the sound medium' and what he describes as auditory rhetoric and acoustic architecture in terms of reception environments, time effects and persuasion in person. It could be argued that Nyre is picking up the baton of Van Leeuwen's interest in the role of sound contextualised by an everyday sociological performance. They both reference Erving Goffman's understanding of the projection of human personality in a daily sonic dramaturgy whereby the speaker can be animator, author and principal in quotidian life as audio-dramatic participation:

> my theory of sound media has four dimensions: 1) a description of sound and listening; 2) a theory of what a medium is; 3) a method for a backwards history of media; and 4) a method for rhetorical analysis of journalism and music. These methods will now be applied to cover the sound media in Europe and the USA for 130 years. From this detached perspective I hope to show that the media are a joint venture of electro-mechanical resources and human creativity. As a hint about the balance of forces in this venture I will quote McLuhan again: 'All media work us over completely. They are so pervasive in their personal, moral, ethical and social consequences, that they leave no part of us untouched, unaffected, unaltered. The medium is the massage.'
>
> (Nyre 2008:30 and McLuhan and Fiore 1967:26)

Lars Nyre provides a historicism and historiography of the social history of sound technological production and reception through music recording from the 1870s to the 1920s, entitled 'The repeating machine', experiments in broadcasting from the 1900s to the 1920s, entitled 'Atmospheric contact', music recording from the 1930s to the 1940s, entitled 'Microphone moods', live journalism from the 1930s to the 1960s, entitled 'The acoustic nation', and the revolution in recorded music from the 1950s to the 1970s, entitled 'Tape control'. I have reversed what he actually presents as 'Backwards history'.

He also presents a compelling and stimulating analysis of present time sound communication in terms of the acoustic computer: 'Nervous experiments with sound media'; synthetic music: 'Digital recording in great detail'; the mobile public: 'Journalism for urban navigators'; phone radio: 'Personality journalism in voice alone' and loudspeaker living: 'Pop music is everywhere'. Nyre's text does not sit alone in its printed graphic existence as he has ingeniously negotiated a collection of thirty-six audio tracks to illustrate his arguments.

MEDIA SOUND LANGUAGE

Theoretical analysis considers how the construction of sound texts creates meaning for the listener. This involves a focus on the structured nature of sound within a media text. An active institutional sound point of listening involves the transmission of meaning by the media institution to a passive audience. The meaning is deconstructed by an appreciation of the logos of the sound text; its social and cultural contexts and previous knowledge of related sound texts. In the analysis it is suggested the student asks who constructed the text, what context has been constructed for it, what other texts have been created by the media institution and what are the codes and conventions that are recognisable from the other sound texts made by the same institution?

If the sound text is being studied from a negotiated point of listening, the meaning is interpreted by the listener in relation to knowledge of previous sound texts perhaps through a decoding of language within the text. The student needs to analyse the genre codes and conventions, its typicality in relation to genre, time and place, representations being used to create meaning, and meaning encoded within the text. An analysis of an active audience point of listening determines how the sound text conforms to audience expectations, any previous experience the audience used in its interpretation, the method of receiving it and how this might influence the meaning being received.

A considerable body of critical vocabulary on the purpose and deployment of sound in film texts has been developed in the context of analysing the mise-en-scène, a term that is used to encompass everything seen and heard and perhaps even imagined from an experience of screen reception. In the setting it is pertinent to evaluate how the sound has been recorded; whether on location or in the studio. How is the sound construction and texture being used to communicate meaning and precipitate an emotional and imaginative reaction from the audience? Are the sounds realistic or surreal and abstract? Is there a metaphorical and ironic meaning charged or encoded into the sound in terms of its function as a symbol?

It may be possible that the soundtrack or design has been constructed to support, reflect, juxtapose and enhance meaning encoded in the media language or grammar of costume and make-up. Is there an abstract sound that has been created to support a thematic tone of colour? Obviously the style and manner of the actors speaking within the mise-en-scène can be of significance. The plotting or scoring of the soundtrack in relation to the lighting is a key factor, and this process is aesthetically demonstrated in the Orson Welles film *Citizen Kane* (1941) where the physically identifiable features of the film's characters are introduced or faded by contrasts of light and darkness, the transition of shadow effects and the accompanying fading up, fading down and cross-fading of sounds, including the speech of the characters. Dynamic movement within the film's text is plotted in sound as well as cinematography. The outstanding artistry of sound design in this iconic film is fully recognised by the film historians Bordwell and Thompson:

> *Citizen Kane* offers a wide range of sound manipulations. Echo chambers alter timbre and volume. A motif is formed by the inability of Kane's wife Susan to sing pitches accurately. [. . .] the plot's shifts between times and places are covered by continuing a sound 'thread' and varying the basic acoustics. A shot of Kane applauding dissolves to a shot of a crowd applauding (a shift in volume and timbre). Leland[JPN1] beginning a sentence in the street cuts to Kane finishing the sentence in an auditorium, his voice magnified by loudspeakers (a shift in volume, timbre and pitch).
>
> (Bordwell and Thompson 1997:320)

We have already been introduced to the critical terms non-diegetic and diegetic sound that are used to define sound originating outside the storytelling frame within the screenplay such as a musical score and sound belonging within the narrative frame that can be heard by the film's characters. This is the difference between the music played and heard by the characters in the record shop Championship Vinyl in *High Fidelity* (2000) and the layering of musical tracks that can only be heard and appreciated by the cinema audience. However, the director Stephen Frears complicates the relationship between the diegetic and non-diegetic in the deployment of the Renaissance theatrical technique of aside and soliloquy, when the central character, Rob Gordon, frequently breaks the cinematic concept of the fourth wall and talks directly to the audience. The other characters remain diegetic, but it could be argued that Gordon's speech and sound fuses with the audience in a quasi non-diegetic relationship.

Critical analysis of filmic sound also considers the extent to which the soundtrack challenges the meaning conveyed by the image or reaffirms it. The theoretical musical term contrapuntal is sometimes used to identify a sound opposed to or in conflict with the image, and the literary critical term parallel or parallelism is used to describe sound that confirms and supports the rational and emotional meaning of the image. It can be argued that the definitions of these terms from the academic disciplines of music and literature studies invite a much richer and more complex understanding of the critical meaning of sound in a wider range of multimedia texts.

The dramatic use of silence is, of course, a valid critical observation in the construction of sound text. It often invites a powerful engagement of audience interaction since the scene or scenes prior to that deploying audio silence may well have invested an anticipation of what the characters may be communicating visually. In the early 1930s a large sound studio was constructed in Königsberg, Germany, containing twenty-two fixed seats and sophisticated acoustics with non-parallel side walls, an inclined ceiling and hanging panels to improve the distribution of sound. Pride of place and in a central position was a large inscription with the words: 'Everything sounds, even silence' (Arnheim 1936:29).

FIGURE 1.2
'Tommy Dorsey (top right) interviews the English pigeon, Beryl Davis, for his first disc jockey stint, with such names as Georgie Auld, Ray McKinley, Mary Lou Williams, Josh White and others visible in the background' (Repository: LoC P&P, William P. Gottlieb Collection). Dorsey interviews Beryl Davis at WMCA in America in 1947. This sophisticated on-air broadcast studio features close microphone interviewing between presenter/DJ and celebrity guest in terms of foreground sound and background sound and potential focus on the performance of singers and other guests to the rear. Sound absorbent panels and clear glass panelling for the producer and studio manager's control room are also visible. The general rule in sound production is that the more busy and over-populated soundtracks tend to generate a greater intensity of dramatic effect through silence.

There are two powerful cinematic demonstrations of this technique in David Mamet's screenplay *The Verdict* (1982) and John Michael Hayes's screenplay *The Children's Hour* (1961). In *The Verdict* the central character Frank Galvin, played by Paul Newman, has been betrayed by a honey trap operation from the well-resourced rival law firm instructed by the hospital responsible for the negligent medical operation that has left his client brain-damaged. Galvin's decision to fight rather than settle the medical negligence case coincides with his romantic liaison with Laura Fischer who happened to be drinking in his local Boston bar. She volunteers to assist Galvin's two man team in their David and Goliath courtroom battle made more difficult by a biased judge and nobbling of their star expert witness. Her deception is discovered by Galvin's partner, Mickey Morrissey, who spots the cheque made out by the defendant's legal firm in Laura's handbag when going to get change for cigarettes. Mickey travels to New York to intercept Galvin who is on his way to meet up with Laura, played by Charlotte Rampling, at a hotel. What Mickey says to Galvin is represented by a long shot scene of gesticulation and discussion on the sidewalk with the soundtrack consisting only of urban traffic and cacophony.

In *The Children's Hour* two young adult women teachers, Karen Wright, played by Audrey Hepburn, and Marthe Dobie, played by Shirley MacLaine, are falsely accused by one of their pupils of having a lesbian relationship, but the actual allegation remains implicit throughout the film and the revelation to each other about the slander that has resulted in the destruction of their reputations is represented by a long shot of the two women visually speaking to each other in the garden, seen through the panes of glass in one of the schoolroom doors, and with the soundtrack silent. The meaning is provided by the imagination, assumption, anticipation and any inherent prejudices present in the audience.

It has sometimes been said that sound tends to be a neglected or undervalued aspect of Media Studies, though as a matter of fact, listening as a process of perception is one of the first sensory experiences of a human being. For example, the ears begin to function when a child is in its mother's womb, and it is also recognised that when eyes close during sleep, ears remain 'awake' or are certainly functioning in terms of receiving sound. As Joachim-Ernst Berendt observed: 'Our ears are open before we are born. Our consciousness begins with them. Is that the real reason why we can never, ever close our ears so long as we live?' (quoted in Sonnenschein 2001:72). Brandon LaBelle in *Background Noise: Perspectives on Sound Art* (2008) reinforces a reflection on the spiritual and aesthetic dimensions of sound with his enthusiastic definition of *auditory relations*:

> Sound is intrinsically and unignorably relational: it emanates, propagates, communicates, vibrates, and agitates; it leaves a body and enters others; it binds and unhinges, harmonizes and traumatizes; it sends the body moving, the mind dreaming, the air oscillating. It seemingly eludes definition, while having profound effect.
>
> (LaBelle 2008:ix)

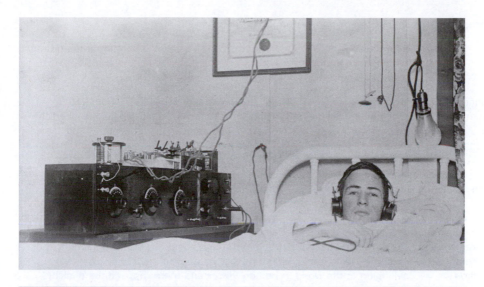

FIGURE 1.3

'Cripplld [*sic*] by fall while putting up aerial this radio fan still "listens in"' (Repository: LoC P&P). Sound entertainment was so alluring that in the early days of radio people would risk their lives to achieve a decent signal. This is 1922 and Lester Picker is lying in bed wearing earphones connected to a shortwave radio; he is convalescing after breaking his back when he fell 55 feet while erecting an aerial for his radio.

Sound perception also has a much wider field of perception. It could be described as all encompassing. It can be argued that the human ears are capable of picking up sound waves from all directions whereas sight is limited by the depth of field of the human eyes. Table 1.1 sets out a proposed critical matrix for an academic textual analysis of sound in any media text, though I readily concede it is not comprehensive and other parameters and considerations could be applied.

The legendary Soviet film director, Sergei Eisenstein, working at the crossroads of so-called silent and sound cinema described the power of listening as the 'synchcronization of the senses' because it had the ability to unify image and sound 'with a single rhythm or expressive quality' (Bordwell and Thompson 1997:317). Sound became the relating synthesis of communicating narrative and meaning, and as David Bordwell and Kristin Thompson so elegantly observed: 'With the introduction of sound cinema, the infinity of visual possibilities was joined by the infinity of acoustic events' (318).

One of the early exponents of elegantly combining the creative possibilities of sound and cinema was certainly Alfred Hitchcock, who in his direction of the screen version of John Buchan's spy novel *The 39 Steps* in 1936 cut and mixed a brilliant example of transitional sound tagging. The bridging between scenes is achieved by symbolising the tension and intensity of drama with the superimposition of a sound

Table 1.1 A proposed critical matrix for an academic textual analysis of sound

Music	Soundscape/ atmosphere and sound effects	Speech	Listening imagination
Non-verbal sound that is organised into rhythm, harmony, melody and is mainly known for its emotional quality. Music can constitute characterisation in itself, operate as a motif/ leitmotiv to support and enhance characterisation, punctuate and accentuate plot and narrative through mood manipulation.	This is the sound environment or sound frame for any mise-en-scène. It punctuates the identification of location, context, world, time and can also constitute characterisation and support characterisation. An atmospheric track belonging to the world of the story that is known to and immerses the participants of a narrative, but sometimes it can exist in a parallel world only known to the audience. Sound effects support and deploy in the events and action of a plot.	Usually the stream of sound that is the paradigmatic anchor of sound communication. In the deployment of verbal language speech can be monologue, dialogue or multi-vocal. It can also be embedded in musical rhythm through song and poetry. It can also be non-verbal and there are dimensions of poetic and musical expression where the spoken voice is avant-garde and abstract in meaning.	In my book *Radio Drama* I described the imaginative spectacle as the fifth dimension of sonic communication and understanding after the dimensions of speech, music, sound noise, intertextual sound or previously recorded archived sound (Crook 1999:62–3). I also applied the thinking behind Chion's concept of negative or phantom sound, which in French can be encapsulated in the term *en creux*; the equivalent in sculpture of the volume defined and cast into the mould. Walter Murch sees it as 'in the gap' (Chion 1994: 123–8). In its purest form the construction of meaning is achieved through the deployment of 'silence'.

Loudness
The method of acoustically plotting and signposting foreground and background and applying dramatic emphasis.

Timbre and pitch
Timbre is a musical tone that is sometimes described as the colour or feel of sound. It characterises the emotional interpretation of sound. Pitch is the sense of highness and lowness of sound and can communicate tension, gender and human mood. With loudness these elements determine sonic texture.

Selection, alternation and combination
This is the juxtapositioning, multi-tracking and mixing of music, soundscape and effects, speech and manipulation of 'in the gap' space or the imaginative spectacle of the listener for the purposes of narrative. This can be achieved by forwards, backwards, flashbacking, overlapping, jump-cutting, paralleling, sound tagging, transitional cross fading, and fading up and down techniques.

Rhythm
This is a key device in the construction of meaning and the manipulation of the emotions of the listener. It is plotting the beat or pulse, accent or stress and tempo or pace of the sound text and can be applied to any sonic stream of communication.

Synchronicity with parallel media
This is the position of sound in multimedia texts for the purposes of determining and constructing overall meaning. Many techniques can be applied including contrapuntal, ironic interplay, emphasis, emotional colouration, additional and expansive information provision.

Spatiality
Determining the imaginative dimensions of the sonic world through a pattern and design of sound elements and the movement of sonic tracks in terms of proxemics (position) and kinesics (movement, strength and characteristics of the sound signal) sometimes described as sonic ostension.

Time and temporality
The representation of story time in sound texts through narrative construction. This dimension can be real-time (*Sekundenstil* or second by second), elliptic time, forward or reverse time, contemporary, historical or future time. Plot time represents the timeframe contained in the *syuzhet* of the sound text. Story or *fabula* time is the frame of the story around the plot represented in the sound text and takes into account parallel plots, background events indicated in flashbacks, back story and future story. Sound text duration is simply the linear timeframe of the audio or film text or any other media with soundtrack.

Diegesis
The place that sound has in the cognition of the characters in the story-world. It is also a matter of empirical sharing of the sound between and within the matrix of reception audience and story-world community. Diegesis can also relate to time and knowledge past, present and future.

Narrative and dramatic function
Every sonic sign can be said to have a function for the purposes of unfolding and developing narrative and dramatic understanding.

Perspective
This is the positioning of the listener in relation to the direction of the sound text's narrative; sometimes referred to as the equivalent of point of view through the terms point of listening (POL) and point of audition (POA).

effect that belongs to the diegesis of the following scene. The effect is similar in pitch and timbre. A cleaning lady discovers the body of a woman secret agent who has been stabbed to death in Richard Hannay's West End mansion flat. Hannay is being framed for the murder. He is fleeing London and Scotland Yard to take up the dead woman's mission in Scotland. When the body is discovered the screen shows the cleaning lady screaming, but the sound emanating from her mouth is the high-pitch whistle of the Flying Scotsman racing out of King's Cross with Hannay on board. The device is recognised by Bordwell and Thompson as an example of what they describe as 'unfaithful sounds' to image: 'A shot of her screaming face is accompanied by a train whistle; then the scene shifts to an actual train. Though the whistle is not a faithful sound for an image of a screaming person, it provides a dramatic transition' (1997:330).

The special qualities of auditory perception and the engagement of the listening imagination was highlighted in a British Open University course, *Understanding Media*, that was first taught in 2006. In a module on 'Analysing speech, music, sound' an audio cluster resource interviewed Andrew Hubbard, a disability equality trainer, writer and consultant who had been invited to analyse his experience of listening to the BBC Radio Three play *Chelsea Dreaming* by David Britton. Andrew went blind in adulthood and he was able to communicate how a sightless person with the cultural memory of previous sight is able to 'appreciate the benefits of a heightened sensitivity to sounds' (Chaplin 2006:17).

It is generally accepted that there is a visual paradigm in sensory perception, though the extent to which sound has a subconscious process of constructing meaning requires further empirical psychological research. Andrew Hubbard's criticism of *Chelsea Dreaming* offers an example of how the closing down of a human being's visual track enhances the auditory sense. The academic analysis of speech used to be the preserve of linguistics and music that of musicology. The production of sound design is studied in a technological context in specialist universities and colleges. The course-team leaders for the Open University argued that sound is a wrap-around medium, sounds are everywhere, are colour-blind and that in the process of hearing only a sound-based text the listener is denied any body language signals to provide visual clues about intended meaning and emotional subtext.

The course drew on an academic semiotic framework of sonic signs developed by Professor Theo Van Leeuwen. Van Leeuwen is an advocate of soundscape philosophising, where he listens to the city as music, and considers music as though it is speaking. The course was also directed to finding an understanding of the media sensorium; in particular, exploring the relationship between senses and social experience.

Van Leeuwen advises that sound should be studied in terms of its intrinsic and social perspective:

> Perspective is a word that comes from the visual. At the same time visual artists covered perspective in painting, perspective in sound was also discovered. Sounds that are closest to me are normally and naturally the loudest, and then when you get a bit further away there are sounds that are still quite well audible, but softer and still further away you get sounds that are softly in the background. So you get degrees of loudness and they relate to degrees of closeness, and therefore to degrees of how much you are involved with an in depth sound.
>
> (*DA204 Understanding Media* Audio CD1 2006: cluster 1, track 14)

Van Leeuwen discussed the distinguishing of foreground sounds where there is close attention, middle ground sound providing contextual clues, and background sound, which we hear though consciously ignore but for which there may well be a subconscious reception. A sense of perspective is achieved by the layering of sounds, or ambient or sonic environmental multi-tracking.

These views intersect with Andrew Crisell's application of the terms proxemics and kinesics in his analysis of sound semiotics. In a consideration of sound and social distance Van Leeuwen says the relationship is to be found in the sound of the voice:

> How voices sound. How loud they are but also more generally what they sound like. They vary with the degree of social distance between the people; the way they are talking to each other. For example, if you are intimate with somebody, or if you are having some kind of conspiracy, you whisper. If you are talking to a good friend about personal things, the voice will not be a whisper but it will still be fairly soft. When you get to more business, formal like interactions, it will be not only louder, but also the whole quality of the voice will change as a result. There will be a little more tension, there will be a somewhat higher pitch, and of course if you are speaking to a large audience, then the voice becomes projected; public.
>
> (*DA204 Understanding Media* Audio CD1 2006: cluster 1, track 14)

Van Leeuwen also emphasised, as many theorists had before him, that sound is responsible for communicating a rich and complex sense of spatiality:

> There are many aspects of sound that indicate what type of space you are in. Where there are bare walls in the floor. Where you may be in a cathedral or an institutional corridor as opposed to some kind of room with carpets, curtains and drapes and so on. [. . .] It can also be used symbolically. You can have a voice that has that extra kind of reverberation and then you think there must be some kind of meaning signified here; some kind of association with meanings attached to the kind of spaces of sound.
>
> (*DA204 Understanding Media* Audio CD1 2006: cluster 1, track 14)

The word 'soundscape' is credited with being coined by the Canadian composer and sound ecologist R. Murray Schafer:

> The sonic environment. Technically any portion of the sonic environment regarded as a field for study. The term may refer to actual environments, or to abstract constructions such as musical composition and tape montages, particularly when considered as an environment.
>
> (Shafer 1994:274–5)

In his seminal book *Our Sonic Environment and the Soundscape: The Tuning of the World*, first published in 1977, Shafer analysed the participation of the human community in:

> our sonic environment, the ever-present array of noises with which we all live. Beginning with the primordial sounds of nature, we have experienced an ever-increasing complexity of our sonic surroundings. As civilization develops, new noises rise up around us: from the creaking wheel, the clang of the blacksmith's

hammer, and the distant chugging of steam trains to the 'sound imperialism' of airports, city streets, and factories.

(1994, cover text)

Shafer debates the issue of whether human society is 'blighted and suffering from an over-abundance of acoustic information and a proportionate diminishing of our ability to hear the nuances and subtleties of sound'. His aesthetic manifesto is to listen, analyse and sustain the ability to make distinctions; to retain what he describes as 'sonological competence'. He even developed a separate discourse on 'ear cleaning' with the publication of a book with this title that set out a 'systematic program for training the ears to listen more discriminately to sounds, particularly of the environment' (1994:272). Shafer tenaciously reclaims critical language for the listening medium in order to make 'earwitnesses' of us all: 'One who testifies or can testify to what he or she has heard' (272).

Van Leeuwen describes 'Soundscape' as the landscape of sound:

> The totality of an environment or place from the point of view of sound and also, and this is important, a particular point of hearing. In a visual landscape you have necessarily a particular angle of viewing. A point of view. You might be in the middle of the forest, or you might stand on the top of a mountain and look down on the forest. So likewise in the soundscape you can only ever experience a form of particular point of view. I can also move away and my point of hearing is different. There is always a subjective point of hearing involved in the soundscape. It is not an objective affair.
>
> (DA204 Understanding Media Audio CD1 2006: cluster 1, track 14)

David Sonnenschein confirms the perspectival property of sound, though he uses the term 'point of audition':

> In the same way that a camera can have a point of view, the perspective of sound, can have a point of audition. This can be purely spatial; for example, listening to an orchestra from far in the balcony with the reverberation of the hall, versus from the intimacy of the conductor's podium. Or this can be a more subjective sense, relating to which character in a certain scene or place in the story is associated with what the audience is hearing. An example is the audible sound of a filtered telephone voice; this would be the subjective point of audition of the telephone listener, not the realistic sound heard in the space where the camera sees the listener with the phone to the ear.
>
> (Sonnenschein 2001:163)

There might be an argument that the analysis of radio/audio drama provides a model and critical tools for academically evaluating all sound texts. And distinguished theorists in addition to Professor Van Leeuwen have already added dimensions and insights into analysis that are sound orientated. Andrew Crisell has focalised on spatial measurement of sonic perspective based on movement and position:

> Noises and SFX can be used as environmental indicators, acoustic means of depicting scenes or settings (birdsong can suggest the countryside, echoing voices and noises a dungeon, and so on) and scene changes (the fading up and down of voices is analogous to the rise and fall of curtains and/or the brightening and dimming of stage lights in the conventional theatre). They can also act as *spatial* indicators – ways of revealing proxemics, the physical distances between the various characters, and kinesics, the physical movements relative to one another and to the listener. Proxemic and kinesic information is most frequently and effectively conveyed by locating the actors at varying distances from the microphone and by moving the actors in and out of its sound-gathering areas. This means that a single sound effect, the fading out of a voice, is often used to convey both environmental and spatial information: it signifies either of two things which would be perceived to be quite different on a stage, the end of a scene or the exit of a character during a scene, but the radio listener would have no difficulty in distinguishing which of them was happening.
>
> (Crisell 1994:146–7)

Crisell argued convincingly for a recognition of the idea of sonic ostension:

> To put it another way, the most natural and obvious mode of ostension, and one which is possible in the theatre, is for an object to be *seen*. On radio this must be replaced by an equally natural if 'secondary' mode of ostension: the object must be *heard*. But if this is impossible or unhelpful the object must be rendered by means of an 'artificial' sign or signs – symbols called *words*, and this process is known as transcodification.
>
> (149)

The semiotics of radio/audio drama were also eloquently considered by Martin Esslin in *The Field of Drama: How the Signs of Drama Create Meaning on Stage and Screen* (1987). He acknowledged a more subjective frame of reference for audio drama's paradoxical and complex semiotic codes. He concluded that radio drama is mimetic action with acting ability at a higher standard than in film, theatre and television largely because he was alluding to the need for a quality of characterisation that could be achieved through voice alone. This undoubtedly demands great concentration and commitment on the part of actors though the evidence in the present and historical archives of audio/radio drama suggests they are more than capable of being 'up to the task'.

Esslin emphasised that sound drama unfolds in time and space with spatialisation communicated physically through the perspectives established by different angles and distances from the microphone. This dynamic is also expressed by the setting of relative strength and volume in an actor's performance. In this way directors and studio managers can communicate a strong suggestion of space through sound perspective. These views coincide with those of Crisell and Van Leeuwen.

Esslin went on to argue that radio/audio drama does have a visual presence in terms of sensory perception. He did not think that visual signs had to be physically present: 'performance in time and space very strongly conjures up visual images' (Esslin 1987:30). He conceded that the quality of radio drama's visual images were not necessarily higher than in television, film or theatre because superlatives were a matter of choice and preferred consciousness for each individual listener. For example, the idea of the most beautiful woman or ugliest man so signposted would be conjured in the imagination in a personal way rather than by any intended anchoring by the director, casting director and performer (Crook 1999:80–1).

Andrew Crisell, with intellectual fortitude, has maintained his view that radio should theoretically be understood as a blind medium: 'What strikes everyone, broadcast and listener alike, as significant about radio is that it is a *blind* medium' (Crisell 1994:3). His persistence in this view does not mean he does not acknowledge the beauty and romantic potential of the role of the listener's imagination:

> In radio, however, we are free – forced – to imagine everything, even the actual dramatis personae who ostend themselves to us in sounds and words. However often we hear them, and in however much detail they are described, we will be required to picture them in our own way, together with further details of them which are *not* described. This is because words can never be as exhaustive or specific as a visual image [. . .] which is another way of saying that images are dogmatic, reductive. The relatively peripheral, or at any rate superficial, role which is afforded to the imagination by the visual media seems to be behind that variously attributed saying 'Television is chewing gum for the eyes' – that is, watching is an insipid, purely physical activity that does not engage the higher faculties.
>
> (153)

Academic criticism of radio continually drives a romantic appreciation of the engagement of the imaginative spectacle along with emotional consciousness. Hugh Chignell described 'Aurality' as 'listening to speech and music' and 'a driving force in cultures around the world' (Chignell 2009:71). He took great pleasure in selecting an upbeat expression of intellectual excitement given by Professor Susan Douglas:

> I don't mean to suggest that listening to Rudy Vallee or Casey Kasem was like a religious experience (although perhaps, for some, it was). I am talking about the medium itself and the way that receivers reel in distant voices out of that incomprehensible dimension called the spectrum and effortlessly bring them straight to us, linking us, through the air, to unseen others. The fact that

radio waves are invisible, emanate from 'the sky', carry disembodied voices, and can send signals deep into the cosmos links us to a much larger, more mysterious order.

(Douglas 1991:41 and Chignell 2009:71)

Even the most cerebral writers on sound seem to be struck by an aesthetic enthusiasm and emotional appreciation of sound's differences. Van Leeuwen observes:

It's all around you. [. . .] You can close your eyes, but you can't close your ears so easily as your eyes. Sound is very much, I believe, dialogic; very much more involved in interaction whereas vision is something that's not so interactive. [. . .] When people start thinking about radio plays you've got to think about it not only in terms of linear, narrative, causal sequence of events. You've got think about another structure, dimension of sound, as things happening at the same time, as dialogic. Different sounds can clash with one another; harmonize with each other. They can be, as it were, polyphonic or unison. There are also lots of patterns that give a quasi-musical time structure which exists at the same time as in relation to a narrative structure.

(*DA204 Understanding Media* Audio CD1 2006: cluster 1, track 14)

Van Leeuwen refers to an intriguing opportunity, often taken up by theorists to extend the discussion of sound aesthetic into the political. When he said 'Sound

FIGURE 1.4
'Radio in a Straw Hat' (Source: Nationaal Archief/Spaarnestad Photo/Het Leven/ Fotograaf onbekend). Radio in a straw hat in the 1920s – an anticipation of the possibilities of portable listening.

unifies' (Van Leeuwen 1999:196) he was inspired by the observation by Umberto Eco: 'The listener must allow a centre to emerge from the sound continuum. Here are no privileged points of view, and all available perspectives are equally valid and rich in potential' (in Van Leeuwen 1999:196 and referenced to Chanan 1994:269).

The concept of multiple grains, utterances and voices within text narrative was substantially discoursed by the Russian theorist Mikhail Bakhtin. The engagement of theoretical concepts of *The Dialogic Imagination* by Mikhail Bakhtin provides a rich source of definition of ironic spaciality in audio texts. The principles of *dialogism*, *polyphony*, *the chronotope* and *heteroglossia* are potentially interfacial and interleaving in ironic reality and expressionism in the sound medium. Bakhtin writes: 'Oppositions between individuals are only surface upheavals of the untamed elements in social heteroglossia, surface manifestations of those elements that play on such individual oppositions, make them contradictory' (Bakhtin 1981:326).

If sound drama and communication can be recognised as a rich territory for utterance then it is the arena for struggle over consciousness, time and place and multi-voiced characterisation as well as the construction of meaning for listeners who in their own memory and imagination resonate chains of cultural identity. Sound communication has the potential to generate cultural spaces for ironic understanding, resistance and independence. I have argued that cultural irony can be located on a number of dimensions in the soundplay: coincidence recognised by characters and/or audience; understanding and knowledge restricted to audience so that the characters have an unwitting and symbolic journey; understanding and knowledge located between audience and a restricted character or number of characters within the *syuzhet*; the idea that the exact opposite is happening and being meant but remains oblivious to one or more characters in the *syuzhet*; by offering a dimension for hypocrisy, self realisation, self deception on the part of character/characters; in the striking of a note of wry humour/comedy. Irony works well in dialogue and action and when it is multilayered because the playing tends to be against the cultural/constructed meaning by audience (Crook 2000).

The significance of Bakhtin's narratological discussion of the multi-voiced properties in literature and their relationship with the dramatic texts of radio drama has been developed with great intellectual force in the 2007 Ph.D. thesis of Paula Knight, *Radio Drama: Sound, Text, Word; Bakhtin and the Aural Dialogue of Radio Drama*, which certainly merits wider publication as an academic monograph.

The radio play *Chelsea Dreaming* was commissioned and broadcast to mark the fifty-year anniversary of the death of Dylan Thomas. The play was a conversation between a characterised or personalised Chelsea Hotel in New York City, where Dylan Thomas was staying, and the writer/poet himself. Temporally it covered the last hours of his life before he slipped into a coma and then death at the premature age of thirty-nine. It might be argued that the play is substantially intertextual with Thomas's Prix Italia award-winning sound play *Under Milk Wood* (1954), which is also constituted as a dream with a narrative voice looking down on a Swansea

Village and seemingly summoning up and interacting with the spirits of imagined personas, ghosts and memories.

The playwright David Britton discussed his semiotic intentions in the authoring of what could be described as the written score for the audio dramatic production. He appreciated a medium where there was a freedom to easily cross the boundaries of space and time:

> Thomas's memory is stuck there within the hotel. The way to listen I think is perhaps something between the experience of listening to narrative play and the experience of listening to a piece of music; that is to say you just have to surrender yourself to the flow of the language.
>
> (Britton quoted in Chaplin 2006)

Van Leeuwen was impressed with how in listening to the play he was aware that the voices were in different kinds of spaces and there were identifiable social distances between the listener and the speakers. As a listener with an acute sight disability, Andrew Hubbard found that the aural text was rich in imaginary meanings and cultural allusions:

> Possibly because I am a blind person it had a strange effect, because I like to pick up particular things about the settings, the sounds, the music, tones of voice established where I am. It opens with a cityscape, which is unmistakably New York through the sounds of sirens and the car horns. But then you are suddenly left drifting, voices come in but they are just voices in a space. [. . .] The thing that is wonderful about it is that you realize there is a bit of a mystery. It immediately asks questions and the listener is obliged or drawn in; Why is this happening? Why is the hotel, a building, speaking? It is a very unusual concept. The hotel, obviously knows about Dylan Thomas. Once he goes and closes his hotel bedroom door he is then actually who he is. So that's when the hotel can actually say 'You are not telling the truth. This is not the real Dylan Thomas.' It's as though the walls were an omniscient narrator, walls are able to say 'So you think you are so special. You think you can drink eighteen double whiskies in a row. That's nothing to the people we have had staying in the Chelsea Hotel.'
>
> (Hubbard quoted in Chaplin 2006)

Andrew Hubbard's powerful appreciation of the listening experience and the complex and detailed meanings he has been able to articulate demonstrate the polysemic properties of radio drama and indeed most sound texts. The variety and imaginary vividness of mental perception can be applied to evaluation of soundplay across the ambiguous boundary of news, documentary and drama (Crook 1999:55–60).

Van Leeuwen's influential book *Speech, Music, Sound* contains a significant chapter on what he describes as 'Modality' (Van Leeuwen 1999:156–88). Modality is defined as:

A set of resources for indicating the *truth* of presentation/representations, for example for indicating as how real (some part of) a soundtrack should be regarded, or as how sincere a tone of voice should be taken. The modality of a sound event (or some part or aspect of it) is then said to be 'high', 'medium' or 'low'.

(208)

Van Leeuwen advises a consideration of configuration in the mixture of high or low modality cues such as when naturalistic sound recordings and musical styles combine in the soundtrack of filmic live action and animation. In great detail he sets out a grid or scale for modality analysis:

The modality configuration of a particular sound event is realised by the values of the various modality scales which characterize that sound (that is, its pitch extent, durational variety, dynamic range, perspectival depth, amount of fluctuation, amount of friction, amount of absorption and directionality). Which of the poles on these scales have highest modality depends on the relevant coding orientation.

(208)

The psychological intensity and value of human perception has been explored in a BBC Radio Four *All In The Mind* documentary broadcast in 2010 on the case of 'SB – The Man Who Was Disappointed with What He Saw'. Sidney Bradford was born in 1906 and lost his sight when he was only ten months old. When it was finally restored with corneal grafts at the age of fifty-two, a lecturer in Experimental Psychology at Cambridge, Richard Gregory, began a series of tests on him. What he found was that Mr Bradford's mind had been so psychologically acclimatised to a sound world and the tuning of his own imagination, he found the connections between his thinking brain and new sight disorientating, confusing and profoundly disappointing. The world he saw with his eyes was never as impressive or interesting as it was in his imagination. The radio programme explored how:

at the Science Museum 'SB' was captivated by the Maudsley screw-cutting lathe from 1800; he enjoyed the flurry of pigeons in Trafalgar Square, and laughed at the giraffes at London Zoo. But in general he found the visual world a disappointing place. He died less than two years after his sight was restored.
(Burgess, 2010)

This contrasted greatly with the experience of Mike May, an American who lost his sight aged three and recovered it when he was forty-three. Psychological research into the nature of perception concludes that human beings have to 'learn' to see and 'without accumulating visual experience from which the brain can make sense of what the eyes see, vision is of little use' (Burgess, 2010).

Psychology has also made considerable progress in the investigation of the phenomenon of synaesthesia whereby the human mind can experience cross-sensory perception; in other words, two or more senses are interconnected. In his study *The Frog Who Croaked Blue* Jamie Ward declares:

> Synesthesia is a real phenomenon with a biological basis that is found in a minority of people. It is not, however, a disorder. Nor is it a condition that requires treatment or sympathy. [. . .] In fact, synesthesia is a condition that many people aspire to. Many artists seek to recreate it. Many cultures induce it using 'magical' plants to achieve spiritual enlightenment.
>
> (Ward 2008:2)

Dr Ward's study references numerous scientifically peer-reviewed articles demonstrating evidence of sightless people being able to hear colours, hence the question posed in a sub-heading 'Can a blind man hear scarlet?' His text opens with an account of the recorded testimony of a three-year-old child:

> Edgar Curtis is the son of Professor and Mrs. O.F. Curtis of Cornell University. At the time of this writing he is three years and seven months old . . . About two months ago his mother noticed for the first time that apparently he has coloured hearing. Their home is not far from a rifle range, and the sound of the guns resounds through the hills with a loud 'boom'. One day Edgar asked: 'What is that big black noise?' A few days later he was being put to bed on the sleeping porch. Two crickets were chirping loudly, one of them having the usual cricket-sound with which he was familiar, the other having a very high, shrill chirp in comparison. He asked: 'What is that little white noise?' When his mother told him that it was a cricket he was not satisfied, and he said: 'Not the brown one, but the little white noise.' Then he imitated both of them, calling the lower brown and the shriller of the two white. At another time, when a cricket-chirp uttered from farther away came with a resonant buzz, he called it red. He calls the sound of the cicada white. The electric fan is orange, and the electric cleaner which has a deep 'burr' is black. The sound of a frog, neither very high nor very low, is bluish. (Reprinted from Whitchurch, A.K. (1922) Synaesthesia in a child of three and half years. *American Journal of Psychology, 33*, 302–303)
>
> (Ward 2008:xiii)

The BBC Radio Four programme *All In The Mind* visited Dr Ward's laboratory at Sussex University in 2008 and learned that the research of his team indicated that synaesthesia was a more widespread and legitimated sensory experience than previously realised. Subjects experiencing 'mirror touch', an actual physical contact feeling, when seeing physical pain in others appeared to have a heightened sense of empathy that was mind experienced. The programme enquired into Dr Ward's investigation of the experience of spatial maps in the mind. Dr Ward said it was:

Certainly one of the most common types of synaesthesia, and between ten and twenty per cent of the population experience, in particular, time as being arranged in space. [. . .] One woman who I've worked with says of BC and AD 'The transitions are about here. The Romans are over there. And dinosaurs are down here on the left towards the bottom.'

(Hill 2008)

There was discussion that synaesthesia might be an inherited and genetic condition and Dr Ward observed that it seemed to cluster in the same families.

The interdisciplinary and multidisciplinary interest in synaesthesia led to a 'Synaesthesia Symposium' hosted by Goldsmiths, University of London, in 2009 entitled 'Future of Sound Future of Light'. It was presented by a creative and dynamic academic synergy of Goldsmiths Screen School, the Sound Practice Research Unit, Centre for Contemporary Music Cultures, the Sonic Arts Network and Illustrious. Dr Julian Henriques synoptically expressed the converging intellectual and aesthetic interest in the phenomenon with his talk 'Multi senses and multi media':

The symposium aims to stimulate new multi media artistic work and discussion – by using synaesthetic experience to question conventional assumption about the senses. It explores the relationships between our multiple sense and multiple media through presentations from key artists. Their work is often concerned with the relationship between sound and vision, for instance, as well as the interfaces between player and instrument, as with the theremin, or Oram's graphic synthe-siser played by shapes drawn on film. Conventionally, the idea of synaesthesia is considered as a confusion between sensory modes – often illustrated in the work of poets, painters and musicians such as Rimbaud, Kandinsky, Boccioni and Scriabin, and increasingly, neurological research. But this idea of synaesthesia rests on the assumption that cross modal perception is abnormal. Second it assumes that the senses are limited in number and separate from one another, rather than inter-related. This is questioned by developmental psycholo-gist Daniel Stern's concept of 'amodal perception' and Russian psychologist B. Galeyev's conception of 'inter-sensory transfer.' A third assumption is that the senses are hierarchically organized, privileging vision. But visual culture's monopoly is questioned, for example, by Barry Truax and Murray Schafer's soundscape research. A fourth assumption is that sensing bodies are separate from the world. This is questioned by ecological psychologist James Gibson's refusal of the dichotomy between 'internal' and 'external' worlds – in favour of the affordances of a 'multi sensory flux.' So, are we all synaesthetes now?

(Henriques 2009)

The sound text student has the advantage of a cultural memory and participation in the sighted world. Any directed listening to an audio drama programme or documentary by closing the eyes to engage a concentration of hearing provides an opportunity of evaluating the sensory value and experience of listening as well as its value as a socially mediated experience. Chaplin suggested the following criteria of analysis for students studying *Chelsea Dreaming*.

- How are speech, music and other sounds arranged and organised to create a drama?
- How are speech, music and other sounds used to convey a sense of space, a setting?
- How do we know what time of day or year it is?
- What is different about the way in which stories are told in a radio, as opposed to a television, drama?

(Chaplin 2006:17)

Such close analysis of any sound text tests any residual knowledge of cultural sounds, codes and conventions, ability to recognise intertextual references and how the construction of sounds in narrative determines and stimulates meaning. It is an opportunity to evaluate 'how our shared knowledge of conventions helps us to interpret sounds, voice and music in particular ways' (2006:17).

Bordwell and Thompson recommend a template of six key questions in the intensive perceptual sound and visual scrutiny of film audiovisual interaction:

1   What sounds are present – music, speech, noise? How are loudness, pitch and timbre used? Is the mixture sparse or dense? Modulated or abruptly changing?
2   Is the sound related rhythmically to the image? If so, how?
3   Is the sound faithful or unfaithful to its perceived source?
4   Where is the sound coming from? In the story's space or outside it? Onscreen or offscreen?
5   When is the sound occurring? Simultaneously with the story action? Before? After?
6   How are the various sorts of sounds organized across a sequence or the entire film? What patterns are formed, and how do they reinforce aspects of the film's overall formal system (narrative or non-narrative)?
7   For each of questions 1–6, what purposes are fulfilled and what effects are achieved by the sonic manipulations?

(Bordwell and Thompson 1997:349)

REPRESENTATION

How does the sound text represent reality? The focus here is in the construction of representations that will have implicit ideology, meanings and values. How does the sound represent social groups and categorise people in terms of gender, sexuality, socio-economic group, disability, age, race and nationality? Does the sound text represent stereotypes or counter-stereotypes? How does the sound text appeal to its target audience and how does it establish its ideology? Other issues to be explored include the positive or negative representations in the text, the aural method of establishment through the use of microphones and sound recording technology, the mise-en-scène, the accuracy and fairness of the representation and the omission of representations that were expected.

The audio cues are, of course, significant. It should also be appreciated that the deployment of audio conveys meaning in the context of juxtapositioned visual media language. A musical track can underpin characterisation in audio drama and film. Allowing documentary subjects to speak for themselves in montage offers cultural autonomy and spatial narrative whereas voice-over or an omniscient narrative commentary can ventriloquise, negotiate and qualify the value and status of interviewees. When the sound is in a matrix of media language, does it have the paradigm in determining meaning? A further consideration includes an analysis of the representation of reality in fictional and non-fictional texts. What are the sound signs used to construct these representations – that is, words, sounds, music and silence – and why are they being used by the media producers? What ideologies are being deployed to interact with the target audiences?

Fundamentally sound is as semiotic as visual imagery so that the word polysemic, meaning carrying a variety of meanings at any one time, has its equivalent power in polyphonic. The influential theorist in the academic discipline of linguistics, C.S. Pierce, argued that socially communicated language has the elements of a signified and signifier; the concrete reality represented by the sign being the *signifier* and the concept of meaning represented by the sign being the *signified*. Crisell discoursed the application of Pierce's categorisation of signs into the indexal, iconic, symbolic and arbitrary in *Understanding Radio* (Crisell 1994:48). Branston and Stafford in *The Media Student's Handbook* discuss how the sound of fictional and non-fictional characters is a coded, signified and indexal representation:

> Imagine: you can't see a person, but you can hear their voice. What does this tell you about them?
>
> - *Pitch*: Is the voice 'high' or 'low'?
> - *Volume*: 'loud' or 'quiet'?
> - *Shape*: 'round' or 'flat'?
> - *Rhythm or cadence*: does the voice rise and fall or keep a continuous pace and tone? Recently an upward inflection at the end of sentences, has spread like wildfire across the English-speaking world, some say from Australian soap operas.
>
> Key components of voices will be in play:
>
> - *Accent*, which usually refers to pronunciation (and often rhythm, cadence) and inflection. British voices are particularly characterised by accents: flattened or 'extended' vowels, missed consonants.

- *Dialect*: everyone in the UK speaks a dialect, a sub-language which differs from a notional 'standard English'. So-called 'received pronunciation' or 'BBC English'' is the dialect of the southern English middle class. Dialects also have differences of vocabulary and syntax as well as pronunciation, and dialect and accent together are read as key signifiers of class origin.

- *Language register*: the vocabulary and syntax (grammar) we use to suit particular circumstances. Most of us are capable of changing this, from formal to informal modes for example.

(Branston and Stafford 2003:29–30)

All sound media texts are capable of being re-presentations of reality, and it is important to identify what representations of people, place, time and culture are being constructed by the text and how these are being employed to create meaning. There may be sound stereotypes or sound countertypes, or complex representations that are ambiguous and ironic and it is useful to bear in mind that they have been socially constructed to appeal to a particular target audience.

When a listening text is studied you are considering what representations are constructed, why they are constructed, and how listeners receive and consume them. Sound plays the same role of other media in often making representations of people, events, history and situations that listeners only obtain from the media. Most listeners are unlikely to meet celebrities they hear or have close tangible experiences with people and events represented in such texts.

Sound representation is a key concept because listeners make conscious decisions about why they accept or challenge the representations they hear. Intellectually it could be said to be a fallacy to make the claim that representations are unbiased in any way. Ideology, meanings and values are implicit in the sound textual representations. As a result media institutions publishing sound, such as radio corporations or public state broadcasters, have considerable power and responsibility in the process of representation.

This would certainly be the case with powerful radio institutions such as the high profile breakfast programme *Today* on BBC Radio Four. The representation of politics, conflicts, crime, asylum seekers, Roma and illegal immigrants can have profound social and political consequences by influencing attitudes. In this way the sound media can be accomplices to crime panics or moral panics in the way they represent people and marginalised or demonised social, ethnic groups.

There are many ways of categorising people and places through representations and they are capable of conjuring pejorative, negative, positive and valorising connotations. Key categories have included sexuality, race, gender, age, disability, nationality and socio-economic grouping. Generally stereotypes are negative representations, heavily invested with cultural capital to undermine the status and credibility of an entire social group through the characterisation of a single individual. Stereotypes are characters in sound media texts who are types rather than complex individuals and they are usually defined by their role in the programme in which they are appearing.

In the US radio comedy series *Amos 'n' Andy* it was argued by the National Association for the Advancement of Coloured People (NAACP) that African American characters were stereotypically represented as 'Uncle Toms' by always being constructed as stupid, gullible and inferior in social status. In contemporary radio drama racist stereotyping would probably lead to prosecution, or regulatory intervention. However, there are many other dramatic roles that appear in commercial radio adverts and BBC radio drama that could be conceived as one dimensionally constructed. Good cops and bad cops in crime mysteries, family matriarchs in sitcoms, docile and dithering grandparents are all examples. Children's radio drama tends to use stereotypes because it is thought this accelerates the way younger listeners can identify with the story. Incidentally, the BBC in Britain during the 1930s had its own equivalent problematisation of sound racial stereotypes in a light entertainment series entitled *The Kentucky Minstrels*, but where the central comedic performers were actually individuals of African and American descent who 'blacked up' in terms of vocal performance and characterisation. There was a considerable cultural irony in that Scott and Whaley were both African-Americans, unlike Freeman Gosden and Charles Correll who were both white southern Americans.

In the field of popular music it could be argued that boy bands are constructed for the sonic imagination by using stereotypical representations of the sporty boy, the casual boy and the quiet boy. It is important to explain how the stereotype engages with the wider context of plot and storyline. Try and appreciate what is the use of the stereotype as well as how the stereotype is constructed.

Representations within a sound text contribute to the definition of ideology. An understanding of the ideology of a text generates expectations of stereotypical roles. This means that the unfolding of many sitcoms within the first minute or two has served to define the roles of family members. Representations are also defined by the deployment of radio and sound genre conventions. Particular stereotypes are associated with specific genres. The relationship between radio and sound audience and textual representation is complex and important. Mabel Constanduros's first radio sitcom on BBC Radio, *The Buggins*, made use of classic comic stereo-typical conventions. The dour and grumpy matriarch Grandma Buggins is an example. Close study of the radio sitcoms and format of the early radio family soap operas conceived and written by Constanduros represent the deployment of ideological codes about middle class life in England in the 1920s, 1930s and 1940s.

AUDIENCE

This is a pillar of media studies analysis and concentrates on why sound texts or media texts constructed with sound are produced. It might be argued that an art for art's sake motivation in producing a sound installation has inevitably to consider audience if created for a community environment or high cultural institution such as the Tate Modern in London or the Guggenheim and Museum of Modern Art in New York City.

Mass media sound forms such as records, CDs, downloadable digital audio tracks, podcasts and radio transmissions are usually produced for mass audiences and with content created to increase audience appeal and satisfaction. A musical production of the national anthem will be created to further the ideology of patriotism and if commissioned by the executive government of state will be produced to ensure that the head of state is pleased with the sound of its message and meaning. Its content in terms of lyrics and music will define a state ideology and identity, but at the same time needs to entertain and please the state's subjects or citizens in order to be respected and sustain the function for which it has been created.

Sound is also produced for niche audiences such as the arts and experimental not-for-profit radio station in South London, Resonance FM. Such dedicated and loyal audiences can also represent a major attraction to commercial advertisers who would be interested in promoting and marketing products to high disposable income and/or affluent and well educated target audience demographics. Sociologists and marketing professionals like to structure and categorise audiences.

Audiences can be segmented in terms of socio-economic modelling, and consequently sound content will be evaluated in terms of its appeal and interest to the age, gender, demographic or social geography, consumer profile and social tribe – that is, communities or groups of people who can be defined by their values, attitudes and lifestyles. This means that a sound advertisement, record or radio programme constructed to target well remunerated and well educated graduate and postgraduate professionals such as doctors, lawyers, chief executives and wealthy entrepreneurs is referencing a marketing group known as Group A. The UK's national classical music radio stations Classic FM, BBC Radio Three or Radio France's equivalent niche channel, France Musique, transmit programming formats that would appeal to 'Group A' people.

Such a radio station might also appeal to Group B – a category defined as teachers, less-well-paid professionals and people in middle management. Advertisers also structure their audience definitions in terms of Group C1 – 'white collar' workers such as bank clerks, call centre workers and nurses; Group C2 – skilled 'blue collar' workers such as electricians, plumbers and builders; and Groups D and E – which include semi and unskilled manual workers such as white van drivers, post office workers, students, the unemployed and pensioners.

Target audiences are said to mediate the way sound is constructed and audience theories such as 'uses and gratifications' or 'media effects' can be applied in order to analyse the impact and negotiation or mediation by target audiences. Sound texts are said to be 'read' in the process of hearing and listening. The categorised definition of 'preferred readings' is applied to messages and meanings that producers of the sound text want the audience to receive, and 'oppositional readings' are said to be heard by an audience who reject the preferred reading and have experienced their own alternative meaning. In 'negotiated readings' listeners have accepted the producer's message but at the same time interpreted the sound in order to mix and interpolate their own independent understanding.

IDEOLOGY

Sound has the ability to communicate implicit and explicit ideology, and media producers either consciously or subconsciously encode sound texts with a dominant ideological discourse. This can be identified in a variety of sound forms from a recorded song in the music business, audio advertisement on a talk radio station, to a propagandist documentary constructed to lower the morale of an enemy population.

It may occur to you that a radio programme may not have an explicit political ideology such as the national newspaper *The Daily Mail*, but there could well be an implicit ideology that is being constructed for the audience. Textual analysis is concerned with the identification of a dominant ideology that is accepted and understood by the majority of the people listening as part of their culture and expectations. For example, how does a radio programme, whether an advert or even a phone-in show, advocate a system of belief constructed and presented by the participants and their words and sounds? How does the radio programme represent the views of the surrounding society and the attitudes of its listeners? You are likely to find the clues in the nuances of language used. In any discussion about conflict who is awarded the status of victory and who is described as having been defeated. In any news report of a strike is it claimed that the workers 'demanded' improved pay and conditions or is it the case that the employers 'resisted' or 'conceded'. The choice of vocabulary reveals ideological attitudes to those groups regarded as unjustifiable aggressors.

In the reporting or discussion of business news it may be the case that a large global bank is being described as doing 'the right thing' when imposing several thousand redundancies because annual profits have dropped from one billion pounds to 'only' half a billion. The language is uncritical and accepting of an economic system that places a priority of enhanced profit over the employment rights of thousands of individuals. The Italian political theorist Antonio Gramsci explained that hegemony is the method by which those with power continue to exercise it. The dominant ideologies in radio texts are often described as hegemonic in that by constructing appropriate ideologies through mass media promotion, those in power keep it. This is a critical Marxist standpoint, arguing that radio listeners are effectively indoctrinated by radio programming into adopting the attitudes and values that the ruling classes wish to impose. This means that the radio media is an accomplice of the ruling classes in exercising control over radio listeners by maintaining the hegemony of cultural and social expectations. This is achieved through a process of narrative persuasion in radio media texts. It is subtle. While there will be reports that criticise the conduct of the police, the overall tone of radio media coverage of police activities will imply that they are doing a good job and are almost always right.

Patriotism is an obvious dominant ideology. When any society is involved in military conflict the dominant ideology is patriotism, the need to support 'our troops'. As a result the radio media coverage of opposition to the invasion of Iraq in 2003 became more muted and attenuated once battle had commenced. Anti-war politicians and messages became marginalised and problematised in an intensity of patriotic consensus. You should be able to identify patriotism as a dominant ideological tapestry in radio broadcasting of England soccer matches in the World Cup or coverage of tours by the Royal Family overseas.

Other significant twentieth-century theorists worthy of mention are Louis Althusser and Noam Chomsky, who investigated the relationship and balance between explicit textual ideologies, where the media institutional identity clearly defines its political bias, and implicit ideologies that encode moral and political philosophy in the sonic messaging. Althusser, as a post-Marxist, discussed how ideological indoctrination and persuasion is communicated through hard and soft power. The military, police and legal societal infrastructures explicitly communicate a rule of law and ideology experienced as sovereign state power. Softer and more implicit ideological state structures of communication are sustained through an inculcation of values and beliefs that are naturalised as commonsensical assumptions and expectations through the institutions of education, religion, everyday political discourse and media reception.

These ideological forces manufacture and maintain a consent and acceptance of the prevailing class hierarchy, social and political order. This direction of thought and analysis motivated and inspired Noam Chomsky to co-write the seminal book *Manufacturing Consent: The Political Economy of the Mass Media* with Edward S. Herman (1988). Chomsky and Herman argued that the mass media operates after the manner of Karl Marx's view of religion, as an opiate of the people, in the sense that its distorted content diverts attention and masks the reality of poverty creation and pervasiveness of self-perpetuating capitalist and corporate elites. Popular culture is manipulated, boosted and celebrated in order to tranquilise the social imagination. Reality television and soap opera dominates and marginalises investigative documentary and critical journalism. It is often referred to as 'the propaganda model' of media theory.

It might be argued that Chomsky and his supporters demonstrated a sound propaganda technique in the 1992 Canadian film documentary of the same name. The text impersonated surgeons and used heart monitor and respirator sound effects with the visual graphics of a scalpel and sutures to deconstruct a newspaper article about human rights abuses in East Timor, invaded by Indonesia in 1975. The production was dramatising Chomsky's argument that because Indonesia was an ally of the USA, the *New York Times* had de-emphasised the reality of atrocities by reprinting a selectively edited London *Times* report (NPR 1993).

INSTITUTION

Media institutions produce sound texts in the context of institutional perspectives shaping content and the need to serve and provide for target audiences. Media studies analyses the media institutional context and institutional codes and conventions. The geography of mass media clearly has a considerable space for media sound producing institutions such as radio stations, multimedia publishers providing podcasts and audio-streamed news, features and programmes, and music entertainment companies that range from global brands such as EMI and Sony to thousands of smaller independent music production companies serving the CD, repro vinyl and digital downloading markets.

As the companion website indicates, in the UK and USA there is an identifiable business sector of independent production companies that pitch for and sell programming to larger media institutions. The process of academic analysis concentrates on the role of funding/money, the nature of ownership and ideological control, aesthetic and social motivations or missions, and the role and power relationship of the audience.

Radio stations and networks in the UK are generally classified as commercial, public service, and community. In the commercial sphere at the time of writing the largest radio group is Global, which has a substantial London-based programme production and transmission centre in Leicester Square, with ownership of the national Classic FM, regional Heart and London Capital and LBC brands. The BBC is a significant micro, meso and macro sound media institution through its ownership and production of local, regional, national and international services as well as a significant sound based multimedia presence online. The BBC's funding base is primarily through a licence fee that is sustained and negotiated in a complex political and constitutional context.

Commercial radio companies are 'regulated' by the state apparatus of Ofcom (the Office of Communications), the direction of which is determined by national legislation. Community radio stations are similarly regulated though constructed under different rules with a limited share-out of central funding and carefully regulated alternative sources of income. In the USA the radio industry, both analogue and digital, is primarily commercial though regulated by the Federal Communications Commission (FCC). It might be argued that there is a public service broadcasting equivalent dimension through 'public radio' networks such as Pacifica, National Public Radio (NPR) and Public Radio International (PRI, formerly American Public Radio) that derive their funds from a centrally constituted federal body, The Corporation for Public Broadcasting, and local listener subscription membership and fundraising. Would these public radio media institutions be classified as independent? The debate and discussion becomes intriguingly complex. There are transnational and global issues arising out of the BBC's involvement and partnership with US public radio organisations and indeed government cross-funding between US and UK radio institutions. Debates are triggered about the role of BBC values and their impact on American public radio cultures as well as the problem of content provision being influenced by the complicated and confusing ideological identity and 'ownership' of radio broadcasting bodies (Dvorkin 2004 and Dowell 2011).

On the 26 and 28 March 2011, BBC Radio Four broadcast an hour-length documentary about the nature of sound collections and archives operated by the British Library's National Sound Archive (NSA). *Walls of Sound* was a production of two media institutions and in its content provided a fascinating demonstration of media studies concepts specific to the sound medium. The archivists at NSA are not said to *produce* programmes. They are described as *curators* of sound. Through central state funding and a commercial realisation of the property value of a previous site in Kensington the programme reported an expansion and infrastructure of studios and sound preservation of audio collections across three floors of the British Library's London headquarters in St Pancras, London. And the programme, presented by Professor Seán Street of Bournemouth University, created a fascinating aural canvas for a consideration of the variety of sounds that have been selected because they are said to have cultural and social value for human civilisation. The NSA's existence began in 1955, many decades after the gestation of sound recording and transmission technologies.

In 1964 a court of the white dominated South African regime sentenced Nelson Mandela to life imprisonment in what became known as the Rivonia Trial in which ten leaders of the African National Congress had been tried for 221 acts of sabotage designed to overthrow the apartheid system. The account of that courtroom event had been primarily consigned to media literature. The media cameras and microphones were not permitted access, a situation true of most court hearings in Britain apart from the new UK Supreme Court that from 2009 was permitted to film its proceedings. Yet the South African judicial system had operated a confidential archiving process of recording the proceedings on 'dictabelt'. Nearly half a century later the NSA was asked to investigate the technological possibilities of retrieving the sound in a post-apartheid South Africa that now realised the historical importance of the sound of this event. In this programme the familiar words of Mandela's defiant speech to the court hauntologically were resurrected in sound.

How should this process be described? Some sound theorists have begun to use the word 'hauntological' as a way of defining the phenomenon of remembering and celebrating events and times past by fetishising, commodifying and socially and politically commemorating the sound recording of the occasion. Marxists and post-Marxist theorists would use the word 'fetishise' to describe the way that the repeated utilisation of the sound can create an investment of political and social power and resonance that is also the equivalent of a commodification exchange value in capitalist and post-capitalist societies.

This archive of sound took listeners in 2011 back to the event so that they not only experienced the text as words of political resistance, but the emotion, courage and dignity of the occasion itself. Instead of a world statesman in his nineties, we were able to hear a young and vigorous man of conscience stating that he was prepared to die for his cause:

> I have cherished the ideal of a democratic and free society in which all persons live together in harmony and with equal opportunity. It is an ideal which I hope to live for and achieve, but, if needs be, it is an ideal for which I am prepared to die.
>
> (Nelson Mandela broadcast in J. May 2011)

There are many recordings whose hauntological value is sometimes enhanced by the clandestine or confidential nature of their original circumstances. Adolf Hitler's frank discussion about the prowess of Soviet military power and resources on the 4 June 1942 with the military leader of Finland, General Carl Gustav Mannerheim, was recorded by the Finnish secret service without Hitler's knowledge and permission. Consequently we have a representation of this notorious dictator as an everyday speaker that is counter-stereotypical to his carefully choreographed performances of public rhetoric in large-scale rallies (Deutches Rundfunkarchiv 2004).

This sound text of Nelson Mandela speaking in the courtroom was invested with a complex array of ideological, representational, and institutional issues. In some ways we had the ghost of Nelson Mandela and this dramatic trial existing and communicating knowledge and being in time present; hence the proposed application of Jacques Derrida's neologism *hauntology*. The programme conjured many more ghosts from the British Library's vaults of sound: the words of Florence Nightingale at the end of the Victorian age urging charitable relief for her fellow Balaclava veterans, the Irish novelist and modernist James Joyce recording a limited edition of 20 discs in a Paris left-bank bookshop, perhaps the first sound recording ever made by Thomas Edison in the 1870s on a tin foil drum only recently reproduced as the result of digital laser three-dimensional modelling of the surviving artefact.

But the hauntological resurrection of human identity and existences from the past and media events charged with social, cultural and political significance through sound is not consigned to the articulation of power elites. The NSA preserves and studies the voices of human community on a bottom up as well as top down scale; albeit in a deliberate process of intent that is dependent more often on serendipity and accident. As the presenter of *Walls of Sound*, Seán Street, so presciently observed, the survival and studying of the voices of 'ordinary' people suggest a democratisation of sound and can be deeply moving. This is particularly so in the example of the sound of the soldier Frank Spragg who was permitted to record a phonograph message for his family in Coventry when serving in an armoured brigade in the North African desert in 1942. NSA radio curator Paul Wilson marked the impact of broadcasting this voice from the past on his *Sound Recordings Blog*:

One touching moment in the programme is the on-air transfer of the previously unheard contents of a booth disc recording picked up by Philatelic curator Paul Skinner at an online auction. It was found to contain a private audio letter from a British soldier based in Egypt during World War 2 to his family back home in Coventry – then still reeling from the blitz which had killed over 1,000 and flattened more than 60,000 buildings. Within hours of its transmission, a message was received from a Mr Keith Spragg, nephew of soldier Frank Spragg, expressing his joy at hearing a 67 year old recording he had no idea even existed, and at the unexpected opportunity of hearing again the voice of an uncle who'd survived the war but finally passed away in 1998.

(Wilson 2011)

Walls of Sound represented a process of mediated social action that went beyond summoning the ghosts of the past by reproducing the sound of history. The NSA archivists also provided Seán Street and BBC Radio Four listeners with the opportunity to hear an ethnographic music recording of the court musicians of the Kabaka of Buganda at the Lubiri Palace in 1949. The personal significance of this recording for myself is that I knew that this performance in all likelihood was heard by my late father who had been a Foreign Office official in Uganda in the 1950s, had known personally King Freddie, the King of Buganda deposed in a violent coup d'état in 1965 that subsequently led to the destruction of the musical culture and the deaths of most of the musicians. When I heard the programme, I pulled from my shelves the books on Bugandan that my father had used to learn and speak the language. As a child I remembered meeting the exiled king in London in the 1960s. The radio programme revealed that this resonance of personal family and Ugandan royal history extended beyond the hauntological experience to a re-materialisation of culture. These valuable recordings of courtly music from 1949 were returned to Kampala University where the sounds helped to reconstitute the musical DNA of the past so that a succeeding generation of court musicians could rediscover their art, culture and identity and resurrect and evolve their musical traditions. A further radio documentary broadcast by the BBC in 2011, *Ghost Music*, focused on the discovery of 3,000 year old silver and bronze trumpets in the tomb of Tutankhamen, one of which was played in a BBC Radio programme in 1939 by soldier bandsman James Tappern, a recording that had been archived and could be resurrected 72 years later. The programme investigated the process of musical archaeology represented by Lost Sounds Orchestra, an international group that recreates the sound of ancient instruments using technology and synthesis (Burgess 2011).

The British Library's NSA embraces a wide portfolio of curating the sound of human community: classical music; drama and literature; oral history; moving image; popular music; radio recordings; wildlife sounds; world and traditional music. The British Library encourages anyone to participate in the recording of voices so that the nature of the evolving English language is catalogued and available for analysis in terms of its representational characteristics. An oral history project in 1999 captured a bottom-up record of English speaking at the time of the 2000 millennium, and for the 2010–11 exhibition *Evolving English: One Language Many Voices*, anyone had the opportunity of contributing their personal accents, words and voices using library recording booths, and an online voice-blogging application, AudioBoo. The accelerating increase of high quality digital recording technology embedded in mobile personal communications equipment means that the capturing of the sound experience is becoming a citizen's prerogative. Everyday life and events are being recorded and preserved outside large-scale and powerful media institutional communicative frames.

In fact the NSA's curators are discovering that sound recordings made in this way in the past inform the historicist perspective and have the effect of transforming historiography. Private recordings of commercial radio of the 1930s and live musical performance not preserved by media institutions such as the BBC make available sonic texts or 'aural documents' that can rewrite as well as gestate history. Regional accents and dialects spoken by British working class soldiers kept prisoners of war by Germany between 1914 and 1918 are discovered in the archives of a study run by an academic socio-linguist, the *heimathörspiel* or *heimspiel* actuality of Karl Jung are discovered because he had been given recording technology to assist with the preparation of a book he was writing during the 1950s. And the sonic hauntology is not restricted to human speech. It turns out that birds have regional accents as well. The programme *Walls of Sound* ends with the birdsong of an extinct species. The Kauai O'o A'a in Hawaii tragically calls out to a mate that had been killed in a hurricane of the previous year and in a note of poignant dramatic irony, Seán Street observes that the bird is 'unaware that he is now completely alone in the world'.

What are the ideological and political implications of this process on a micro-personal scale? I was personally involved in a secret judicial hearing in London in 1994, the nature of which I am prohibited from communicating to anyone for all time. The ruling of the court *in camera* was in fact recorded electronically, but it is more than likely, unlike the dictabelts kept from Nelson Mandela's sentencing in 1964, that the reel-to-reel audio tape has been re-used, wiped or destroyed. Decades or centuries in the future neither the sound nor written content of this secret hearing may ever emerge into the light of knowledge and understanding. However, I may have old audio-cassettes of recordings I was permitted to make of the dramatic courtroom hearings of a sensational inquest in 1982 concerning the death of a British nurse called Helen Smith in Jeddah, Saudi Arabia. Her father believed she had been murdered. The coroner in Leeds permitted journalists to make audio recordings to assist them with note-taking. There is a court order preventing their use in any other form. Is it possible that this prohibition might be discharged or redundant sometime in the future? Is it possible I may still have these cassettes in dust and cobweb covered cardboard boxes in my attic? Might the NSA be able to curate the sound of a British inquest proceeding from 1982 sometime in the future?

A tape recording I made in that year in the Lord Chief Justice's court in London has, however, survived. Extracts have been broadcast and in its entirety it is available on the companion website for this book. I was given permission to record the entire valedictory ceremony of the retirement of the then celebrated Master of the Rolls, Lord Tom Denning. In a hearing of some forty minutes, the establishment of England's legal profession packed the huge courtroom to pay tribute to his life and career. The voices of the Lord Chancellor, Lord Chief Justice, Attorney General, Lord Denning himself and many other senior judicial and legal figures materialise the existence of people who have since died. It is an event invested with emotion, power, ideological and cultural significance and in its hauntology is charged with past and present resonance that becomes a fascinating experience of mediation for the listener. This phenomenology is explored in the elegant poetic and philosophical prose of David Toop in his 2010 text *Sinister Resonance: The Mediumship of the Listener*:

> *Sinister Resonance* begins with the premise that sound is a haunting, a ghost, a presence whose location in space is ambiguous and whose existence in time is transitory. The intangibility of time is uncanny – a phenomenal presence both in the head, at its point of source and all around – so never entirely distinct from auditory hallucinations. The close listener is like a medium who draws out substance from that which is not entirely there. Listening, after all, is always a form of eavesdropping.
>
> Because sound vanishes into air and past time, the history of listening must be constructed from the narratives of myth and fiction, 'silent' arts such as painting, the resonance of architecture, auditory artefacts and nature. In such contexts, sound often functions as a metaphor for mystical revelation, instability, forbidden desires, disorder, formlessness, the supernatural, for the breaking of social taboos, the unknown, unconscious and extra-human.
>
> (Toop 2010:xv)

NARRATIVE

This key concept has a general relevance to the study of all media sound texts since sound, even in its non-verbal abstract forms, intends to or is understood to communicate a story. Aristotle's classical text on tragedy *Poetics* and the Greek theatrical tradition have underpinned the narrative concept of the unity of the three act play where crisis cliff-hanging plot points at the end of the first two acts become resolved, usually with an ideological, acceptable and 'happy' finish at the close of the third act.

It could be argued that there is a clearly defined line of narrative theory from classical antiquity to the modernist age and postmodernist surrendering of authorial control of meaning in structuralism and post-structuralism. If the engagement of sound narrative involves a paradigmatic application of emotional and imaginative consciousness it might be possible to highlight where this would be served by narrative conventions. *Poetics* is an influential criticism of Greek tragedy by Aristotle and it is possible to appreciate how sound productions, whether fact or fiction, can combine the elements of plot, character and 'imaginative spectacle' to produce 'pity and fear'. Any counterpoint of 'pity and fear' reacts at the core of emotional consciousness. In the sound form any narrative *topos* of creation, performance and reception is likely to generate a special pleasure in exploring and experiencing the emotional and psychological pain of 'pity and fear'.

Aristotle's preoccupation with what he described as mimesis (imitation), hamartia (error) and catharsis must have locations in the transmission and reception of sound texts. It must also be possible to investigate any merging of poetics and rhetoric in sound narrative and whether this can promote a better and proper understanding of the human soul. Classical narrative discourse raises an interesting question about sound media texts even in the twenty-first century. Sound texts can be tested in their ability to provide an interface between a skill dedicated to persuading an audience through rhetoric and the art of poetry, which in the classical tradition was considered an imitative art that seeks to produce a particular pleasure. Classical theorists were interested in ideas about story telling and narrative unity. Horacian 'organic unity' emphasised that:

> every part and every aspect of that work must be appropriate to the nature of the work as a whole: the choice of subject in relation to the chosen genre, the characterisation, the form, the expression, the metre, the style and the tone.
>
> (Murray 2000:xl)

The idea that cathartic and balanced storytelling supports a sense of socio-psychological equilibrium is an active cross-disciplinary academic debate:

> In a parallel way, narrative theorists (Labov, 1982; Bruner, 1990; Linde, 1993) describe how we tell stories about troubling events in our everyday experience in order to regain some sense of equilibrium in our lives. The important shared concept at the heart of both Gestalt theory and narrative theory is that we are constantly addressing and attempting to make sense of 'disequilibrium' in our experience.
>
> (Mortola 1999:308)

The nature of the arrangement of the constituent elements of narrative have a role in a perception of pleasing and emotional and cultural stability (Crook 1999:159). Sonnenschein has successfully argued that 'Gestalt psychology (the theory that a pattern or unified whole has specific properties that cannot be derived from a summation of its component parts) uses terms in regard to visual perception, which can find equivalents in aural perception as well' (Sonnenschein 2001:79).

The Latin poet Horace in his *Art of Poetry* counselled against mixing genres, emphasised the value of dramatic characters that are true to life and the avoidance of characters who lacked verisimilitude: 'the skilled imitator should look to human life and character for his models, and from there derive a language that is true to life' (Horace, 2000:107). Longinus, in 'On the Sublime', classified oratory as grand for rousing the emotions, plain for setting out arguments, and intermediate for giving pleasure. He discussed the ritual and art of spoken oratory in terms of a sublimity that was marked by an ability to amaze and transport the audience and overwhelm with its irresistible power. He breaks away from the position of Plato, Aristotle and Horace by advocating a fusion rather than separation between poetry and prose. Most allusions to narrative theory at the end of the nineteenth century and early part of the twentieth century were generally built around allusions and respect for classical Greek and Roman writers who dominated the education of the elite at this time.

The deployment of narrative conventions and codes is often linked in analysis to the producing media institutions and the attendant debates about ideological imperatives. The use of narrative critical terms is also usually dependent on the genre or form of sound storytelling communication. Drama, documentary and word based content is often examined for its use of story action, usually described as drama with events being represented to impact on character.

'Narrative voice' is usually defined as word based telling rather than showing. There is often a discussion about the representation of time in narrative and a distinction being made between discourse time – the time taken to describe the events – and story time; the 'real time' of the events so described. Realist and naturalist conventions relate to the presentation of reality, and surreal and dream-like conventions relate to imagined and phantasmagorical representations of mythological and folkloric stories; the kind of conventions associated with the genre of magic realism so prevalent in the *Harry Potter* novels of J.K. Rowling or *Disc World* novels of Terry Pratchett.

Up until the later part of the twentieth century, narrative was understood as a combination of story and plot, and there was little awareness of the move in Russia to establish a distinction between *syuzhet* and *fabula*. These terms were first applied by the Russian theorists Vladimir Propp and Viktor Shklovsky. In short *fabula* is the chronological order of retold events and *syuzhet* is the exposition of narrative within a text. *Syuzhet* can also be regarded as the 'plot time' in the narrative and *fabula* the timeframe for the overarching of the narrative in relation to its back story, present time and forward story context.

Ellipsis is a technique identified with keeping the story moving by shot or scene juxtaposition that leaves an imaginative understanding of a timeframe having been experienced diagetically by the characters. Flashbacks are used to take the audience back in the linear progression of the narrative. Stretch narrative is used to slow-motion or freeze the story time for emotional focus on the part of the audience.

The critic Frank Kermode wrote about *chronos* and *kairos* narrative. The critical term *chronos* is said to mean endless successiveness without direction or purpose. *Kairos* has given points of time filled with significance that are charged with meaning and derived from their relation to the end. In *kairos* narrative ends, resolutions and conclusions command and determine the flow of the preceding narrative (Martin 1991:19–20).

Narrative theory also tends to concentrate on the focalisation of the story telling. In film theory and practice, this is known as the point of view (POV). Obviously in sound it makes sense to discuss the concept in terms of point of listening (POL) (Beck 1998).

These critical narrative terms are obviously associated with word based sound and multimedia texts such as audio dramas, film, documentaries and forms of talk programming. The academic discipline of music has a long-established and independent frame of critical vocabulary for defining the story or narrative in the musical form. For example the *discord* is a technique in music that can be a powerful way of making music move forward by the striking of a discord on the strong beat of a bar. The hearer is compelled to listen forward for the discord to be resolved. Another example of a musical narrative phrase is *Wagner's method*. This is a continuous piece of music woven out of endless melody. The combination of separate musical leitmotivs are written and played to represent objects, persons and emotions and in the operative tradition Wagner intended to show what his characters were thinking when they remained still or silent on the musical theatrical stage. It can be argued that the narrative of the music is manipulated by composition to determine and influence the audience's thinking and emotions.

The phrase 'Once upon a time' situates the story in the past and suggests that it takes place in a different world, one far removed from that of the teller, listener or reader. It is a narrative agent on space and time. Mikhail Bakhtin discoursed the concept of 'chronotope', which in terms of its Greek roots means 'chronos' – time and 'topos' – space. Bakhtin argued that time-space is inseparable and therefore a consideration of the shifting locations of time-space provide a key to understanding the philosophical geography of prose. The relationship of time and space is therefore relevant in literary criticism and it can be argued that it is fundamentally relevant to any criticism, or theorising on sound media narratives.

In addition to Bakhtin's essays published as *The Dialogic Imagination: Four Essays*, other influential texts on the theory of storytelling, which are valid lenses for analysing sound media texts, are Vladimir Propp's *Morphology of the Russian Folktale*, Tzvetan Todorov's *The Fantastic* and 'The Typology of Detective Fiction' in *Modern Criticism and Theory: A Reader*. When the opening phrase 'Once upon a time' is considered further it is possible to recognise its practical purpose. In the context of sound texts it indicates the need to attract the attention of the listener. Practically speaking it operates as a narrative hook, leading us into a narrative world, setting up the puzzle/enigma, and asking questions. The modern narrative theorists cited agree that the audience reads the meaning at different levels. Those levels could be cultural, conscious, subconscious and political. Roland Barthes's *S/Z* analysed literary prose in terms of several 'voices' that he streamed into structuralist codes.

Barthes said 'art is a system which is pure, no unit ever goes wasted, however long, however loose, however tenuous may be the thread connecting it to one of the levels of the story' (Barthes 1990:89–90). Openings sometimes contain seeds of the themes, setting up the dynamic of predictability and orientating the audience so that the following questions arise in the mind of the listener: who is the hero and villain? (containing binary code of conflict) what is the setting? what is the style? is this going to be satisfying the cultural consensus of convention in the storytelling? The nature of genre tends to settle the context of story. This locks into the cultural memory of the audience to engage their ready-made framework of understanding the meaning. Non-genre texts raise more enigmatic openings. There is also the technique of narrative masking. This is where one genre might be disguised by another. Reading the text through an invisible genre window sets up a kaleidoscope of conscious and unconscious reading. This is perhaps obvious when it is realised that the opening of the plot or the text is not the same as the beginning or opening of the *fabula*.

Barthes set up an inter-relational nexus of narrative codes through the complex study he did of Balzac's short story 'Sarrasine' in *S/Z*. Barthes appears to align himself closely with Bertolt Brecht's view of the bourgeois conceit in the pretence of 'reality' in dramatic entertainment and communication. The 'realist' text is in fact a braid or interweaving of different narrative codes. The importance is in the way that they are combined to provide an impression or representation of reality.

A sound text like a novel or poem has its own internal logic of combined narrative codes and references to other existing storytelling/communication texts. This reference to other texts is known as 'intertextuality'.

Barthes believed that the audience becomes a 'writer/reader', which coincides with the theory of the listener engaging actively with their consciousness with a personal imperative of narrative understanding that I defined as the imaginative spectacle of the listener – a combination of mind's eye and powerful human emotions (Crook 1999:53–69).

Barthes's Hermeneutic Code or Enigma Code raises questions in the mind of the listener/audience. When the answer is delayed there is an enigma and the internal logic of the play requires a solution. The narratives capture the audience by making them want to know what is going to happen next. The delay between proposition and resolution of this code motivates 'reading'. It is the motor of the narrative. Barthes uses the word hermeneutic as it is a Greek word meaning the philosophy of interpreting texts.

In his Semic Code a text must be analysed for the way characters, objects and settings take on particular meanings. This equates with Propp's spheres of action.

In the Symbolic Code, the media analyst looks for signs that signify binary oppositions, for example, good/bad, youth/adult, etc. This code provides a map of the antitheses in the sound text and how these reflect cultural aspects and social anxieties. They appear natural enough in the realistic setting. This is the code that defines and explains the narrative of oppositions.

In Barthes's Proairetic or Action Code, the analysis concentrates on action tags. Things are done, normally at the end of scenes to predict what is likely to happen next. It is a shorthand way of advancing the action. This code can unveil whether it is acceptable to show certain kinds of action and serve the interests of censorship by implying or being implicit without being explicit or presentational. There might be a throw-ahead of intimacy or sexual relations but the reader is not actually shown what happens in detail.

Barthes's understanding of a text's Cultural or Referential Code is meaning that does not belong to the actual narrative of the text but belongs *outside*. It is one step beyond diegetic engagement. It is not part of the play's language and only present in the understanding and interpretation by the audience. It depends on the common stock of politics, art, ethics, history and the psychology of the listeners. Barthes called units of meaning *lexias*. He argued that the illusion of realism is founded on the integrated functioning of these five levels of codes. They all combine together to create meaning on the part of the audience. It might be argued that the referential codes are the psychological and cultural mechanisms to perpetuate mental equilibrium, self actualisation and social harmony (Lacey 2000:72–7).

Barthes, Propp and Todorov belong to a structuralist and post-structuralist tradition where narrative codes and functions are really signs with meaning derived from context (syntagmatic dimension) and that context tends to be binary oppositions. It is a system of differences. The French structural anthropologist, Claude Levi-Strauss, argued that binary oppositions are at the heart of people's attempts to come to terms with reality. They do this by creating myths through storytelling. Myth is an anxiety-reducing mechanism that deals with unresolvable contradictions in a culture and imaginative ways of living with them. It might be argued that the heart of conflict in storytelling proves this point. Binary oppositions in storytelling rituals often include: Heroes to Villains; Helpers to Henchmen; Princesses (love objects) to Sirens (sexual objects); Magicians (good/white magic) to Sorcerers (evil/black magic); Donors of magic objects to Preventers/hinderers of donors; Dispatchers of heroes to Captors of heroes; Seekers to Avoiders; Seeming Villains who turn out to be good to False Heroes who turn out to be bad.

Binary oppositions represent a process of privileging factors and setting up hierarchies. Normally the hero represents the triumph of what society holds to be good. The guarantee of success is part of the function of entertainment. Media narratives are therefore sometimes criticised as being socio-politically delusionary and the opiate of false-consciousness. When in life good often fails, storytelling serves to reassure us about the uncertainties and injustices of life. This means that in narrative analysis of sound texts attention needs to be paid to the ideological direction by asking what has changed in the world of the story, what has been transformed, what has been added or lost in the process/plot development and how have the characters' relative positions and status or their hierarchy changed? It might be argued that the process of answering these questions helps the audio authors and readers to apply an interrogative tool to understand their own ideological objectives and purposes.

Vladimir Propp's *Morphology of the Russian Folktale* was originally written and published in 1928 but not introduced to western readers and academics through translation until 1958. It has become an influential text on defining and explaining the 'shape' of narrative or storytelling. The object for analysis was Russian folktales and in the process he has identified cultural conventions in narrative techniques and in particular a theory about the function of characters in the construction of myths and folkloric traditions.

Rather than concentrating on the motivation and internal psychological 'ticking' of a character, Propp was more concerned about the function of characterisation in the narrative. He concentrated on the actions of character in the story and the consequences of these actions for the story. Propp identified a range of storytelling functions in folktales. He said that not all these functions had to be present and that several functions could be grouped together to form a set of 'Moves'. For example he defined the first seven functions as 'Preparation' and that many 'plot/narratives' actually began at function eight where the disruption or crisis manifests itself. Some writers have argued that Propp's approach equates to that of Todorov, and Table 1.2 sets out a comparison along with the functions and story moves that underpin Propp's theory.

GENRE

Genre is a type of sound form. The process of analysing such forms intersects with media institutional, ideological, representational, language and audience issues. Genre theory in sound studies can clearly develop interesting debates since an individual genre can often be defined by a range of critical characteristics such as plot, technical features, characters, format, mise-en-scène, motifs and setting. For example in radio drama practice professionals are aware of what distinguishes 'soap opera' from classical or literary dramatisation, suspense thrillers from comedy, science fiction from new cutting edge realistic writing. In the BBC institutional environment there is an understanding of difference in genre between the strand of programming on the BBC Radio Three national network *Between the Ears* – an experimental and avant-garde programme that pushes the boundaries in sound expressionism – and BBC Radio Four's *Archive Hour* – one hour documentaries that tend to have a linked narrative frame and are rooted in historical and contemporary story telling dependent on surviving and previously recorded sound material, *Walls of Sound* being an example discussed earlier.

Table 1.2 A comparison along with the functions and story moves that underpin Propp's theory

Todorov 1: Propp 0 to 7	A state of equilibrium at the outset
Todorov 2: Propp at 8	A disruption of the equilibrium by some action
Todorov 3: Propp at 9	A recognition that there has been a disruption
Todorov 4: Propp 10 to 17	An attempt to repair the disruption or disequilibrium
Todorov 5: Propp 18 to 31	A reinstatement of the equilibrium
Propp's 7 moves	Propp's 7 spheres of action, and narrative functions
1–7 PREPARATION	The Villain who creates the narrative complication.
8–10 COMPLICATION	The Donor who gives the hero something that aids in the process and resolution of narrative.
11–15 TRANSFERENCE	The Helper who supports the hero in the struggle to restore the equilibrium.
16–19 STRUGGLE	The Princess – The character most threatened by the villain and who has to be saved by the hero. (The father usually gives the princess away in the role of King at the end of the plot.)
20–26 RETURN	The Dispatcher sends or launches the hero on his or her 'holy grail' or 'journey'.
27–31 RECOGNITION	The Hero/Heroine is the characterisation force who restores the narrative equilibrium – usually through searching and saving the princess. Propp subdivides the hero/heroine into Victim Hero – the object of villain's malice and subterfuge; and Seeker Hero – the character who helps others who are victims of the villain. The hero is often the central character and plot protagonist.
	False Hero. Facade of goodness but is revealed as the wolf in sheep's clothing.
Propp's character function He argued that fairy tales could be studied consistently in terms of the function of their *dramatis personae* (Propp 1968:20).	Explanation. ('1. Functions of characters serve as stable, constant elements in a tale, independent of how and by whom they are fulfilled. They constitute the fundamental components of a tale. 2. The number of functions known to the fairy tale is limited. 3. The sequence of functions is always identical. 4. All fairy tales are of one type in regard to their structure.' Propp 1968:21)
0 INITIAL SITUATION	Members of the family are introduced; hero is introduced.
1 ABSENTATION	One of the members of the family absents himself or herself (death of parents; sometimes members of the younger generation absent themselves).
2 INTERDICTION	Interdiction addressed to hero (can be reversed by 'An inverted form [. . .] represented by an order or a suggestion', Propp 1968:27).

3 VIOLATION	Interdiction is violated ('Thus, a villain has entered the scene. He has come on foot, sneaked up, or flown down, etc., and begins to act', Propp 1968:28).
4 RECONNAISSANCE	Villain makes attempt to get information. ('1. The reconnaissance has the aim of finding out the location of children, or sometimes of precious objects, etc. 2. An inverted form [. . .] is evidenced when the intended victim questions the villain [. . .] 3. In separate instances one encounters forms of reconnaissance by means of other personages', Propp 1968:28)
5 DELIVERY	Villain gets information about victim. ('1. The villain directly received an answer to his question [. . .] 2–3. An inverted or other form of information-gathering evokes a corresponding answer', Propp 1968:28–9)
6 TRICKERY	Villain tries to deceive victim. ('1. The villain uses persuasion [. . .] 2. The villain proceeds to act by the direct application of magical means [. . .] 3. The villain employs other means of deception or coercion', Propp 1968:29–30)
7 COMPLICITY	Victim submits to deception and thereby unwittingly helps his enemy. ('1. The hero agrees to all of the villain's persuasions [. . .] 2–3. The hero mechanically reacts to the employment of magical or other means', Propp 1968:29–30)
8 VILLAINY	Villain causes harm to a member of the family; or lack: 8a. One member of the family lacks something, desires something. Propp says the 'forms of villainy are exceedingly varied' and he sets out 19 different examples from 'The villain abducts a person' to 'The villain declares war' (Propp 1968:31–4).
9 MEDIATION (the connective incident)	Misfortune made known; hero is allowed to go or dispatched. ('1. A call for help is given, with the resultant dispatch of the hero [. . .] 4. Misfortune is announced', Propp 1968:37)
10 COUNTERACTION	Hero (seeker) agrees to or decides upon counteraction.
11 DEPARTURE	Hero leaves home.
12 FIRST DONOR FUNCTION	'Hero tested, interrogated, attacked, which prepares the way for his receiving either a magical agent or helper' (Propp 1968:89).
13 HERO'S REACTION	Hero reacts to agent or donor. Propp gives ten examples from 'He frees a captive' to 'The hero vanquishes (or does not vanquish) his adversary' (Propp 1968:42–3).
14 PROVISION OR RECEIPT OF AGENT	Hero acquires use of magical agent (Propp 1968:43–50).

15 SPATIAL CHANGE ('transference between two kingdoms, guidance', Propp 1968:50)	Hero transferred, delivered or led to the whereabouts of an object of search. ('1. The hero flies through the air [. . .] 6. He follows bloody tracks', Propp 1968:51)
16 STRUGGLE	Hero and villain join in direct combat. ('1. They fight in an open field [. . .] 3. They play cards . . .', Propp 1968:52)
17 BRANDING, MARKING	Hero is branded.
18 VICTORY	Villain is defeated. ('1. The villain is beaten in open combat [. . .] 6. He is banished directly. . .', Propp 1968:53)
19 LIQUIDATION ('The narrative reaches its peak in this function', Propp 1968:53)	Initial misfortune or lack is liquidated.
20 RETURN	Hero returns.
21 PURSUIT, CHASE	Hero is pursued. ('3. He pursues the hero, rapidly transforming himself into various animals, etc [. . .] 5. The pursuer tries to devour the hero. . .', Propp 1968:56)
22 RESCUE	Hero is rescued from pursuit.
23 UNRECOGNISED ARRIVAL	Hero, unrecognised, arrives home or elsewhere.
24 UNFOUNDED CLAIMS	False hero presents unfounded claims.
25 DIFFICULT TASK	Difficult task is proposed to hero. ('Ordeal by food and drink [. . .] Hide and seek [. . .] Test of endurance: to spend seven years in the tin kingdom', Propp 1968:60–1)
26 SOLUTION	Task is proposed to hero. Propp said 'THE TASK IS RESOLVED' (Propp 1968:62).
27 RECOGNITION	Hero is recognised.
28 EXPOSURE	False hero or villain is exposed.
29 TRANSFIGURATION	Hero is given a new appearance. ('2. The hero builds a marvellous palace [. . .] 3. The hero puts on new garments', Propp 1968:63)
30 PUNISHMENT	Villain is punished.
31 WEDDING	Hero is married, ascends the throne.

Source: Lacey 2000:46–8 and Propp 1968:25–65

In the radio or audio-documentary form there is an identifiable distinction between montage, continuous stream of consciousness programmes and those depending on an omniscient or voice of god narrative frame. Sound genre classifications can cross-over to media that use sound in a significantly communicative manner. For example, in a first person shooter (FPS) computer game the player takes on the role of the main protagonist, but can it not be argued that there are strands of fiction and non-fictional audio programming where the listener is directed by the POL (point of listening) to identify with the main protagonist who may well be silent or not represented by verbal language? This might arguably be the case with Gemma – the character in Anthony Minghella's famous BBC Prix Italia and Giles Cooper award-winning radio play *Cigarettes and Chocolate* (1988). All the other diegetic characters in the play communicate with her, but we never hear her voice. This may also be the case with the noises and non-verbal human expression of the character being chased in Andrew Sachs's play without words *Revenge*, broadcast by BBC Radio in 1978.

Music theory can equally be said to be concerned with genre. For example, styles of music are said to be divided between the Baroque, Pre-Classical, Romantic and Post-Romantic periods. Is it not the case that Jazz and Musique Concrète represent genres of musical expression?

Narrative analysis seeks to confirm and categorise by identifying the presence of formulas, enigmas, linear, flashback, flash-forward and episodic phases, changes in location and time, single or multiple points of focalisation in character, montage or linking narrative voice that is omniscient and separate from the diegesis, overt and covert ideological rituals and emblems. It might be said that the presence of a cynical hard-boiled central character's voice given to commentating on present, past and future, and interacting flirtatiously with a 'femme fatale' means that there is as much a tradition of audio-noir in radio drama as there is film-noir in cinema. The character roles of hero, heroine and villain and the functions of ideological attitude conform with audience expectations.

MODERN CRITICAL TRADITIONS

It can be argued that the leading 'contemporary' critical traditions gaining prominence in the twentieth century were existentialism and phenomenology. There arose out of these movements a challenge to the concept of the Cartesian self in the sense that personal identity was objectified and structured by the social environment rather than essential consciousness. As a result recent critical traditions have been strongly influenced by: structuralism; post-structuralism; semiotics; new feminism; post-Marxism; modernity and postmodernity.

Modern academic disciplines consequently pay homage to Michel Foucault's post-structuralist theory on discourse and power and the politics of the personal, Jacques Lacan's argument about the instability of the subject, Jean Baudrillard's writing on the power of simulacra, the hyperreal and the political economy of the sign, and Jean-François Lyotard's desire to subvert the hegemony of metanarratives (Mundy 1999:2). All modern academic disciplines expect their students to reference twentieth-century post-Marxists such as Theodor Adorno and Jürgen Habermas, whose literature criticises capitalist cultural production and focuses on the political economy of the media. Adorno, in particular, has produced some key writings on the social significance of music and radio.

The fashion at the time of writing is to investigate sound beyond the branch of modern philosophy known as phenomenology. A leading philosopher of consciousness from this school is Maurice Merleau-Ponty whose seminal work *Phenomenology of Perception* seems to be highly relevant for any appreciation of a philosophical enquiry into the meaning of sound. Yet Merleau-Ponty's work did not directly address hearing and listening. And this neglect has been enthusiastically bridged with an exciting plethora of publications in recent years. Many have emerged from the discipline of music:

> I am a sound chauvinist or perhaps (better) a sound evangelist. I believe the medium in which I work is fundamental to life; indeed I believe it has a life of its own, potentially independent of visual accompaniment. I shall argue that a recognition of this independence and its strengths is essential for a mature relationship of sound art to visual art. [. . .]
>
> Having been separated for at least two thousand years, the arts of light and sound cannot arbitrarily be flung together again. I am suggesting that sound has the power to create its own visual response in humans – one which is sometimes not accounted for by visual artists – a sense of place, of aural landscape.
>
> For a real relationship to develop there is a need for each artist in a collaboration to understand the inherent 'crossover' nature of each art independently: the visual as suggested by the aural alone and vice versa. This will involve experimenting and working together with mutual respect, accentuating the craft of the work over the romantic egotism of 'art'.
>
> (Emerson 1999:135, 139)

Simon Emerson is by no means alone in tackling the issue of sound phenomenology and human consciousness, and the sonic relationship between the individual, society and the wider environment. As he explains further in his journal article on 'Aural Landscape: Musical Space':

> Acoustics can no longer be separated from the sciences of perception (bioacoustics and psychoacoustics); but further, perception can only be understood as part of a greater network which includes environment and evolution (zooecoustics and ecoacoustics).

Murray Schafer (based at the time at Simon Fraser University in Vancouver where he founded the 'World Soundscape Project') was the first to look systematically at this field – at least the environmental aspects.

His classic work, The Tuning of the World, published in 1977, sets an agenda for awareness and action which has scarcely (outside Canada, at least) had the impact it deserves. His designation of 'hi-fi' and 'lo-fi' soundscapes of our real environment remains a classic:

> The hi-fi soundscape is one in which discrete sounds can be heard more clearly because of the low ambient noise level. [. . .] In the hi-fi soundscape, sounds overlap less frequently; there is perspective – foreground and back-ground [. . .]. In a lo-fi soundscape individual acoustic signals are obscured in an overdense population of sounds. The pellucid sound – a footstep in the snow, a churchbell across the valley [. . .] – is masked by broadband noise. Perspective is lost. On a downtown street corner of the modern city there is no distance; there is only presence. There is crosstalk on all channels [. . .] (Schafer 1977:43).
>
> (Emerson 1999:137)

THE INTERDISCIPLINARY, THE MULTIDISCIPLINARY, AND THE CROSS-DISCIPLINARY

At Goldsmiths, University of London, sound is studied and practised in virtually every department: Anthropology, Art, Computing, Design, Drama, English and Comparative Literature, History, Music, Politics, Media and Communications, Sociology, and Psychology. And in recent years sound has become a common ground for intellectual, aesthetic and creative discussion. Academic papers and conferences are being convened and sound is being analysed with a mixture of theoretical application (the interdisciplinary) and sound is also being written about discretely across separate academic doctrines (the multidisciplinary). In practice film sound designers are studying and addressing radio. Radio producers have been studying and addressing sound art in exhibition and installation. Computer engineers have been constructing algorithms and programming language to blend digital visual and sonic animations. It might be more accurate to describe the relationship between the practice and theory of these areas as cross-disciplinary. Is there an explanation? I would like to speculatively develop the theme of romanticism that I started with.

AESTHETIC TRADITIONS

I think it is being increasingly appreciated that in our artistic and existential being sound can be intensely romantic. It is intellectually and aesthetically magical.

My colleague in the Department of Media and Communications, Julian Henriques, teaches students on his course 'Music as Communication and Creative Practice' that the first recorded author to describe sound in terms of waves is said to be the Roman neo-classical architect Pollio Vitruvius (circa 80–15 BC):

> Voice is a flowing breath of air, perceptible to hearing by contact. It moves in an endless number of circular rounds, like the innumerably increasing circular waves which appear when a stone is thrown into a smooth water . . . but while in the case of water the circles move horizontally on a plane surface, the voice not only proceeds horizontally, but also ascends vertically by regular stages.
>
> (Vitruvius 1960:138–9)

The significance of this passage is that centuries before pure science was able to identify and measure the 'real' nature of sound waves, their existence was perceived and rationalised by the human imagination. Vitruvius was discoursing on metaphysics, a division of the traditional academic discipline of philosophy. It could be said he was a science fiction writer in the age of ancient Rome. In essence his interest in *metaphysics* was an early method of trying to understand what was responsible for the phenomena of the physical world, in this case sound. He was reflecting on what could be derived after or *meta* the physical.

Francis Bacon in the early seventeenth century could be described as a late renaissance science fiction writer with this inspiring passage from *The New Atlantis* on 'sound houses':

> Wee have also Sound-houses, wher wee practise and demonstrate all Sounds, and their Generation. Wee have Harmonies which you have not, of Quarter-Sounds, and lesser Slides of Sounds. Diverse instruments of Musick likewise to you unknowne, some sweeter then any you have; Together with Bells and Rings that are dainty and sweet. Wee represent Small Sounds as Great and Deepe; Likeweise Great Sounds, Extenuate and Sharpe; Wee make diverse Tremblings and Warblings of Sounds, which in their Originall are Entire. Wee represent and imitate all Articulate sounds and Letters, and the Voices and Notes of Beasts and Birds. Wee have certaine Helps, which sett to the Eare doe further the Hearing greatly. Wee have also diverse Strange and Artificiall Eccho's. Reflecting the Voice many times, and as it were Tossing it: And some that give back the Voice Lowder than it come, some Shriller, and some Deeper; Yea some rendring the Voice. Differing in the Letters or Articulate Sound, from that they receive, Wee have also meanes to convey Sounds in Trunks and Pipes, in strange Lines, and Distances.
>
> (Quoted in Briscoe and Curtis-Bramwell 1983:52 and Crook 1999:30–1)

Bacon's prophetic writing captures in imaginative and exciting language many of the essential creative connections that are being recognised in sound communication and reception. The very idea of projecting sound from boxes and pipes suggests radio reception and transmission, cabled public address systems, sound art installations, and Internet podcasting. The sounds of music and nature can be cut (quarter sound) and processed (slides, trembles and warbles). The 'Sound Houses' quotation is highlighted in *The First 25 Years: The BBC Radiophonic Workshop* by Desmond Briscoe and Roy Curtis-Bramwell, a non-academic book now regarded as seminal. Published in 1983, it sought to celebrate the achievements of an aesthetic and industrial workshop or laboratory that was established to creatively generate sound for radio and television programmes. Copies of the book rarely become available in the second-hand market, and when they do they are so much sought after by sound professionals and enthusiasts they command values of well over a hundred pounds.

ALCHEMISTS OF SOUND

The BBC's Radiophonic Workshop has become the source of mythology, a recognised and celebrated tradition, and serious academic study. One of its composers and producers, Delia Derbyshire, is certainly a cult figure with her reputation and legend retrieved and reset by the Soundscape Art and Electronic music movement. There may also be a feminist resetting of electronic music history since the academic study of the workshop by Louis Niebur, *Special Sound: The Creation and Legacy of the BBC Radiophonic Workshop*, published by Oxford University Press, quotes Byron Adams that this 'feat of virtuoso research [. . .] places in a wholly original context the extraordinary accomplishments of such pioneers as Maddalena Fagandini, Daphne Oram, and the fabulous Delia Derbyshire' (in Niebur 2010). It might be argued that these celebrated women audio 'alchemists' certainly had richly sounding names to match their craft, science and artistry.

In its praxis, the workshop, situated in the art nouveau wedding cake style and former ice rink Maida Vale studios, operated as a cultural and aesthetic crossroads of music, technology, audio/radio drama, television/film drama, BBC broadcasting institution, sound art, and pure science (electronics and mathematics).

The early workshop pioneers were inspired and influenced by Pierre Schaeffer and Pierre Henry, Club d'Essai, Radio France and the '*musique concrète*' movement. Equally influential was the output from the Norddeutscher Rundfunk broadcasting studios in Cologne – which specialised in the generation and application of synthetic sound generally known as elektronische musik. The book contributes to the canonising of radio drama texts where the creative and philosophical focus of expression is through sound, such as *All That Fall* by Samuel Beckett, directed by Donald McWhinnie, and broadcast in 1957 on the BBC's Third Programme, and audio plays with memorable and evocative titles such as *The Disagreeable Oyster* and *Under the Loofah Tree* by Giles Cooper, first broadcast in 1959 and 1960. The poetic and psychological expression inherent in the short feature *Private Dreams and Public Nightmares* written by Frederick Bradnum and directed by Donald

McWhinnie, on the BBC Third Programme in 1957, was also marked as a pioneering achievement in synthesising abstract symbolism in the sound medium.

The canonising in this text also began to invest the musical arrangements and compositions of Delia Derbyshire with celebrated legacy. She is culturally identified and recognised for the radiophonic arrangement of the *Doctor Who* theme tune, a sonic icon if you can tolerate the lexicographical contradiction, and the beautiful and playfully entitled compositions 'Blue Veils and Golden Sounds' and 'Ziwzeh Ziwzeh Oooh Oooh Oooh'.

In 2005 the BBC produced an hour-long documentary on the history of the Radiophonic Workshop, transmitted on its digital cultural channel BBC 4 and given the delightful title 'Alchemists of Sound'. This summoned the poetic mysteries and magic of Dr Faustus, Mephistopheles and the religious and occult legends of transformation and transubstantiation. The suggestion is that the very idea of turning iron into gold is a metaphysical dream because of the barriers and limitations of material and physical existence. But as sound cannot be seen and cannot be touched and is an imagined perception, perhaps sound is truly alchemistic.

The BBC's Radiophonic Workshop has become a cultural metaphor for the growing recognition that sound is a transformative and transitive phenomenon bridging and conjoining human existence through the arts, social networks of communication, and everyday performance of social life. But as Niebur observes the cultural appreciation of electronic sound stimulating the human imagination through storytelling and frames of aural narrative extends beyond the high cultural frequencies of the BBC's Third Programme.

SONIC *GOONS* AND NONSENSE

The Light Programme entertained millions of listeners throughout the middle 1950s with the abstract, surreal and farcical phonic fantasia of *The Goon Show*. Sound performance 'with effects' professionally annotated as 'F/X' could conjure the perception of 'François the Flea' (series 7, episode 12, 1956). Absurd streaks of imaginative humour were struck in words, music and nonsensical sounds. As the Goon characters Bloodnok, Moriarty and Eccles pursue their enquiry into the potential world destroying threat of the flea ('François the Flea is in my sock. He likes to travel on foot.'), they enter a coffee house in London at the time of the Great Plague in 1665 ('1665? Good Heavens! I must hurry or I'll miss my bus.'), and after references are made to 'Master Pepys' not wanting a cappuccino, there is an exquisite exchange of dialogue: 'I'm sorry I didn't see you standing in a coffee pot? I know we had the lid down. We? Where's your friend? He's up the spout.' François enters the story jumping while blindfolded ('I see he favours the Western roll!'). His presence is conjured through the performance of live effects and imagistic language that links with the listener's imagination to participate in a truly phantasmagorical realm. When the plot moves rather illogically to a trial in a courtroom with the offending biting flea summoned, he arrives sonically by the sounds of a galloping horse:

> Whoa, Whoa, Woa, Wow.
> Great Jupiter mate! Is that thing a flea?
> No, it's an 'orse mate.
> A horse?
> Yeah.
> Take its hat off.
> Yeah.
> You're right it is an horse.
> Where, Where's the flea?
> He's on the 'orse mate. I thought he'd get here quicker that way.
> I see. As he's not riding side-saddle I presume he's a male flea? Will the flea raise his right leg and swear to tell the truth?
> ABSTRACT WHIZZING TWO BELL TYPE SOUND
> Thank you.
>
> (Milligan and Stephens 1956)

Niebur's interest in *The Goon Show* was that the surreal deployment of effects 'began to alter and distort standard effects, becoming more willing to push audience's abilities to understand what (if anything) these distortions were meant to represent . . . ' (Niebur 2010:9). Niebur has recognised the significance of 'Radio Drama and the Birth of Electronic Music', which is the title of the first chapter of his book and pays homage to experimental British radio feature makers and audio dramatists such as Lance Sieveking, Douglas Cleverdon, Donald McWhinnie and the apparent 1950s *convivencia* with the importation of continental 'Theatre of the Absurd' traditions articulated by a one-time Editor of BBC Radio drama, Martin Esslin: 'sense of the senselessness of the human condition and the inadequacy of the rational approach by the abandonment of rational devices and discursive thought' (Esslin 1980:399).

Niebur elegantly tracks the origins of electronic sound in audio dramatic texts and productions, and as is becoming fashionable in sound studies and artistic discourse, retrieves and fashions a critical vocabulary to explain and define what is being created and experienced in the sound medium: '*musique concrète*, elektronische Musik, Hörspiele, Shoenbergian expressionism, radiophonic, audiogenic, acousmatic, *acousmêtre*, synchresis, synchretic *acousmêtre*, virtually synchretic, virtually acousmatic, virtual synchretic *acousmêtre*, *musique concrète* renforcée'. This exotic collection of neologisms is a mere sample of the new language of sound criticism and in their utterance it could be argued the vocabulary has an immediate sonic resonance. Intellectually and philosophically these terms need to be mapped in terms of meaning and understanding. I have made an effort in the glossary and will try my best to render their application in plain English wherever possible.

THE UNDECIDED MOLECULE

Audio drama broadcast on the radio had convened the pioneering development of electronic sonic expressionism not only in Britain, France and Germany. An American radiophonic auteur, Norman Corwin, scripted, directed and produced a play that convened science, politics, art, aesthetics, music and dramatic performance and fortunately, although broadcast live, it has been fully preserved in archive and published as a literary text.

Corwin's work, *The Undecided Molecule*, represents modernism and postmodernism at the same time, which was a remarkable achievement when it was broadcast on the CBS radio network on 17 July 1945 – twenty days before the atomic explosion over Hiroshima. As with the Goons, it might seem somewhat paradoxical that this significant advance in sound aesthetics was rooted in a comedy albeit with salty dimensions of ironic satire. There would be a prophetic link with mass human destruction nearly three weeks later. The detonation of a human and scientifically created chemical bomb that in some ways interrupted and stopped time would be represented in the debris by the discovery of a clock frozen with its hands pointing to the hour and minute of the atomic bomb's explosion. It is a tribute to Corwin that he wrote contextually and could engage contemporary moral and political philosophy with poetic ingenuity.

Norman Corwin has been described as the poet laureate of the radio. He had an extraordinary position as a rhetorician and poet of the radio spectrum from the late 1930s through the Second World War until black-listing and market economics made his art – that of the poetic drama, drama-documentary and didactic audio drama – redundant. Corwin thrived when radio was the paradigmatic electronic medium. Seven days after the Japanese attacked Pearl Harbor it was Corwin's script that became the symbolic dramatic embodiment of constitution and US national dignity. *We Hold These Truths* commanded an audience estimated at sixty million.

Corwin's art and role could be described as that of the modern court hailer or repro medieval fool. He was Shakespeare's fool to America's King Lear. In their cultural resonance and reception, Corwin's dramatic verse productions were the equivalent of William Shakespeare's plays in Elizabethan London. They were immensely popular and culturally powerful. They rallied the emotional and political anxiety of American identity. His cultural message combined aesthetics with politics. He would combine the hermeneutics of the courtier with the ironic subversion of the court jester. His style would be a reception of classical poetic mnemonics, modernist thinking and expressionism, Renaissance rhetoric, Enlightenment rationality and postmodernist mischief.

As with most audio-dramatists he would approach the design of his work (described in England as the feature) by anticipating phenomenological existence on the part of his audience. He would construct a reception on the basis of what he saw and felt in the mind of his listener. That design would be a perception of what he saw in his mind's eye, felt emotionally and ethically in his sense of consciousness, and this would be projected into an expectation of how he believed the common listener would conjure the *existenz*, *dasein*, and *humanitas* (terms used by twentieth-century phenomenologists such as Karl Jaspers, Martin Heidegger and Hannah Arendt to describe existence, day-to-day reality and human character). *The Undecided Molecule* was, according to Corwin's biographer R. Leroy Bannerman, his all-time favourite (Bannerman 1986:170–1). Robert Benchley opened the programme with this greeting:

> Lucky you! You have happened to dial
> this program in time to attend a trial
> Stranger than any since we first learned the knack
> Of breathing – and that was a long time back.
> The poor folks listening to other stations
> Will lose all this. But congratulations
> To you for being no such fool
> As to miss The Undecided Molecule!

(Corwin 1947:3)

The verse play is a trial to decide the fate of a rebellious molecule who speaks or squeaks electronically through the operation of an early musical oscillator. With a sense of poignant prophesy Corwin explores the ethical dilemma of the potential of splitting the atom and unleashing a force that requires adoption and responsibility because the power is unlike anything experienced in terms of animal, vegetable or mineral. Groucho Marx is given the role of the judge and he provides the same lilting, leering humour that typified his Marx Brothers movies (Bannerman 1986:170).

> Clerk: The court will rise and face
> The justice who will adjust the case.
> See that your concentration centers
> On his Honor the Justice as he enters –
> Which he is doing even now.
> Everybody bow. Everybody bow.
> Judge: (coming on) Arrumph . . . garrumph . . . ahem . . . to wit . . . contrary notwithstanding . . . you may sit.

(Corwin 1947:6)

The script and performances are satirical, culturally and politically mocking. Corwin taunts the inherent fascism in American social being that would emerge with chilling absurdity in the McCarthy style witch-hunts characterised by the House of Un-American Activities. Drugs, sex and politics are served up with loosely veiled subtextuality and irony in a Thanksgiving banquet of American parody:

Anima: Then there's Franco Spain
And the common cold.
[. . .]
A Fascist will fight you,
And then there is asthma.
[. . .]
Judge: A fey character.
Interpreter: Like a film by Disney.
Judge: Disney's not involved in this.
Interpreter: Why isney?
[. . .]
Judge: I'm famished. Been a tiring day. I sure would like to crunch
A nice fresh salad bowl of crispy, tangy hasheesh!
[. . .]
Judge: How could I be a Fascist? Why, I am so benign
I hardly ever beat my wife; my children bow before me.
I'm much admired by rattlesnakes, and birds of prey adore me.
I'm tender and I'm sensitive and anti-insurrectionist;
I wouldn't hurt a cobra, and I'm anti-vivisectionist.

(Corwin 1947:12, 14 and 28–9)

Corwin versifies with wry and exquisite aural brushstrokes aspects of feminism and anti-Semitism. The actor Robert Benchley serves as a ventriloquising interpreter for the molecule. The atom is anthropomorphised after being constructed as the Other. Vincent Price is the prosecutor. Keenan Wynn performed no fewer than four roles. As the trial progresses, representatives of the vegetable and mineral kingdoms recount the advantages of their classifications. But the wayward molecule remains undecided. At Goldsmiths the play is workshopped every year with postgraduate students from the MA Radio and Scriptwriting programmes performing all the roles and one student being given an old-style Marantz cassette sound recorder and a handheld microphone. The speaker volume is turned up along with the recording level dial and the student, with creative alacrity and enthusiasm articulates the Molecule by manipulating the feedback in sweeping upward and downward movements of the microphone against the inbuilt speaker. The low and hi frequency wowing of feedback invests the molecule with an abstract electronic musical composition that is improvisational and unique to each workshop and every student.

Corwin in his postscript analysis admitted 'I found it was best to use the effect sparingly, else it became monotonous. And the inflection should parallel that of a child's sing-song recital of a poem' (Corwin 1947:42). The legendary audio playmaker acknowledges that electronic music remains something of an acquired taste and in excess tends to push the tolerance aesthetic to extremes. But his reflection confirms an early experimentation of art and technology that you will not find in the frothy enthusings of contemporary 'sound lords' who are so fashionable in our universities:

Sound. The old handyman of sound effects is the oscillator. It is an electrical device that looks like a small receiving set, and it produces a squeal not unlike that which arose from an early radio when closely approached. The musical instrument called the theremin (after its inventor, Léon Theremin – and what has happened to both?) was based on the principle of the oscillator. No more versatile piece of baggage exists in the sound department. Its tone can be held steady or interrupted, as in code; its pitch can be varied; it can be made to flutter, whine, or imitate the inflections of speech. The last of these talents is the one I selected to serve as the voice of X. I myself (every director is a ham at heart and wants to perform in some way or other) operated the spark key and tuning dial that gave expression to the molecule's inner struggle.

(Corwin 1947:42)

The opportunity to perform Corwin's script more than sixty years later and give an electronic sonic identity and expression to the undecided molecule is frequently cited as one of the most enjoyable moments in the course.

Eventually 'Anima', performed by Sylvia Sidney, speaks for the animal kingdom and despite her candid appraisal of mankind, sways the molecule. The defendant, speaking as an oscillating tone, is interpreted by Benchley to acknowledge:

The common guy
Both thinks and feels
Nothing's too high
For his ideals.
Though it cost him sadly
To put down jerks,
He's not done badly-
Look at this works!
For all his pains
We owe him thanks.
And I do gladly
Join his ranks.

(Corwin 1947:32)

For the molecule to join the ranks of the American common guy is to invite the culpability of Hiroshima and Nagasaki only a matter of three weeks away. Corwin was not unaware of the political subtext:

X is anti-social, antiuniversal. It is bad enough that man, the end product of certain molecular combinations, should be more or less neurotic. But if his raw material – the dust from which he cometh and to which he returneth – if that, too, goes off into a psychic sulk, then woe to everybody and everything.

(Corwin 1947:36)

The judge meanwhile is attracted to the smouldering and erotic starlet of the animal kingdom, and flirtatiously advances:

> As for you, Miss Anima, you were great.
> It's slightly extralegal – but have you a date
> For later in the evening? Do you like to dance?
> Have you any marked tendency toward romance?

(Corwin 1947:32–3)

A place for the molecule is found when Anima agrees to marry the judge and, together, they decide to adopt friend X (the molecule) as their offspring. The molecule oscillates a happy yes and the clerk of the court heralds the ending:

> Will the court musicians kindly advance
> To the mike and play a wedding dance;
> And then, after that, please segue and sally into a sort of a king of finale?
> MUSIC: A SORT OF A KIND OF FINALE.

(Corwin 1947:34)

Justice and Humanity have absorbed the implications of atomic power into a family that can live happily ever after by dropping 'Fat Man' and 'Little Boy' on the people of Japan. The American family is complete. The Supreme Court has ruled. The molecule has decided its rightful allegiance. The atom could not be killed by execution. It had to be appropriated by constitution and the affirmation of justice in the context of political rhetoric that could justify the decision in terms of 'the just war'. And although its first dramatic use in the twentieth century would be for the purposes of unleashing deliberate terror, what would be coined in the Anglo-American led 'coalition' invasion of Iraq in 2003 as 'shock and awe', the ameliorating and soothing claims that nuclear power could be the energistic saviour of mankind would lose confidence in the post earthquake and tsunami disaster at Fukushima in 2011.

The significance of Corwin's play and my aesthetic and intellectual enthusiasm for it was first presented to an academic conference at Goldsmiths in the year 2000, which was attended by a BBC radio drama producer who would a few years later interview Corwin and facilitate the play's rebroadcast in Britain. At the conference I somewhat mischievously sought to argue against a longstanding proposition that sound and radio reception was 'a blind medium'. My point has always remained that the mind's perception of hearing, sometimes defined as 'listening' is not stripped of visual encoding and decoding. This is because the physiological sense of sight is a process of perception and perception psychologically is a mind process and not just a sensory experience. Consequently, as for most people, sound is perceived with sight and the other senses. The mind encodes and decodes an imaginative experience that is both visual and sonic.

Against this background my paper playfully drew inspiration from the famous book *Art and Illusion: A Study in the Psychology of Pictorial Representation* by

E.H. Gombrich. If my desire to continue to draw on critical and philosophical discourse from the visual arts is seen as a continuing menace to so-called 'Radio Studies' and the emerging academic discipline of 'Sound Art' and 'Sound Studies', I am more than happy to plead guilty to heresy and any charge of academic dysfunctionalism. My riposte is that to do so is both fun and educational since issues in art and illusion are fully relevant and pertinent to issues of sonusion – oh dear, another neologism.

Gombrich's introduction was entitled 'Psychology and the Riddle of Style' and he headed it with a maxim by Max J. Friedlander from *Von Kunst und Kennerschaft*. I found it interesting to substitute 'Art' with 'Sound' so that the quotation ran: 'Sound being a thing of the mind, it follows that any scientific study of sound will be psychology. It may be other things as well, but psychology it will always be' (Gombrich 2000:3, with my alteration). As I read and absorbed each chapter of Gombrich's influential work I realised that the aphorisms he drew from historical sources of pictorial art criticism when spun or morphed into the sound context offered fundamental and informing observations about the art of sound as well.

Gombrich approached his first chapter by exploring the artistic journey of turning light into paint. This is the same as turning the phenomenal reality of sound existence into the representation of a sound design. It seemed interesting and meaningful to adopt the quotation from Jean-Étienne Liotard in *Traité des principes et des règles de la peinture* and again substitute the word 'painting' with 'sound design': 'Sound design is the most astounding sorceress. She can persuade us through the most evident falsehoods that she is pure Truth' (Gombrich 2000:29, with my alteration). In Chapter 2 the art historian discussed the subject of 'Truth and the Stereotype' and in quoting Emile Zola that a work of art is 'a corner of nature seen through a temperament' I would venture to suggest Zola only needed to have considered hearing nature through the emotional sensibility of human temperament. The idea that listening is a unique interpretation of truth through an apparent stereotype of sound or visual representation would be similarly articulated.

The chapter opens with the observation by the great German Enlightenment philosopher Immanuel Kant from *Critique of Pure Reason* that 'The schematism by which our understanding deals with the phenomenal world . . . is a skill so deeply hidden in the human soul that we shall hardly guess the secret trick that Nature here employs' (Gombrich 2000:55). As Gombrich so cleverly states 'Even in scientific illustrations it is the caption which determines the truth of the picture' (59). The very nature of operating sound technology is a personally interpretative experience. The enregistrement ('recording' in French) of a sound is dependent on the frequency response of the microphone and its position, the different setting and controls of the recording equipment and the quality of its electronic circuitry to 'phonograph' the sound onto a recording medium; be it tape or digitally encoded disk. And the juxtaposition or mixing of music, words, and other sounds is an individual creative choice on the part of the sound engineer, producer or director. The decisions will anchor the experience of creating sound and listening to it with further truth and meaning that is unique to the individuals concerned.

Gombrich's third chapter is called 'Pygmalion's Power' and he explores the interrelationship between representation in art and human fantasy. He discusses the issue through two captivating legends. In Ovid's Latin classic *Metamorphoses*, Pygmalion is the sculptor who in seeking to create a woman after his own heart makes a statue with which he falls in love. He then prays to Venus to give him a bride who mirrors the sculpted image he has made himself and the goddess converts the cold ivory statue into a living body. Gombrich echoes the poignancy of this story with the recounting of a fairy tale of the Guiana Indians:

> Once there was an old man whose name was Nahokobani. He was troubled in his mind because he had no daughter, and who could look after him if he had no son-in-law? Being a witch doctor, he therefore carved himself a daughter out of a plum tree . . .

> (Gombrich 2000:80)

It might be argued that both legends are dealing with emotional psychology. The sound of a living being and a human social event however crafted and edited will always remain a representation and the style and nature of that representation is in the 'eye' or mind of the creator. There is no Venus to rematerialize human life from sound waves in the way that devotees of spiritualism after the Great War of 1914–18 hoped the souls of their loved ones contained in some kind of suspended aural miasma could reach out and offer them post-mortem companionship. Ovid is fantasy, but the tale from Guiana is very real in the sense that Nahokobani's 'daughter' is a carved plum tree to everyone but Nahokobani himself. As Leonardo da Vinci said 'If the painter wishes to see beauties to fall in love with, it is in his power to bring them forth, and if he wants to see monstrous things that frighten or are foolish or laughable or indeed to be pitied, he is their Lord and God'. What the painter sees can be very much what the sound designer and artist hears (Gombrich 2000:81 and Richter 1939:19).

Gombrich discusses the enigma of evaluating historical voice and sound. Richard Hughes's radio play, *Danger*, broadcast by the BBC in 1924 and hailed somewhat erroneously as the first radio play, sounds risible and bizarre today. As Plato said in *The Greater Hippias* 'Our sculptors say that if Daidalos were born today and created such works as those that made him famous, he would be laughed at' (Gombrich 2000:99). Visual art criticism has long dealt with 'The Beholder's Share' in the construction of meaning and the ancient texts have always warned us that 'these cloud shapes have no meaning in themselves, they arise by pure chance; it is we who by nature are prone to imitation and articulate these clouds' (Gombrich 2000:154). In Shakespeare's *Antony and Cleopatra*, the contingency of receiving the anticipated geometric of the image in the clouds applies equally to the ambiguity and interpretation of sound design:

> Sometimes we see a cloud that's dragonish;
> A vapour sometime like a bear or lion,

A tower'd citadel, a pendant rock,
A forked mountain, or blue promontory
With trees upon't, that nod unto the world,
And mock our eyes with air . . .

(IV, 14:2–7)

And inevitably William Shakespeare could make the same point about sound that in the Elizabethan open-air and wooden theatres heavily depended on music as a source for imagination and suspension of disbelief:

If music be the food of love, play on;
Give me excess of it, that, surfeiting,
The appetite may sicken, and so die.
That strain again! It had a dying fall:
O, it came o'er my ear like the sweet sound,
That breathes upon a bank of violets,
Stealing and giving odour! Enough; no more:

(*Twelfth Night*, I, 1:1–7)

Sound illusion relies on the conditioning of cultural memory. Gombrich's quotation from *The Painting of the Ancients*: 'The mind, having received of sense a small beginning of remembrance, runneth on infinitely, remembering all that is to be remembered' (Gombrich 2000:170), was included in the context of his reflections on being employed for six years by the BBC during the Second World War as a radio transmission monitor. Gombrich concluded that he was heavily affected by an anticipation of meaning conditioned by his own knowledge and memory:

once your expectation was firmly set and your conviction settled, you ceased to be aware of your activity, the noises appeared to fall into place and to be transformed into the expected words. So strong was this effect of suggestion that we made it a practice never to tell a colleague of our own interpretation if we wanted him to test it. Expectation created illusion. [. . .] the greater the probability of a symbol's occurrence in any given situation, the smaller will be its information content. Where we can anticipate we need not listen. It is in this context that projection will do for perception.

(2000:171–2)

Gombrich stated that it was:

the 'guess' of the radio monitor [. . .] that turned the medley of speech sounds into speech; it is the guess of the beholder that tests the medley of forms and colours for coherent meaning, crystallizing it into shape when a consistent interpretation has been found.

(204)

To what extent are sound perspectives different from visual perspectives? Ptolemy in *Optics* warned that 'When the sense cannot discern and place the object through its own mode of action, it recognises it through the manifestations of other differences, sometimes perceiving truly and sometimes imagining incorrectly' (Gombrich 2000:204). Perhaps it comes back to the wisdom of Philostratus through his hero Apollonius that no one can understand the painted horse or bull unless it is known how they look and how they sound.

SOUND ART AND THE TURNER PRIZE

Goldsmiths, University of London used to have a 'Fine Art' Department. It decided to remove the adjectival qualifying word 'Fine' and 'Art' has long since expanded its remit beyond canvas, oil paint, and watercolours, sculpture in stone, clay and wood. The success of Susan Philipsz in being awarded the 2010 Turner Prize for her sound installation *Lowlands 2008/2010* confirmed that 'sound art' has a prominent and recognisable position. It can be argued that the assertion of an artistic aesthetic in a community sound installation that is also enclosed in a gallery exhibition informs and invests artistic credibility in the genres of creative feature making traditionally placed in radio transmission and elsewhere.

'Feature' sound programme makers would also recognise the creative imperatives present in Susan Philipsz's work. She had researched and located a traditional sixteenth-century Scottish folk lament in which a drowned lover returns to haunt her sweetheart. She discovered there were three different versions and sang each of them and combined them through multi-tracking to be played beneath three bridges spanning the River Clyde: The George V Bridge, the mighty Caledonian Railway Bridge and Glasgow Bridge. She used her own voice in the 'installation' to retrieve cultural and folk memories in music and social history to be resonated in a sound ecology that interrogated and echoed in the environment.

The singing resonated in a location with natural and urban architecture and the poetic dimensions were multi-faceted. The installation places the artistic expression of crafted and aesthetically rendered sound in a visual context and reinforces the fact that sound is made, communicated and received in an inter-media, multimedia and complex natural ecology. When multi-tracked the words are the same at the beginning of the lament, veer off almost contrapuntally in their own paths of melody and then return synchronically in a unison for a choral sounding refrain.

The experience in Glasgow for visitors to the bridge underpasses could be described as virtually entering a movie-scape where the space entered is immersed and enveloped in a musical atmosphere for the here and now. In the *Guardian*, the Director of Tate Britain and chair of the judges, Penelope Curtis observed: 'It was both intellectual and instinctive. You could understand it conceptually, but it also had an emotional pull that you can't quite explain' (Higgins 2010). Philipsz did not think of herself as a 'sound artist'. She was originally a sculptress and it might be more accurate to say that she had 'sculpted' her work in sound using her own voice about a folk legend from her own community and there was nothing aesthetically incongruous about her creation being something that you could not see or touch:

> I see it as a sound sculpture under the bridge of the Clyde with the sound of the trains trundling overhead and the sound of the water. When it's presented in a gallery it's a much more intimate experience because you can spend more time with it in a more contemplative space.
>
> (*Guardian*, 6 December 2010)

SONIC AND AUDIOGENIC LITERATURE

The early twentieth-century literary movement described as 'modernism' coincidentally accompanied the social experience of mass media sound reception in the development of radio broadcasting. Early dramatic and literary output was both novelistic and stage dramatic. The early BBC relayed stage drama and vaudeville from West End theatres. Early audio dramatic and producing auteurs such as Compton Mackenzie and Cecil Lewis pioneered the dramatisation of contemporary literature, others such as Reginald Berkeley and Lance Sieveking fashioned a new dramatic genre called the 'microphone play'.

Modernist thinking and expression could be described as a global cultural phenomenon. In Italy the poet, Filippo Tommaso Emilio Marinetti, was experimenting with dividing the sound of language from its literal meaning and indeed would use literal language to create a representation of sound design utterances. The title of his seminal avant-garde poem set off in unconventional angles on the cover of the book published in 1914 'Zang Tumb Tumb Tuuumb Tuuuum Tuuuum Tuuuum' was the indication of his new theory of language and communication: 'Parole in Libertà', a commitment to abandoning traditional grammar and embracing the idea of words in freedom. Marinetti was influenced by a manifesto on sound published a year earlier by Luigi Russolo on *The Art of Noises* in which he declared: '. . . we find far more enjoyment in the combination of the noises of trams, backfiring motors, carriages and bawling crowds than in rehearsing, for example, the "Eroica" or the "Pastoral"' (Russolo 1987).

The much celebrated Bloomsbury group of poets, novelists and philosophers convened around the publications of the Hogarth Press founded by Leonard and Virginia Woolf. Virginia Woolf focused on creating characterisation where personality was defined by the voice of speech that represented individuality. This special attention to language, it might be argued, engaged with the accompanying enthusiasms in poetry for symbolism and imagism. In her 1925 novel *Mrs Dalloway* Woolf succeeds in expressing character through the individualistic sound of speech and language identity that is both verbal and non-verbal. In her prose she summons the literary devices of alliteration, assonance and onomatopoeia. An illustrative passage from the novel involves the character Peter Walsh walking from Regent's Park in London, crossing the Marylebone Road, just by Regent's Park Tube station:

> A sound interrupted him; a frail quivering sound, a voice bubbling up without direction, vigour, beginning or end, running weakly and shrilly and with an absence of all human meaning into
>
> ee um fah um so
>
> foo swee too eem oo –
>
> the voice of no age or sex, the voice of an ancient spring spouting from the earth; which issued, just opposite Regent's Park Tube Station, from a tall quivering shape, like a funnel, like a rusty pump, like a wind-beaten tree for ever barren of leaves which lets the wind run up and down its branches singing
>
> ee um fah um so
>
> foo swee too eem oo,
>
> and rocks and creaks and moans in the eternal breeze.
>
> Through all ages – when the pavement was grass, when it was swamp, through the age of tusk and mammoth, through the age of silent sunrise – the battered woman – for she wore a skirt – with her right hand exposed, her left clutching at her side, stood singing of love – love which has lasted a million years, she sang, love which prevails, and millions of years ago, her lover, who had been dead these centuries, had walked, she crooned, with her in May; but in the course of ages, long as summer days, and flaming, she remembered, with nothing but red asters, he had gone; death's enormous sickle had swept those tremendous hills, and when at last she laid her hoary and immensely aged head on the earth, now become a mere cinder of ice, she implored the Gods to lay by her side a bunch of purple heather, there on her high burial place which the last rays of the last sun caressed; for then the pageant of the universe would be over.
>
> As the ancient song bubbled up opposite Regent's Park Tube Station, still the earth seemed green and flowery; still, though it issued from so rude a mouth, a mere hole in the earth, muddy too, matted with root fibres and tangled grasses, still the old bubbling burbling song, soaking through the knotted roots of infinite ages, and skeletons and treasure, steamed away in rivulets over the pavement and all along the Marylebone Road, and down towards Euston, fertilising, leaving a damp stain.
>
> (Woolf 1925/1992:88–9)

I would argue that this passage of prose represents a beautiful expression of the auditory imagination as part of an expansive multi-dimensional geometry of artistic planes. Woolf was concerned about psychological perspective and when the academic critic Elaine Showalter discussed the author's modernist engagement with cinema, it is apparent that the bridge between the silent visual of urban image is struck with the impending sound of the 'talkie' culturally advanced by the aesthetic of the onset of radio literature through BBC broadcasting:

> Woolf makes use of such devices as montage, close-ups, flashbacks, tracking shots, and rapid cuts in constructing a three-dimensional story. [. . .] The historically meaningful and symbolically apt transitional devices of *Mrs Dalloway* show how effectively Woolf used the lessons she had learned from the cinematic medium. Urban life, she believed, was made for cinematic representation: 'We get intimations only in the chaos of the streets, perhaps, when some momentary assembly of colour, sound, movement suggests that here is a scene waiting for a new art to be transfixed' (p. 272 *Collected Essays*, ed. Leonard Woolf [4 vols., Hogarth Press, 1966–7] esp. 'The Cinema', II, pp. 268–72). [. . .] One of the most cinematic linking devices in *Mrs. Dalloway* is the sky-writing plane which is seen by the crowd around Buckingham Palace, and also by Septimus and Rezia in Regent's Park. Clarissa hears its 'strange high singing' right after she leaves her house when she crossed Victoria Street, but never sees it; when she returns home, she asks the maid what people are looking at.

> The sound of an aeroplane bored ominously into the ears of the crowd. There it was coming over the trees, letting out white smoke from behind, which curled and twisted, actually writing something! Making letters in the sky! Every one looked up (pp. 21–2) [. . .]

> In its final arc, the plane is compared to Shelley's skylark, 'curving up and up, straight up, like something mounting in ecstasy, in pure delight,' while 'out from behind poured white smoke looping, writing a T, an O, an F.'
>
> (Showalter 1992:xxi–xxiii)

Throughout these passages of the novel, Showalter is emphasising this aesthetic cohesion between visual and sound expression and metaphor. Peter Walsh's evocation of the street-singer is a sound language stripped of linguistic code and dissolving the human form 'like a funnel, like a rusty pump. Like a wind-beaten tree' (Showalter 1992:88). Woolf is striking a powerful fusion of imagery and rhythm with the street-singer transliterated into a powerful symbol whose meaning is visual and sonic.

Woolf's contemporary T.S. Eliot, wrote the modernist play *Sweeney Agonistes: Fragments of an Aristophanic Melodrama*, first published in 1926 and first performed in 1934. The audio-dramatic production for the Open University in 1991 in support of the course 'Literature in the Modern World' indicates that Eliot may have been sonically influenced by the euphony and rhythm of what might be described as the 'Jazz age of radio drama'. Graham Martin observes that '*Sweeney Agonistes*, though incomplete, is Eliot's most strikingly Modernist play. Its language is 'poetic' in a style very like Beckett's. Syntax and vocabulary are straightforward and familiar, but the compression, repetition of words and sentences, and rhythmic excitement achieve effects impossible for naturalist dialogue' (Martin 1991:107–8).

The audio production engages a musical score that seems to find a style of playing and saying rather than a style of composition. There is a confrontation between tonal Western music and vocal rhythm and indigenous African music. It is almost as if Eliot's writing has a Western high cultural instrumentation, melody and harmony and at the same time he attempts to score it with rhythms and phrasing that alludes, albeit with racist connotation, to the African and Semitic musical tradition. This is particularly the case in the choral song attributed by Eliot to 'Klipstein and Krumpacker' (Eliot 1974:133).

Graham Martin argues that:

> since Aristophanes wrote comedies, hints at Eliot's combination of farcical comedy and violent melodrama. The songs, on the other hand, belong to the world of minstrel shows, music-hall and Gilbert and Sullivan operetta. [. . .] Could we not say merely that what we have of *Sweeney Agonistes* amounts to a radio play well in advance of its time?
>
> (Martin 1991:108)

In 1933 Eliot wrote an essay entitled 'The Auditory Imagination' in which he explored the sonic feeling for syllable and rhythm in poetic language and how he believed that this penetrated far below the conscious levels of thought and feeling and had an invigorating impact on the poetic perception of words (Eliot 1955).

ROMANCING THEATRE SOUND

War Horse, a thrilling and spectacular production based on the novel by Michael Morpurgo has been a theatrical success since 2007 and successfully transferred from the National Theatre production in London to New York City's Broadway. It might be argued that its central appeal is the way that actors, working with life-sized horse puppets created by the Handspring Puppet Company, create an emotional and physical representation of the characters of the horses of soldiers in the Great War of 1914–18. The production engages with a sophisticated sound design and uniquely composed music. But it is the theatrical illusion of live horses that many critics identify as so moving and captivating. All of the traditional and modern arts and technologies of stage theatre were deployed and the character of the horse Joey in the New London Theatre production had separate actors playing his foal head, heart, and hind, and adult horse head, heart and hind. Joey's physical characterisation on stage actually had a total cast of nine actors. The live music was performed by five musicians playing trumpet, flugelhorn, bugle, French horn, tenor horn, cornet, piccolo, clarinet tenor trombone, and euphonium. One of the original National Theatre co-directors Polly Findlay reported that detailed research was conducted 'trying desperately to find out the exact pattern of First World War bugle calls to make sure that the cavalry charges were accurate' (Findlay 2009:7). While there was a stylistic representation of horse characterisation through an advanced and sophisticated aesthetic of theatrical puppetry, the production was directed to achieve an aspiration to realism:

> Tom Morris, one of the directors, was particularly adamant that we avoid any traces of sentimentality or anthropomorphism ('humanising' or reading human traits into animal behaviour) when dealing with the horses: we were going to portray them as if they were absolutely real. That's why at times during the show you might see the horses whinnying or making noises at seemingly dramatically inappropriate or sensitive movements; like real horses, our puppets give the sense that they are pursuing their own agenda rather than turning too unnaturally into what is going on in the human world.
>
> (Findlay 2009:9)

A similar theatrical sensation based on the illusion of sound and a large-scale set physicality was created at the Garrick Theatre in 1926 to represent the characterisation of a steam-train in the production of Arnold Ridley's play *Ghost Train*. The play concerned a group of travellers stranded at a remote country railway station in Cornwall said to be haunted by a ghostly train. The travellers challenge the fear created by this legend and discover a more mortal and criminogenic explanation for the supposed haunting of the station by steam and whistle. Frank Napier's 1936 'handbook of sound effects' *Noises Off*, described how the steam train experience was created on stage for the theatregoers of the time:

> The train effect in 'The Ghost Train' at the Garrick Theatre in 1926 was produced with the following apparatus: a garden roller pushed over slats of wood nailed to the stage at regular intervals, to represent the train passing over the rail joints; three cylinders of compressed air, one to blow the whistle, the second for an uninterrupted steam effect, and the third used with a tin, covering and uncovering the jet rhythmically, for the exhaust; a large tank; a large thunder-sheet; a thick, oval thunder-sheet and mallet; a whistle, for distant whistle effect; a side-drum and jazz-drummer's wire brush; another side-drum and a small padded mallet; a bass drum; some heavy chains; and sand-paper for distant puffing effect. Seven men were employed to work it all.
>
> This effect was arranged for a large theatre, and was very good indeed. For a smaller theatre no doubt less apparatus would be needed. The tank and oval thunder-sheet could be omitted, and the work of the air-cylinders, which cost 7*s.* 6*d* each, could be done with foot-pumps and inflated tyres or camp mattresses. Even so it would be quite a large undertaking requiring considerable space and personnel.
>
> (Napier 1936:39–40)

More than 80 years later the contemporary theatre has surround sound recording and transmission technology with the sound design blueprint digitally compressed microscopically on computers to reproduce the illusion of 1926. But the legend of the Garrick Theatre's ghost train endures with John A. Leonard in *Theatre Sound* (2001) supposing that eleven technician/performers were needed to create and perform the train:

> The instructions on how to [. . .] make the sound of a phantom steam engine may seem very funny to today's sound designer, but just think of the ingenuity that went into designing those effects and into making them happen night after night. I believe that it must have been more satisfying than going to the effects library and pulling out a stock steamtrain recording.
>
> (Leonard 2001:5–6)

Leonard is alluding to the fact that live sound is a creative performance uniquely experienced between stage presentation and audience; something that makes the *War Horse* puppetry so romantic and magical as an art form. Consequently the drawing of the train machine in the 1958 *Stage Noises and Effects* by Michael Green in the *Practical Stage Handbooks* series published by Herbert Jenkins has an authenticity and innocence; something of a sonic truth:

> Sometimes the whole effect has to be produced 'live.' This calls for several different sounds to be made in the proper order and strict organization is essential. The stage manager should first study the precise combination of sounds needed by listening to trains or records. A goods train requires an effect different from that of a passenger train – the rhythm of the wheels is different and there are the added noises of clanking couplings and buffers. The surroundings also make a difference. The noise of a train passing through a station is echoed by the surrounding buildings and the roof.
>
> A piece of apparatus can be built to imitate the sound of wheels rumbling and clicking over the rails. Basically, it is rather like a wind machine one of which may be adapted. It consists of a wooden drum, with framework sides, which is fitted to a stand so that it rotates when a handle is turned. Over the framework is fixed thin metal sheeting. Small wooden slats are fixed across this in two places, or slots may be made in the metal.
>
> For the effect of a train passing the drum is turned and a roller-skate is pressed against the metal sides of the drum. This gives the rumble of the wheels and the two slots cause the roller-skate wheels to jump, giving the 'clickety-click' caused by the rail joints. This method is particularly suitable for the sound of a train passing through a station at high speed.
>
> Another method of imitating the rumbling of wheels is to nail wooden slats to the floor about two feet apart and to run a garden roller over them.
>
> (Green 1958:34–5)

The art of creating and performing live sound in real performance before audiences has a central position in the nexus of modern entertainment media. For the analogue theatrical sound performer binds the onset of film produced in front of live audiences in its so-called 'silent' period, the development of dramatic entertainment and communication on broadcast radio, and the burgeoning art of sound sculpture. The memories and traditions of creative improvisation in sound were called up to inform each new wave of blossoming media technological platform avariciously consumed by the demands of infotainment markets. The art is still studied and celebrated as it is needed to inspire and enlighten the contemporary world of digital logarithms and multi-tracked pre-production. Reproducing a fist thudding into flesh by whacking a watermelon with an axe, the guillotining of a King by slicing a red cabbage with a carving knife, and the effect of a T-1000 cyborg passing through cell bars by slimy dog food sliding slowly out of a can hails to a time when there was no electricity, no amplified sound systems, no sound playback machines, and no recording technology. The imagination would be served by an intuitive and creative understanding of how human and natural objects and music can create sonic illusion.

In 2010, BBC Radio Three applied thirty minutes of its *Between the Ears* series to the legend of theatrical sound that is the breaking harp-string effect in *The Cherry Orchard*. John Goudie's documentary 'The Chekhov Challenge: The Sound of a Breaking String' investigated the history of this phenomenon as well as the contemporary challenge and interpretation. Chekhov's actual stage direction is both precise and ambiguous in terms of having fixed and unstable meaning: 'A distant sound is heard. It appears to come from the sky and is the sound of a breaking string. It dies away sadly.'

The programme referenced the great Frank Napier, celebrated by Tyrone Guthrie as the genius of theatrical sound effects who was able to create Maeterlinck's stage direction from *Les Aveugles* 'The nightbirds exult in the tree-tops' with an empty matchbox and three bent pins' (Napier 1936:v). Chekhov held no terrors for Frank Napier:

> I must tell how it was done at the Old Vic, namely, with a musical saw. Any ordinary saw, except of course a tenon saw, will make a similar sound, but a proper musical saw gives the best results, being longer, heavier, and of special temper. For those reasons it is an expensive article, the cheapest costing fifteen shillings.

> To play the saw the performer sits gripping the handle between his knees. He grasps the other end and bends it over to the left. It is important that the bend should be correct. Having bent the blade over and down, he must bend the end upwards again, as though he were trying to snap it off, thus forcing the saw into an S curvature. He can then play it, either by striking the flat of the blade on its convex curve with a small padded stick (the method used for the harp-string effect) or by bowing with a 'cello bow on the smooth edge.

> The sounds produced are marvellously eerie and good use can be made of them in 'spook' plays. I have played this instrument in the cauldron scene of 'Macbeth', and have had a part written for it in incidental music for 'The Tempest.'
>
> (86)

For a modern production of *The Cherry Orchard* for BBC Radio Drama, the director Peter Kavanagh was anxious to locate the sound in the meaning of the play. He found two sound motifs: one the sound of a cable breaking in a mine, a very likely scenario in Russia; the other a gun going off, a political idea planted in five or six places during the play. He therefore aimed to create a symbolic rather than a literal representation of the stage direction:

> I married the sound of the mine-shaft metal scrunching at a great distance, given a slightly strange unearthly sound with literally the sound of a gun going off, but taken down in pitch so that it sounded like a vast explosion with reverberation. [. . .] I referred to Chekhov's famous dictum that 'If you have a gun placed in Act One, in fact if you have a gun hanging on the wall in Act One, it must go off in Act Three.' I wasn't interested in the sound of a literal breaking string because to me it didn't signify something. Being a hardy Ulsterman, I thought well, I'm going to try and convey the meaning of what I think he's getting at. I think he was constrained politically. He wasn't able to say up on stage 'Vive La Revolution.' He wasn't going to do that. He was going to bring this strange sound that will be eerie, that will be a presage that would get the audience frightened or involved, but for our audience would mean nothing.
>
> (Goudie 2011)

SOUND AND FILM

The legendary film-maker and artist Derek Jarman lost his sight when his HIV turned into AIDS. In consequence he created a film called *Blue* that was also an audio drama. In its transmission and exhibition it was broadcast on UK Channel Four television and BBC Radio Three in 1993 at the same time. Radio Three later broadcast the soundtrack separately as a radio play and it was released on CD and as a film in video and DVD. In featuring only the unchanging screen of Yves Klein-inspired blue, the viewer's and listener's concentration focuses on the collage of voices performed, sometimes chorally by John Quentin, Tilda Swinton, Nigel Terry and Jarman himself. In 2010 Jarman's long-standing musical collaborator Simon Fisher Turner and the poet and musician Black Sifichi recreated the original sound design live at Brighton's Duke of York's cinema.

The screen is saturated with the colour blue, but the parallel soundtrack is certainly not saturated sound. Jarman died four months after its release and it stands as his last film. Aesthetically could the reverse sound and visual dynamic operate in the same way? Is there an equivalent blue noise as distinguished from what is normally understood to be white or pink noise? I would argue that it is a beautiful fusion of sound expression across the media of poetic literature, radio, film and television. The visual image appears to be a fixed screen canvas of blue, the audio soundtrack a combination of narrative performance, drama, music and sound design. The opening words establish the atmosphere and spirit of the film:

> You say to the boy open your eyes
> When he opens his eyes and sees the light
> You make him cry out. Saying
> O Blue come forth
> O Blue arise
> O Blue ascend
> O Blue come in.
>
> (Jarman 1994:3)

The script and audio drama are a magnificent contrapuntal requiem between realism and poetic reflection on immortality, disease and rage against dying:

> Teeth chattering February
> Cold as death
> Pushes at the bedsheets
> An aching cold
> Interminable as marble
> My mind
> Frosted with drugs ices up
> A drift of empty snowflakes
> Whiting out memory
> A blinkered twister
> Circling in spirals
>
> (Jarman 1994:23–4)

The language is suffused with intertextuality and the narrative voice switches between Jarman himself and the actors Tilda Swinton, Nigel Terry, and John Quentin. The music by Simon Fisher Turner, John Balance, Momus, Peter Christopherson, Karol Szymanowski and Erik Satie is a powerful interweaving of mood and accompaniment and contributes to Jarman's literary lament on mortality: 'The shoes I am wearing at the moment should be sufficient to walk me out of life' (Jarman 1994:28). Eight years before 9/11 Jarman's text has the portentousness of Nostradamus:

> As I slept a jet slammed into a tower block. The jet was almost empty but two hundred people were fried in their sleep.
>
> The earth is dying and we do not notice it.
>
> (25)

In the context of Michel Chion's critical vocabulary how does the sound follow the rule of the acousmatic in being without visual source and continually offscreen? It certainly summons the most powerful idea of Chion's *acousmêtre* in deriving 'mysterious power from being heard and not seen' (Chion 1996:221). With the cinema's audience gazing upon blue screen saturation how are we to articulate Chion's concept of synchresis in being the 'forging of an immediate and necessary relationship between something one sees and something one hears at the same time?' (224). Jarman fashions an exciting interpolation of naturalistic being as a dying patient of AIDS and a heightened expression of poetic literature that becomes self-elegiac in his final lines:

> In time,
> No one will remember our work
> Our life will pass like the traces of a cloud
> And be scattered like
> Mist that is chased by the
> Rays of the sun
> For our time is the passing of a shadow
> And our lives will run like
> Sparks through the stubble.
> I place a delphinium, Blue, upon your grave.
>
> (Jarman 1994:30)

However, the experience of the listener, whether attending the Edinburgh International and New York film festivals in 1993, live soundtrack performance in Brighton's 2010 film festival, or as cinematic and domestic film audiences, is a complex journey of perception. The academic and sound designer David Sonnenschein in 'Sound Spheres: A Model of Psychoacoustic Space in Cinema' has constructed an interesting method of critiquing sound in film that could be applied to Derek's Jarman's *Blue*:

> The importance of localisation of sound in our real world is explored and compared with the use of diegetic sound in film, which has been usefully codified by Michel Chion as onscreen and offscreen. To further develop the theory of filmic psychoacoustic space, the Sound Spheres model offers six levels of sonic experience, beginning from the most inner personal sphere and expanding toward the most outer unknown sphere: I Think, I Am, I Touch, I See, I Know and I Don't Know. Real world experiences and perception exercises of these spheres informs us how they can be applied to the creation of filmic stories.
>
> (Sonnenschein 2011:13)

Sonnenschein describes the innermost core of this sound sphere as representing 'personal audio thoughts that are simply not available to other listeners, unless we are told about them' (17). As examples he suggests these could be 'memories, daydreams, dreams, mental rehearsal or notes to oneself, internal music' (17). How would this engage with the passage in *Blue* when one of the narrative voices says:

> The damaged retina has started to peel away leaving the innumerable black floaters, like a flock of starlings around in the twilight. I am back at St Mary's to have my eyes looked at by the specialist. The place is the same, but there is new staff. How relieved I am not to have the operation this morning to have a tap put into my chest. I must try and cheer up H.B. as he has had a hell of a fortnight. In the waiting room a little grey man over the way is fretting as he has to get to Sussex. He says, 'I am going blind, I cannot read any longer'.
>
> (Jarman 1994)

Sonnenschein's model engages the inner 'I Think' zone with 'I See' and 'I Know'. The filmic notion of 'onscreen' audio is there though the image remains saturated blue and although this is 'I See' most of the perception is focused on 'I Think' as the viewer/listener engages imaginatively with Jarman's description of the onset of blindness through decaying and diseased retina and what he observes and perceives himself of his return to St Mary's hospital. The imaginative spectacle of 'I Think' and 'I Know' is stimulated by ambient soundtrack, narrator's words and the fading in of emotional rendering through Erik Satie's evocative music. Sonnenschein describes 'I Know' as the 'sense of offscreen sounds, where the source is not visible to the listener. The context of the environment and types of sounds expected to occur in that environment create a sense of familiarity with the soundscape' (2011:18). However, some parts of the soundtrack of Jarman's *Blue* may belong to the realm of Sonnenschein's outer sound sphere of the 'I Don't Know': 'if the person is an unknown character, this may fall into the I Don't Know sphere; we know it is a human voice, but we don't know exactly who it is'. He refers to the mystery of the strange tone associated with the black obelisk in Kubrick's *2001: A Space Odyssey* and explains how transitioning sound between the spheres is a device central to moving drama on and 'creating tension, anticipation, release and surprise' (2011:24–5).

SOUND – THE FLIGHT OF IMAGINATION

When the BBC first started broadcasting sound programmes from its fledgling London station 2LO in the 1920s, it may not be fully appreciated that the wizards and witches of sound were young men and women in their early twenties. Indeed, this was also the case in the USA where the image reproduced in this book of a young woman listening to sound radio on headphones indicates the excitement and enthusiasm for sound entertainment and story telling.

FIGURE 1.5
'The shut-in's Sunday service' (Repository: LoC P&P). In the early days of sound broadcasting radio was about young people enjoying storytelling across the airwaves, and this elegant American woman is listening on headphones to live radio in the splendour of her Art Deco drawing room in 1923.

In Britain this generation had recently engaged in total industrialised war. Pioneers of early BBC programming and engineering Lance Sieveking, Cecil Lewis and Peter P. Eckersley had all been in the Royal Flying Corps where it was rare for pilots to survive more than two weeks of aerial combat. Lewis described his role as Director of Programmes as 'riding the tiger' and his courage and adventure in creating sound story telling from drama and literature captured the spirit of his descriptions in *Sagittarius Rising* of piloting a reconnaissance plane above the slaughter and horror of 1 July 1916, the first day of the Battle of the Somme when only 19 years old:

> As we sailed down above it all, came the final moment. Zero!

> At Boisselle the earth heaved and flashed, a tremendous and magnificent column rose up into the sky. There was an ear-splitting roar, drowning all the guns, flinging the machine side-ways in the repercussing air. The earthy column rose, higher and higher to almost four thousand feet. There it hung, or seemed to hang, for a moment in the air, like the silhouette of some great cypress tree, then fell away in a widening cone of dust and debris. A moment later came the second mine. Again the roar, the upflung machine, the strange gaunt silhouette invading the sky. Then the dust cleared and we saw the two white eyes of the craters. The barrage had lifted to the second-line trenches, the infantry were over the top, the attack had begun.

> (Lewis 2000:72)

There is a sense that these pioneers of sound story telling were Ariels playwriting with a sense of the flyer's horizon and riding the storm clouds and streaks of lightning that the universe could throw at them. Sieveking's writing seems to suggest he was as mercurial and adventurous as his flying brother in arms and broadcasting. In his 1934 book *The Stuff of Radio* he smarted at the dismissal by his producing rival and colleague Val Gielgud and contemporary playwright Tyrone Guthrie of the early sound mixing desk (described then as a dramatic control panel) as a mere machine to be operated. For Sieveking 'equipment' that could create sound were the tools of life and creativity; to be played and not contemptuously dismissed as something to be operated, to merely produce output:

> I am strongly reminded of an old friend of mine who was shot down in a battle towards the end of the war. He was a brilliant flyer. Quick, hard, precise – precise to a degree, and quick as lightning in decision. And he flew his aeroplane with a sensitiveness that called forth exclamations of delight and admiration time and again. He would land her even in rough weather within a few yards of his hangar and she would roll just exactly the right distance. To see him side-slip, for just so far, spin for just so far, and end in the neatest loop you ever saw in your life was something one never forgot. And yet that man hated machines. 'Gosh!' he used to say to me, 'I loathe these ruddy kites. They're dead. I wish I'd gone into the cavalry. Horses for *me*!' And I once answered: 'You're an ungrateful blighter. Why! That little Sopwith of yours has saved your life over and over again, by being so nimble, so spry, so quick to answer to your least touch.' 'Yes, damn it!' he laughed. And now he's dead . . .

> How he would chuckle and nod and understand, if only I could tell him about Gielgud and Guthrie and the dramatic control-panel.

> (Sieveking 1934:59)

For Lance Sieveking making art out of sound was the fulfilment of a romantic dream. For him the stuff of radio was the essence of being. It was the thrill of going into battle. He could have been Callimachus before the Battle of Marathon, or Alexander before taking on the Persians at Arbela, or Joan of Arc before her victory over the English at Orleans:

> I dressed myself in a white tie and tail coat and dined alone in the upper room of the Blue Cockatoo in Cheyne Walk. The play was to begin at nine-fifty.

> I got into my old Morris Oxford car and drove slowly along the Embankment to Savoy Hill. I parked under the back windows of the Savoy Hotel and entered just exactly in the state of mind in which, one imagines, a young composer might have entered the Opera House at, say, Prague in 1840 to conduct for the first time an opera of his own composition. [. . .] I went into our old Savoy Hill building and climbed the stairs to my quaint office, that once had been an actress's bedroom, and later the room in which I was demobilised. I threw down my coat and hat and took from its hiding-place (for of course I had hidden it – in case!) my producer's script of the play, struck into a large blank

book, on the right-hand pages. I put it under my arm and lit a cigarette. There was plenty of time. More than half an hour to go yet to 'Zero'.

(Sieveking 1934:18)

Sieveking's recollection of the joy and the romance of crafting sound with all the charming references to Art Deco style and Jazz Age London, driving open-topped on a summer's evening along the Chelsea embankment to his orchestrating and conducting of a sonic symphony at the BBC's former riverside headquarters in the West End, and his appreciation of sound machines as alchemist's stones is our cue for contemplation of sound technologies.

THE ACADEMIC STUDY OF SOUND

The academic study of sound across disciplines should be a creative and stimulating experience at all educational levels. Academic projects and outcomes include research, essay/thesis writing, and publication. Academic essays are intellectually driven written arguments based on the analysis of primary and secondary sources or 'texts' and fieldwork research that includes qualitative and quantitative surveys. It may combine all of these characteristics or only one or two. Reference has already been made to the cross-disciplinary nature of this book's enquiry into the practice as well as the theory of sound. This interface is set out in Table 1.3. It might be argued that the intellectual and creative production interplay among these production and academic disciplines through sound represents a productive *praxis* synergy.

Primary sources are likely to be sound texts that you have acquired or recorded yourself, or borrowed and gained access to at library and archive institutions, such as the BBC, Library of Congress or the British Library's National Sound Archive. They may be DVDs of films with soundtracks you wish to textually analyse or digital files of radio programmes. Many primary source sound texts are accessible in the contemporary world of digital cyberspace. The BBC now makes available a free access weekly audio drama and documentary podcast. Equally, primary texts may be sound recordings, digital video files that you have made (with permission) of sound art installations. Primary sources can also be acquired in the field through original interviewing on your part of sound communicators, designers, producers and artists.

You may wish to conduct research or laboratory studies on the perception and reception of sound media texts and depending on your objectives and academic discipline it should be possible to establish the methods and protocols for your surveying. Psychological research into radio listening began as early as the 1920s and the first publication in the UK was the work by Professor T.H. Pear of Manchester University in *Voice and Personality* (1931). He had the cooperation of the BBC in distributing survey samples to radio listeners throughout the United Kingdom in issues of *The Radio Times* and the specific broadcast of the voices of different people reading the same text (Crook 2009:53–61). In the USA the seminal foundation of studying the social psychology of sound and radio was the text *The Psychology of Radio* edited and written by Hadley Cantril and Gordon W. Allport (1935). The book convened research into radio as a psychological novel, the influence of radio upon mental and social life, institutional and ideological issues contextualising radio content and reception, and listener's tastes and habits. In laboratory research the book published the findings of surveys into voice and personality, gender differences in radio voices, the differential impact of sound reception between human speaking and voice communication through loud-speaker, the nature of perceiving and socially receiving broadcast sound, and the cognitive issues concerning listening versus reading. The book also discussed radio social and cultural function in the process of broadcasting messages, providing entertainment, the role and impact of advertising, the function and impact of education through sound radio and a debate about whether radio broadcasting extends the social environment by creating, developing or changing the nature of human communities. It might be argued that neither the subject of media and communications studies/radio studies has changed much in more than 75 years.

You may wish to concentrate on a qualitative methodology that aims to understand and interpret social and cultural phenomena (in this case sound texts or reception) rather than measuring them and this is usually achieved through one to one interviews. It may also be achieved through interviews with 'focus groups' where there is a wider discussion and quick opportunity to gather small-scale quantitative patterns of response and reaction.

Quantitative methods aim to measure and statistically analyse the social and cultural issues connected with sound media and sound textual reception. This is usually achieved through large-scale, representative samples of people, opinions or data. If you embark on surveying research of this kind you will be obliged to have your project evaluated in terms of the research ethics. This will determine the research contract between you and your human subjects in terms of their anonymity, their understanding of how you will be using the information they are providing, method and length of data storage and permission and indications of how the data will be published. The quantitative category of research also includes content analysis where you may wish to count and measure the frequency of specific elements in sound texts.

When researching most academic essays you will be reading and notating broadly six categories of published texts:

(1) Notes of lectures you have attended and specific lecture notes, hand-outs and virtual learning environment resources.

You should ask your course convenors how any quotations from these sources should appear in your theses in terms of notation and bibliography.

Table 1.3 An interface of the cross-disciplinary nature of this book's enquiry into the practice as well as the theory of sound

Radio	Theatre	Music	Film	Animation and games	Art exhibition and installation	Internet and podcasting
Music and speech programme. A wide frame of sound programme genres including journalism, factual documentary, drama, drama-documentary, phone-in talkback, reality shows, light entertainment, niche ideological agendas, propaganda and commercial persuasion.	An accompanying component of the art of stage theatre through recorded or live music, recorded or live-performed sound effects/design and on-stage and off-stage pre-recorded/produced sequences that intersect with live physical performance by actors on a stage. The technology requires projection and transmission of sound in physical space in conjunction with performances that interact with present audiences. 'Theatre in the dark' and 'auricular theatre' is a growing strand of audio-dramatic reception in darkened stage auditoria with either live sound/performance or through speakers and live physical presence.	A long-standing performative sound specific art-form consisting of composition and live and recorded sound sequences. In its cultural expression and dissemination it is a private and public phenomenon and convenes public events and performances that are musically discrete as well as participating in multimedia publication.	Sound had a role in the film medium even when it was supposedly 'silent'. Early visual films with no soundtrack were accompanied during exhibition by live musicians and sound noise performers – a borrowing of a performance art tradition from live stage theatre and vaudeville. With the development of filmic sound prints and technology film-sound became a fundamental stream in the construction of meaning for cinema.	Sound was the foundation for early animation production in the sense that drawing and designs were created to link with an initially sound-produced narrative. In computer games sound is a dramatic and environmental determinant of linear and lateral direction of first person shooter experience as well as being part of the multimedia illustration of computer gaming on CD-ROMs or Internet/web-space networks.	In the twentieth century the concept and practice of art evolved and developed from being physical drawing, colouring and sculpture. The development of multimedia technologies provided artists with new materials for expression and inevitably sound has been embraced as a tool or material for 'sculpture' and multi-dimensional expression in community and exhibition space.	Digital matrices and technologies and their social and transnational cohesion through cyberspace and the Internet means that sound has a new space for expression in the postmodern information and Internet age. Sound can stand alone in live streaming and downloading and in multimedia converged web-space can contrapuntally intersect with the visual and text-based frame. Two sound-based forms have developed in this new media context: the podcast – a downloadable sound text; and audio-slideshows or film-soundtracks – multilayers with visual sequences of photographic stills as filmic shots.

The practice and social significance of radio communication is studied in the social sciences, sociology, media and communications studies and cultural studies. Radio drama and poetic texts are studied in English. In recent years a separate discipline of 'Radio Studies' has developed usually aligned to university degrees teaching practice radio skills.

The study of theatre sound has been something of a minority strand of academic interest and was solidly placed in theatre or drama studies. In practice, sound theatre design has been part of stage management though in the modern age, the theatre sound designer has taken on greater significance in the context of large state-funded and commercially successful theatres. Digital and surround sound technology offers creative and technological possibilities. In many respects opera and stage musicals are also a form of sound in theatre though they have tended to be the preserve of music as an academic discipline.

Music has been one of the key Renaissance practice and academic disciplines and has a well-established cultural and intellectual framework. It certainly shares the practice-theory dynamic of radio and theatre. In the twentieth and twenty-first century it has developed its multidisciplinary and inter-disciplinary vectors in the consideration of the social and cultural roles of classical and popular music and the development of sound art practice and philosophising largely around the electronic music movement.

Film studies has emerged as an academic discipline in its own right and has also thrived in university and college film practice and film school clusters. The textual, social, cultural and contextual analysis of film has developed through cultural studies and media and communication studies and is very much an interdisciplinary and multidisciplinary subject. Film music composition is both an industrial output for composers and performers, and a focus for film studies analysis. The role of the soundtrack has been convened and celebrated academically through seminal conferences and journal publications, notably the decision by *Screen* to devote its entire May/June 1984 issue 'On the Soundtrack'.

The study of animation academically belongs to media and communications studies and its later evolution into the independent discipline of 'Film Studies'. The practice of animation sound is very much a specialist skill taught within film and art schools teaching animation or universities convening undergraduate and graduate degrees in sound design. This is also true of the sound design for computer games and the skills required in this area are sometimes being taught in digital computer and design departments. The cultural, aesthetic and social significance of sound in computer games is being developed academically in the developing disciplines of radio and sound media/art studies.

Art has always had a considerable realm of theoretical and aesthetic reflection in art schools and universities and art's transition out of the confines of 'Fine Art' to 'Art' as an all-embracing or open-ended rather than closed-textual practice and intellectual discipline has in a sense opened a Pandora's box in terms of practice, expression and philosophical discourse. The creative and almost evangelical *convivencia* and osmosis between the art and music academic practice and theoretical disciplines has generated a revolution or certainly identifiable movement in writing, debate, discussion, conferencing and exhibition.

Internet and podcasting tend to be objects and spheres of interest for media and communications studies though cyberspace clearly offers huge potential in relation to music and art exhibition and interactive participation of listeners on global and transnational vectors. The excitement of bottom-up and horizontal-to-horizontal power relations is generating a considerable amount of quantitative, qualitative and ethnographic participant observer academic surveying in media studies, anthropology, sociology and politics.

(2)   Textbooks cited as core readers for your course and which consist mainly of academic discussions of other primary and secondary sources with little original research.

These books are essentially surveys and summaries of the scholarship of the prevailing subject. In a way this book falls into this category although there are instances of original observations and argument.

(3)   Academic monographs consisting of original research and contributing new arguments and information advancing and developing knowledge and understanding of the subject area.

Examples of this category would be *Crossing the Ether: British Public Service Radio and Commercial Competition 1922–1945* by Seán Street and published in 2006, *Ezra Pound's Radio Operas: The BBC Experiments, 1931–1933* by Margaret Fisher and published in 2002, *Radio, Television and Modern Life: A Phenomenological Approach* by Paddy Scannell and published in 1996 and *Ocean of Sound: Aether Talk, Ambient Sound and Imaginary Worlds* by David Toop and published in 1995. They all hail from different academic disciplines. Street's book is an original contribution to the history of British radio culture during a critical period of the twentieth century and changes a previous view of BBC dominance of radio broadcasting reception. Fisher's book makes an original contribution to the scholarship on Ezra Pound's literary output and is revelatory about his participation in early BBC radio content production. Scannell's book is a creative and original exploration of broadcasting's role in the context of twentieth-century social and political philosophy. Toop is a musician, author and music curator who writes an original and creative text expressing new insights into the social and cultural relationships of music and sound. It could be argued that the first academic monograph on radio/sound was probably *Radio: The Art of Sound* by Rudolf Arnheim, a German-born art and film theorist and perceptual psychologist, that was first translated for English publication in 1936 by Margaret Ludwig and Herbert Read. Arnheim had produced an equally seminal and influential text on the art of film, first published in German as *Film als Kunst* in 1932. Arnheim's early discourse on radio focused on issues and debates that have hardly changed in radio and sound studies: the imagery of the ear; the world of sound; direction and distance in hearing; spatial resonance; sequence and juxtaposition (the art of editing sound); the necessity of radio-film; in praise of blindness; emancipation from the body; author and producer; the art of speaking to everybody; wireless and the nations (issues of transnationality in communications); psychology of the listener and television. The opening paragraph of his book recounted an anecdote and image that initiated the debate about modern media communications (in this case sound radio) as being some kind of *global village*:

> Not so long ago I was sitting by the harbour of a south Italian fishing-village. My table stood on the street in front of the café door. The fishermen, their legs a-straddle, their hands in their pockets and their backs turned to the

street, were gazing down on the boats which were just bringing home the catch. It was very quiet, but suddenly from behind me there came a spitting and a spluttering, then screams and squeaks and whistles – the wireless was being tuned in. The loudspeaker had been set into the front wall of the café and served to catch customers. What the net was to the fishers the loudspeaker was to the café proprietor. When the screaming had stopped we heard an English announcer speaking. The fishermen turned round and listened, even though they could not understand. The announcer informed us that they were going to broadcast an hour of German folk-songs and he hoped we would enjoy them. And then a typical German male voice choir sang the old songs that every German knows from childhood. In German, from London, in a little Italian place where strangers are almost unknown. And the fishermen, hardly one of whom had been in a big town, let alone abroad, listened motionless. After a while the waiter seemed to think we should have a change, so he got on to an Italian station, and as an hour's gramophone records was on just then, we heard a French chansonette. French, from Rome, in that village!

This is the great miracle of wireless. The omnipresence of what people are singing or saying anywhere, the overleaping of frontiers, the conquest of spatial isolation, the importation of culture on the waves of the ether, the same fare for all, sound in silence. The fact that forty million sets are scattered over the world to-day appears to be the central problem of broadcasting.

(Arnheim 1936:13–14)

The aesthetic and political romanticism and innocence about sound radio's hope, possibilities and humanistic potential expressed in this passage is at the heart of this book's appreciation of the spirit of romancing the sound. In a matter of years after Arnheim wrote this passage, radio would be used to promote and advance the designs of militaristic and genocidal regimes lead by Adolf Hitler and Benito Mussolini and Arnheim would flee Europe to arrive in New York in the autumn of 1940 with only ten dollars in his pocket. He would go onto participate in the pioneering social research into radio at Columbia University and remain in the states as a leading academic of psychology.

Also included in the category of monographs are collections of original research articles published in what are known as *Readers*. A typical example would be the appropriately titled *Radio Reader: Essays In the Cultural History of Radio* (2002) edited by Michele Hilmes and Jason Loviglio and *Broadcast Talk* (1991) edited by Paddy Scannell, which includes 'Referable words in radio drama', by Peter M. Lewis, who focuses on contestation and institutional struggles over the content of language in radio drama:

in order to illustrate the relations of power between the different parties. But there is also some correspondence with what actually happens in the day-to-day exchanges between those concerned. Language – and especially 'language'

– is indeed abstracted, literally bracketed, from its context and made to do duty for underlying political, social and psychological realities whose importance tends consequently to be overlooked.

(Scannell 1991:15)

Peter Lewis's research was unique in being derived from ethnographical observation. He had been permitted access to the internal operations of the BBC Radio Drama department and sat in on meetings and production processes.

Two influential readers on the cultural and multidisciplinary analysis of music and sound art are *Audio Culture: Readings in Modern Music* (2008) edited by Christoph Cox and Daniel Warner and *The Auditory Culture Reader* (2003) edited by Michael Bull and Les Back. These collections of original and thought provoking essays by leading researchers and academics discourse thinking about sound, histories of sound, anthropologies of sound, sounds in the city, living and thinking with music, music and its others: noise, sound, silence, modes of listening, music in the age of electronic reproduction and musical and sound art practices with a focus on electronic music and electronica, DJ culture, musical improvisation, experimental musics and the notion of 'The Open Work' – 'the indeterminate world of quantum physics and a post-theological universe, an authorless world without a unique origin, essence, or end' (Cox and Warner 2008:166).

(4)   Academic journals providing a space and platform for original scholarship that has a published output in shorter lengths of between 5,000 and 10,000 words.

These also review and monitor key developments in their respective disciplines. Research and intellectual argument about sound is published in a number of journals; some without the sign-posting of the word sound in their title. Universities running practice and theory sound-related courses may subscribe electronically or in terms of bound volume library cataloguing to the following journals known to focus on social, philosophical, cultural and textual analysis of sound phenomena:

- *The Soundtrack* and *The New Soundtrack*
- *The Radio Journal: International Studies in Broadcast and Audio Media*
- *Organised Sound: International Journal of Music and Technology*
- *Journal of Radio and Audio Media* (journal of the Broadcast Education Association [BEA], USA)
- *Screen* (founded in 1959 as *Screen Education*, an academic journal for international scholarship research and education in screen studies, published by Oxford University Press and associated with the University of Glasgow, which organises an annual '*Screen* Studies' conference)
- *Journal of Gaming and Virtual Worlds*
- *Historical Journal of Film, Radio and Television* (the journal for the International Association for Media and History, an interdisciplinary journal

concerned with the evidence produced by the mass media for historians and social scientists, and with the impact of mass communication on the political and social history of the twentieth century).

Your first port of call when researching academic journals is to examine the abstract that should inform you of whether it is likely to assist you with your topic or subject area. In volume 51, issue 3 of *Screen* in Autumn 2010, Sean Cubitt published an article entitled 'The sound of sunlight'. The title might be a promising source for an essay on synaesthesia, or the representation of sunlight in cinema through soundtrack. The abstract reveals:

In films as disparate as The Garden of Allah (1935), Lawrence of Arabia (1962) and Kingdom of Heaven (2005), sunlight is given an aural presence of considerable distinction. Perhaps only the tradition of the nocturne has acquired such a recognizable audio palette. This paper investigates the types of sounds used to characterize heat and light, with special reference to desert scenes. As the sun is so difficult to film, because it manifests an extreme where vision and blindness, warmth and pain intersect, its image requires a supplement, or indeed a substitution. Among the cinema's repertoire of codes, in general it is sound and music that have most commonly stood alongside, beneath or in place of visual depictions of sunlight in cinema. This case study of a highly recognizable motif illuminates the history of sound design through the sonification of an essentially silent phenomenon.

(Cubitt 2010:118)

In 2009 Georg Klein published an article entitled: 'Site-Sounds: On strategies of sound art in public space' in the academic journal *Organised Sound*, published by Cambridge University Press. If you are researching an essay on sound art in community and public space this may well be an important publication that will inform your argument. Again the journal helpfully makes available on most university electronic databases an abstract that will guide you on whether you should follow up with extended reading:

During the mid twentieth century, space was developed as a composable dimension. Composers used the three spatial dimensions in their own fashion, but space was understood primarily as an abstract concept. It was not until the development of sound installation art that space was discovered in a concrete manner, explored, performed in and could even acquire its own specificity, called *site-sound (Ortsklang)*.

The article shows consequences and strategies of sitesound installations in three sections – from spatial sound to site-sound, public space as performance venue, and public strategies (acoustic interventions, interactive installations and participatory projects) – with three examples of site-sound installations *(Site-Sound Marl Mitte, meta.stases and towersounds.2: watch tower)*.

> Acoustic art in public spaces basically involves installing a space in another existing space, both physically and sensorially, and metaphysically and mentally – an interior space in an exterior space, so to speak. The original quality of sound art lies in the *oscillation of interior and exterior space*. Thus public spaces intensified by sound art cause transitional spaces to come into being, in a political and a psychoanalytic sense.
>
> (Klein 2009:101)

It is quite common for academic journals that by their titles are unlikely to cover analysis of media sound texts to include substantial and significant instances and collections of scholarship. For example *Journal of Adaptation in Film and Performance*, Volume 3, Number 2 in 2010 included the article 'Radio Drama Adaptations: An Approach Towards an Analytical Methodology' by Elke Huwiler in which he sought to establish:

> a methodology with which radio drama pieces can be analysed. It thereby integrates all features the art form has to offer: voices, music, noises, but also technical features like cutting and mixing contribute to the narrative that is being told. This approach emphazises the importance of seeing radio drama as an art form in its own right, and not as a literary genre. An analysis of radio drama adapted from literary pieces shows how varied the features with which the 'same' story can be told in the two art forms can be.
>
> (Huwiler 2010:129)

Significant conferences investigating converging issues around sound sometimes lead to special issues of academic journals in pre-existing disciplines. The example of *Screen*'s influential 1984 issue 'On the Soundtrack' has already been mentioned. The articles in this publication again point to the meeting points of cross-disciplinary discussion and debate: 'The Acoustic Dimension: Notes on Cinema Sound'; 'Carnal Stereophony: A Reading of "Diva"'; 'Composing for the Films'; 'From "Aida" to "Zauberflöte" Jennifer Batchelor Considers the Opera Film'; 'Towards a Semiotics of the Transition to Sound: Spatial and Temporal Codes'; 'Mood Music: An Inquiry into Narrative Film Music'. A groundbreaking conference in Cardiff in 2000 called 'Radiocracy' was an inaugural event for the United Kingdom's 'Radio Studies Group' and the *International Journal of Cultural Studies* published a collection of some of the papers given. In 1991 *Theatre Journal* (USA, John Hopkins University Press) devoted an entire issue to the subject of 'Radio Drama' with a number of articles by practitioner directors who were invited to engage on the theoretical underpinning and framework of their aesthetic output.

(5)   Books written by practitioners on the how and why of producing and creating sound texts and hybrid books that blend theory with practice.

These books are credible and reputable sites of scholarship since they inform the theory as well as express how theory informs the practice. An impressive example of this kind of book would be *Sound Design: The Expressive Power of Music, Voice, and Sound Effects in Cinema* by David Sonnenschein, published in 2001. Books that are written and aim to inculcate only knowledge of high quality practice include *Audio in Media* by Stanley R. Alten, which was published in its 9th revised edition in 2010. This book's contribution of theory is purely technological and deriving from the science subject of physics and electronics.

(6)   Internet sources.

The more contextualised these are by way of peer-reviewing or university hosting the better. Students are normally advised about the potential unreliability of Wikipedia entries though they sometimes provide links and gateways to cyber-sources that have more authority. It is advisable to always file the urls of sites that contribute to your research with the date and time of access.

Educational institutions provide full training and resources on the protocols of academic attribution and sources, avoidance of plagiarism, and recommended criteria for qualitative essay argument, development and conclusion writing. Much enjoyment can be derived from reading and researching as widely as possible. Texts that are initially difficult to absorb on first reading can be better assimilated by breaking up the reading process. Understanding and interest are often increased on second and third examination. It is always a good idea to collect quotations and points that impress your understanding of the question or issue through posting notes or updating a computer/word-processed file. Researching and reading primary source texts whether sound, visual or written are always a more satisfying and interesting experience than relying on another academic's interpretation or summary. It is also much more fulfilling to give yourself time to think and reflect so that the quality of your critical autonomy in expressing your views and opinions will be much higher.

You will find extensive resources and audio-visual interfaces supporting and extending many of the topics and subjects raised in this chapter on the book's companion website.

CHAPTER 2

Sound technologies

ACCELERATING FUTURES

The advance of sound technologies over the last thirty years has been breathtaking. We have moved from the analogue into the digital age. Sound editing based on physical cutting in relation to hearing moved to digital manipulation on multi-tracks and audio-montage space in audio-visual computer screen interfaces. The portable recording machine has changed from shoulder-carried boxes weighing several pounds mechanically and electro-magnetically recording on plastic tape to mini-computers the size of credit card wallets and weighing less. The process of editing and production is now moving from keyboard tapping and mouse-clicking to touch-screen tablets. The sophistication of sound production through digitisation has substantially reduced the economies of scale in the producer and consumer technological interface and cyberspace makes us all potential sound designers. Stereo and binaural is no longer the cutting edge of experience. Digital all enveloping surround sound is the standard across much multimedia.

The student and novice of sound practice is faced with an overwhelming array of digital products and technologies available with the wide range of pricing. Advice provided in 2011 is likely to be go out-of-date very quickly; hence the continual updating of new editions of standard audio-production books. It is hoped that the companion website for this book will help the sound practitioner keep up with innovation and development.

FIGURE 2.1
Historical artefacts in the storage of sound (Photo: copyright Marja Giejgo). Reel to reel tape, cassette, 5 and a quarter inch 'floppy disk', mini-disc, hard disk for laptop computer, SD card and mini-SD card.

PRACTICE TECHNOLOGY AND AESTHETIC

The technological grasp and practice of sound can always be articulated in terms of its aesthetic. John L. Bracewell observed: 'The designer's imagination is critical [. . .] The metaphor must appeal to the senses and the emotions through the qualities of the medium within which the artists works' (Bracewell 1992:1). Table 2.1 sets out the creative aims and objectives of the essential sound designers' technological skill set. They fundamentally blend the tool of sound characteristics, its crafting through production to dramatic and communicative purpose:

It's very important that we understand the principles of sound in order to accurately capture music, sound effects, or even noise. The sound source helps define the tools we should use to record it. Most of the time, we strive to preconceive the sonic impact of the recording, imagining the sound that provides the desired musical or artistic result, and then go after it. Other times, we stumble across a sound that inspires a complete redirection of the artistic process. In either case, a thorough understanding of your recording tools is essential.

(Gibson 2007:35)

Table 2.1 The creative aims and objectives of the essential sound designers' technological skill set

Scope	Functions
To transmit the human voice in speech or song (adequate audibility is always the first requisite)	Audibility
To establish locale (bird songs, traffic noises)	Extension of dramatic space/time
To establish atmosphere (wind and rain)	Vocal substitution
To create and sustain mood (combinations of devices uses for locale and atmosphere; distortion of speech; soft music)	Mood
As an independent arbitrary emotional stimulus (music, non-associative sounds)	Music
To reveal character (the unspoken aside)	Vocal substitution
To advance the plot (sound bridges)	Motivation
Controllable properties	
Intensity	
Frequency	
Duration	
Timbre	
Envelope	
Directionality	
Key technologies and skills	
Physics of sound	Understanding its nature and properties
Acoustics	Understanding and shaping its properties environmentally
Hearing, listening and psycho-acoustics	The physiology of reception
Microphone and recorders	The technology of recording the sound of people and events outside the studio
Mixing and editing	The technology of digitally manipulating and producing sound
Use of sound studios	Using studio technology to record and produce sound through live and pre-recording panel/console operations and sound stages
Transmitting sound in live spaces	Loudspeaker and live sound systems outside the studio

Source: Burris-Meyer *et al*. 1979:2 and Bracewell 1993:1

THE NATURE OF SOUND AND HEARING

Most technical writers use the metaphor of the stone being dropped into a pool. Essentially the sound wave comprises of five key elements: phase, velocity, frequency, amplitude and wavelength. The wave begins with the vibrating of an object, which sets molecules closest to it in motion and they ripple out. The momentum of one displaced molecule to the next 'propagates the original vibrations longitudinally from the vibrating object to the hearer' (Alten 2008:1). Air molecules around the vibrating object contract and expand until it completes its cycle and the 'vibrations cause continuous variations in the existing air pressure' (Gibson 2007:35). Molecules pushed together in high pressure are said to be in compression. Those pulled apart in areas of low pressure are in rarefaction (Hausman *et al.* 2000:96). Elasticity occurs when the displaced molecule pulls back to its original position. The number of vibrations per second is known as frequency and the first vibration is called the fundamental with subsequent multiple vibrations being known as harmonics. Consequently music has a wide frequency range with speech being more limited (Walne 1990:20).

In normal atmospheric conditions, sound moves through air rather slowly relative to light. It is usually at a rate of about 1,120 feet (340 metres) per second, at 70° Fahrenheit at sea level, though it is important to understand that elevation, temperature and humidity will affect the conditions of the air and consequently the velocity of sound. When a sound source has produced one wave crest and one wave trough it is said to have completed one cycle.

The sound wave produces frequency and pitch. Frequency is the number of times that a sound wave vibrates per second and is usually expressed in hertz (Hz) and pitch is the subjective hearer's perception of this frequency in terms of highness or lowness. The pitch/sound frequency range is usually divided between low bass, upper bass, midrange, upper midrange, and treble. This means that a sound at 100 Hz has completed its wave cycle 100 times each second. Each musical note is related to a specific frequency. For example, middle C has a fundamental frequency of 262 Hz.

Each frequency has a wavelength, which is the distance that a sound wave has to travel to complete one cycle of compression and rarefaction. Frequency and wavelength change inversely in relation to each other so that a sound with a lower frequency has a longer wavelength. A higher sound frequency will have a shorter wavelength. Understanding wavelength gives the sound designer a tool of measurement to evaluate the acoustics of performance and recording spaces.

Amplitude and loudness are values that are directly related to each other. Again, like frequency and pitch, you have the scientific objective value first and then the value of the listener's perception second. Amplitude, as the number of air molecules in motion and therefore the size of the sound wave, produces on the human ear the subjective understanding of a sound's loudness or softness. Amplitude is measured in decibels. As Gibson explains 'Loudness is a subjective, perceptual aspect of sound. The human ear is not equally sensitive to all frequencies. [. . .] In fact, as the amplitude decreases, our ears become dramatically more sensitive to this frequency range' (Gibson 2007:41).

In 1933 Bell Laboratories carried out surveying in order to determine the nature of perceived volume in human beings. The survey results are known as the Fletcher-Munson Curve and demonstrate that for the human ear, music sounds fuller at loud volumes and thinner at soft volumes, but the human ear is not equally sensitive to all audible frequencies. We do not hear low and high frequencies as well as we hear middle frequencies. This is called the equal loudness principle though Alten is correct to suggest that it should be called 'unequal loudness principle' (Alten 2008:13). This is the explanation of why listeners sometimes complain that radio and television commercials are 'louder' than the programming around them and that they are forced to turn the volume down. It is more a case that human perception is better at midrange than high and low frequencies.

A sine wave is a graphical illustration of what is known as pure tone, a single frequency without harmonics and overtones, because most sound is a combination of different frequencies to create the complicated waveforms seen in software editing programmes. The combination of frequencies contributes to what is usually defined as a sound's timbre or tonal quality. This is further 'coloured' by the sound's shape or envelope, a sound's change in loudness over time, which is broken down into attack, initial decay, sustain and release. As a result the concept of timbre becomes associated with the tonal quality of a human voice or musical instrument. In the attack phase a sound rises in amplitude from zero to its attack peak. A snare drum would be an example of sound with a fast attack time and an approaching helicopter would be the opposite. The decay is the quick decrease following a sound's amplitudinal peak. The sustain is the period a sound is still generating from its source after the attack and decay, and the release describes the sound after the sources stop its generation. This process of attack, sustain and decay is known as the transient response.

The ability of the human ear to hear frequencies is dependent on age and health. Most young people can perceive pure tones of 16,000 to 20,000 Hz (16–20 kHz). People exposed to long periods of loud noise beyond the threshold of hearing tend to lose the ability to hear high-end frequencies and this ability also deteriorates with age. The ear works with three key parts: outer ear, middle ear and inner ear. Sound enters and travels down the auditory canal to the ear drum that vibrates and these sensations travel to the hearing nerves in the inner ear. Sensitivity to frequencies is dependent on the size of the auditory canal. The physiognomy of the hearing organ is complex and beautiful in its combination of biology, chemistry and physics. It consists of bundles of microscopic hair-like projections called cilia attached to a sensory call that vibrate when meeting sound waves and these vibrations are transformed into electrical and chemical signals sent to the brain. The machine of the ear, if it can be described as such, works in three clusters of signal reception, encoding and decoding. The outer and middle ear operate as the sensory receptor, the inner ear and eight cranial nerves operate as the neural encoder, and the auditory cortex and brain sphere are responsible for constructing identity and meaning operate as the sound date processing system. Sound is a temporal sense because acoustic data is a stream of stimulus energy extending through time.

When the threshold of hearing is at 0 decibels (dB), a quiet whisper is usually measured at 10 dB, quiet street noise or residence at around 30 dB, a normal human conversation from five feet at around 60 dB, loud street traffic at five feet in the region of 80 dB, thunder at 100 dB, a loud rock band from five feet at 110 dB and the sound of a jet aircraft from 100 feet in the region of 130 dB, which is normally regarded as the threshold of pain (Gillette 2008:515).

Practitioners in the sound medium have to be conscious of three vitally important health risks in working professionally with decibel levels that can become powerful and operate around the threshold of pain as well as with prolonged exposure to high levels in noisy background environments. Auditory fatigue also known as temporary threshold shift (TTS) is a process of desensitisation when working with loud sound over long periods. The problem is reversible if breaks are taken and intense production work under the stress of deadlines is staggered or paced. Experience of 'violent' instances of loud sound at over 130 dB can precipitate the condition of tinnitus, which is a ringing, buzzing or whistling in the ears. Permanent threshold shift is the effective wearing down of the nerve endings in the inner ear and the damage is unfortunately irreversible.

There is a facility in electronics that has the effect of restricting the signalling of sound in circuitry. This is known as impedance. In simple terms the flow of alternating current (AC) is limited and the measurement or value is in ohms – a unit of resistance to current flow. This facility explains situations where you might find plugging microphones and other sound equipment together does not result in a clear optimum signal being routed, or the very opposite of a loud, distorting and unusable sound signal being produced. This is because sound equipment with low and high impedance is being plugged into incompatible channels, connections and circuits. Professional microphones of low impedance have three benefits over high-impedance models manufactured for amateur/domestic use: 'they generate less noise; they are much less susceptible to hum and electrical interference, such as static from motors and fluorescent lights; and they can be connected to long cables without increasing noise' (Alten 2008:58–9).

A handbook of this kind does not pretend to provide a comprehensive outline of the complex science of sound theory and acoustics, but it is useful for the entry level student and sound professional to have a basic understanding of phenomena that account for variations and impacts on the quality of sound production and reception. Acoustical phasing can generate a sudden loss of signal and sound quality, and a sensation of sonic confusion or lack of coherence; particularly in stereo or surround sound. The sound phase is in scientific terms the time relationship between two or more sound waves at one specific point in their cycles. Phase in simple terms is the up and down point of one sound wave in relation to the other. Two waves starting at the same time will coincide at various intervals, thus reinforcing each other, increasing amplitude and the perception of loudness. This means that they will be *in phase*, but if the waves go out of step, are not coinciding, and the waves impact against each other, weakening their strength and diminishing their amplitude, the listener will perceive a reduction in loudness. To summarise if waveforms rise and fall in synchrony they are in phase and if they do not they are out of phase. This will mean the pressure wave from one sound source arrives at a listener's position before the pressure wave from the other. An out of phase situation can also be understood as sound sources arriving earlier or later than another.

Masking is a sound phenomenon where a weaker sound interferes with the perception of a stronger sound when each sound is vibrating simultaneously but at a different frequency. It is possible for a sound to be made inaudible by simultaneous masking. It is a perceptual concept dependant on a listener's reception of frequency and loudness. This condition arises because of the psychoacoustic nature of hearing. The human ear has to evaluate multiple and competing sounds and this involves our ability to discriminate spatial depth through processing equal loudness as well as our ability to localise sounds and discriminate their identity, distance, and direction. Masking occurs when the cochlea has to respond to two or more sounds at the same time. There is a tendency for lower frequencies to mask higher ones and higher frequencies not to mask lower ones. As Bracewell explains:

> The sound of jet engine produces a large amount of low-frequency noise, and low frequencies mask high frequencies. If your friends shout, you can probably understand what they are saying. If one member of the group were a girl with a high pitched vice, she would be much more audible than the men in the group, because the effect of masking diminishes as second stimulus frequency gets progressively higher.
>
> (Bracewell 1993:186)

ACOUSTIC ENVIRONMENTS

A basic understanding of acoustics is a useful tool of knowledge for all kinds of practical sound producers so that they know how to control and determine the sound environment for recording and transmission/exhibition purposes. All sound has a life cycle in any interior and exterior ambience. Inside buildings this cycle is usually talked about in terms of reverberant sound, early reflections and direction sound. When recording journalistic, documentary and speech programmes the usual objective on the part of the sound producer is to achieve more direct sound than indirect sound to the microphone, and sometimes to eliminate the maximum amount of indirect sound. The way sound behaves in any interior acoustic is usually shaped by room acoustics, the interior wall and ceiling dimensions, the overall shape of the room and the extent to which there is sound isolation or proofing.

When sound meets a surface it can be reflected, diffracted, partially absorbed, fully absorbed, or diffused. Diffraction is a spreading of its energy around the surface. Diffusion is a uniform distribution of the sound energy. The meaning of the word implies absorption; the surfaces take in the sound's energy so that its ability to be reflected and come back to the source or echo to a listener is reduced. Sound studios are usually designed to achieve good noise reduction and sound dispersion to support and achieve the purposes of a microphone pick-up or direct recording.

Control rooms are constructed in terms of their sonic architecture (also known as acoustics) to maximise the quality of listening to studio sound through loudspeakers. Sound production studios will be equipped with portable panels, wall, baffles to provide flexible options in setting diffusion, absorption and reverberation time. At its extreme end, an anechoic chamber, usually an ante-room will have maximum sound absorption panels so that it creates a dead or dry atmosphere; the equivalent of sound in open air, external environments where there is no reflection. Interior environments with one second or more reverberation time are described as 'live' or ambient environments and those with reverberation times of one half second or less achieve the dry or dead characterisation. Essentially acoustic environmental properties in studio recording are designed, changed and amended for the purposes of the recording project. This is also true of the design and selection of sound art exhibition space.

While sound proofing to the extent of minimising background noise and indirect sound can be an objective, the early BBC studios were so heavily draped with curtains the complete absorption led to complaints from broadcasters and performers that they felt their vocal communication was in suffocating, coffin-style ambiences. Their experience was not helped by the lack of air conditioning. Consequently reverberation may well be a quality that sound studio managers and producers want because of the way it contributes spatiality, gives body to a sense of loudness, texture and tonal energy.

Psychoacoustics is the mental perception engagement with acoustics so that, again, we are talking about objective values in terms of how sound physically behaves in the world and is processed in production technology and how the human being encodes and decodes the signal subjectively. The brain can process a sense of time and intensity in relation to sound reaching the ears and judge its directionality. When this is done three-dimensionally the brain is experiencing binaural hearing. This means that we hear and listen to direct sound first and when the sound reflects from environmental surfaces we then hear and listen to the indirect sound. The indirect sound is bifurcated between early sound and reverberant sound. Early indirect sound reaches the listener so quickly (usually within 30 milliseconds) that they are heard as part of the direct sound; these early reflections generate the perception of loudness and fullness and the sense of perspective about the interior space. But the reverberant sound bounces off interior surfaces after the original source has been cut off and the longer the time it takes to die away will determine the sense of spatiality and may well create a perception of echo if delayed by 35 milliseconds or more. There will be a distinct sensation of a repeat of the direct sound.

PORTABLE RECORDING AND THE COMPUTER – DIGITAL EMPOWERMENT AND GETTING STARTED

In my lifetime as a radio programme producer the technological revolution in digitisation has liberated professionals and artists in having access to qualitative and production economies of scale. A professional standard reel-to-reel tape recorder such as the stereo Uher in 1978 would have cost over £1000 or $2000 at that time. Now a higher standard quality of recording in the digital format is realisable at one twelfth of the cost. In Table 2.2 a practical guide to the operational possibilities of a competitively priced digital audio recorder is set out. The package provides its own microphone kit and the omnidirectional microphones offer huge flexibility in pick-up ranges and situations; particularly when fixed on a professional boom. Even without such a tool, a plastic coat-hanger improvises effectively as a hand-held directional support unit.

FIGURE 2.2
Two condenser lapel microphones from American Audio Pocket Record on stereo boom (Photo: copyright Marja Giejgo). How budget equipment can be adapted to generate stereo sound fields: in this case the two omnidirectional microphones are positioned similarly to the position of somebody's ears and the pick-up field is more like the experience of hearing in the sense that sound is being received from all directions stereophonically.

Table 2.2 A practical guide to the operational possibilities of a competitively priced digital audio recorder

Guide to Operating Portable SD Digital Recorder 'Pocket Record' (American Audio)

1 At the time of writing this package of digital portable audio recorder (They call it a 'record') plus universal serial bus (USB) cable, two mono omnidirectional condenser lapel microphones and headphones was being sold at a competitive price compared with other higher-end digital recording devices.

2 The two external microphone facilities at the top, with mono jack microphone connections, provide excellent quality recordings on WAV format. The MP3 format is not so good. So it is recommended that for professional recording purposes only record WAV files. It is easy to set the machine to record WAV files using the 'mode' switch. The internal microphones built into the structure of the machine are not of a standard suitable for professional work and must be de-activated on the side switch marked: 'Mic level' – this switch should be far right on 'off'.

3 Although the machine has a built in 'flash' digital drive with a maximum of 128 megabytes of storage it is advisable to use an external SD card, and this forms a drive that can support up to 4 gigabytes of space. What actually happens when you connect the machine to your computer by USB cable is that the internal flash card becomes 'SMI Label' with a letter for the next additional drive for your computer and the external SD card becomes an additional drive with the next letter of the alphabet. So if your computer has three drives, for example, two hard disks and a CD/DVD player, your computer structure will probably show SMI Label D and then a new external drive E for the SD card in your American Audio machine.

4 If you have a mini stereo socket-to-2-jack-plugs adapter (difficult to obtain in the UK but can be ordered online from USA), it is possible to dub from an external playback machine using a mini stereo lead. To do this you would need to change the 'Audio in' switch from M (microphone usage) to far right L (line usage). 'G' is switched in if you are connecting your machine to record an electric guitar.

5 Microphone level adjustment is achieved by turning the knobs at the top of the machine clockwise for more level and anti-clockwise for less level. It is recommended that you use the earphones provided to monitor the level. There is a LED metre on the front screen that can tell you if you are at risk of digitally distorting. But the better judgement is achieved by listening.

6 Machine is switched on by pressing middle button and holding it down. Then pressing this button again plays back file 1 in whatever folder you have open, pressing again pauses, and then pressing again engages the playback. To stop the playing back you simply press the 'Stop' button above. Holding down the big middle button switches the machine off. An excellent feature of this machine is that it plays back files on an external built-in speaker. So playback does not require headphones, but if your headphones are plugged in, it will not play back on the speaker.

7 Pressing the menu (top far right) button twice enables you to select whether you want to record MP3 sound files (smaller digital size – compressed but broadcastable in many contexts) or WAV files (much larger digital size – high quality audio). Both formats record at 44 kHz. Be careful not to move along this menu bar to change the WAV sample rate to 8, 11, 16, 22 or 32 kHz. Obviously recording MP3 files means you can record more time as WAV files take up more digital space so the maximum amount of time you can record in WAV format is less. But for high professional level programmes and outputs the MP3 compression means that American Pocket Record MP3 files will not be as 'warm', with good timbre texture even at 128kbs. The functions 'Rep' and 'BL' relate to the repeating of tracks and the back light on the LED display. The latter is useful is you are working in poor light.

8   The machine is powered by two AA batteries. Always carry spares and additional batteries that you might need to power any additional hand-held microphones you might be using. A single mono hand-held microphone (reporter style) needs a cable connector that distributes the signal into a pair of left and right jack plugs. If you use a single jack plug connected to either the left external or right external microphone channel, you have to bear in mind that your sound files in these circumstances will have a one legged stereo recording. Unfortunately the machine does not have a switch that carries a mono signal across both tracks if a mono microphone is plugged into the left channel. If you have a one channel stereo recording most multi-track editing software programmes can mirror copy/paste to the other stereo channel, but I have found that even using this facility it still tends to sound rather hissy. I have also found that with hand-held microphones, the issue of electronic impedance and signal-to-noise ratio means that it is sometimes best to have the record level at maximum in order to get a usable recording. In the end I have found it best to adapt the two condenser lapel microphones provided with the machine for all recording purposes. For news and documentary interviewing it is very straightforward putting one lapel on oneself and the other on the guest/interviewee. For actuality and reporting action purposes, I have found that clipping the two microphones onto an improvised bar (for example a plastic coat hanger!) gives you the equivalent of a stereo microphone arrangement and very effective stereo spatial recordings.

9   The record button is marked with a red ring on the left and holding it down starts the recording process. The machine adds files as it records. It is probably better to delete files using your laptop/mainframe computer when you have connected the pocket recorder to it and it has become two external drives. Bear in mind that the LED display indicates the nature of the recording format (WAV or MP3) of the last file recorded. So do not be put off if you have switched from MP3 to WAV and the LED display indicates prior to recording that you might be in MP3 mode.

10 It would appear that the lapel condenser, omnidirectional microphones have been manufactured to work with the machine's digital circuit-board and achieve the optimum signal-to-noise ratio. As they are powered by the batteries in the machine you do not have to worry about microphone battery power fading. You can use the pair in any long-form documentary interview – lapel yourself as the interviewer and your guest as interviewee. If you are doing montage documentary you can of course lapel mic two of your guests/interviewees so that they are recorded 'in conversation'. You can adjust the recording levels between the two.

11 These microphones can also be mounted on a boom to create a rather impressive binaural stereo field, which is excellent for on location drama recordings or documentary audio-vérité. By clipping them to a bar on the end of the boom at an equal distance in relation to the position of the ears on somebody's head, and making any adjustments you wish to make in relation to each microphone's recording level (it is advisable to have them equally positioned), the boom then becomes an external stereo microphone with its own special field of recording spatiality.

12 Operational quirks: a) try not to allow your SD card to be 'maxed out', that is, a disk full situation; for some reason the entire SD card is at risk of becoming corrupted with recordings lost in this situation; b) watch out for your external hand-held reporter's microphone battery going flat or your failing to switch on the microphone if it has its own 'on/off' button; c) try and achieve a maximum threshold of recording level without distortion – there is a risk that low level recordings carry background hiss that is exacerbated by any declining power from the microphone or machine batteries; d) take care to transfer your sound files quickly to your mainframe/laptop computer for storage and editing – there is always a risk that your SD card might become corrupted, or files on it accidentally lost. (Be careful to label your files by 'renaming' with identifying information and date of recording. SD cards can be erased and re-formatted on Windows computers; particularly if your computer has an SD drive facility.)

13 The 'Hold' switch on the side can be switched on if you want to record long sequences and do not want the machine to shut itself down, but do remember to put the switch back to 'off' when you have finished. All the other operational buttons are pretty self-explanatory. They include play forward and play rewind, volume up and down. The machine has an analogue 'line out' socket on the side for the external SD card and USB connection.

14 The American Audio pocket recorder can be used for personal description recordings while engaged in action. For example it can sit easily in a pocket or on a belt hook and the lapel condenser microphones can be clipped either as a stereo pair or single mono for a subject who wishes to be recorded in 'audio diary' mode.

15 The machine can also be used for synching in television and film. This is demonstrated by the item on YouTube at: www.youtube.com/watch?v=zzdwN80G0is and a trade exhibition promo from 2008 at www.youtube.com/watch?v=spintNd1m3o. The machine also has guitar and line-in recording sources if there is a need to record non-microphone sound inputs.

16 The package comes with 'American Audio Pocket Record User Instructions' (see www.adjaudio. com/pdffiles/pocketrecord.pdf). It is advisable to photocopy them and keep a separate copy somewhere in your portable recording gear. It is also a very good idea to take the time to read and re-read the instructions at least two times and try out each function to bring your skills on operating the machine up to speed as well as evaluating how useful and effective each function actually is.

17 Another useful skills drill is to practice operating the machine in the dark so that you can connect machine to microphones/headphones, switch on, record, and playback 'blind' in situations of darkness/semi-darkness or when your attention is required on a 360° plane due to environmental or social circumstances.

18 Clear plastic food bags, rubber bands and 'blue tack' style adhesive putty are very useful accompaniments to protect the machinery from rain and wind and give you adaptability in microphone usage in the field.

The other revolution is that computer digitisation means that by a simple USB connection, portable digital recorders operate as drives from which recorded sound files can be clicked and dragged for editing. The higher end portable digital recorders have in-built qualitative stereo microphone capsules, which means that complex and sophisticated recording projects can be achieved in the palm of a directed hand pressing side-buttons, in the way texting entered the communications lexicon in mobile phone communications. But the touch-screen tablet is accelerating potentialities now so that portable recording units can expand into sophisticated postproduction units with the capability of multi-tracking construction of programmes and mix-down/rendering to master programme file.

Portable digital recording units can now secure 24 bit/96 kHz sound files, thus even bypassing the consumer 16 bit/44.1 kHz standard and the accelerating movement towards the use of micro-SD cards means that the old Uher of 1978 that could hold 15 minutes of recording tape at seven and a half inches per second (broadcastable) in the two gigabyte form can hold more than 33 hours of MP3 recording time of broadcastable quality. Portable recording units, the size of wallets, can play back recordings on speakers, be operated by remote controls, have specially manufactured absorbent casings so that there is no handling noise and clear light-backed organic LED displays with accurate level metres and peak indicators. But that is not all. Built-in limiter, low cut and mic gain processors accentuate the guarantee of qualitative recordings that prevent distortion through unexpected rises in noise or the heavy rumble of indirect background noise. At the time of writing these machines mean that high quality recordings can be made of

Table 2.3 Formats for reading sound

MP3	A compressed sound file achieved using software that preserves much of the audibility of a WAV standard file. Can be used in professional productions and in reality is of a standard that is equivalent to professional digital broadcasting and podcasting.
WAV	High professional standard at 24 bit/96 kHz. CD and high broadcastable standard at 16 bit/44.1 kHz.

Professional Standard	WAV 24 bit/96 kHz	Professional recording quality	15 minutes = circa 600 megabytes
CD consumer quality	WAV 16 bit/44.1 kHz	Suitable for burning into audio CDs	15 minutes = circa 150 megabytes
Internet/podcasting standard	MP3 128 kbs/ 44.1 kHz	Internet downloading of music and radio programmes	15 minutes = 15 megabytes

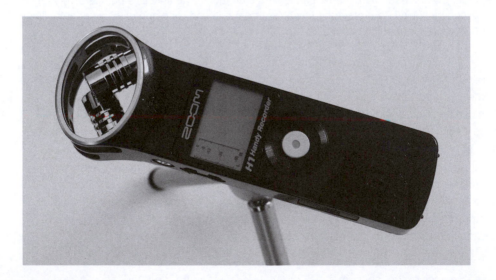

FIGURE 2.3
Zoom H1 Handy Stereo digital recorder on tripod (Photo: copyright Marja Giejgo). An example of a budget digital sound recorder. Its 2 gigabyte micro SD card can record more than thirty-three hours of broadcastable MP3 sound files, and it is the size of a small fingernail.

grand piano performances, electric guitar or bass, synthesisers and organs, drums and other forms of percussion, wind and stringed instruments. Many high quality and reasonably (always a relative term) priced portable digital recorders have the capacity to record two extra pairing or four additional tracks thereby widening the possibilities for control over mixing and more sophisticated stereo and surround sound productions.

STANDARD KIT FOR THE PROFESSIONAL SOUND PRODUCER

There is no definable answer to the question of what the professional sound producer and designer needs when out in the field, but at the time of writing and with what would be regarded as a professional budget, a consensus of replies from UK professional radio documentary and creative sound-art and drama producer/directors indicated a package of the following:

- Small in-the-bag high quality handheld digital recorder with built in stereo microphone capsules that can be operated instantly to record interviews, actuality and sound atmospheres as well as close sound sources. An example would be the Roland Edirol.

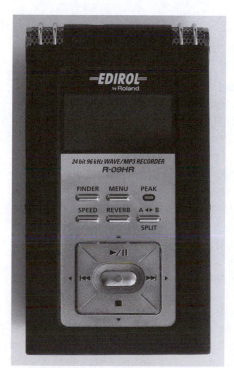

FIGURE 2.4
Edirol R-OH9 digital sound recorder by Roland (Photo: copyright Marja Giejgo). The Edirol R-OH9 digital sound recorder, hand-sized, with two inbuilt qualitative microphone capsules arranged for coincidental stereo recording. Versatile and flexible with professional standard recordings achieved through pressing of buttons and simple positioning.

- High quality stereo digital recorder with professional and robust cable sockets for hand held microphones and stereo microphone single capsules or paired coincidental arrangements. An example would be the Marantz PMD671, which was designed for professional use and XLR cabled microphone input with the capability of recording at 24-bit 96 kHz standard.

- High quality omnidirectional monophonic robust dynamic moving coil microphone with internal shock-mount that minimises handling noise and thick coated minimal handling noise cable for XLR input. An example would be the Beyerdynamic M 58, which was designed for electric news gathering and electronic field production. It is known to withstand physical and environmental punishment, its slim profile and non-reflective finish means that it has a low profile on camera in television applications.

- Competitively priced digital stereo recorder with condenser microphones for lapel use. The American Audio Pocket Record package contains two condenser external lapel/lavalier microphones with clips, an additional piece of kit that offers adaptable options such as a microphone and recording arrangement for interviewees who are nervous in the presence of hand-held microphones, or subjects who need to be filmed with unobtrusive microphone presence. The facility is also useful for a stereo boom field and close-microphone pick-up for a moving actor or actors. The relatively low cost of the unit means that it is potentially disposable in robust or physically challenging recording environments.

- Multiple cables, sockets, plugs and adaptors, SD cards, batteries and mains units, tripods and accessories, windshields and pop filters to reduce potential distortion from wind, interviewee and performer plosives and loud bursts of noise.

- Stereo and surround sound microphones. This option is more suitable for drama and ambitiously creative music and sound-art producers and the budget would probably need to match the level of ambition. An example for stereophonic use would be the Beyer MCE72 for X-Y stereo recording. The microphone XY arrangement is the equivalent of two separate cardioid microphones arranged into a coincidental pair and set between 90 and 135° in order to create a stereo field or sound stage in front of it. It has the advantage of integrated windshields and shock mounts to cope with on-location recording. Soundfield is one example of a reputable sound equipment company producing high quality location recording units for surround sound production. The ST350 Portable Microphone System generates surround and stereo simultaneously on balanced line level outputs (balanced is a term that relates to electrical line cabled with two stranded positive and negative wire conductors and a third ground wire, encased in foil wrapping and with thick outside plastic sheathing). The company also manufactures a lightweight four capsule SPS200 Software Controlled Microphone that does not require an accompanying control unit. All the processing – such as stereo and surround sound decoding and manipulation – takes place in inclusive Surround Zone software.

MICROPHONES

In sound production you could think of your microphones as your cameras in terms of being the tools to obtain the brightness and quality of your sound. The further away from the source signal, the more likely you will be recording equivalent long-shot/background sound. The closer you are to the sound source the more likely your recording will be medium/close-shot/foreground sound. As with cameras, microphones have varying ratios and properties of listening pick-up potential. Microphones usually operate with three modes of pick-up; omnidirectional (360°); bidirectional, meaning from the front and rear; and directional – from the front only. A good design on the microphone shield will usually indicate which side is 'live'.

Stereo and surround microphones contain capsules of individual microphones that can record in percentage ratio sound stages that could be fixed or movable. For example, a popular stereo microphone used in the early 1990s with professional Sony Walkman cassette recorders, ECM909, had a stereo ratio sound stage, or spatiality of 90 or 120°. Table 2.4 sets out a summary of the standard technology and varieties of microphone used in professional applications and also endeavours to explain the meaning of the technical specifications.

The essential aim of the professional is to select a kind of microphone suitable for the recording project. And it is useful to identify its low impedance (electrical circuit characteristic) signal-to-noise ratio (quality of sound and minimising of hum and background indirect sound – measured in decibels) and whether it requires its own electrical supply (by portable battery, or additional electrical power from the recorder/mixer into which it is plugged). You should also be assessing the microphone's 'frequency response', and this term relates to the range of high and low frequencies that it can reproduce through the recording process at an equal level. The instruction manual should display a frequency response curve in the form of a graph. The quality of unidirectionality is established by a design with casing on the sides (and back where pick-up is from the front) that blocks unwanted indirect sound. Unidirectional microphones increase in their performance when recording higher frequency sounds.

Consequently, the task for the professional is to match the microphones to the recording project. A reporter going to a noisy event such as a demonstration needs a microphone that is robust and has a directional pick-up. A moving coil microphone with a built in pop shield protection in shock absorbing casing to reduce handling noise and thick coated cable with a lock-in connection with the recorder such as XLR would probably be the best option. It is necessary that the reporter understands that this kind of microphone loses sound quality substantially when more than about a foot away from the sound source. On location or studio recordings of audio drama

Table 2.4 A summary of the standard technology and varieties of microphone used in professional applications with an explanation of the meaning of the technical specifications

Dynamic microphones	Ribbon microphones	Condenser electret microphones
These microphones are also known as moving coil mics because the pattern of sound waves is transduced by the action of a moving diaphragm and coil within the poles of a magnet. The microphone transduces energy electromagnetically and the term can apply to ribbon mics. But the difference lies in the fact that dynamic mics respond to changes in pressure applied to the surface of the diaphragm whereas ribbon mics respond to changes in the pressure gradient. The mics are similar to small electric generators. When the coil moves, a current is induced in the coil. Dynamic microphones have a frequency response of between 50 and 18,000 Hz. Moving coil microphones are the most durable and robust. They withstand high volume before distorting within their own circuitry. They tend to have a thin sound pick-up when more than a foot from the sound source. They are better used in close-microphone applications.	These microphones work with a strip of corrugated foil mounted on a coil within the poles of a magnet. They are usually constructed with a figure of eight pick-up pattern. The name is derived from the fact that a ribbon diaphragm is suspended in the magnetic field. Ribbon microphones are better at responding to changes in high frequency energy. Historically ribbon microphones were rather fragile and not suitable for hand-held reporter, outside broadcast use. They have become relatively more robust with the development of smaller and stronger magnets though they are still more susceptible to damage. Usually ribbon microphones do not require a power source. The ribbon capsule is inherently bidirectional with the front and back being equally sensitive. They have the advantage of a full sound and frequency response, which is often considered warmer and smoother than its moving-coil sister/brother.	In these microphones, the sound wave signal induces the interaction of a moving diaphragm and a fixed plate and these form a capacitor. The capacitor transduces acoustic energy electrostatically. These microphones tend to be very sensitive and produce an even response. These microphones have small amplifiers placed inside them in the form of capacitive plates. The electret element is a pressure-sensitive, self-polarising structure that requires no external polarising voltage and thereby means the microphones can be miniaturised and operate as lapel/lavalier microphones. Condenser microphones usually require power to charge the metal-coated membrane and amplify the signal from the capsule up to microphone level. Condenser microphones have a more accurate recording sensitivity. They respond better to fast attacks and transients and add the least amount of colouration.

Phantom power

Phantom power is an operating voltage supplied to a condenser/capacitor microphone by an external source such as a mixer in order to eliminate the use of internal batteries.

Omnidirectional	Bidirectional	Unidirectional	Cardioid
A microphone that picks up sound from all directions so could equally be called nondirectional! Such microphones do not reject sound from any direction and provide the fullest and most accurate sound from distance. They are good for recording direct sound in atmosphere or its context. On a live set with PA (playback) they are likely to generate rapid feedback/howl-round.	A microphone that picks up sound to its front and back and has very limited pick-up potential on its sides. These microphones are more suitable for situations where there are two sound sources that need to be recorded with intimacy onto one track (mono or stereo). They have the advantage of minimising adverse phase interaction and indirect room noise. However, they are susceptible to generating heavy feedback on live sets.	A microphone that picks up sound from one direction only so could equally be called a directional microphone! Most directional microphones have a heart-shape pattern of pick up with a rounded sound field at the front and dimpled pick up pattern at the rear. It is obviously most sensitive at the front and least sensitive at the back. They are best used if you wish to isolate sound and need a robust handling of loud direct noise. However, the frequency response rapidly deteriorates more than one foot away from the source. They are more appropriate in live public performance/ address situations in their ability to prevent feedback.	A unidirectional microphone with a heart-shaped pick-up pattern of recording. The standard cardioid microphone has a full frequency response at the front and a decrease in sensitivity of up to 25 or 30 dB at 180° off-axis. If you need a sharper focus of directional sound pick-up you need to consider selecting supercardioid, hypercardioid and ultracardioid microphones that increasingly narrow their front pick up pattern and decrease off-axis sound. A subcardioid microphone widens the pick-up pattern around the front to the sides and is the next step to omnidirectional characteristics.

would invite the use of binaural (a stereo arrangement reproducing the process of human hearing with two microphone capsules placed in a distance arrangement equal to the position of ears on a human head) surround sound in order to pick up sound field direction in terms of stereo sound stage front, stereo sound stage back and stereo direction front to back. Wireless microphones are more suitable for stage drama, public music performance, large studio talk-show formats and the sound engineering needs to take into account issues of power supply, transmission range, frequency assignment, as well as sound quality. Where there is an engagement of sound with the television or film medium then adaptive microphones to these audio-visual situations would be more suitable in terms of being operated on a boom, selected for their unobtrusiveness and mini-size, such as lavalier microphones.

The lapel/lavalier option is also very useful where the recording project requires audio diary, multiple conversational forum, or subject moving situations as it guarantees a close-microphone pick-up in relation to the subject(s) thereby always providing the choice of POL (point of listening) focus. Present-day technology offers high technical flexibility and specifications that can deliver advanced matching to project requirements. For investigative, wildlife and film productions enhanced directional 'gun' microphones that have narrowing sensitivity in pick-up – and are described as supercardioid, hypercardioid, and ultracardioid – clearly offer the advantage in pinpointing qualitative recording of sound sources from long distances. They even have their use in journalistic coverage at press conferences or media events where crowds distance the reporter/crew from the subjects being covered.

Sports broadcasting has substantially advanced a surround sound ambience to a combined visual and audio image and special microphones are designed for use on boundaries and contact surfaces. Some microphones actually have built in recorders. USB microphones have been developed that contain a built-in digital audio interface that amplifies and converts the analogue signal to digital directly onto computer hard-disk recording.

The key challenges in the recording process with microphones are usually: level too high, level too low, and interference from other sound sources. The solutions include balancing microphone selection for intrinsic properties, microphone positioning, record level adjustment, application of limiters and bass roll-off (to cut back on low frequency proximity effect) and matching microphone level to achieve a high threshold of recording level on the recording device. Microphone overload is variously known as distortion, 'overmodding' – from the days of analogue – and in the digital dimension is an irrecoverable situation in terms of sound processing repair. Low-level recordings are more recoverable but when using sound processing to remove the hiss, indirect noise that becomes enhanced with adjustment dubbing, there will usually be a loss of frequency response.

Further safeguards and adjustments can be achieved through the application of external pop filters and windscreens (as well as directing speakers and performers to make changes to their articulation of plosive sounds such as 'b' and 'p' as well as an excess of exhalation in enunciation) and shock absorbers and shock mounts that help to block external vibrations reaching the microphone pick-up components. Balanced microphone cables with XLR connectors combined with robust and flexible microphone clips and stands all contribute to improving the sound recording infrastructure.

EDITING AND MIXING

In the twenty-first century it could be argued that laptop or computer palmtop tablet media consumption will be expected to provide sophisticated sound production. But while a considerable amount of professional standard editing and mixing can now bypass the expensive large-scale sound studio production environment, there will always be a need to use sound studios for a large range of productions. And, of course, all the advantages of the digital audio workstation (DAW) have also been transferred into the sophisticated mixing desk, console or, to use the quaint original early BBC description, 'Dramatic Control Panel'.

Games sound designer G.W. Childs IV in *Creating Music and Sound for Games* demonstrates how the individual can generate a substantial power of mixing and editing skills and capabilities with the appropriately selected computer and software:

> We all have that one computer, those several pieces of software, and the specific database that we most like to use. The list can get quite extensive. Why do you cling to these particular items? They worked when you needed them most. Sure, they have their quirks, but you've learned through experience what they are and how to work around them.
>
> (Childs 2007:35)

And as Karl Coryat observed in the delightfully subversively titled *Guerrilla Home Recording* with the subtitle *How to Get Great Sound from Any Studio (No Matter How Weird or Cheap Your Gear Is)*:

> Contrary to the newer/faster/better culture that permeates the recording-equipment industry, you *can* record a really good-sounding CD with minimal tools. All you need are a few key pieces of gear, and more important, knowledge of a handful of important concepts – along with some experience learning to hear what does and doesn't sound good.
>
> (Coryat 2008:1)

The computer has a sound card that converts analogue sound signals into digital audio. The software programmes provide keyboard, mouse and touch-screen operating power to edit sound on the hard-disk of the computer and manipulate the sound files into multi-tracked arrangements of mixed sound through parallel positioning, processing and level setting. The software can also produce a fixed mix-down/rendered master recording. This combination of software and hardware effectively reproduces all the functions of digital recorder, mixer, sound processing and studio monitoring. Sound editing is best undertaken with monitoring from high quality speakers. Headphone editing and mixing is usually only efficient for short periods of time because of the onset of hearing fatigue. It is also easier to cause permanent damage to hearing with loud volume headphone use when the ears desensitise to potentially damaging levels.

Childs recommends the acquisition and confident use of basic software wave editors that can trim and tail beginnings and ends of sound files, quickly apply effects/sound processing, undo mistakes, stack effects/processing operations and batch convert/change multiple quantities of files (Childs 2007:38). He also recommends the selection of sound software that is capable of complex multi-track editing and mix-downs. The companion website provides demonstrations and detailed guides to the digital editing and mixing process. It would be churlish to claim that one software programme is 'better' than another. Childs honestly and courteously explains that it is perfectly reasonable for him to describe his preferences (35–54). At the time of writing there is widespread use and respect for the professional sound editing software programmes Adobe Audition (incorporating the formerly known Cool Edit Pro), Wavelab, Protools, Nuendo, and Sadie, all of which can be uploaded and used by hardware systems with compatible and supporting soundcards, hard-disc ROM (read only memory), processing RAM (random access memory) and audio-visual display. The soundcard is one of the crucial electronic components in this package as it inputs, manipulates and outputs sound. It should have a signal-to-noise ratio of −70dB and below.

In addition to the availability of these and other software programmes, a share-ware multi-track sound editor called Audacity is freely downloadable and very flexible and usable for sound producers needing to or preferring to operate in 'budget conditions'. It is always advisable to ensure that the software obtained is compatible and matches the computer operating system on your editing computer, for example, Windows XP, Windows Vista, Windows 7, Apple Mac, etc.

Digital sound has two systems of measurement and representation that equivocate to the terminology in analogue sound. The time component, known in the analogue age as frequency, is now represented in the digital dimension by the word 'sampling'. The analogue description for the loudness/level of sound was amplitude. Its digital equivalent is known as 'quantisation', and this is represented in the term *bits*, which stands for 'binary digit'. Bit depth relates to audio resolution. The sampling rates in digital audio were normally in a range of 32 kHz (compressed standard on old mini-discs), 44.056 kHz, 44.1 kHz (CD standard), 48 kHz, (standard on old digital audio tape) and 96 kHz (seen as high range professional standard). The quality of digital sound depends on the depth of its representation in binary code. The greater the bit rate/depth, for example, 16 or 24 bits, the higher the resolution of the sound reproduction.

One of the advantages of digitisation in sound editing is that many of the functions in multi-track software programmes use word-processing terms that effectively carry out the same actions such as 'insert audio file', paste, copy, delete and cut. Another advantage is that the editing is non-destructive. No original recording need be lost apart from by carelessness. (Destructive sound editing is removing by deletion unwanted sequences of sound, non-destructive sound editing is extracting by copying required sequences of sound.) Digital copying does not result in any loss of quality and most programmes have considerable undo functions. Many also default save work in programmes.

The editing process is also non-linear, which means that previews and auditions, adjustments and changes can be done at any stage with level changes, additional processing and restorations are always possible without any risk of destroying or permanently changing master audio files.

There are two key processes in digital sound editing: first the recording, dubbing, preparing and polishing source files in terms of speech, music, effects and sound archive; and then the multi-track sound design phase, which in fact consists of recording information data about the manipulation and changes in the positioning and components of the sound files being used. In the editing software programme Wavelab this facility is labelled 'audiomontage'. It is effectively a decision-making file that intersects and places markers on the sound files. This is why it is recommended that sound files sourcing the multi-track decision-making data file are all of the same sampling and bit rate. Furthermore, it is advisable that digital sound editing takes place on the hard-disk itself rather than through the desktop of the operating programme and that all of the sound files and data files used in the multi-track editing operation are in the same folder. This increases the speed of processing, ensures accuracy in playback and mix-down operations and militates against digital freezing and computer crashes.

It is recommended that continual practice in editing speech and music will increase dexterity and listening appreciation of the component sounds that make up the articulation of words, the breathing and pauses between words. It always needs to be remembered that the wave-form audio-visual representation in colour on computer screens, while providing such precise information about sound, particularly when zoomed in, can sometimes detract from correct judgements that need to be made when listening only.

There are a number of standard sound processing and editing tools set out in Table 2.5 that are also demonstrated by sound and video sequences on the book's companion website. It is recommended that the student of sound production practices and applies these and other available editing resources provided by the sound editing software that has been selected so that confidence and creativity in decision-making is maximised.

When editing speech there is always a need to match background ambience and appreciate the difficulties of editing speech with a linear background musical track. Music editing experience builds an understanding of style and texture, rhythm and repetition. At all times, the professional sound editor seeks to avoid sound mismatches that are unnatural and without dramatic purpose. This occurs when music editing is out of time, out of key and sequence, and when speech editing removes the natural breathing and pauses present in the intonation of vocal expression.

In film sound-editing some consideration needs to be given to the multi-dimensional and multi-transitional potential of sound. Dialogue, atmosphere, effects and music can often parallel together in complex mixes and the placing of these sounds will, of course, be related to narrative and creative purposes inherent in the visual sequence. Where audio-visual or sound only, editing techniques can establish intensity through contrasting juxtapositions in texture such as tonal to atonal, non-rhythmic to rhythmic, fast to slow and loud to quiet.

Table 2.5 Standard sound processing and editing tools (these are also demonstrated by sound and video sequences on the book's companion website)

Time-compression and time-stretching – the technique can expand and contract the length of the sound within a linear timeframe and in the process pitch and frequency can change. (Alten 2008:157–8 and Childs 2007:56–7)

Pitch-shifting/correction – changing the pitch of a sound file without changing its duration. (Alten 2008:165–6 and Childs 2007:58)

Pitch Bending – creating an upward or downward swing in the pitch before and after the bend. (Childs 2007:59)

Fade-in/Fade-out – gradual increase or reduction in audio level. The process can be quickened to suit the desired rhythm in the editing process. (Alten 2008:391–2 and Childs 2007:60–1)

Silence – a digital editing function that can insert 'true silence' or varying levels of potentially looped background noise. (Childs 2007:62)

Gain change – lowering or raising audio file level by the addition or subtraction of decibels. (Coryat 2008:49–50, Alten 2008:100 and Childs 2007:62)

Reverse – making any highlighted audio file/track to play backwards. (Childs 2007:63)

Cross-fade – overlapping of two sound files with one fading down and the other fading up. Also known as segueing. (Alten 2008:407–9 and Childs 2007:63–6)

Reverb – the adding of echoes to a sound file so that the original sound has the tone of being in varying spaces with sound reflecting off hard surfaces. (Alten 2008:171–2, 427–8, 436–8 and Childs 2007:67–8)

Chorus – 'Recirculating a doubling effect to make one sound source sound like several' (Alten 2008:468). Doubling is making an original sound seem fuller and stronger by adding slightly delayed signals with the original. As Childs explains this 'makes it sound like there are two versions of the sound playing back almost in unison' (Childs 2007:69), hence the description 'chorus'.

Delay – the imposition of a definite sounding echo that can be sped up and some digital software 'plug-ins' can expand the effect into multi-delay. This processing can precisely regulate the duration of given sounds. (Alten 2008:470 and Childs 2007:70)

Distortion – overdriving a sound file without peaking into the red sector of the digital volume unit (VU) meter (past 0dB). This is a simulation of actual distortion and has the effect of giving ferocity to sounds in different contexts. (Childs 2007:71)

Compression – boosting sound signals that are too soft and lowering sound that is too loud. Also a sound-shaping tool that enable sounds, in particular musical instruments, to better integrate into the overall mix. (Alten 2008:425 and Reece and Gross 2002:203)

Equaliser – a digital sound software facility that can remove unwanted frequencies and add or enhance selected frequencies. It is usually a plug-in or processing function in multi-track software that can brighten muffled sound and soften over-metallic and harsh sounds. (Alten 2008:423–5 and Childs 2007:73–4)

Batch converting – a processing facility that can select large numbers of sound files and change them all after applying preset parameters. (Childs 2007:109–128)

The companion website for this book provides a range of multimedia resources demonstrating the topics and sound concepts as well as sound editing and mixing techniques.

STUDIO PRODUCTION

As with DAW production, the sound producer needs to develop confidence and assurance in setting up and operating a sound production studio and this involves researching what tools and facilities will be needed for the project being allocated to it. Will microphones be needed for speech, music or effects? Generally, digital sound processing can provide any subsequent reverberation and ambience in editing, though acoustic screens with reflecting surfaces can enhance some aspects of classical musical instruments. When recording or transmitting (in the case of radio broadcasting) speech, reverberation-free acoustics are usually what is required. Alten advises an evaluation of speech microphones for their versatility, presence, clarity and richness: 'The closer a microphone is placed to a sound source, the closer to the audience the sound source is perceived to be and the warmer, denser, bassier, drier, more intimate, and more detailed is the perceived sound' (Alten 2008:189). The opposite in positioning expands the sense of perspective and ambience for the listener so that it sounds more open and spatial. Stereo sound stages set up through the arrangement of coincidental cardioid microphones or self-contained multiple capsule microphones should be tested and blocked by way of monitoring, setting the pans on the microphone channels and placing markers on the floor of the studio; particularly if actors will be performing speech with action.

Where a programme is being recorded/transmitted with a presenter and one or more guests, care should be taken to ensure that the loudness levels from the microphone channels are similar and there is an application of the three-to-one-rule precisely defined by Alten as:

> A guideline used to reduce the phasing caused when a sound reaches two microphones at slightly different times. It states that no two mics should be closer to each other than three times the distance between one of them and its sound source.
>
> (486)

The companion website takes you through the nature of the control room in a professional production studio, the functions of the mixer channels in terms of gain, equalisation (EQ) and filter, pre-fade, mute switch and pan pot. A good sound studio will have a peak performance/programme meter (PPM) to provide warning of distortion because its rise time is rapid and fallback is slow – a superior function to the VU meters that are standard on portable recording machines. The control room/sound studio has a system of monitoring that provides accurate sound representation of what is being recorded in the studio through speaker monitors in the control room and foldback through headphones to presenter/performers in the studio. The foldback can also route sounds from other sources, which is useful in the case of interviews and interactions with people on telephone or outside broadcast lines. Talkback is the system of communication between the studio manager/producer and presenter/performers in the studio. A further key piece of machinery in the control room is the patch-bay, which is something like a railway junction control/signalling panel whereby sound sources can be connected in various ways to the mixing channels on the console.

Digitisation has resulted in the introduction of touch-screen and console automation so that computer hardware and software can have channel levels and functions pre-programmed with continually retrievable memory files available in mixing operations. This is the advance of technology that no doubt will continue well into the twenty-first century probably with an acceleration and scale of function advancement already experienced in the twentieth century.

LOUDSPEAKERS AND PROJECTING SOUND IN INTERIOR AND EXTERIOR SPACES

A key area of the sound designer and producer's role is playing out sound as a form of performance projection and entertainment in interior and exterior locations. This is sometimes referred to as live sound performance. It is the dimension by which stage theatre sound designers function and is also fundamental to the technical and artistic requirements of live music producers and artists curating and designing sound for installations and exhibitions. To this end knowledge and skills are needed to be able to understand how sound travels through space and reacts to the architecture and texture of interior surfaces. This skill set needs to be extended to an appreciation of how wind, temperature and the presence of different sizes and arrangements of human audience can change the absorption and dynamics of sound. Essential electrical safety standards need to be applied; not least an understanding of earthing and the safeguards needed to deal with rain or accidental water damage.

Loudspeakers effectively reverse the transducing process of microphones. Microphones and loudspeakers can be seen as twins in the world of transducers. The loudspeaker transducer converts electrical signals into sound wave energy and the internal technology of sound production is similar to microphone operations: ribbon, capacitor and moving coil. Speakers requiring an external power source are known as passive and those powered internally are called active. Most loudspeakers are middle-sized and send out good low and high frequencies, but for an enhanced framework of sonic reproduction, additional frequency range 'drivers' are required. Large drivers produce low bass frequencies. Small drivers produce high treble frequencies. The low frequency projection has an all round dispersal property and generates noise that penetrates through walls and reflective and absorbent surfaces. The high frequency projection is much more directional and is easily absorbed and reflected faster. The more familiar term for a bass enhancing speaker driver is woofer and that for the treble enhancing speaker driver is tweeter. Owners of surround sound home cinemas will be familiar with the additional square speaker-box called a 'sub-woofer', which generates a low-frequency band of sound waves in a decoded surround field such as Dolby 5.1. This speaker is channelling what is known technically as the low frequency enhancement (LFE) and is also known as the '0.1 Channel'.

In an auditorium the sound designer has to be conscious of the enduring struggle to acoustically balance speech and music. This is caused by the problem that human speech in dramatic or singing performance requires a short reverberation time and sounds much better with longer periods of reverberation. The ideal solution is an auditorium with adjustable panelling that can provide flexibility and options for acoustic balancing. It will be obvious now that hard surface finishes such as plaster, wood or metal generate faster and more reverberation and soft surface finishes such as curtain fabric, clothing and insulation (including the presence of human beings as members of the audience – unless they are wearing polished armour and chain-mail!) reflect much less and absorb more. The way in which sound is absorbed by the audience is known as the 'grazing effect' and is compensated for by stepping or raking the seating since this reduces the absorption as well as improving sight lines.

Ideal conditions for spoken word performance would be a decay time of one quarter to three quarters of a second. The right balance for musical performance is between three quarters and one and a half seconds. The challenge, of course, is going to be greater for a sound designer and stage management team preparing for both dramatic speech and musical performance in equal quantities. They are assisted by the presence of adjustable acoustical baffles that are mounted on and over the stage as well as in the walls and ceilings around the audience seating (Gillette 2008:517).

Monitoring through amplification and speaker positioning in a control room is designed to enable sound designers and producers to accurately position and mix sound in direct proportion to the intention of sound field design in recording and with the ability to make creative adjustments and decisions in editing and mixing. Loudspeaker production and projection in the 'open air' and in interior auditoria is designed to maximise the entertainment and appreciation experience of the audience. Obviously there needs to be a close connection between the latter and the former.

There are some principles that apply equally well in terms of loudspeaker positioning in the control room or larger theatrical and performance space. There is an argument that a sound's arrival time at the monitoring position in a control should not be in excess of 1 millisecond (Alten 2008:56). This rule does not necessarily apply to the position of the audience in an auditorium wishing to enjoy a musical performance where the entertainment aesthetic, requiring added reverberation, is paradigmatic over the sound design decision-making aesthetic in mixing and editing. It is generally understood that a loudspeaker in the middle of a room-space produces the least concentrated sound, whereas positioning at the intersection of a ceiling or floor produces a much greater concentration.

At the time of writing there are three broad categories of sound field production and reception: monophonic, stereophonic and surround sound. All mixing consoles should have a monitoring option for all these standards so that the producer/sound designer always knows how the mix-down will be experienced. Some reference is made in this textbook to *binaural*, and for the purposes of achieving an immediate understanding the best way of explaining the stereo/binaural difference is that stereo production has the purpose of creating a sound field reception for listeners that can be experienced with two-dimensional loudspeaker projection and hearing. Binaural recording positions microphones to simulate a quasi-representation of actual hearing through the ears (cardioid microphones are clipped on a boom about eight to ten inches apart equivalent to the distance between ears on a human head) that can only be properly appreciated when received through headphones.

In order to experience the breadth and depth of two-dimensional stereo, it is advisable to position the two (left and right) loudspeakers being amplified symmetrically so that the sound image is an accurate and balanced reproduction side to side and front to back. In the monitoring location it is also recommended that far-field speakers are fixed onto the room wall above and several feet from the listening position and near-field speakers are positioned close to the listening point.

SURROUND SOUND

Surround sound production, monitoring and audience reception is an expansion of the depth of listening perception. In short the listener is positioned more at the centre of the aural image with a dynamic of sound design that is greater than left-to-right and right-to-left panning characteristics. Surround design production for cinema and theatre is aimed at directing the attention of the audience's perception towards the screen or stage, which is usually at the front. Thrust or black box theatres provide the opportunity of a completely different dynamic of sound to audience and performance experience. The situation in relation to radio, computer notebook/laptop or iPad sound reception is much more complicated. Most radios transmit sound out of one monophonic speaker. Some up-market car manufacturers install surround sound radio/playback systems, but even the stereo matrices raise interesting questions about the efficiency of the reception. It might be argued that in stereo car listening it will be difficult to achieve qualitative sound image representation. What is heard and good for listening appreciation for rear-seat passengers might be very different for the driver. How many radio listeners sit in the middle of their home cinema systems listening to sound only? Much radio listening is experienced on the move, in mobile social contexts either in the home or in public. It might be argued that a more precise matching of sound design image to listener experience can be better achieved in sound art installation and exhibition where visitors are seeking to experience the sound aesthetic intended by the artist. There is more of a cultural audiogenic contract.

Surround sound and complex sound imaging design and reproduction is a complicated subject that is beyond the frame of comprehensive treatment in this textbook, though the companion website endeavours to extend the discussion. Tomlinson Holman in his influential book, *Surround Sound: Up and Running*, issues pertinent cautions about assumptions of what is possible. In particular he argues that the very nature of a former four-channel standard 'quadraphonic' that was experimented with extensively in the 1970s has been misconstrued.

> The misconception that Quad works as four stereo systems ranks right up there with the inanity that since we have two ears, we must need only two loudspeakers to reproduce sound from every direction – after all, we hear all around don't we? This idea neglects the fact that each loudspeaker channel does not have input to just one ear, but two, through 'crosstalk' components consisting of the left loudspeaker sound field reaching the right ear, and vice versa. Even with sophisticated crosstalk cancellation, which is difficult to make anything other than supremely sweet-spot sensitive, it is still hard to place sounds everywhere around a listener. This is because human perception of sound uses a variety of cues to assign localization to a source, including interaural level differences, that is, differences in level between the two ears; interaural time differences; the frequency response for each angle of arrival associated with a sound field interacting with the head, outer ears called the pinnae, shoulder bounce, etc. and collectively called the head-related transfer function (HRTF); and dynamic variations on these static cues since our ears are rarely clamped down to a fixed location. The complexity of these multiple cue mechanisms confounds simple-minded conclusions about how to do all-round imaging from two loudspeakers.
>
> (Holman 2008:7–8)

The standard monitoring matrix for 5.1 surround sound consists of five separate speakers and the 0.1 sub-woofer. The sound producer and listener usually face front-left, centre and front-right speakers with two left and right rear speakers that are normally described as the 'surround' speakers. In the older Dolby Pro-logic standard the left and right surround speakers were fed one monophonic signal though the surround encoding could achieve panning between the rear mono pair to the mono front centre speaker and back in decoded reception. This dynamic is still possible though Dolby 5.1 now has a more complex array of panning fields. It is now possible to pan rear left and right surround speakers in either direction. By presetting the front/surround panning dynamic, 5.1 can achieve a more enveloping dynamic of sound movement between the front left and the rear (surround) right speaker. It is also possible to position two sub-woofers in the 5.1 surround set up on either side of the listener.

These advances in surround sound design have been accompanied by equally enriching expansions of multiple capsule microphone recording potentialities. The SoundField microphone system uses four rotating capsules to capture genuine three dimensional sound by working with a 5.1 controller. The pick-up array captures a sound perspective that is up and down, front and back with additional side/ambient fields channelled into a controller that produces mixing outputs to feed a 5.1 surround array of front left, centre, front right, rear left and rear right. SoundField argues that the listener is provided with a more fully immersing sound experience that they have named as 'ambisonic'. But as Alten points out, this three dimensional sound texture can only be appreciated through listening within a four speaker matrix (Alten 2008:71). It is also apparent that the 5.1 matrix produced through mixing and panning with six channels of sound (five full frequency response and one LFE) has its limitations in reproducing the experience of immersion that new microphone technologies are able to achieve. Dolby has responded by introducing Surround 7.1, adding a further two channels for rear side left and right speaker output, and positioning the back 'surround' speakers further behind the audience/listener. The new format of encoding produces four surround zones, improves the precision of panning and sound localisation, enhances sonic definition, and widens what is described as the 'listening sweet spot'.

OPEN AIR SOUND PROJECTION

The projection and reproduction of sound outdoors has to take into account the fact that there are no reflections and the reverberation time is usually zero unless it is taking place in hyper-urban space with hard surfaces. The sound operator needs to understand how wind and temperature affect sound. When wind and sound are travelling in the same direction, the wind cools the lower levels of air making the sound waves refract towards the listener. When the wind blows against the sound waves they are refracted upwards and away from the listening position. Consequently, it is advisable to point open air loudspeakers with the prevailing wind in order to cover the largest area or against the wind if the intention is to restrict reception to the smallest area. Sound pressure level measurement and monitoring is required in the selection and construction of speaker power and systems to the environment where they are going to be deployed. Loudspeakers will probably have to be elevated on towers, trucks or buildings in order to reduce the grazing effect and lessen the problem of the inverse square law (ISL) of noise generation. In short the ISL in sound is a principle that stipulates a fall off in sound pressure level as the distance from the sound or loudspeaker increases. This rule can also be applied to the distance of microphones from sound sources. In essence sound pressure level (SPL) drops 6dB for every doubling of the distance.

Health and safety expertise will be required to ensure proper earthing, weatherproofing and the use of suitably powered and insulated electrical circuitry. Low-impedance interior wiring would suffer much signal loss where signals have to be carried over long distances. The principle of earthing covers protection from electrocution and unwanted sound interference. The protective earth (PE) connection ensures circuit breaking will disconnect the power supply if any device has an insulation fault. There is also a protection against 'earth looping' whereby the shields for mains wires and sound system cables become sensitive to radio and mains interference. A useful safeguard would be to ensure separate electrical grounds for musicians' power supplies, amplifiers and the lighting system.

FURTHER READING: RECOMMENDED BOOKS ON SOUND RECORDING AND PRODUCTION

There is no shortage of high quality books providing detailed guidance and explanation of a wide variety of sound production skills in multimedia, and the following list makes a brief selection of those with which the author is familiar.

Alten, Stanley R. (2010) *Audio in Media* (9th edition), Belmont, California: Thomson Wadsworth.

Childs, G.W., IV (2007) *Creating Music and Sound for Games*, Belmont, California: Thomson.

Coryat, Karl (2008) *Guerrilla Home Recording: How to Get Great Sound from Any Studio (No Matter How Weird or Cheap Your Gear Is)* (2nd edition), New York: Hal Leonard Books.

Gibson, Bill (2011) *The Ultimate Live Sound Operator's Handbook* (2nd Revised edition), New York: Hal Leonard Books.

Hausman, Carl, Messere, Fritz and O'Donnell, Lewis (2009) *Modern Radio Production: Production, Programming, and Performance* (8th edition), Belmont, California: Thomson Wadsworth.

Hiitola, Bethany (2010) *Getting Started with Audacity 1.3*, Birmingham: Packt Publishing.

Holman, Tomlinson (2008) *Surround Sound: Up and Running* (2nd edition), Boston: Focal Press.

James, Daniel (2009) *Crafting Digital Media: Audacity, Blender, Drupal, GIMP, Scribus, and other Open Source Tools*, New York: Apress.

Katz, Bob (2007) *Mastering Audio: The Art and the Science* (2nd edition), Boston: Focal Press.

Lansley, Andrew (2011) *Sound Production: A Guide to Using Audio within Media Production*, London and New York: Routledge.

Moylan, William (2007) *Understanding and Crafting the Mix: The Art of Recording* (2nd edition), Boston: Focal Press.

Reese, David, Gross, Lynne and Gross, Brian (2009) *Audio Production Worktext: Concepts, Techniques, and Equipment* (6th edition), Boston: Focal Press.

Riley, Richard (2008) *Audio Editing with Adobe Audition* (2nd edition), Norfolk: PC Publishing.

Senior, Mike (2011) *Mixing Secrets for the Small Studio*, Boston: Focal Press.

Sonnenschein, David (2001) *Sound Design: The Expressive Power of Music, Voice, and Sound Effects in Cinema*, California: Michael Wiese Productions.

White, Paul (2003) *Recording and Production Techniques*, London: SMT.

CHAPTER 3

Sound practice and theory in radio

PRACTICE

Making audio documentaries – Finding 'true' stories and constructing realities

One of the celebrated advantages of audio documentaries is that it is an ideal experience of individualistic production and communication. It is the ideal *auteur*'s genre. It is democratically realisable, not constrained by the alienating top-down exclusion zone of global capitalist economies of scale. The technology has been micro-realised into portable digitisation and the method of distribution and publication has been transnationally liberated across the public and private spheres of cyberspace. Sound is an emotional *lingua franca*. Sovereign state linguistics are no longer barriers. The passport and visa are signified by audiogenics. The radiophonic is no longer controlled by the licensing and state appropriation of electromagnetic wavelengths. It has a realm of freedom of expression that digitally channels with a speed unheard of in living human memory.

The walls of discrimination in audio programme genre also appear to be dissolving. The 'feature', 'the documentary', 'the sound art', 'the drama-documentary', 'audio mockumentary', fact and fiction, faction and drama are becoming interchangeable terms that serve or become tools of audio production projects that primarily communicate individualist journeys, enquiries and modes of story telling. There may be ideological and aesthetic frames of interest and aspiration. The publication in 2010 of *Reality Radio: Telling True Stories in Sound*, edited by John Biewen and Alexa Dilworth, arises from an annual festival in the USA called Third Coast that celebrates audio/radio documentary. Across the world there has been a convening of radio programmes and web-based cultures supporting, encouraging and valorising creative sound programmes and outlets such as *Radiolab*, *Soundprint*, *Hearing Voices*, *Between the Ears*, *This American Life*, Transom and PRX. Table 3.1 sets out a selection of audio programme making sites where there is a creative aesthetic and commitment to idealist and ideological aspirations for communicating storytelling through sound.

Biewen and Dilworth are based at a research and practice Center for Documentary Studies at Duke University. Their edited volume of essays provides a space for an eclectic, diverse heterogeneous community of audio programme makers to discourse what they make, how they make and why. Although audio creative programme makers are diverse in the construction of their content and their style of expression, Biewen argued that what they do have in common is using 'sound to tell *true* stories *artfully*' (Biewen and Dilworth 2010:5). While he acknowledges the structuralist and post-structuralist background ethic that 'there is no absolute, objective truth "out there" – certainly not one that we can vacuum up through a microphone, assemble into a perfect bundle of sonic reality and transmit to the listener', Biewen, along with his essayists and other publications from audio story artists, assembles a patchwork of ideological care and consideration for humanity through its storytelling tradition that could be said to philosophically bridge the optimism and hope of Enlightenment rationality with a sober sense of epistemological and ontological realism of the present age. Might they be described as sound *philosophes* of the twenty-first century? To help answer this question, it might be interesting to retrieve and rediscover how the first encyclopedia, a creation of the enlightenment, defined the notion of the *philosophe* at the end of the eighteenth century.

The Age of Enlightenment is substantially marked by an ambitious and pioneering publishing project in France between 1751 and 1772 edited by Denis Diderot called the *Encyclopédie*. This sought to map human knowledge in a society that was heavily censored and where writers earned virtually no money from their work because there was no system of royalties and no enforceable copyright laws. It was a product of a group or movement of individuals known as the *philosophes*. It could be argued that they consolidated the advances established by pioneers of rational journalism in the previous century. Alan Downie argues that 'rational journalism' emerged in England/Britain well before the *philosophes*, arguably after the breakdown of censorship in 1642 and certainly after the end of pre-publication censorship in 1695 (Downie 1994 and 1981:35–6).

They were committed to investigating and writing about law, technology, the arts, public affairs, politics, medicine and science. The *Encyclopédie* could be said to be the embodiment of their ideas. Certainly the very definition of *philosophe* in the *Encyclopédie* itself seems to resonate the founding tenets of public service journalism and many objectives that underpin journalistic codes throughout the world to this very day. The description of the *philosophe* here is male gendered because of the nature of the original text. Women did have a role in the Enlightenment, particularly

Table 3.1 A selection of audio programme-making sites where there is a creative aesthetic and commitment to idealist and ideological aspirations for communicating storytelling through sound

The Third Coast International Audio Festival (TCIAF) www.thirdcoastfestival.org/	'Celebrating the best audio stories produced worldwide for radio and the Internet'. An annual conference conferring awards and discussing the professional practice and art-form. It began at Chicago Public Radio in 2000 to support producers and other artists creating audio documentary and feature work of all styles and to bring this fresh and vital work to audiences throughout the world. Inspired by the popularity of documentary film festivals in the US, and motivated by the lack of attention given to outstanding audio work, the organisers of the TCIAF created their own blueprint for a radio festival.
Between the Ears www.bbc.co.uk/programmes/ b006x2tq	Programme on the UK national culture channel BBC Radio Three. 'Innovative and thought-provoking features on a wide variety of subjects', usually broadcast weekly with audio-streaming on 'listen again' for seven days within the radio transmission.
Radiolab at WNYC (New York City based NPR station) www.wnyc.org/shows/radiolab/	'Radiolab believes your ears are a portal to another world. Where sound illuminates ideas, and the boundaries blur between science, philosophy, and human experience. Big questions are investigated, tinkered with, and encouraged to grow. Bring your curiosity, and we'll feed it with possibility.'
Transom www.transom.org/	'Transom.org channels new work and voices to public radio and public media. We offer tools, advice, and community. We focus on the power of story and the ways public media can be useful in a changing media environment.'
Sound Portraits and StoryCorps www.soundportraits.org	'Sound Portraits Productions was the predecessor to the national oral-history project, StoryCorps. While Sound Portraits Productions is no longer an active organization, we would like to share with you the history of this award winning not-for-profit organization and encourage you to learn more about the work of StoryCorps.'
Hearing Voices – National Public Radio http://hearingvoices.com/	'Radio for people who love radio. A weekly hour series of "driveway moments" culled from broadcasts, podcasts, sound-portraits, slam poets, features, found-sound, audio archives, audio art and docs.'
PRX http://podcast.prx.org/	'Weekly podcasts on the natural world, curated by Atlantic Public Media, sponsored by The Nature Conservancy and the Public Radio Exchange.'
This American Life www.thisamericanlife.org/	'This American Life is a weekly public radio show broadcast on more than 500 stations to about 1.7 million listeners. It is produced by Chicago Public Media, distributed by Public Radio International. There's a theme to each episode, and a variety of stories on that theme. It's mostly true stories of everyday people, though not always.'
360Documentaries ABC Australia www.abc.net.au/rn/360/	'ABC Radio National's 360documentaries presents the best radio features and documentaries from Australia and around the world. You'll hear tales of ordinary and extraordinary lives, sound adventures

and fresh perspectives on the way ideas and culture intersect with contemporary life. Our online visuals and stories will take you to places and introduce you to people you'll want to know more about, from the corner shop to the rainforests of Kalimantan. The full 360documentaries-degree view.'

The Curious Ear www.rte.ie/radio1/doconone/ docs_curiousear.html Documentary on One www.rte.ie/radio1/doconone/ about.html	'The Curious Ear' is a programme strand of short creative documentaries from RTE in Ireland and edited by Ronan Kelly. 'Documentary on One' are weekly 40 minute programmes, 'productions are radio stories about real life. It's all about ideas, life, events, experiences, perspectives but most importantly – stories.'
Battery Radio www.batteryradio.com/	Newfoundland, Canada, based creative audio production workshop 'Battery Radio produc[es] radio features, information documentaries, historical series, comedy features, audio guides and acoustic films and special projects'. Producers: Chris Brookes; Paolo Pietropaolo; Bill Brennan; Kathryn Welbourn; Doug Bird; Ivan Morgan.
In the Dark www.inthedarkradio.org/	'In the Dark is a collaborative project between radio producers and radio enthusiasts. We aim to create a mini-revolution in the way we think about the art of spoken-word radio by lifting it out of its traditional settings and curating it in new and unusual ways. We are run by an enthusiastic team of volunteers. Each of our events are lovingly put together in collaboration with some of the best radio producers in Britain and abroad.'
Hackney Podcast http://hackneypodcast.co.uk/	'The Hackney Podcast was set up in 2008 to record the borough's different faces: one of Britain's poorest places but culturally one of its richest; an area of London profoundly marked by its history but, as the Olympics loom, caught in a frenzied period of change. From its first days, the podcast – available free to download – has provided an eclectic mix of politics, environmental issues and scenes from local life alongside cutting-edge art, literature and music. As professional producers working as volunteers, we're eager to broaden our sonic horizons and push our creativity to the limit. We favour montage, allowing the people of Hackney to tell their stories in their own words; create rich soundscapes, giving listeners an atmospheric sense of the borough; and commission local writers, musicians and poets to create new work.'
Resonance 104.4 FM London http://resonancefm.com/	'Imagine a radio station like no other. A radio station that makes public those artworks that have no place in traditional broadcasting. A radio station that is an archive of the new, the undiscovered, the forgotten, the impossible. That is an invisible gallery, a virtual arts centre whose location is at once local, global and timeless. And that is itself a work of art. Imagine a radio station that responds rapidly to new initiatives, has time to draw breath and reflect. A laboratory for experimentation, that by virtue of its uniqueness brings into being a new audience of listeners and creators. All this and more, Resonance104.4fm aims to make London's airwaves available to the widest possible range of practitioners of contemporary art.'

Falling Tree Productions www.fallingtree.co.uk/about	'Falling Tree's team of producers crafts features and documentaries for the BBC's UK networks, the BBC World Service and broadcasters in Ireland, Europe, north America and Australia, as well as audio tours and podcasts for a range of cultural institutions. Awards over the years include Prix Italias, Third Coast Awards, the Prix Bohemia and several Sonys'. Falling Tree's founder is Alan Hall, who teaches Creative Radio at Goldsmiths, University of London.
Too Much Information WFMU public radio USA http://itunes.apple.com/us/podcast/too-much-information-benjamen/id349682430 http://wfmu.org/playlists/shows/35653	'Too Much Information is the sober hangover after the digital party has run out of memes, apps and schemes. Host Benjamen Walker finds out that, in a world where everyone overshares the truth 140 characters at a time, telling tales might be the most honest thing to do.'
UbuWeb http://ubu.com/	UbuWeb is a large web-based educational resource for avant-garde material available on the internet, founded in 1996 by poet Kenneth Goldsmith. It offers visual, concrete and sound poetry, expanding to include film and sound art MP3 archives. UbuWeb is not affiliated to any academic institution, instead relying on alliances of interest and benefiting from bandwidth donations from its partnerships with GreyLodge, WFMU, PennSound, The Electronic Poetry Center, The Center for Literary Computing, and ArtMob.

as patrons of the salons that became the *polis*/marketplace for political and cultural debate in eighteenth-century France. Elite women could participate if they had the power of wealth and aristocratic influence. Nevertheless this public space of Enlightenment salon discussing and debating politics, arts and philosophy in eighteenth-century Europe was primarily elitist.

The entry in the *Encyclopédie* for *philosophe* was anonymous. Intriguingly, it defines a manifesto for ethical conduct in terms of communicating in society. The reasoning is late eighteenth century yet the principles appear to be extant in a variety of modern legal, quasi-legal and voluntary journalistic codes.

The house stylebooks/editorial guidelines of public broadcasting organisations such as the BBC in Britain, National Public Radio in America, and the ABC in Australia emphasise the importance of using reason in an empirical process of research and newsgathering with distancing from the passionate and emotional aspects of human partiality. Despite a recent penchant for 'conviction journalism' particularly with media charged celebrocrats avowedly setting out their points of view, there is still an enduring professional ethic that it is better for people to be able to speak for themselves. However, the certainty of impartiality behind that is challenged by the discourse of Bill Nichols, which will be explored later.

The idea of truth based on the evidence available is also a common feature in these stylebooks. A commitment to humanity and society through the exercise of

Table 3.2 A variety of modern legal, quasi-legal and voluntary journalistic codes

1 The *philosophe* uses reason because even when passionate he does not act until after full reflection.

2 The *philosophe* approaches topics and investigations in an empirical manner. He bases his principles on an infinite number of particular observations.

3 The *philosophe* makes a balanced assessment of truth by not committing himself beyond the evidence available. He can suspend judgment. He only seeks to distinguish truth when he is in a position to perceive it. Here is a clear precursor to the traditional public service definition of impartiality.

4 The *philosophe* is committed to society. The anonymous entry in the *Encyclopédie* emphasised that reason requires the *philosophe* to know, study and work to acquire sociable qualities.

5 The *philosophe* enjoys life because he is a civilised man who wants to give pleasure and make himself useful. Is this not an acknowledgment of the advantages to audience of combining information, education with entertainment?

6 The *philosophe* has humanity. He is interested and concerned about the 'bad or good fortunes of his neighbour'.

7 The *philosophe* has integrity. The *Encyclopédie* defines him as being filled with the idea of the good of civil society – 'The more reason you find in a man the more integrity you find'.

8 The *philosophe* is against unbalanced emotion when 'fanaticism, superstition, passion and anger dominate'. *Nathan the Wise* – a thought provoking play from the time of the European Enlightenment (1779) by Gotthold Ephraim Lessing is an example of a text demonstrating this maxim. It dramatically challenged the immorality of anti-Semitism and through a philosophical interplay of characters and dilemmas uses the past (the time of the Crusades in Palestine) to provide his present society a paradigm of *convivencia*.

9 The *philosophe* 'is a civilized man who acts in all things according to reason and who combines a spirit of reflection with social manners and qualities'.

integrity and good manners is also present in publications that are, in a sense, manifestos for journalistic ideology. The cultural historian Peter Burke has acknowledged the contribution of the *philosophes* in the development of the notion of public sphere:

> they have sometimes been described as the first intellectuals, independent of patrons, or even the first intelligentsia, in the sense of being systematically critical of the regime under which they were living . . . Above all, the famous Encyclopédie published between 1751 and 1765, was an important vehicle for politics.
>
> (Burke and Briggs 2002:96–7)

In each of the contributions to *Reality Radio* there is an expression of security and hope in the properties of sound story telling and its new cyberspace possibilities. The Canadian Chris Brookes enthuses how Internet archive sound inspires present day producers to understand how radio did bring down emotional, geographical and imaginative barriers:

> What radio does best is stimulate the imagination. And we should have realized this in the very beginning. After all, the first of our senses to develop is that of hearing. Lying in the darkness of the womb at first we can only hear. We can tell there's something out there – it may be Mom playing Mozart to us with headphones on her belly or having a shouting match in the kitchen with Dad – but we can't see it or smell it or touch it or taste it. We don't have those senses yet. All we can do is listen, and imagine what it might be.
>
> (Biewen and Dilworth 2010:17)

Davia Nelson and Nikki Silva, known as *The Kitchen Sisters*, in their essay 'Talking to Strangers' explored the personal and emotional impact of their audio story telling:

> The power of listening, of talking to strangers until they are no longer strangers, of passing on wisdom and humor and knowledge and music, of adding the voices of people whose stories aren't usually part of the national conversation, of creating something haunting and beautiful together, gets us every time.
>
> (Biewen and Dilworth 2010:43)

Jad Abumrad mischievously entitled his essay 'No Holes Were Drilled in the Heads of Animals in the Making of This Radio Show' in order to argue that the programmes he made, edited and sponsored sought to appeal to the analytical left side of the brain wanting explanation and the free-associative right side of the brain desiring experience:

> A good story shows there's magic in experience. [. . .] (It occurs to me now that maybe the reason we improvise so much, sometimes to the point of crushing inefficiency, is that's our way of staying connected to the actual 'experience' of storytelling). On the other hand, the best stories connect experience to something larger. An idea, a slightly new perspective, a sense of something universal that's shared, human to human. Maybe even human to duck.
>
> (Biewen and Dilworth 2010:53)

I would argue that as these eclectic and diverse audio storytellers explain their view of 'telling true stories in sound' they are close to matching an understanding of the liberal ethos of humanity that was extensively discussed by the twentieth-century German philosopher Karl Jaspers, who unlike his contemporary Martin Heidegger, became a dissident of the Nazi regime and through his marriage and commitment to his Jewish wife philosophically, spiritually and in practice resisted the ghastly curse of anti-Semitism. Jaspers explored the idea of the completion of truth in time in that:

Religion, art, and poetry are the ordinary designations of what, for Jaspers, are the intuitions that afford visions of the ground of truth. They are thus the life-founding completion of truth for man in time; they accomplish this in a manner that is original, i.e., not primarily reflective, though their expression and traditions can reach pinnacles of spiritual sophistication.

(Jaspers 1986:291)

Kurt Salamun defined Jaspers' existential philosophy as well as his reflections on reason and politics as portraying a *liberal ethos of humanity* where a number of moral attitudes or values could be identified as underpinning his understanding of the individual's role and existence as a communicative human being:

First, courage without self-deception, composure, patience, self-possession, and dignity [. . .] are also important in so far as they enable the individual to act within the social, political and economic realms without ideological bias or dogmatic fanaticism. Second, a permanent readiness to assume personal responsibility for consequences of our actions in the world. [. . .] Third, a sincere intention to accept communication-partners in their own personal freedom and potential for self-realization, and not to force one's own dogmatic standards of behavior upon them. [. . .] Fourth, the non-egoistic intention to help the communication-partner to realize *Existenz* (see glossary) without using the other as a mere instrument for one's own purpose or self-realization. [. . .] Fifth, an intellectual integrity and open-mindedness which enable a person to struggle against prejudices and political tendencies that suppress personal freedom . . .

(Salamun 1999:219–20)

Jaspers argued that 'communication is seen as the ultimate vehicle of the concretion of truth in time' (Jaspers 1986:294) and in a homespun way, Ira Glass in his chapter 'Harnessing Luck as an Industrial Product' touches on the praxis of Jaspers' existential discourse:

the easiest way to make something that other people will love is to be out for my own fun.

So that's how I see my job now: To try a thousand things until something interesting happens. To push on the half-baked ideas and stories as hard as they can be pushed. And to follow my curiosity. To keep trying different things until luck kicks in. Luck will always kick in.

(Biewen and Dilworth 2010:66)

Katie Davis in 'Covering Home' explored the nature of radio/audio programme making as a dimension of civic activism: 'I have started to think of myself as a witness-participant, keeping in mind what writer James Baldwin said – that a witness is at times called to testify' (74). She talked about being asked to speak in community meetings, intervene with cops and parole officers and in the many hours she now spends with her neighbours she has discovered a social process of 'deeper listening', where she no longer expects or need answers immediately:

> The man who runs the local teen center heard my radio story about the false accusation at the bike shop, and he told me he's glad there's a storyteller in the community to gather up the threads of the many stories. That is how I've started to think of myself – as a storyteller. And I use 'storyteller' in the traditional sense. I am a keeper of stories that guide. I capture the stories and keep them in trust for my community. And I retell them, and yes, sometimes I shape them.
>
> (Biewen and Dilworth 2010:75)

Many of the essays in *Reality Radio* celebrate in different styles and ways the cross-generational, ethnic, gender and transnational properties of radio and audio broadcasting for the purposes of empowering dignity in identity and expanding understanding and respect. As Maria Martin said in 'Crossing Boundaries':

> Radio in places like Guatemala, Bolivia, and Uruguay is truly a people's medium. I was greatly impressed with the journalists I met and worked with – *comunicadores sociales* who possess a strong commitment to serving the public and to helping their listeners become active participants in a peaceful democracy.
>
> (Biewen and Dilworth 2010:163)

Karen Michel in 'Adventurers in Sound' talked about the wonderful nature of radio as a medium for 'hearing one's own and others' voices, for the growth that allows teens and the rest of us to share and reflect' (170). Perhaps unknowingly she was extolling the very ethos of the Jaspersian dream:

> Hopefully, some of these teens will reach us through whatever technologies exist, and hopefully, too, there will some day be regular spots on the air for their stories and insights. They will become the adventurers in sound, heading off into that territory that we once claimed as our own. We all know the sound of civilized radio; let's hear it for the teens who can cannabalize the good parts, chew them up, and come up with something new. Attention will be paid.
>
> (170)

Fifty or so years ago, the child of the British imperial establishment called Charles Parker, enjoying all the privileges of an Oxbridge background and full-time job as a producer in the British Broadcasting Corporation, was seeking to cross class boundaries in mythologising and giving valorisation to the working classes through a series of documentaries mixing interview with folk music called *Radio Ballads*; perhaps out of emotional and ideological frustration that as a political Marxist himself, he was unable to wear the badge of the very class his doctrine sought to elevate

FIGURE 3.1
Broadcasting House in Portland Place,
Headquarters of the BBC, completed in 1932
(Photo: copyright Tim Crook).

and legitimise with political, economic and cultural power. Parker is canonised in British radio studies (Street 2004:187–94). He has an archive organisation (Charles Parker Archive Trust at Birmingham Central Library), annual conference and award convened by universities to encourage innovative and exploratory radio documentary making by students.

Parker hails from a tradition of programme-making long gone at the BBC. These were individual poets of sound, who according to the award-winning feature maker Piers Plowright speaking on Martin Spinelli's *Radio Radio* reputedly spent most of their time discussing programme ideas in a pub round the corner from London's Broadcasting House, and making only one outstanding programme a year so that they had enough time to think (Spinelli 2005). Plowright himself is also something of a legend in British broadcasting. Current generations of radio feature makers who had the privilege and pleasure of attending his training workshops in Marylebone High Street recall his poetic metaphor on what to aim for in good documentary production:

> Listening I think. If you're not listening and interested in listening to people and stories and sounds, then I don't think that will communicate to any other listeners. [. . .] I think of myself as the listener really. I am the listener when I listen to people. And I'm the listener I'm designing my programme for. It's got

to be very personal. I've often said there are three things that go into a really interesting feature programme. And I do a little diagram, which has a sort of black cone shooting upwards, the tip of the cone is upwards, a green circle and in the middle a red heart. And the cone means adrenaline raising excitement; something that really makes you want to go on listening. The green circle is focus, because it is no good having the most wonderful range of sounds and ideas and panoramas if you haven't got something at the centre, which is of great interest. I think very often small things illuminate big things too; particularly in radio. And the red heart, and if you ask me this is the thing that matters more than anything else, is the human passions and the human stories that have to touch you. So although I am not against abstraction on radio, and indeed I think it is quite exciting and perhaps we don't in Britain experiment nearly enough with what sound can do, with what concepts can do. We are rather tied to the journalistic tradition from which the BBC has come. Nonetheless, if it hasn't got heart, if it hasn't got a passionate tale, that doesn't reach out and touch you, then I don't think you have got a very interesting piece of radio.

(Spinelli 2005)

Martin Spinelli's enlightening series of 16 *Radio Radio* documentaries extends intelligent interviewing, reflection and debate across the entire spectrum of radio and sound programming poetics including episodes with Gregory Whitehead, Charles Bernstein, Jennifer and Kevin McCoy, Stephen Erickson, Paul D. Miller (aka DJ Spooky), Christof Migone, Michael Basinksi, Bob Cobbing and Lawrence Upton and the British sound artists Jane Draycott and Elizabeth James whose work can be heard on the Internet. The interview with Piers Plowright includes long excerpts from three of his seminal and much-celebrated 'features': *Mr Fletcher the Poet*, *Fanny and the Plaster Saints*, and *Miroo*.

Goldsmiths, University of London, has hosted an MA in Radio programme (the first of its kind in Britain) for twenty years at the time of writing. Every year it has the privilege of receiving visits from contemporary creative sound story programme makers who generously provide talks to students. They have included Laurence Grissell (BBC), Francesca Panetta (*Guardian* and Hackney Podcast), an array of independent producers, Ronan Kelly from Ireland and Simon Elmes (Creative Director, Features and Documentaries, BBC Radio). Simon explored through sound illustration from audio documentaries produced in Britain and abroad how they contain the essence of stories from all sorts of people. He observed that there is a unity factor that is at the heart of all great poems: 'distil the essence of a moment, of a thought, of a feeling, of a person's life' (Elmes 2010). He referred the students to the opening few lines of Philip Larkin's poem *The Whitsun Weddings*. This is the impact on the imagination of words and sounds and Larkin's line 'a hothouse flashed uniquely' conjured the immense emotional and mind's eye power of glass reflecting the sun. Simon talked about how the constant subconscious nature of listening means:

there exists a deep, deep silt of layer upon countless layer of sound-information, semi-defined, able to be focused and sharpened into understanding, but existing more as a sort of gloop, with ill-defined borders that can fuse and coalesce and connect with all sorts of other sense memories. Rather like poetry does, but with sounds and words. That's *why* the pictures on radio are better.

(Elmes 27 January 2010)

Simon Elmes celebrated how contemporary programme makers such as Lawrence Grissell could generate the dignity of poetics in the lifetime of ordinary as well as extraordinary people sometimes referred to in legal jurisprudence as public figures of *par excellence*. The radio critic of the *Daily Telegraph*, Gillian Reynolds, had observed about Laurence Grissell's *An Interior Life* (BBC Radio Four 2009):

You would wait forever to hear a programme like An Interior Life (Radio 4, Sunday) on commercial radio. Come to think of it, it's not often these days that Radio 4 broadcasts something of such quality. This 40-minute feature was by Laurence Grissell, a monologue by a man in his 80s, looking back on his life, walking round his house, taking his pills, talking about music, his childhood, the war, the two partners with whom he shared his life. It was simple, careful, frank and beautiful. It was also made with the sort of craft that only comes when it can be practised. Such programmes require time to make and a place in the schedule.

(Reynolds 2009)

Simon Elmes reflected on how the audio feature in terms of its storytelling had the power to be time-transpositional and again demonstrating the power for such communication to seek truth through time in the spirit of Karl Jaspers' existential phenomenology and humanistic liberal ethic:

However, it was a more humdrum, British story that really captured my imagination, one that perhaps sums up my thirty years in feature-making for Radio 4. I'd travelled to Australia in pursuit of Joseph Lingard, a man from Chapel Milton near Glossop in Derbyshire who, 200 years ago, had been accused of stealing an ordinary little door-latch, worth sixpence-ha'penny. Melvyn Bragg and I were working on a series called Voices of the Powerless, and we'd discovered Lingard's written account of his transportation in a dusty, unread Victorian volume in Derby municipal library. Lingard's individual story remained, 160 years after he wrote it, very moving and in its simple honest way had the power to bring into sharp focus the fate of the thousands of powerless men and women taken to Australia and elsewhere for their often insignificant misdemeanours.

And thus it was that I found myself in the chill of the Tasmanian winter, amid the world's experts in Transportation studies, surrounded by rainforest, and in sight of the penal settlement of Sarah Island. It seemed an enormous distance to travel in pursuit of a fragment of a single human life, yet it characterised what all of us who make features for Radio 4 seek to champion, and that is the illumination of a corner of our present, past, or perhaps future world, through spinning riveting stories, told with passion.

(Elmes 2007:126–7)

Critical debates on truth telling or the representation of reality

The most detailed, and some would argue the most compelling analysis of the interface between 'truth telling' and representation of reality in the documentary form was completed by Bill Nichols in 1991. His focus was on the film/television medium, but I have argued that this theorising was wholly relevant to the radio form (Crook 1999:207–9). Nichols divided the documentary form into four categories in his book *Representing Reality*: expository; observational; interactive; reflexive – and then four years later discussed a further genre: performative (Buckland 1998:103–23):

- Expository: 'Voice-of-God commentary and poetic perspectives sought to disclose information about the historical world itself and to see that world afresh, even if these views came to seem romantic and didactic' (Nichols 1991:33).

- Observational: 'An observational mode of representation allowed the film maker to record unobtrusively what people did when they were not explicitly addressing the camera. But the observational mode limited the film maker to the present moment and required a disciplined detachment from the events themselves' (Nichols 1991:33).

- Interactive: 'Interactive documentary [. . .] arose from the availability of the same more mobile equipment and a desire to make the filmmaker's perspective more evident. Interactive documentarists wanted to engage with individuals more directly while not reverting to classic exposition. Interview styles and interventionist tactics arose, allowing the film maker to participate more actively in present events' (Nichols 1991:33).

- Reflexive: 'Reflexive documentary [. . .] arose from a desire to make the conventions of representations themselves more apparent and to challenge the impression of reality which the other three modes normally conveyed unproblematically. It is the most self-aware mode; it uses many of the same devices as other documentaries but sets them on edge so that the viewer's attention is drawn to the device as well as the effect' (Nichols 1991:33).

- Performative: A style of documentary that stressed the 'subjective aspects of a classically objective discourse', where the 'loss of referential emphasis may relegate such films to the avant-garde: "excessive" use of style' (Nichols 1995:95).

Nichols' analysis raised the potential ethical difficulties in distinguishing between fact, fiction, faction, drama-documentary and the new genre of *mockumentary* that has become an increasingly popular platform for irony and parody. However, the performance of creative games with the listener always risks social, political and cultural misunderstandings. Winston recognises that sound/radio programming, particularly with its space for emotional and imaginative intensity, has severely tested the debate in media history:

> The use of documentary characteristics dates back at least to Orson Welles's radio version of *War of the Worlds* (1938). It is astonishing that even at the time anybody could have thought it really matched the conventions of actual disaster broadcasting, so artificial was it, but it did. It has become one of the most notorious examples of radio's power as thousands of listeners were seemingly convinced that Martians were taking over New Jersey.
>
> (Winston 2000:24)

Professional documentarists and their media institutions have met the twentieth-century charge from Roland Barthes about the death of the author and the structuralist condemnation that objectivity is a fantasy with a commitment to the ethic of aspiring to impartiality. But Bill Nichols warns that the 'impression of distinterestedness is a powerful reassurance and a seductive ploy' (Nichols 1991:198). He argues that:

> What objectivity itself cannot tell us is the purpose it is meant to serve since this would undermine its own effectiveness (lest that purpose be one that adopts the shroud of objectivity as a final purpose: the pursuit of truth, the quest for knowledge, the performance of service for the common good.).
>
> (198)

Roscoe and Hight built an entire book's analysis around the penchant for mocking the conventions of documentary in television, film and radio. There appears to be a playful enthusiasm on the part of radio communicators to test the assumptions and expectations of their listening audiences. The game of intended entertainment or unintended carelessness can have catastrophic consequences. When BBC Radio Four began a stream of phone-in style programming *Down the Line*, there was a deliberate attempt not to signpost it as dramatised performance so that the attending publicity from angry and confused listeners expecting to hear more professionally produced discussion and talk programme generated media interest and served as a marketing tool.

But carelessness on the part of BBC Radio Four *Today* reporter Andrew Gilligan who misrepresented the identity and content of an anonymous source in 2003, and misjudgement on taste and decency by BBC Radio Two entertainers Russell Brand and Jonathan Ross in 2008, when making prank calls to the veteran actor Andrew Sachs over Brand's previous relationship with his granddaughter resulted in resignations, wider moral panics, enquiries and regulatory fines and crises over credibility and authority. The Radio Two event became a curious enquiry into the behaviour and lack of courtesy shown by two 'low popular cultural' performers in relation to an actor and writer, Andrew Sachs, who is strongly associated with 'high cultural' values in radio's history.

Roscoe and Hight reflect that:

> As documentary's ability to capture reality has been undermined, it is paradoxically bolstered by technological advances that allow the documentary to penetrate the social world in newer and deeper ways. In some sense, the development of Reality-TV (including an infatuation with surveillance footage) and the docu-soap represent a search for a more 'authentic' form of documentary representation. Despite its enduring popularity through these forms, the genre's privileged cultural status is arguably more tenuous now than at any time in the past.
>
> (Roscoe and Hight 2001:188)

The modus operandi of radio/audio programme storytelling

Detailed guides and resources for developing the essential skills of audio writing, documentary and feature programme making, editorial judgement and creative programme structuring as well as recommendations on time-management for research, content origination and editing to different time frames such as 5, 10, 15, 30, 45 minute and 1 hour programmes are set out in multimedia on the companion website.

The resources provide advice and demonstrations on the process of producing three genres of radio/audio programmes each of 10 minutes duration:

1   Montage documentary – without narrative links.
2   Linked, narrated documentary.
3   Dramatised feature – either factual, fictional or hybrid, but using audio dramatisation techniques.

Table 3.3 sets out recommended reading for the broad categories of skills acquisition in radio/sound journalism, creative feature/documentary and radio drama.

THEORY

Media and cultural studies concentrate on a focus of intellectual axis that could be represented in the triple enquiry track of audience-media production-media text. Textual analysis oscillates between semiotic and narrative analysis. In *Analysing*

Table 3.3 Recommended reading for the broad categories of skills acquisition in radio/sound journalism, creative feature/documentary and radio drama

Radio/sound journalism	
Practice	**Theory (extending beyond journalism in terms of genre)**

Practice

Adams, Sally and Hicks, Wynford (2009) *Interviewing for Journalists* (2nd edition), Abingdon: Routledge.

Baird, Lois (ed.) (1992) *Australian Film, Television and Radio School. Guide to Radio Production*, Allen and Unwin Australia.

Beaman, Jim (2006) *Programme Making for Radio*, London: Routledge.

Beaman, Jim (2011) *Interviewing for Radio* (2nd edition), London and New York: Routledge.

Boyd, Andrew, Stewart, Peter and Alexander, Ray (2007) *Broadcast Journalism. Techniques of Radio and TV News* (6th edition), London: Focal Press.

Chantler, Paul and Stewart, Peter (2009) *Essential Radio Journalism: How to Produce and Present Radio News*, London: A&C Black. (Highly recommended.)

Crook, Tim (1999) *International Radio Journalism: History, Theory and Practice*, London and New York: Routledge.

Emm, Adèle (2001) *Researching for Television and Radio*, London and New York: Routledge.

Frost, Chris (2010) *Reporting for Journalists* (2nd edition), Abingdon: Routledge.

Gage, Linda (1999) *A Guide to Commercial Radio Journalism* (2nd edition), Douglas, Lawrie and Kinsey, Marie (revising eds), Boston: Focal Press.

Geller, Valerie (2009) *Creating Powerful Radio: Getting, Keeping and Growing Audiences, News Talk, Information, Personality*, London and New York: Focal Press, an imprint of Elsevier.

Hudson, Gary and Rowlands, Sarah (2007) *The Broadcast Journalism Handbook*, London: Pearson Longman.

Ibbotson, Trevor and Rudin, Richard (2002) *An Introduction to Journalism: Essential Techniques and Background Knowledge*, London: Focal Press.

Kaye, Michael and Popperwell, Andrew (1992) *Making Radio: A Guide to Basic Radio Techniques*, London: Broadside Books.

Theory (extending beyond journalism in terms of genre)

Adorno, Theodor (2000) *The Psychological Technique of Martin Luther Thomas' Radio Addresses*, Stanford, California: Stanford University Press.

Barlow, William (1999) *Voice – The Making of Black Radio*, Philadelphia, Pennsylvania: Temple University Press.

Barnard, Stephen (2000) *Studying Radio*, New York and London: Arnold, Hodder Headline Group.

Chapman, Jane and Kinsey, Marie (ed.) (2008) *Broadcasting Journalism: A Critical Introduction*, London: Routledge.

Chignell, Hugh (2009) *Key Concepts in Radio Studies*, London: Sage Publications.

Crisell, Andrew (1994) *Understanding Radio* (2nd edition), London and New York: Routledge.

Crisell, Andrew (2002) *An Introductory History of British Broadcasting* (2nd edition), London and New York: Routledge.

de Burgh, Hugo (2008) *Investigative Journalism – Context and Practice* (2nd edition), London and New York: Routledge.

Delmer, Sefton (1962) *Black Boomerang: The Story of His Secret 'Black Radio' Operation in World War 2 – and How It Has Boomeranged Today*, London: Secker & Warburg.

Douglas, Susan J. (1999) *Listening In: Radio and the American Imagination, from Amos 'n' Andy and Edward R. Murrow to Wolfman Jack and Howard Stern*, New York: Times Books, Random House.

Fleming, Carole (2010) *The Radio Handbook* (3rd edition), London: Routledge.

Franklin, Bob, Hamer, Martin, Kinsey, Marie and Richardson, John (2005) *Key Concepts in Journalism Studies* (SAGE Key Concepts series), London: Sage Publications.

Garnett, David (2002) *The Secret History of PWE – The Political Warfare Executive 1939–1945*, London: St Ermin's Press.

Hendy, David (2000) *Radio in the Global Age*, Cambridge: Polity Press.

Kern, Jonathan (2008) *Sound Reporting: The NPR Guide to Audio Journalism and Production*, Chicago: University of Chicago Press.

Lynch, Joanna R. and Gillispie, Greg (1998) *Process and Practice of Radio Programming*, Lanham, Maryland: University Press of America.

McLeish, Robert (1994) *Radio Production* (3rd edition), London and New York: Focal Press, an imprint of Elsevier.

Milam, Lorenzo Wilson (1988) *Sex and Broadcasting: A Handbook on Starting a Radio Station for the Community*, San Diego, California: MHO & MHO Works.

Mills, Jenni (2004) *The Broadcast Voice*, London and New York: Focal Press, an imprint of Elsevier.

Mitchell, Leslie (2005) *Freelancing for Television and Radio*, London: Routledge.

Rosenbaum, Marcus D. and Dinges, John (eds) (1992) *Sound Reporting: The National Public Guide to Radio Journalism and Production*, Dubuque, Iowa: Kendall/Hunt.

Stewart, Peter (2006) *Essential Radio Skills: How to Present and Produce a Radio Show*, London: A&C Black.

Trewin, Janet (2003) *Presenting on TV and Radio*, London and New York: Focal Press, an imprint of Elsevier.

White, Ted (2002) *Broadcast News Writing, Reporting, and Producing* (3rd revised edition), Boston: Focal Press.

Hilmes, Michele (2002) *Only Connect: A Cultural History of Broadcasting in the United States*, London and New York: Wadsworth, Thomson Learning.

Hilmes, Michele and Loviglio, Jason (2002) *Radio Reader: Essays in the Cultural History of Radio*, London and New York: Routledge.

Krause, Keith (2007) *The Radio Station: Broadcast, Satellite and Internet* (7th edition), Boston: Focal Press.

Mitchell, Caroline (ed.) (2000) *Women and Radio: Airing Differences*, London and New York: Routledge.

Rudin, Richard (2011) *Broadcasting in the 21st Century*, London: Palgrave Macmillan.

Shingler, Martin and Wieringa, Cindy (1998) *On Air: Methods and Meanings of Radio*, London and New York: Arnold, Hodder Headline Group.

Soley, Lawrence C. and Nichols, John S. (1987) *Clandestine Radio Broadcasting: A Study of Revolutionary and Counterrevolutionary Electronic Communication*, Westport, Connecticut: Praeger.

Squier, Susan Merrill (ed.) (2003) *Communities of the Air – Radio Century, Radio Culture*, Durham, North Carolina, and London: Duke University Press.

Starkey, Guy (2004) *Radio in Context*, London: Palgrave Macmillan.

Sterling, Christopher H. (ed.) (2004) *Museum of Broadcasting Radio Encyclopedia in Three Volumes*, Chicago: Fitzroy Dearborn/Taylor Francis in association with the Museum of Broadcast Communications in Chicago.

Strauss, Neil (ed.) (1993) *Radiotext(e)*, New York: Columbia University.

Street, Seán (2002) *A Concise History of British Radio: 1922–2002*, Tiverton, Devon: Kelly Publications.

Street, Seán (2006) *Crossing the Ether: British Public Service Radio and Commercial Competition, 1922–1945*, Eastleigh, Southampton: John Libbey Publishing.

Walker, Jesse (2001) *Rebels on the Air: An Alternative History of Radio in America*, New York and London: New York University Press.

Williams, Gilbert A. (1998) *Legendary Pioneers of Black Radio*, Westport, Connecticut: Praeger.

Creative feature/documentary

Practice

Biewen, John and Dilworth, Alexa (eds) (2010) *Reality Radio: Telling True Stories in Sound*, Chapel Hill, North Carolina: The University of North Carolina Press.

Boardman-Jacobs, Sam (ed.) (2004) *Radio Scriptwriting*, Bridgend, Wales: Seren.

Crook, Tim (1999) *Radio Drama: Theory and Practice*, London and New York: Routledge.

Horstmann, Rosemary (1991) *Writing for Radio* (2nd edition), London: A&C Black.

MacLoughlin, Shaun (1998) *Writing for Radio: How to Create Successful Radio Plays, Features and Short Stories*, Oxford: How To Books.

McInerney, Vincent (2001) *Writing for Radio*, Manchester: Manchester University Press.

Siegel, Bruce H. (1992) *Creative Radio Production*, Boston, London: Focal Press.

Theory

Augaitis, Daina and Lander, Dan (1994) *Radio Rethink: Art, Sound and Transmission*, Alberta, Canada: Walter Phillips Gallery, The Banff Centre for the Arts (book and CD).

Briscoe, Desmond and Curtis-Bramwell, Roy (1983) *The BBC Radiophonic Workshop*, London: BBC Books.

Nichols, Bill (1991) *Representing Reality: Issues and Concepts in Documentary*, London: John Wiley & Sons.

Roscoe, Jane and Hight, Craig (2001) *Faking It: Mock-documentary and the Subversion of Factuality*, Manchester: Manchester University Press.

Street, Seán (2012, forthcoming) *The Poetry of Radio – The Colour of Sound*, London and New York: Routledge.

Winston, Brian (2000) *Lies, Damn Lies and Documentaries*, London: BFI Publishing.

Radio/audio drama

Practice

Ash, William (1985) *The Way to Write Radio Drama*, London: Elm Tree Books.

Beck, Alan (1997) *Radio Acting*, London: A&C Black.

Boardman-Jacobs, Sam (ed.) (2004) *Radio Scriptwriting*, Bridgend, Wales: Seren.

Brooke, Pamela (1995) *Radio Social Drama: Communicating Through Story Characters*, New York: University Press of America.

Crook, Tim (1999) *Radio Drama: Theory and Practice*, London and New York: Routledge.

Dancyger, Ken (1991) *Broadcast Writing: Dramas, Comedies, and Documentaries*, Boston: Focal Press.

De Fossard, Esta (2005) *Writing and Producing Radio Drama*, London: Sage Publications.

Horstmann, Rosemary (1991) *Writing for Radio* (2nd edition), London: A&C Black.

Kisner, Don (2004) *Theatre of the Mind: Writing and Producing Audio Dramas in the Classroom: A Manual for Teachers* (revised edition), Sanger, California: Balance Publishing Company.

MacLoughlin, Shaun (1998) *Writing for Radio: How to Create Successful Radio Plays, Features and Short Stories*, Oxford: How To Books.

McInerney, Vincent (2001) *Writing for Radio*, Manchester: Manchester University Press.

Traynor, Mary and Hand, Richard J. (2011) *Radio Drama Handbook: Audio Drama in Context and Practice*, New York: Continuum Books.

Theory

Cory, Mark Ensign (1974) *The Emergence of an Acoustical Art Form*, Lincoln, Nebraska: University of Nebraska Press.

Drakakis, John (ed.) (1981) *British Radio Drama*, Cambridge: Cambridge University Press.

Fisher, Margaret (2002) *Ezra Pound's Radio Operas: The BBC Experiments, 1931–1933*, Cambridge, Massachusetts, and London: The MIT Press.

Gilfillan, Daniel (2009) *German Experimental Radio*, Minneapolis, Minnesota, and London: University of Minnesota Press.

Lewis, Peter (ed.) (1981) *Radio Drama*, Harlow, Essex: Longman.

Rattigan, Dermot (2002) *Theatre of Sound: Radio and the Dramatic Imagination*, Dublin: Carysfort Press.

Rodger, Ian (1982) *Radio Drama*, London: Macmillan Press.

Note: Some of the texts indicated above are also hybrid and combine practice/theory perspectives and focus.

Media Texts, Gillespie and Toynbee concentrated on the paradigmatic-syntagmatic relationships where syntagmatic is said to refer to 'the linear dimension of a text, its "sequentiality"', and paradigmatic is said to refer as '"storage shelves" where one finds and takes out the words one needs to fill certain places in the syntagms' (Gillespie and Toynbee 2006:24). Narrative analysis focuses on how texts represent the binary opposition of equilibrium and disequilibrum. It would seem the theoretical drive is to identify the patterns of linguistic representations of differences and oppositions.

Adorno's propaganda template for academic analysis

Hitherto neglected texts such as Theodor Adorno's *The Psychological Technique of Martin Luther Thomas's Radio Addresses* provide an opportunity to elucidate a wider frame of academic analysis of media texts in terms of the genre of talk radio and the masking of talk radio techniques during information wars. The intertextual interest in talk radio as a cultural phenomenon is apparent in the 1988 film, *Talk Radio*, directed by Oliver Stone. There continues to be an active debate about the political role of charismatic and conservative radio talk show presenters. Philip Seib in his 1993 text *Rush Hour: Talk Radio, Politics, and the Rise of Rush Limbaugh* speculated that 'Behind the popularity of talk radio is frustration that has given rise to an electronic activism. Rather than taking to the streets, dissatisfied Americans are taking to the airwaves' (Seib 1993:177). He argued that the charges against Limbaugh of political demagoguery giving rise to the threat of regulatory intervention left 'half his brain tied behind his back to make it a fair fight' (276), but he declared with the aggression and assertiveness of his subject study 'the Godzilla of broadcasting will battle on. Dittoheads rejoice; liberal wackos despair! Rush Limbaugh is likely to be with us for a long time'.

The intermedia connections and contestation about US talk radio representation First Amendment freedom of expression or irresponsible and violence provoking propaganda are set out in Table 3.4.

'Der Chef' is German for 'The Chief' and was the title of a charismatic fictional character who provided the central voice for a British 'Black Propaganda' radio station broadcast to Germany between the 23 May 1941 and the 18 November 1943 (Garnett 2002:210). As the historian for the Political Warfare Executive David Garnett documented:

> The aim of our Black transmissions to Germany was to corrupt the discipline of the enemy. This could be done in various ways, GS1 denounced corruption in order to show it was safe, profitable and widely prevalent, and appealed indirectly to the 'inner swine hound' in the German.
>
> (195)

Table 3.4 *Talk Radio* **and the cultural phenomenon of the 'Shock Jock': The intermedia connections and contestation about US talk radio representation, First Amendment freedom of expression, and irresponsible and violence-provoking propaganda**

Talk Radio and the cultural phenomenon of the 'Shock Jock'.

Talk Radio directed by Oliver Stone was made in 1988 and stars the actor and playwright Eric Bogosian who co-scripted a stage play that formed the basis of part of the film. The screenplay was also drawn from the assassination of the left wing radio host Alan Berg in 1984.

Barry Champlain is a controversial host presenting the evening phone-in on a radio station in Dallas, Texas. His popularity is dependent on the exercise of bitter and vicious irony and making sure he has the last word by pulling down the fader and cutting off callers expressing bigoted and simple opinions. The entertainment is based on bullying and baiting the ugly and pathetic.

The film's plot covers a short period when Champlain's radio show is about to go nationwide. There are flashbacks to his life as a former suit salesman, and demonstrating how he achieved fame through a guest shot on the Jeff Fisher radio show. The location is the radio station and studio with Barry confronting hostile callers trying to intimidate him and having to deal with threatening 'hate mail' including a bomb threat, a fake bomb including a Nazi Swastika flag. The status of his fame and talent is predicated with his insecure private life, affairs at work and alienation of his wife who he still clearly depends on emotionally. The screenplay explores the principle that people destroy and hate that which they love most.

Alan Berg (1934–84), like Barry Champlain, espoused left-wing views and his politics made him a target in 'middle America'. He also shared Champlain's Jewish background and style of on-air rhetoric when confronting anti-Semitism and callers with 'Ku Kux Klan' style attitudes.

Alan Berg became a martyr for free speech because an extremist white nationalist group decided to assassinate him for his politics. He was cut down by gunfire as he was about to get into his car at his home in Denver, Colorado on 18 June 1984. Steven Singular's history of the events *Talked to Death: The Life and Murder of Alan Berg* describes the highs and lows of the police investigation into his death. This led to convictions for criminal offences in connection with the killing.

Michael C. Keith writes that by the late 1990s AM and FM speech formats were up nearly 300 percent and that surveys indicated News/Talk stations 'were the most tuned format in the United States' (Keith 2007:97). It might be argued that the demise of the 'fairness doctrine' in 1987, which used to be regulated by the FCC, unleashed an expansion of politically partisan, mainly conservative, presenters. The doctrine had obliged stations to give a right of reply to people wishing to rebut expressions of controversial opinion. In the UK the equivalent statutory regulator, Ofcom, imposes controls on stations to be balanced politically and stylistic brakes on the muscular speech of US so-called 'shock jocks' such as Rush Limbaugh and Glenn Beck. The companion web site provides links to so-called right wing and left wing presenters in the US and UK though sometimes the ideological position of talk show hosts is difficult to pin down.

The right-wing political heritage of talk radio can be drawn from the mid-1930s, when controversial radio priest Father Charles Coughlin's radio broadcasts were reaching millions per week. There were a number of other pro-fascistic broadcasters, including Martin Luther Thomas of whom the Frankfurt School theorist Theodor W. Adorno carried out a detailed academic content study that was published in English by Stanford University Press in 2000. Adorno studied the phenomenon in terms of: 1) The personal element: self-characterisation of the agitator; 2) The method of broadcasting in terms of technique, 'movement' trick, 'flight of ideas', 'listen to your leader', excursus of 'fait accompli', 'unity' trick; 'democratic cloak', 'if you only knew', 'dirty linen' device, 'tingling backbone' device, 'last hour' device, 'black hand' device and 'let us be practical' rhetorical narrative device; 3) Using radio as 'the religious medium', and 4) Ideological bait using: imagery of communism, 'Communists and bankers' device, president-baiting, 'pick up thy bed and walk' device 'the Jews are coming' and the 'problem' device (Adorno 2000:v).

The 'shock jock' or talk radio phenomenon is the subject of continuing media hagiography and criticism. This ranges from the supportive profile of Rush Limbaugh by Philip Seib, *Rush Hour: Talk Radio, Politics, and the Rise of Rush Limbaugh* (1993), to the 15 minute *Profile* by BBC Radio of Glenn Beck. 'Glenn Beck, the provocative tv and radio talk show host, represents the polarised politics of American media. Those who like him describe him as an "inspiration" and those that don't call him "toxic". His TV show on Fox News averages a daily audience of two million viewers. Beck doesn't shy away from controversy, recently describing progressivism as "the cancer in America eating our Constitution" and referring to President Obama as having "a deep-seated hatred for white people or the white culture". Along with Sarah Palin, he's often invoked as a spiritual leader by the Tea Party Movement' (Sieghart 2010).

The author and director for the dramatic content and performance of this genre of audio deception was Sefton Delmer, who had been a foreign correspondent for the *Daily Express* before the outbreak of the Second World War in September 1939. The black propaganda operation depended for its effect on a belief by its audience that they were consuming factual narrative. Any analysis of the textual content of the fictional narrative that framed this genre of deception may resonate and intersect with Adorno's *The Psychological Technique of Martin Luther Thomas's Radio Addresses* for several reasons. Adorno was a left wing Jewish exile from Nazi anti-Semitic tyranny. He was studying a genre of sound texture in the USA that was arguably mirrored by Adolf Hitler in his political rhetoric and double-mirrored by Delmer and the Political Warfare Executive in their desire to create an audio demagogue more right-wing and extremist than Hitler himself. Adorno was studying the age of the right-wing, anti-liberal, neo-fascist broadcaster, the ancestors of the 'shock jock' 'hate-radio' personalities of contemporary radio.

Martin Luther Thomas is not mentioned in Erik Barnouw's *The Golden Web – A History of Broadcasting in the United States Volume II – 1933 to 1953*, but from a footnote in Adorno's book (Adorno 2000:75) there did not seem to be any shortage of right-wing charismatic radio preachers. Adorno cites the names of Winrod, Jeffers and Hubbard. Indeed an argument could be made out that the radio demagogue was the catalysing focus for a specific strand of American fascism, which also attracted some support from big business (Crook 2001:238).

It is difficult to appreciate just how politically normative fascism actually was in Britain and America during the 1930s. The fact that the BBC would unselfconsciously, and without any critical context, publish a photograph of British fascist leader Sir Oswald Mosley in their 1934 Yearbook demonstrates the establishment friendliness of this genre of totalitarian politics. Communist leaders were not accorded the same privilege and had been effectively demonised as the Bolshevik Other. Anti-Semitism was also rife in both countries. In the USA voting restrictions on Jews had not been lifted in Rhode Island until 1842, North Carolina until 1868, and in New Hampshire until 1877 (Piotrowski 1998:38).

At the time Adorno was working with Paul Lazarsfeld and Herta Herzog on the social significance of radio (Crook 2001:238). The Martin Luther Thomas analysis was written during the Second World War and first published in German in 1975. The English translation was first published in 2000 and the reason for its emergence 60 years after it was written is ethically interesting as well as sociologically or potentially New Historicist.

Historicising the radio demagogue

As Richard Danson Brown observed about Stephen Greenblatt's 1981 essay on Shakespeare's History plays 'Invisible Bullets': 'Greenblatt . . . [was] attuned to how power was used in Renaissance England at precisely the historical moment when the right-wing Republican administration of Ronald Reagan governed twentieth-century America'. Brown is correct in stating that analysing the agonies, conflicts and dislocations of your own culture sometime in the past is an understandable way of exploring the related dynamics of the contemporary age (Brown 2000:5) (Crook 2001:239).

Adorno's thesis becomes an intellectual artefact from the first half of the twentieth century and a primary source of socio-psychological writing. In a sense it was journalistic being contemporary to the praxis of fascism and anti-Semitism. Clearly it was not journalistic in output but it is an ethical study of communications power. Adorno sought to make a cogent intellectual and cultural appraisal of an aspect of popular political culture. Radio was the primary electronic medium. The content of the broadcasts had profound cultural anchorage to their time. The addresses are an expression of the ideology of envy and *ressentiment*.

The main target is Bolshevism and Jews. The consequences of demonising categories of humanity within the boundaries of a democracy are that the people in the totalitarian autocracy that might follow will have been conditioned to hate and indifference. Two models of genocide in the twentieth century are associated with extreme racist hate propaganda by radio: Nazi Germany 1933–45 and Rwanda 1994–96.

Adorno's study is content analysis without social survey. However, the right-wing radio demagogue remains a socio-political phenomenon of US broadcasting. Perhaps the more complex inter-media of our present age suggest that a contemporary neo-fascist charismatic broadcaster is likely to have less power than he or she did when radio was the paradigmatic electronic medium (239).

The techniques of hate radio

Adorno criticises Thomas's techniques and concentrates on the how rather than what of his media phenomenon. The book is divided into four parts: 'The Personal Element'; 'Self-Characterization of the Agitator'; 'Thomas's Methods'; 'The Religious

Medium' and 'Ideological Bait' (239–40). Intriguingly the historian of Britain's Political Warfare Executive, David Garnett, talked about how Sefton Delmer, the author of the black station propagandist and fake German Nazi dissident broadcaster Gustav Siegfried Eins used pornography as 'Listener's Bait':

> Delmer did not scruple to introduce passages of extreme indecency which undoubtedly did much to attract an audience quickly. But, unfortunately for the peace of the Department, the 'ground-wave' of the beamed broadcasts could be picked up easily near Woburn, and sometimes in London, and programmes intended to attract the thugs of the SS had their British eavesdroppers. There were repeated protests from the Foreign Office, and Mr Leeper (Head of PWE) had to become the unwilling apologist for a matter which was extremely distasteful to him.
>
> (Garnett 2002:44)

One member of the war cabinet, Sir Stafford Cripps complained to Leeper: 'I am sorry you belong to that beastly pornographic organisation'.

In essence Adorno's book is a radiogenic exploration of his central belief about the way commodification conceals truth, how radio propaganda can serve as a mechanism for reifying consciousness, and how Christian Fascism used audio rhetorical techniques to mask and convene a phantasmagoric trail of anti-Semitism and totalitarianism (Crook 2001:240).

In a way Martin Luther Thomas's addresses on the radio were the audio cues for the open-air prison perceived by many people in areas of the world subjugated by German Nazi, Italian Fascist and Japanese military aggression. In other respects Adorno's critique of Thomas was an explanation of Nazi radio propaganda techniques. There are a number of comparisons with the use of radio by Hitler and Goebbels. Adorno precisely explains how the sound medium and the fascist radio star have an intimate marriage when exercising the ideology of personality in private psychological space (240).

Fascist radio orators personalised talk, bridged the gap between broadcaster and listener in an intimate psychological dance of real or fabricated confessional. Adorno claimed that the cold objectified world of despair, isolation, and loneliness within the listener could be emotionally manipulated when replaced with a vicarious psychological leader who had cleverly equivocated the ambiguity of characterisation. Strength was juxtaposed with weakness, the human with the superhuman, and the distant emotional perspective with the close. Here was a fabrication of truthfulness and it therefore did not matter if the confessions were actual or faked.

Adorno equates this technique with the so-called true stories of media celebrities and the role that these narratives played in pandering to the base human instincts of voyeurism. Fascist demagogues were therefore exploiting the advertising and communication techniques used to sustain present day celebrocratic dynasties.

These could be perceived as the neo-fascist inheritors of a media elite status in contemporary global market capitalism. Sexuality, pornography and voyeurism all play a part (240).

Adorno says 'Revelations about briberies or thefts supposedly committed by the foe, or discussions of his wife's illness or his financial difficulties which may even be invented' are equally effective (Adorno 2000:2–3). Adorno is acknowledging that it is useful to maintain an arbitrary attitude to accuracy and verisimilitude. The personal touch is therefore a camouflage or audio mask designed to hide or obscure his real aims. Adorno also recognises the function of satisfying the libido of the listener through being treated as the psychological insider. Adorno explains that Thomas is 'essentially an advertising expert in a highly specialized field' (28). In order to reify religious bigotry into political and racial hatred the advertising techniques are more important than the ideas to be sold. Whether the audience is esoteric or exoteric – a dichotomy explained in terms of committed ideological audience and general listeners – it does not matter if the content is illogical and contradictory.

It is more important to strike the politics of lack and engender fear, insecurity, sexual inadequacy, emotional and spiritual loneliness and personal worthlessness. Here we have another link between the fascist propaganda techniques of the 1930s and the contemporary marketology of global capitalism. The emotional nature of the radio medium conjoins with the emotive racket of religion. Adorno distinguishes the anti-religionist style of German fascism with the manner in which Thomas and presenters like him perverted religion into an instrument of hate-propaganda (Crook 2001:241).

The location of Christian bigotry in the 'false myths of Christ-killers, of the Pharisee, of the money-changers of the temple, of the Jew who forfeited his salvation by denying the Lord and not accepting Baptism' (Adorno 2000:77) were torches for anti-Semitism. The emotional nature of radio as a medium could be exploited through ideological baiting and hitting the nerve points of political controversy. Adorno concludes by claiming that Thomas is aiming for 'authority by brutal, sadistic oppression' and his ultimate dream is 'the unification of the horrible and the wonderful, the drunkenness of an annihilation that pretends to be salvation' (130–1) (Crook 2001:241).

Parallels with Sefton Delmer's fake demagogue *Der Chef*

Lawrence C. Soley and John Nichols observed that the purpose of 'strategic stations' such as *Der Chef* on GS1 was to:

> transcend the immediate combat situation. [. . .] Strategic clandestine stations are operated over an extended time period with a long-range purpose. The purpose is only rarely to promote a battlefield victory. The long-range objective of the British clandestine station [known as] Gustav Siegfried Eins was, for

example, to promote divisions between Nazi commanders and professional military men. Its objectives were not linked to an immediate military goal.

(Soley and Nichols 1987:42)

It is fortunate that a sociological audience research study on the efficacy of the GSI was conducted by an American academic in the years immediately after the Second World War. Although the field-work interviewing depended on audience memory, at least the recall was relatively immediate. This was set out by Howard Becker in the *American Sociological Review* in April of 1949 in a paper entitled: 'The Nature and Consequences of Black Propaganda'. His research indicated that initially the deception had a useful impact, but there was also a rapid decline in recognising verisimilitude:

> A survey conducted immediately after the war found that 75 percent of German listeners reported initially believing that Gustav Siegfried Eins was broadcasting by mobile truck from inside Germany, as it claimed. The initial belief declined as the station continued to operate. Less than 10 percent of the respondents reported believing the station after it had operated for 14 months.
>
> (Soley and Nichols 1987:22)

The British PWE was a counterpart to the German Büro Concordia. GSI could have stood for 'George Sugar One' and Soley and Nichols state that it was the literal translation of Gustav Siegfried Eins. The name also sounded like a code for Geheimsender 1 (Secret Transmitter 1) and Generalstab 1 (General Staff 1). Soley and Nichols write:

> The ambiguous name was intentionally selected so that listeners would provide their own interpretation for the station's name [. . .] For two and a half years, *Der Chef* hammered at the same theme, emphasizing the divisions between German military commanders and Nazi party leaders. By 1943, when the station was finally silenced, its credibility was low. Few German listeners believed the fiction that the clandestine transmitter eluded detection and confiscation by authorities for so long a period (Becker 1949). Despite the loss of credibility, the station maintained until the very end the myth that it broadcast from German territory. The station signed off with the claim that it was being seized.
>
> (47)

The performing voice of *Der Chef* was a refugee from Nazi Germany called Corporal Paul Sanders, who had moved to Great Britain from Berlin before the outbreak of the war. As well as characterising *Der Chef*, he worked during the Blitz with a London bomb disposal squad. Another German exile, the journalist Johannes Reinholz, wrote the scripts. He had also fled Germany before World War II started (Soley and Nichols 1987).

The participating creativity and performance of dissident and exiled Germans in this fictional deception on clandestine radio intersects with the deconstruction of the neo-fascist radio demagogue Martin Luther Thomas by Adorno.

Many of the narrative techniques of right-wing cynicism identified by Adorno in Martin Luther Thomas's rhetoric are present in the style and strategy of communication by *Der Chef* in his addresses. They include the concept of the 'Lone Wolf', the 'little, big man', the exploitation of emotionalism, nostalgic reference points, his role as messenger, the punctuation of his language with racy human interest, 'the pornographer's bait', and the idea that he is being hunted and persecuted. Both forms of manipulative radio rhetoric exploit a personalised conspiracy between broadcaster and isolated listener. *Der Chef* substitutes Luther Thomas' ideological and religious bait with the tawdry and sleazy bait of pornographic gossip.

Der Chef was characterised and plotted through a psychological dramaturgy rooted in the reality of US broadcasting facticity. Mimesis and the construction of apparent authenticity were the vital strategies to deceive and manipulate German listeners. The suspension of disbelief depended on narrative poise and accomplishment in writing, direction and performance.

The director and dramaturgist of *Der Chef*, Sefton Delmer, wrote a violent and climactic end for the character when he concluded that the phenomenon had outlived its usefulness. As Delmer wrote 'So "Der Chef" had to die – "caught at last". Alas, in dying "The Chief" suffered the only bad slip-up of his long career. For he died twice!' (Delmer 1962:76).

Unfortunately, the production standards of transmission did not match those of dramaturgical creativity:

> A transmitter engineer, knowing no German and unaware of the final nature of the broadcast – complete with tommy-gun salvo and gruff 'Got you, you swine!' – went through his usual routine and repeated the record an hour after the broadcast that was supposed to be his last. Fortunately I heard it. I have never met anyone else who did.
>
> (Delmer 1962:76)

RADIO STUDIES METHODOLOGY

The UK's Quality Assurance Agency for Higher Education commissioned and agreed a benchmark statement for the teaching of communication, media, film and cultural studies in 2002 and revised it in 2008. What follows to the end of the chapter is an attempt to provide an expression of this reference in terms of radio studies (QAA 2008).

An academic enquiry will endeavour to examine the ways in which radio cultural and media organisations intersect with general political and economic processes (questions of 'political economy'), the ways in which radio accounts of the world

FIGURE 3.2
Mr J.C.W. Reith, Managing Director of the British Broadcasting Company (Lewis 1924: opposite page 21). Reith, Managing Director of the BBC from 1922–29, was then Director General until he left in 1937. He is said to have founded the ethos of public service broadcasting and advocated the 'brute force of monopoly'.

are created and how they mediate symbolically between the individual and society (questions of 'representation'). The first managing director and Director-General of the BBC, John Reith is continually referenced in histories of the BBC and British broadcasting. Reith was in charge and the effective leader of a monopoly during Broadcasting's radio age between 1922 and when he left in 1937. His complicated personality, and political and social prejudices, might be said to have resulted in the embodiment of the BBC as a media institution or ideological materialisation in the content of its programming during this period. Table 3.5 sets out some issues arising from this intersection between powerful individuality and institutional and cultural context.

We also need to explore the ways in which social radio interactions may operate through circulating meanings and systems of representations (questions of 'discourse'), the ways in which people appropriate and use radio cultural texts and practices (questions of consumption) and the ways in which understandings of self and the world are formed in relation to such radio texts and radio communicative practices (questions of 'identity').

We should also investigate the relations between systems of radio meanings and relations of social and political power in radio institutions, broadcasting and reception and the nature of inequality in this cultural matrix ('questions of ideology'). BBC Radio Four is seen as the United Kingdom's most powerful radio institution. Its breakfast news and current affairs programme *Today* is said to be the programme of choice for decision-makers and the political, social and cultural elite. But as a broadcasting institution it has found that its journalism can be its Achilles heel in the context of the country's involvement in a controversial war in Iraq in 2003. The death of the weapons' inspector Dr David Kelly and the subsequent Hutton Enquiry resulted in the resignation of the BBC's chairman and Director General, an event unprecedented in its history. A profile of issues arising out of Radio Four's role as a media institution is set out in Table 3.6.

Table 3.5 Some issues arising from the intersection between powerful individuality and institutional and cultural context

---

Cultural imperatives raised by the personality and role of John Reith – First Managing Director and Director-General of the BBC

Platonic and authoritarian leadership of the BBC as a cultural and political media institution
Reith believed his leadership of the BBC from 1922 to 1937 was a vindication of the idea that there should be a monopoly of broadcasting in Britain. In his book *Broadcast Over Britain*, in 1924 he wrote '. . . I believe it has been proved conclusively that in a concern where expansion is so rapid and the problems so unique, unity of control is essential' (Reith 1924:70).

Self-fashioning in the manner of a Renaissance Prince
It might be argued that the BBC was an embodiment of Reith's personality.

Quick and decisive judgements and leadership
Reith had a reputation for making up his mind and not being prepared to compromise or relent e.g. his attitude to commercial radio, television, etc.

Setting out a public service agenda: information, education and entertainment
Reith believed the understanding of entertainment should extend beyond 'to occupy agreeably'. He suggested: '. . . it may be part of a systematic and sustained endeavour to recreate, to build up knowledge, experience and character, perhaps even in the face of obstacles. Broadcasting enjoys the co-operation of the leaders of that section of the community whose duty and pleasure it is to give relaxation to the rest, but it is also aided by the discoverers of the intellectual forces which are moulding humanity, who are striving to show how time may be occupied not only agreeably, but well' (18).

Negotiating interests of the audience and interests of the state
Historical research indicates he was deft at recognising the extent and limits of contextual executive power and how to advance the development and survival of the BBC, e.g. management of the BBC during the General Strike of 1926.

The brute force of monopoly: allaying state anxiety about licensing mass media electronic communications power
Reith recognised that public corporation status put the BBC at constitutional arm's length of government and in its privilege of monopoly gave government and legislature a sense that they had potential control over broadcasting, which at the same time benefited the BBC.

Stifling diversity of ownership and content

From local initiative and enterprise to national control and censorship 1922 to 1929
It is not widely appreciated that wireless technology meant the BBC started as local radio stations, but when it was possible to transmit nationally, Reith took the opportunity of imposing a homogenous rather than heterogeneous policy of content production.

The public corporation: a social democratic ideological concept, distancing the source of funding and buffering interference of state executive and legislature

---

Cult of personality
Reith was an admirer of Mussolini and Hitler; in the new Broadcasting House, he had an admiral's bridge style office with its own open fire, and a Latin inscription:
TEMPLUM HOC ARTIUM ET MUSARUM ANNO DOMINI MCMXXXI RECTORE JOHANNI REITH PRIMI DEDICANT GUBERNATORES PRECANTES UT MESSEM BONAM BONA PROFERAT SEMENTIS UT IMMUNDA OMNIA ET INIMICA PACI EXPELLANTUR UT QUAECUNQUE PULCHRA SUNT ET SINCERA QUACUNQUE BONAE FAMAE AD HAEC AVREM INCLINANS POPULUS VIRTUTIS ET SAPIENTIAE SEMITAM INSISTAT.
Translation:
This Temple of the Arts and Muses is dedicated to Almighty God by the first Governors of Broadcasting in the year 1931, Sir John Reith being Director–General. It is their prayer that good seed sown may bring forth a good harvest, that all things hostile to peace or purity may be banished from this house, and that the people, inclining their ear to whatsoever things are beautiful and honest and of good report, may tread the path of wisdom and uprightness.

Reith's personal hypocrisy and ethical ambiguity present in BBC programming, staff and content
Sunday Mass, 'The Sabbath' programming, progress in women's employment, pensions and conditions, but discrimination against and intolerance of homosexuals, men and women involved in divorce and responsibility for any explicit expression of communism and 'political controversy'.

Table 3.6 A profile of issues arising out of Radio Four's role as a media institution

BBC Radio Four developed from the BBC Home Service **Radio Four replaced the Home Service on 30 September 1967** **It is regarded as the 'Crown Jewels' of BBC National Radio**
Almost 90 per cent of the station's 9.98 million weekly listeners are 35 or older. Its core audience is over 50. In the autumn of 2009, the then BBC Radio Four Controller Mark Damazer went on autumn tours to the universities of Cardiff, Derby and Bedfordshire to 'bring Radio Four to audiences more au fait with YouTube than *You and Yours*, the station's consumer programme' (Dowell 2009). He said: 'The centre of gravity for Radio Four will always be older, but it's not a club. Anybody can join in, whatever the age'. The controller at the time of writing is Gwyneth Williams who was director of BBC World Service English.
How the previous BBC Board of Governors reviewed Radio Four in 2003–4: 'BBC Radio Four's remit is to use the power of the spoken word to offer programmes of depth which are surprising, searching, revelatory and entertaining. The network aims to offer in-depth and thoughtful news and current affairs and seeks to engage and inspire its audience with a rich mix of factual programmes, drama, readings and comedy'.
Audiences to Radio Four oscillate with a reach between 9.5 and nearly 11 million listeners. In London, the UK's most competitive radio marketplace, the network remains top for reach and share.
News and current affairs provide the spine for Radio Four and the network has maintained its strong position in this genre. Audience research shows that six out of ten radio listeners consider BBC Radio to be the best source of radio news – and Radio Four leads the other BBC radio stations in being considered the best provider of news. These figures were not significantly affected by the Hutton Inquiry arising from a controversial live radio question and answer with reporter Andrew Gilligan on the *Today* programme just after the invasion of Iraq in 2003.
In 2007–8 BBC Radio Four's annual budget was just over £100 million. By comparison, BBC Seven's annual budget was £6–9 million. BBC Seven was rebranded as BBC Radio Four Extra in 2011.
In-house dramas in London and in Manchester and the North cost 50 per cent more than the other English regions and Wales, and over three times those in Scotland. The median cost per hour of in-house productions of plays for Radio Three and Radio Four are £23,965 and £24,000 respectively. This is higher than plays commissioned from independent production companies (for Radio Three, by 29 per cent; for Radio Four, by 8 per cent). The cost of independently produced plays is 20 per cent higher on Radio Four than it is on Radio Three.
In 2008 the National Audit Office was commissioned to carry out a review of the 'efficiency of radio production at the BBC', and in the following year reported that: 'The remit of Radio Four is to be a mixed speech service, offering in-depth news and current affairs and a wide range of other speech output including drama, readings, comedy, factual and magazine programmes. The service should appeal to listeners seeking intelligent programmes in many genres, which inform, educate and entertain. Radio Four should be available every day for general reception in the UK on FM, Long Wave, Medium Wave in some parts of the UK, DAB digital radio and digital television platforms, and it may be simulcast on the internet'. The report stated that Radio Four intended to produce a net saving on costs efficiencies of £4.3 million between 2009 and 2013.
In 2007 BBC Radio Four celebrated its fortieth birthday with the publication of several books including its authorised history by David Hendy, *Life On Air: A History of Radio Four*, published by Oxford University Press and *And Now on Radio 4: A Celebration of the World's Best Radio Station* by features editor Simon Elmes, published by Random House.
The BBC 2 TV documentary 'Close Up' transmitted in 1999 could be seen as a critical and mocking portrayal of BBC Radio Four culture and the controversial tenure of the controller James Boyle who was succeeded a year later by Helen Boaden, now Director of BBC Journalism.

Radio studies also seeks to develop wider understandings of the diversity of forms of culture, as well as new understandings of the increasingly pivotal role that radio communication plays in the social, economic and political organisation of contemporary societies. In exploring the centrality of forms of radio media, radio communicative and expressive practice in contemporary life, there may be some merit in focusing on the continuing regeneration and development of radio creative professional practice within the media and cultural industries.

These practices could be subjected to systematic, critical and reflective analysis. There may also be some advantage in attempting to reappraise received cultural traditions and canons and explore the ways in which radio media, communication and cultural activities and processes are central to the organisation of everyday social and psychological life, and to the ways in which human social groups conceive their identities.

This academic enquiry raises a number of important questions. To what extent are radio communicative, cultural and aesthetic systems and practices imbued in people's lives? To what extent are radio industries significant areas of employment and responsible for creative professional practice that requires systematic, critical and reflective practice? To what extent do the radio industries play key roles in generating symbolic resources through which people individually and collectively imagine the past, define the present, and develop projects for the future? To what extent does 'radio culture' play an increasingly pivotal role in economic and political organisation at local, regional, national, international and global levels? To what extent do large-scale institutions whose structures, operations, regulation and performance require sustained analysis increasingly organize the public forms of radio?

We can investigate whether it can be said that the opportunities to participate actively in the central sites of radio public culture and communication are differentially distributed in ways that are linked to prevailing structures of economic and symbolic power and central axes of social division such as ethnicity, gender, nationality, sexuality and social class. Can we identify beyond mainstream institutions, many other groups, communities, and alternative producers who contribute to the communicative life of any society, often in ways which produce challenging or oppositional forms of understanding and symbolic and affective life?

What are the informed debates on the political, legal and ethical aspects of radio communication and culture, which take into account the above points and which consider the importance of access and inclusion in public communicative life for a democratic society?

Radio communication, culture and society

In many respects we are on a journey exploring radio communications, culture and society. We are seeking an understanding of the roles of radio communication systems, modes of representations and systems of meaning in the ordering of societies, an awareness of the economic forces that frame the radio media, cultural and creative industries, and the role of such industries in specific areas of contemporary political and cultural life. If possible we want to achieve a comparative understanding of the roles that radio media and/or cultural institutions play in different societies. Furthermore, we would also gain from studying the roles of radio cultural practices and radio cultural institutions in society and understanding the nature of particular radio media forms and genres and the way in which they organise understandings, meanings and effects. It would also be useful for us to seek to achieve an understanding of the role of radio technology in radio media production, access and use, an understanding of the ways in which participatory access to the central sites of radio public culture and communication is distributed along axes of social division such as disability, class, ethnicity, gender, nationality and sexuality.

As radio communication is so diverse it would be useful to achieve an understanding of the dynamics of public radio and everyday radio discourses in the shaping of culture and society. There would be merit in analysing the ways in which different social groups may make use of radio cultural texts and products in the construction of social and cultural realities, cultural maps and frames of reference.

Radio histories

Clearly, the study of the history of radio communication is a key area of our subject. We want to achieve an understanding of the development of radio media and cultural forms in a local, regional, national, international or global context. We also want an understanding of the social, cultural and political histories from which different radio media and cultural institutions, modes of communication, practices and structures have emerged.

To achieve this objective we should do our best to acquire an historically informed knowledge of the contributions of radio media organisations to the shaping of the modern world. It would also be useful to find an understanding of the interconnectedness of radio texts and contexts, and of the shifting configurations of radio communicative, cultural and aesthetic practices and systems. In our enquiry we shall be investigating the historical evolution of particular radio genres, aesthetic traditions and forms, and of their current characteristics and possible future developments.

In our investigation of radio studies we need an understanding of the history of radio communication and media technologies and recognition of the different ways in which the history of and current developments in media and communication can be understood in relation to technological change. We will be analysing the historical development of practices of radio cultural consumption (including subcultural forms and everyday lived practices), in order to gain an awareness of the ways in which critical and cultural theories and concepts have developed within particular radio contexts.

Radio processes and practices

The subject of radio studies inevitably touches on the creative dynamic of radio theory and practice. We will gain much insight into this dynamic by trying to understand the processes linking radio production, circulation and consumption. We will also benefit from appreciating the processes, both verbal and non-verbal, whereby people manage radio communication face-to-face and in the context of groups.

When we achieve an awareness of the processes of radio cultural and subcultural formations and their dynamics, we can go on to seeking an understanding of the key radio production processes and professional practices relevant to media, cultural and communicative industries, and of ways of conceptualising radio creativity and authorship. The radio professional, technical and formal choices that realise, develop, or challenge existing practices and traditions, and the possibilities and constraints involved in radio production processes, all merit consideration.

The real practice of radio engages knowledge of the legal, ethical and regulatory frameworks that affect radio media and cultural productions, circulation and consumption and an understanding of how radio media, cultural and creative organisations operate and are managed. Much enjoyment of the subject will be gained from trying to understand the material conditions of radio media and cultural consumption, and of the cultural contexts in which people appropriate, use and make sense of media and cultural products. In a global capitalist world we need to achieve an awareness of how radio media products might be understood within broader concepts of culture.

Radio forms and aesthetics

Many practitioners of radio production and communication talk about their expression in terms of art as much as product. Our academic journey should, therefore, seek an understanding of the aesthetic and formal qualities at play in radio and their relation to meanings, in particular cultural forms. We can gain an insight into the cultural and social ways in which radio aesthetic judgments are constructed and radio aesthetic process experienced. In our examination of the role that radio aesthetic and other pleasures and judgments play in the production and maintenance of social arrangements we can also gain an awareness of the range of works in radio, which generate different kinds of aesthetic pleasures. For example we can gain an appreciation of the narrative processes, generic forms and modes of representation at work in radio media and cultural texts and an understanding of the ways in which specific radio media and their attendant technologies make possible different kinds of aesthetic effects and forms.

It could be argued that the practice of radio communication can be interpreted by achieving an understanding of the audio and verbal conventions of radio. How do people engage with radio cultural texts and practices and make meaning from them?

Radio culture and identity

We need to appreciate the complexity of the term 'radio culture' and an understanding of how it has developed. We also need to investigate the ways in which
identities are constructed and contested through engagements with radio culture.
A useful approach would be to analyse how disability, class, ethnicity, gender,
nationality, sexuality and other social divisions play key roles in terms of both access
to the radio media and modes of representation in radio media texts.

Our studies should enable us to acquire some insight into the different modes of
global, international, national and local radio cultural experience. How do they interact in particular instances? How are the forms of radio media and cultural
consumption embedded in everyday life, and how do they serve as ways of claiming
and understanding identities? One of our overall objectives is to try and define the
relationship between discourse, culture and identity in the context of radio studies.

Analysing media radio texts

Our subject area inevitably involves the development of critical vocabulary that can
assist us in our analysis of radio communication as a 'text'. We can be assisted
by the use of language and terminology created and developed by the practitioners
and participants of radio communication. This is a communicative phenomenon
informed by thinking practitioners as well as analytical theorists.

The aesthetic

In all radio communication there is an aesthetic appreciation of the nature of sound
story telling. Radio texts involve the use of narrative and action, the performance
of presenters and actors, the casting of actors and presenters, the process of
sound design, the style and art of editing, the style and art of musical composition,
the selection and use of music and the quality of radio writing, which can also be
described as 'radio literature'.

There is a philosophy of sound expression that transcends ideas of phenomenology,
art for art's sake, cultural materialism and propaganda. The nature of radio communication is also talked about in terms of genre, formalism, montage, and the
role of auteur/masterpiece versus collaborative ensemble. Radio editing involves
the multi-tracking of streams of narrative sound direction. There appears to be
concentration on the intertwining or weaving of at least five potential parallels that
include the word, sound effects (SFX), music, and the postmodern use of archive,
documentary interview. The very idea of postmodernism in radio demands analysis,
reflection and considerable intellectual discussion.

Radio practice has a considerable technological vocabulary that becomes symbolic and culturally significant. There are debates about the implications of the binary
oppositions in analogue and reel-to-reel, and digital and hard-disc, live versus

pre-recorded, concealed versus revealed recording presence, surveillance versus participation.

It could be argued that there is an established grammar of sound editing and production software. What were the implications of the process of splicing in analogue editing and audio montage in digital multi-track editing? What is meant by the point of listening and microphone fields, microphone angles, kinesics versus proxemics – that is, movement and distance, sonic panning, and the purpose and effect of designing sound in terms of the monophonic, the stereophonic and the surround? How do we define and understand the concepts of sound processing, rendering, compression, location and more binary oppositions in the tension and choice between mise-en-scène versus studio sound stage, and live orchestration versus pre-recorded precision? This can also be understood as the difference between creative chances versus mathematical logarithm in the aesthetic of mixing sound.

What is meant by the establishing edit, extreme close up/close microphone and extreme long shot/ambient acoustic, high angle, low angle and reverse pick up? A 'new media' world raises the dimension of split perspectives of media perception. What are the differences between analogue, digital and Internet dimensions of transmission, sound and text, sound and visual design?

The social

The social analysis of radio texts explores issues of ideology, representation, construction of identity and contemporary politics. We need to understand the process of radio textual canonisation, the application of power, hegemony and the role of gatekeepers, the implications of conflict studies, censorship, moral panics and content. Radio institutions and texts will be influenced and determined by issues of economy of scale, race, class and alienation, access to the means of production, broadcasting and distribution, audience studies/reception, cultural imperialism, the idea of the dominant culture and subcultures of radio. What is the difference between mainstream radio and art house radio and how can this be defined? Are there specific media radio events that can be identified and studied in terms of social action? How do we understand the nature of popular culture and high culture in radio broadcasting? How are radio stereotypes constructed? How do we apply theories of feminism and an analysis of radio genders in relation to radio texts? What is the relevance of theoretical discourse on tabloidisation or McDonaldisation of production in relation to radio?

The economic

This aspect of our studies explores the economic dimension of radio culture. How are radio institutions and products budgeted and financed? What are the implications of access to state grants and issues of politico-economy in relation to radio communication? There are also binary oppositions in our analysis in terms of capitalism versus socialism, and market economy versus the social market. How does competition and monetarism relate to radio production and consumption? What are the implications of the concepts of 'New Deal' and public investment? How do we analyse the economic nature of institutions of production and transmission, and oligopolies in the radio industry? What are the implications of tradecraft and union agreements, closed shops, cartels, etc., contracts and the law of financing? How do we understand radio in the context of multimedia merchandising, sponsorship and advertising, pay on demand, copyright fees, distribution of budget and programming income and business synergies?

The hermeneutic

The word hermeneutics is derived from ancient Greek and relates to the construction of meaning. In radio studies we borrow from other academic disciplines such as literature and film studies to engage the concepts of the diegetic and non-diegetic. We have already been provided with an academic discourse of texts, deconstruction, critical autonomy, semiotics and codes that can enable us to talk about aural signs and binary oppositions. Issues in docudrama, documentary and the factual/fictional debate can obviously be applied to radio practice and content. *Cinéma-vérité* can be transmogrified into an understanding of *audio-vérité*. We can discuss sound improvisation, sonic iconography and sound motifs. The representation of control, voice of god, voice of participants negotiated by editing, voice of participants with own negotiated content, subjectivities and aspiration to the myth of objectivity, and intertextuality (relation to other texts and media) all have their place and function in the analysis of radio texts.

RADIO STUDIES THEORY – SOME CONCLUSIONS

Fundamentally, the subject of radio studies is about articulating a sense of understanding and meaning about radio media texts. This is in a dynamic social relationship whereby the radio texts are the result of radio media production and consumed by radio media audiences. Radio media institutions play a significant role in this triple nexus of radio production-texts-audiences. These radio studies factors are negotiated and mediated by some key intellectual themes. They include the determining concepts of power, change and continuity, knowledge, values and beliefs. In a sense the determining concepts are also key cultural multipliers.

The student of radio studies will be preoccupied with the creation and construction of radio and its discovery and revelation by audiences. We have been able to identify perennial questions: Should the development of radio be seen as expressions of underlying social trends or change? Might radio be a catalyst for particular forms of social change? Is the radio representation of politics as spectacle debasing political knowledge, shifting the focus from political processes to an unhealthy preoccupation with image and performance often described as 'dumbing down'?

Can our political beliefs really be influenced by the demeanour and relative glamour of political individuals in radio texts? Do the radio media really have the power to shape the values of a nation/society?

In our study of the history of radio we are likely to consistently consider a social anxiety of cultural decline particularly when a capitalist political economy drives radio production to serve the interests of free market populist democracy. We investigate the processes of radio mediation, celebritisation, celebrity culture and celebrocracy. When we engage in textual analysis we are looking to define the preferred reading and meaning, the context, the radio communicative conventions, the radio genre and the deployment of stereotypes, celebrity personas and the cultural trend towards tabloidisation. The evolution of the BBC's national music channel The Light Programme into BBC Radio Two is an interesting potential case study since it demonstrates how the BBC as a media institution responds to the changing fashions in moving demographics. The music played on BBC Radio Two in 2011 and listened to mainly by middle-aged people was followed by teenagers fifty years earlier. The music then was associated with youth culture, marginalised from mainstream broadcasting and could only be listened to on pirate radio stations, moored outside British territorial waters, and foreign stations transmitting from Europe, such as Radio Luxembourg. In 2008 two of the station's highest profile comedy artists, Russell Brand and Jonathan Ross were found to have misjudged the acceptable limits of taste and decency in prank calls to the actor Andrew Sachs. The case history became an intriguing challenge to celebrity power and a cross-generational confusion over social and cultural values (Ofcom Adjudication 2009). Table 3.7 outlines some of the issues arising out of BBC Radio Two's role as a media institution exercising considerable influence and communicational power.

When considering the production of radio we evaluate the organisational approach, the political economy approach, and the post-structuralist approach. We ask how the various institutions of radio production construct media messages. We ask whether radio media messages are wholly or mainly a result of the internal dynamics of radio media institutions, the profit motive or of discourse. We also try to determine how the main theories understand the production of radio media messages.

When considering the issue of power, the organisational approach views radio media workers as autonomous agents with an ability to cooperatively shape media content. The political economy approach, or 'cultural industries' approach, views power as systemically unequal, with more powerful institutions exercising control of the media production of radio messages/texts. Michel Foucault's notion of power sees radio media messages as circulated through radio media technologies and internalised into the very core of individual and collective identities.

When considering the influence of social knowedge, values and beliefs it is possible to see the mutual negotiation of radio texts by publicists and journalists as one premised upon a shared understanding of cultural codes and icons. Political

Table 3.7 Some of the issues arising out of BBC Radio Two's role as a media institution exercising considerable influence and communicational power

BBC Radio Two – BBC Radio's most listened to national channel
Radio Two is used by the BBC to reinvent a middle-aged/mature person's music format that attracts the largest popular audience in the radio market. BBC Radio recognises that youth culture changes with fashion and generation and that music selection policy and presentation profile needs to shift with the evolution of tastes and cultures through time.
Radio Two took over from the 'Light Programme' in 1967. Its schedule still maintains a balance between music disc jockeying, comedy, documentaries and events, but with the music format predominating.
Current format could be defined as 'Adult Contemporary' or AOR, although the station is also noted for its specialist broadcasting of other musical genres. The day-time playlist features music from the 1960s to various current chart hits, album and indie music.
Radio 2, like the BBC's other national radio networks 1, 3 and 4, is transmitted on a variety of platforms including analogue wavelengths, online, mobile, digital radio and television, and Internet downloads. At any time around 70 of the station's programmes are available for listen again download/podcasting and the station's music playlist is published with a spirit of accountability. Listeners can go online and find out each week which new releases are being added.
Its national audience share was 15.9 per cent as of June 2010. Its speech programming could be described as 'infotainment'. The old 'Light Programme' channel was a significant broadcaster of popular audio drama 'soap' serials such as 'Mrs Dale's Diary' and 'Waggoners' Walk'. In the 15 minute current 'Archers' episodic length, though, it currently does not appear to brand itself as a carrier of audio drama programming.
In its history it has been associated with 'middle of the road' music and middle-aged broadcasting voices such as Terry Wogan on breakfast, Ken Bruce, Derek Jameson, Jimmy Young, 'Diddy' David Hamilton, and John Dunn at what became known as drive-time. Radio Two became the first 24-hour radio station in the UK in 1979. The only 'senior' woman broadcaster strongly associated with the station's history was Sarah Kennedy.
As this generation of broadcasting personalities became as old as its original audience a new generation of presenters, who had previously been associated with the pirate radio of the 1960s and Radio One youth culture through the 1970s and 1980s joined: Steve Wright, Chris Evans, Simon Mayo, Mark Radcliffe, Stuart Maconie, Janice Long, Johnnie Walker and Bob Harris. Jeremy Vine – the introducer to Panorama – has become the consumer investigative champion and political interviewer, which had been the legendary role of Jimmy Young.
The station's controversies have contributed to a number of intense political debates about the BBC's failure to reflect the ethnicity profile of British society and the excessive 'greed' of BBC talent contracts being associated with poor taste humour. Sarah Kennedy was reprimanded in October 2007 after joking that she had almost run over a black pedestrian because she could not see him in the dark and a further 'off the cuff' comment in July 2009 that she thought Enoch Powell had been 'the best prime minister this country never had'.
Johnnie Walker was suspended in April 1999 after being surreptitiously filmed by the *News of the World* offering to sell cocaine. He was fined £2,000 and agreed to do drug rehabilitation and was then reinstated by the BBC.
In October 2008 an edition of the Russell Brand show with guest and fellow BBC Radio Two presenter Jonathan Ross featured the leaving of four prank messages on actor Andrew Sachs's answer-phone. This included offensive remarks about his granddaughter and use of foul language. The content was exposed by the *Daily Mail* newspaper group and generated a moral panic about the lack of regulation of poor taste and inappropriate behaviour by excessively paid presenters. The BBC Trust and Ofcom investigated complaints arising out of the broadcast. Ofcom imposed a fine. Russell Brand announced his resignation from the BBC shortly followed by the controller at the time, Lesley Douglas, and middle management executives. Jonathan Ross was suspended from the BBC without pay for twelve weeks and eventually left the corporation.

economists see the marketing of radio cultural codes and icons in terms of a certain kind of knowledge being manipulated and formatted to make profits. A post-structuralist position sees radio cultural codes/messages/icons as discourses that are types of knowledge that regulate the values and belief patterns of mass audiences.

When considering the issue of continuity and change, the organisational theoretical approach registers some of the small scale processes behind the changes in radio messages/codes/icons within the organisational continuities provided by media institutions. Political economists emphasise the changing structure of the radio market in cultural products and the increasing concentration of radio media ownership and control as guided by the permanent pressure to maximise profits and market share. Post-structuralists tend to see the production of radio discourses as part of an ongoing struggle over audience identities.

Different approaches to the study of radio audience start from different assumptions about whether the audience is active or passive – they start from different theoretical positions that involve assumptions about what people are like. In the context of the reception of radio broadcasting what happens between audiences and the media? What are the gender perceptions and the role of fandom? Different approaches to the study of radio audiences pay different amounts of attention to what audiences actually say about their experiences – they adopt different methodological positions. Answers to the question 'why are radio audiences attracted to radio messages/codes/icons?' depend on the theoretical and methodological assumptions of the person who is providing the answer.

We are interested in the role of charisma in radio characterisation, the nature of radio as a culture industry, how audiences derive pleasure and pleasurable re-working of texts, the politics of lack (particularly in radio advertising), subversive readings of radio texts and the nature of radio cultural capital. What are the tactics of the socially weak in relation to powerful radio communication? What work goes into the making of a radio media product? What social values and beliefs are radio media products associated with? Why are radio audiences attracted to radio media products?

CHAPTER 4

Sound practice and theory in stage theatre

PRACTICE

John L. Bracewell believes that the purpose of a sound designer's creative engagement is professionally aesthetic and essentially collaborative:

> the idea or ideas expressed in the playwright's script together with the director's interpretation of what that script means. The designer's function is to create, within the range of ideas expressible within his or her medium, a set of conditions that will promote the insights and the emotional character implicit in the script and the director's interpretive purpose. Those conditions may be the color and shape of the clothing worn by the characters; the depth, texture, color, and form of the surroundings in which the characters act; or the qualities of the auditory environment and/or the musical analog of the characters' feelings and interactions.
>
> (Bracewell 1993:206)

Consequently Bracewell argues that the stage sound designer must be engaged with the auditory world of the drama and that can only be achieved with a fundamental immersion and creative commitment to the entire drama in all its dimensions. Sound design in theatre is physical, dynamic and three-dimensional. Michael Gillette then grounds the student with six practical considerations:

1   What is the budget for sound?

2   What equipment does the theatre own? What is its status?

FIGURE 4.1

The Three Witches in a rehearsal of *Macbeth* (Arnheim 1936: facing p. 145). Radio drama in performance from the 1930s. The three witches of Shakespeare's *Macbeth*, arms outstretched, scripts in the air seen from the perspective of the microphone.

3   Are there any local shops where I can rent equipment?

4   Will the actors' voices need to be reinforced?

5   What are the director's thoughts regarding the use of non-specific background sound?

6   What is the rehearsal schedule for sound? When will the director want the effects tape? When will he or she want the microphones working for the reinforced sound?

(Gillette 2008:518)

Beyond these precepts, Gillette advises the sound designer to research everything within the script and fathom the director and writers' (if living) creative aspirations or thoughts on what the sound could achieve by way of dramatic purpose, incubate ideas for a while, make a clear selection of sound archive and already produced materials that are appropriate for the production, implement the plan by: 'stop talking and start recording' and evaluate with the production team through rehearsal and sometimes adjustment during the performance run.

Bracewell advises the sound designer to keep in mind seven functions of sound in theatre that divide into the categories of the dramatic in terms of directly advancing or conditioning the progress of the drama, the aesthetic in terms of designating 'matters that have to do with personal interpretation of the immediate emotional character of the drama' (Bracewell 1993:207), and the practical in terms of referring to audience comfort and effectively perceiving the actors' voices. He further subdivides the functional tools as: audibility; motivation (environmental ambience); music; vocal alteration; vocal substitution; extension of dramatic space/time; and mood. He explains the function of extension of dramatic space/time as using 'sounds in ways that refer to events outside of the physical space and/or time frame of the dramatic action' (208). In picking up the technical principles referred to in Chapter 2, Bracewell reminds the sound designer that the controllable properties of sound are: intensity; frequency; duration; envelope; timbre; and directionality. More often than not the style of the production will determine many aspects of the sonic texture and its content.

This consideration is contextualised by the conventions of theatrical practice that in the western tradition tend to fall into the fields of naturalism, realism, stylisation, formalism and abstraction. Sound designed for naturalistic stage drama usually aspires to fidelity to real-world environments. Realism is faithful to the real-world soundscape, but according to Bracewell 'not so slavishly as in naturalism', and he suggests that realism 'admits artistic license in arranging the events and components of the dramatic surroundings' (209). In stylisation Bracewell suggests distortion 'for the purpose of aesthetic emphasis is permitted' (209). In formalism Bracewell explains that the patterns of sound 'are more important in and for themselves than realistic patterns that might be characteristic of an actual locale' (209). In abstraction Bracewell says the production of sound is 'reduced to their most fundamental shape or form' and 'usually demands the juxtaposition of several elemental entities in a collage of elements designed to make a larger and more complex pattern' (210).

The acoustic ecologist, composer and sonic artist John Levack Drever has analysed the indexical, to use the semiotic vocabulary of C.S. Pierce, origin of sound design in British stage theatre and referenced 'the emanations into the auditorium of an off-stage sound resembling that of a baby's cry – apt that a baby's cry should be given the honours – in Arthur Law's *The Judge* on 2 August 1890' (Drever 2010:192). This derives from the original research of J.W. Stedman who retrieved the event from theatrical history and reported it in 'Enter a Phonograph' in the *Theatre Notebook: A Journal of the History and Technique of the British Theatre*. Stedman's fascinating article revealed that the sounds played out to the live audience were those of a real infant who had been recorded by one of the earliest Edison Phonographs (Stedman 1976:125). The technology of the time in playing back through a horn apparatus would be highly primitive by today's standards and in the discussion of the signal to noise ratio issue, Drever argues:

> In its day the use of such technology would have been of high novelty even pioneering value. It is an attempt at a literal rendition of the script's instruction.

Such a naturalist reading may well have been influenced by Edison's marketing prowess.

(Drever 2010:192–3)

In 1996 I had the privilege of being invited by the director Tom Morris to sound design a production of Samuel Beckett's *All That Fall* to be performed in complete darkness before live audiences in one of the theatres at the BAC in Battersea, South West London:

a sound design operated for every second of the performance from seventeen speakers, two surround sound fields of transmission and three stereophonic fields of reproduction. Two computers, a sub-woofer to enhance base frequency and a substantial array of digital technology were deployed to provide near 'virtual reality' acoustic space to operate in time to the actors' script cues.

(Crook 1999:67)

Morris would develop the concept of theatre in the dark in subsequent festivals and it might be argued that he instigated a genre of theatrical experience equivalent to the sound film aesthetic advanced by Derek Jarman in *Blue* (1993). Sixteen years further on, computer digitisation and three-dimensional sound production and reproduction means that the *All That Fall* experimentations are somewhat commonplace. Sonic immersion and directionality is so much more realisable and flexible. But while technological progress gives the director and sound designer realms of creative possibilities, John A. Leonard wisely cautions that less is sometimes best:

Tempting as it is to fill our studios and theatres with all the latest kit, and our productions with continuous sound effects and music, very often less is more. To give a final example, in W. Somerset Maugham's play, *Our Betters*, the stage directions call for the sound of a pianola (a mechanical piano using punched rolls and a vacuum system operated by the player pedalling a pair of bellows) to be heard off stage. A point is given for the music to begin, and another for the music to stop, however in a recent production, the director was concerned that the constant background music would distract from some fairly crucial plot development. The answer was extremely simple: during the scene, various characters enter and leave the room; when the door was open, we heard the pianola, and when the door was closed, we did not. The problem was solved by reducing the amount of sound in the show rather than increasing it.

(Leonard 2001:9)

PRODUCTION PRACTICE

The companion website provides detailed resources on the practical approach to designing the sound for theatre productions. Many directors willing to harness the

FIGURE 4.2
Flight of steps in a new dramatic radio studio in Berlin in the 1930s (Rudolf Arnheim 1936, *Radio*, London: Faber & Faber, p. 48). Live radio drama needed to operate in spatiality and generate realistic acoustics; not unlike the sound in modern stage theatre.

creativity offered by actors and other artists participating in the collaborative experience of theatre are increasingly recognising the contribution that can be made by original sound designers and the developing potential of digital surround technology.

Practice Project One: Developing a full portfolio of soundtracks for a traditional classical stage play that meets or addresses the original text's sound stage directions. What further layers of sound and effects can you contribute to a contemporary production given the possibilities offered by digital technology and surround sound?

Practice Project Two: Select the script of a radio play and evaluate how you would produce the script for a theatre space. Maximise the potential for theatrical use of sound in your production and design the portfolio of soundtracks that would engage with your envisioned use of set, physical acting performance and blocking and lighting.

THEORY

It might be argued that in the English-speaking world there is great potential for more academic writing and analysis of the role of sound in theatre. An outstanding entry into the field was made by Ross Brown in his 2009 text *Sound: A Reader in Theatre Practice*. It would appear this volume is the first serious attempt to intellectually discourse the relationship between sound and theatre, with a focus on sound's interdependence and interaction with human performance and drama. Brown intelligently examines how sound can be interpreted to create meaning and the volume includes an additional range of sources on sound design and symbiotic perspectives from beyond the discipline.

There is certainly evidence of a significant exploration of creative sound practice in contemporary theatre. In 2010 the directors Faith Collingwood and Jacqui Honess-Martin presented two seasons of *Auricular* at Theatre 503 in London. Collingwood explained the intentions of *Auricular* as:

> Auricular is a season of staged, live audio drama. Theatre director Jacqui Honess-Martin and I set up the season to push the boundaries of audio drama and staged drama, and to investigate the potential for a hybrid medium by combining the two. We've been experimenting with fusing pre-recorded aural landscapes, live spot/foley FX and theatrical performance techniques for a live audience to great effect.
>
> (Collingwood 2010)

There are a few examples of excellent academic analysis of theatre sound in various journals such as *Contemporary Theatre Review*, *Theatre Journal*, *Theatre* and *Dance and Performance Training*. For example, in 'Scenographies of the Everyday in Contemporary German Theatre – Anna Langhoff and Sasha Waltz Restage the Family Drama', Denise Varney explored 'beyond the text' and discoursed the aural image-making of two German stage productions that were celebrated for shedding light on tensions and debates in postreunification Germany. In her consideration of *Frieden Frieden* and *Allee der Kosmonauten*, Varney observed that the choreography:

> like the performed written text in theatre, is immersed in layers of visual and aural signification. The musical score, for instance, is a collage of contemporary music, folk accordion, classical strings, jazz and 'DDR-Schlager' (East German hit songs) compiled by Lars Rudolph and Hanno Leichtmann. Sound effects, which include the sound of rewinding and fast-forwarding of tape, refer to the overall mediatization of culture that is the context for the work.
>
> (Varney 2008:63)

There is no doubt that the palpable signs of creative and dynamic experimentation with sound in live theatre are beginning to stimulate intellectual reflection and analysis of the aesthetic, cultural, social and political role of the sound dimension in the stage arts. A selective suggestion for further reading is set out below.

A SELECTIVE SUGGESTION FOR FURTHER READING: THEATRE/STAGE/DRAMA PRACTICE AND THEORY TEXTS

Bracewell, John L. (1993) *Sound Design in the Theatre*, Englewood Cliffs, New Jersey: Prentice Hall College Division.

Brown, Ross (2009) *Sound: A Reader in Theatre Practice*, London: Palgrave Macmillan.

Burris-Meyer, Harold (1959, 1979) *Sound in the Theatre* (1st edition, 1959, Radio Magazines, Revised edition 1979), New York: Theatre Arts Books.

Collison, David (2008) *The Sound of Theatre*, Eastbourne and New York: Professional Lighting and Sound Association (PLASA).

Finelli, Patrick M. (2002) *Sound for the Stage (Applications and Techniques)*, Cambridge: Entertainment Technology Press.

Gillette, Michael J. (2008) *Theatrical Design and Production: An Introduction to Scenic Design and Construction, Lighting, Sound, Costume, and Makeup* (6th edition), London and New York: McGraw-Hill Higher Education.

Green, Michael (1958) *Stage Noises and Effects*, London: Herbert Jenkins, Practical Stage Handbooks.

Kay, Deena and LeBrecht, James (2009) *Sound and Music for the Theatre: The Art and Technique of Design* (3rd edition), Oxford and Burlington, MA: Focal Press, an imprint of Elsevier.

Leonard, John A. (2001) *Theatre Sound*, New York: Routledge.

Napier, Frank (1948) *Noises Off: A Handbook of Sound Effects* (3rd edition), London: Frederick Muller.

Walne, Graham (1990) *Sound for Theatre (Stage and Costume)*, London: A&C Black.

CHAPTER 5

Sound practice and theory in music

PRACTICE: VOICE AND INSTRUMENTAL PLAYING

The first human musical instrument was the voice. And it may seem odd, but the first paragraph in this chapter is emphasising how important it is to be able to play the human voice like a musical instrument. Anyone professionally working, performing or designing sound, should, in my opinion, participate in singing groups and/or learn a musical instrument. It provides practical and emotional understanding of rhythm, timbre, tone, melody and the grammar of music. This enhances editing and expands an appreciation of the potentialities of sound structuring and mixing. I would strongly urge taking up any musical instrument even if there is no chance whatsoever of playing it well. Indeed the beauty and charm of playing it badly is now recognised in sound art as a legitimate and culturally valid expression of musical sound as is certainly the case with the Portsmouth Sinfonia:

> The Portsmouth Sinfonia is unusual among orchestras in that it does not require members to display any particular proficiency in their instrument of choice. Of course, there are talented members, some of whom even play their regular instruments. The result is a – how should we put this? – unique sound. The genius is that there are sufficient players with sufficient mastery of their instruments that the resulting sound is recognisable. Just.
>
> (BBC 2001)

In fact the Portsmouth Sinfonia is celebrated throughout the world, has been recorded and continues to play sell-out concerts. Its website at www.portsmouthsinfonia.com

archived its achievements. Indeed, it might be argued that you do not have to have the so-called 'musical ear' and to be in tune to produce music. The celebrated John Cage created '4′33″', which has been broadcast on the national classical BBC channel Radio Three. '4′33″' has no musical notation in its score. The pianist goes to the piano, sits down and does not play any keys. He or she might operate a stopwatch in order to precisely time the performance of silence. But the key question is, are the pianist and his or her audience actually hearing complete silence? As the late Mr Cage once said:

> I have nothing to say
> and I am saying it
> and that is poetry
> as I needed it
>
> (Cage 1973)

The sound philosopher Brandon LaBelle picks up the debate eloquently when writing:

> what we hear in the work of Cage, and reflected in works such as 4′33″ as well as Cartridge Music (1960), which calls for the amplification of small objects, is an emphasis on the very source of sound itself, as objects, electronic circuits, and real bodies: a reference to sound as found upon the actual object of its source, as in the piano and the sounds of the audience, shopping malls and their soundtracks (and their proposed removal), or the multiplicity of the live action and their unimpeded and chance-driven juxtapositions.
>
> (LaBelle 2008:24–5)

The companion website provides training resources on improving the vocalisation and articulation of the voice. It is the instrument that all audio communicators and broadcasters need to use when interviewing, narrating and talking to the listener. Audio broadcasters need to develop and train the seven variables of the speech personality: pitch, volume, tempo, pronunciation, vitality or enthusiasm, voice quality and articulation (Hyde 1971:59). As the legendary voice coach of Britain's Royal Shakespeare Company, Cicely Berry, once said:

> Ideally, I suppose, every actor wants to know that his voice is carrying what is in his mind and imagination directly across to the audience. He wants it to be accurate to his intention and to sound unforced. He wants to know that he is carrying the listener with him for, in the end, it is the voice which sets up the main bond between him and his audience. Certainly this is true of Western theatre. He knows that the audience want to be let into this character, and that this will happen to a large extent through his voice and speech. Above all, he wants it to be interesting.
>
> (Berry 1987:14)

PRACTICE PRODUCTION

Practice Project One: Arrange to record a singing soloist or a performing poet or speaker in a public location using coincidental XY microphones or a portable recording unit with inbuilt capsules with an XY configuration. The project requires coordination with the companion website resources. You will need to carefully consider selecting the appropriate microphones and recording unit and position them a little below the mouth to reduce the sound of breathing and thereby pick up more of the lower frequencies. You will also need to select and control the recording environment to minimise indirect sound. The reverberation time in the interior space needs to enhance rather than interfere with the resonance of your singer/speaker's voice.

Practice Project Two: Arrange to record a pianist playing a grand piano. Again the musical style is not important. Because the piano produces sound from its whole structure you might find that omnidirectional microphones pick up a richer stereo field. You should try to position the microphones between the strings and the soundboard in order to achieve a balance between the attack and sustain of the piano's sound waves and varying distance should enable you to adjust the brightness and softness of the recordings.

Practice Project Three: Arrange to record an acoustic guitarist performing any style but without singing vocals. Again, using a tripod/stand and clip, position your microphones pointing towards the sound hole between the fifteenth and seventh fret at an angle from the neck of the guitar. This position should offer enhanced pick-up of the mid and low frequencies that give the guitar its rich and specific sound as an instrument. Also attempt a recording with the microphones pointing where the neck is attached to the soundboard in order to have a recording of the sharper sound of guitar strumming.

The companion website offers advice and exercises with multimedia resources on recording further arrangements of instruments: drums/percussion, electric guitar or bass, classical ensemble, synthesisers and electric organs and even orchestras and symphonies. A further multimedia resource explores recommended guidelines and practice for using a recording studio.

THEORY

It would seem that the focus of academic musical theory at the time of writing is exploration of sonic philosophy in the context of the Post-Second World War avant-garde and the cultural study of popular music. This preoccupation is by no means unhealthy. In fact, as has already been acknowledged in Chapter 1, the seminal readers *Audio Culture: Readings in Modern Music*, edited by Christoph Cox and Daniel Warner, and *The Auditory Culture*, edited by Michael Bull and Les Back, are a healthy result of this preoccupation.

A selection of further recommended reading can be found at the end of the chapter. However, the companion website pays homage to the wider framework of music as a discipline though with some limitations. Music has been a key source of social, cultural, religious and political sound communication across centuries of human civilisation. It seems somewhat negligent not to investigate jazz, chromatic harmony, twentieth-century music, French music from 1870, Romanticism and Post-Romanticism, musical nationalism, mid-eighteenth-century Russian music, Mendelssohn and Schumann, Beethoven, Hadyn and Mozart, the Pre-Classical Style between 1740 and 1780, Bach, Handel and eighteenth-century music, late Italian and French Baroque music, Renaissance music from Germany and the Netherlands, French and English music from the seventeenth century, early, middle and late Italian and English Renaissance music, and the plainsong and choral traditions from the medieval period. This long list does in fact constitute merely a single chapter in the history of music since it journeys across the story of only Western music.

The creative engagement with avant-garde forays into electro-acoustica, *musique concrète* and postmodernist abstractions has enriched the critical vocabulary of music and sound studies. The boundaries between human musical synthesis and musical environmental ecology appear to have dissolved and the debate certainly seems to be informing the discipline of academic music and its associated cross-disciplinary subjects. The English translation of *Sonic Experience: A Guide to Everyday Sounds* originally produced at the *Centre de recherche sur l'espace sonore et l'environnement urbain* in Cresson in 1995 gives us sonic definitions and concepts to understand, interpret and apply. We have compositional effects in the form of Doppler, rallentendo, Tartini; mnemo-perceptive effects in the form of asyndeton, ubiquity, metamorphosis; psychomotor effects in the form of Deburau, niche and repulsion; semantic effects in the form of dilation, perdition and sharawdji; and electroacoustic effects in wha-wha, wobble, wow and fuzz.

One of the more widely applicable cross-disciplinary terms used is anamnesis:

> An effect of reminiscence in which a past situation or atmosphere is brought back to the listener's consciousness, provoked by a particular signal or sonic context. Anamnesis, a semiotic effect, is the often involuntary revival of memory caused by listening and the evocative power of sounds.
>
> (Augoyard and Torgue 2006:21)

Augoyard and Torgue discuss the concept in terms of the personalisation of sound and the tradition of symphonic poems such as *The Sorcerer's Apprentice* and *Peter and the Wolf* (157).

Explanations for a selection of Augoyard and Torgue's critical terms are given on the companion website. For the present the very sound of their pronunciation conjures mantras and magical chants that might be said to invest the study of sound with a new romanticism.

FURTHER RECOMMENDED READING

Music and philosophy of senses and perception

Birdsall, Carolyn and Enns, Anthony (2008) *Sonic Mediations: Body, Sound, Technology*, Newcastle-upon-Tyne: Cambridge Scholars Publishing.

Bull, Michael (2000) *Sounding Out the City: Personal Stereos and the Management of Everyday Life*, Oxford and New York: Berg.

Bull, Michael and Back, Les (eds) (2003) *The Auditory Culture Reader*, Oxford and New York: Berg.

Cox, Christoph and Warner, Daniel (eds) (2008) *Audio Culture: Readings in Modern Music*, New York: Continuum.

Dolar, Mladen (2006) *A Voice and Nothing More*, Cambridge, Massachusetts: The MIT Press.

Ihde, Don (2007) *Listening and Voice: Phenomenologies of Sound* (2nd edition), Albany, New York: State University of New York Press.

Kahn, Douglas (2001) *Noise, Water, Meat: A History of Sound in the Arts*, Cambridge, Massachusetts: The MIT Press.

Levin, David Mitchell (1989) *The Listening Self: Personal Growth, Social Change and the Closure of Metaphysics*, London and New York: Routledge.

Nancy, Jean-Luc (2007) *Listening*, Mandell, Charlotte (trans.), New York: Fordham University Press.

Serres, Michel (2008) *The Five Senses: A Philosophy of Mingled Bodies (1)*, Sankey, Margaret and Cowley, Peter (trans.), New York: Continuum.

Szendy, Peter (2008) *Listen: A History Of Our Ears*, Mandell, Charlotte (trans.), New York: Fordham University Press.

Toop, David (1999) *Exotica: Fabricated Soundscapes in a Real World*, London: Serpent's Tail.

Toop, David (2001) *Ocean of Sound: Aether Talk, Ambient Sound and Imaginary Worlds*, London: Serpent's Tail.

Toop, David (2005) *Haunted Weather: Music, Silence and Memory*, London: Serpent's Tail.

Toop, David (2010) *Sinister Resonance: The Mediumship of the Listener*, New York: Continuum.

Voegelin, Salomé (2010) *Listening to Noise and Silence*, New York and London: Continuum.

Voice and speech

Alburger, James R. (1999) *The Art of Voice Acting: The Craft and Business Performing for Voice-Over*, Boston and Oxford: Focal Press.

Berry, Cicely (1990) *Your Voice: And How to Use It Successfully*, London: Virgin Books.

Berry, Cicely (1992) *The Actor and His Text*, London: Virgin.

Gondin, William R. and Mammen, Edward W. (1970) *The Art of Speaking*, London: Made Simple Books, W. H. Allen.

Hyde, Stuart W. (1971) *Television and Radio Announcing* (2nd edition), Boston: Houghton Mifflin Company.

Karpf, Anne (2006) *The Human Voice: The Story of a Remarkable Talent*, London: Bloomsbury.

Mills, Jenni (2004) *The Broadcast Voice*, London and New York: Focal Press, an imprint of Elsevier.

Shaw, Bernard Graham (2000) *Voice-Overs: A Practical Guide*, London: A&C Black.

Trewin, Janet (2003) *Presenting on TV and Radio*, London and New York: Focal Press, an imprint of Elsevier.

Turner, J. Clifford (1993) *Voice and Speech in the Theatre* (2nd edition), Morrison, Malcolm (ed.), London: A&C Black.

Music and cultural theory and history

Chanan, Michael (1994) *Musica Practica – The Social Practice of Western Music from Gregorian Chant to Postmodernism*, London: Verso.

Chanan, Michael (1995) *Repeated Takes: A Short History of Recording and Its Effects on Music*, London and New York: Verso.

Emmerson, Simon (2000) *Music, Electronic Media and Culture*, Aldershot, Hampshire: Ashgate.

Goodman, Steve (2010) *Sonic Warfare: Sound, Affect, and the Ecology of Fear*, Cambridge, Massachusetts, and London: The MIT Press.

Hegarty, Paul (2009) *Noise/Music: A History*, New York and London: Continuum.

Katz, Mark (2004) *Capturing Sound: How Technology Has Changed Music*, Berkeley and London: University of California Press.

Kittler, Friedrich A. (1999) *Gramophone, Film, Typewriter*, Winthrop-Young, Geoffrey and Wutz, Michael (trans.), Stanford, California: Stanford University Press.

Leyshon, Andrew, Matless, David and Revill, George (eds) (1998) *The Place of Music*, New York and London: Guilford Press.

Milner, Greg (2009) *Perfecting Sound Forever: The Story of Recorded Music*, London: Granta Books.

Schwarz, David (1997) *Listening Subjects: Music, Psychoanalysis, Culture*, Durham, North Carolina: Duke University Press.

Stern, Jonathan (2003) *The Audible Past: Cultural Origins of Sound Reproduction*, London and Durham, North Carolina: Duke University Press.

Music and popular culture

Bennett, Andy (2000) *Popular Music and Youth Culture*, London: Macmillan Press; New York: St Martin's Press.

Bennett, Andy (2001) *Cultures of Popular Music*, Buckingham and Philadelphia, Pennsylvania: Open University Press.

Brewster, Bill and Broughton, Frank (1999) *Last Night a DJ Saved My Life: The History of the Disc Jockey*, London: Headline Book Publishing.

Chapman, Robert (1992) *Selling the Sixties: The Pirates and Pop Music Radio*, London and New York: Routledge.

Frith, Simon and Goodwin, Andrew (eds) (1990) *On Record, Rock, Pop, and the Written Word*, London and New York: Routledge.

Martin, Peter J. (1995) *Sounds and Society: Themes in the Sociology of Music*, Manchester and New York: Manchester University Press.

Mundy, John (1999) *Popular Music On Screen: From the Hollywood Musical to Music Video*, Manchester and New York: Manchester University Press.

Negus, Keith (1999) *Music Genres and Corporate Cultures*, London and New York: Routledge.

Negus, Keith and Hesmondhalgh, David (2002) *Popular Music Studies*, London: Bloomsbury Academic.

CHAPTER 6

Sound practice and theory in film

PRACTICE

The first sound heard with film in the early cinemas was music, performed live on acoustic instruments. Although musical composition is a subject that cannot be contained in a short chapter it has aesthetic properties that blend strongly in the mix with dialogic speech, narration, sound effects and ambience. It has been widely argued that one of the most successful collaborations between a film director and musical film composer was that of Alfred Hitchcock and Bernard Herrmann. Herrmann embraced film as 'the most important artistic development of the twentieth century' (Herrmann 1999). He realised that a composer who writes for the cinema reaches a worldwide audience. He was bold enough to argue that any film could not 'come to life' without the assistance of the musical track. Herrmann observed that Hitchcock knew how to use music to increase the intensity of suspense, whereas Orson Welles knew how to use music to develop and identify the emotions and attitudes of his characters as though the music operated a leitmotif.

Herrmann recalled that in musical composition he had to think of the landscapes of Hitchcock's screenplays. In the case of Orson Welles' films he had to concentrate on characters in specific time and place harbouring attitudes of hatred, love or revenge. Herrmann provides a succinct definition of the discipline that a stream of sound must provide in the overall mix of vision, narration, dialogue and mise-en-scène:

> Film music must supply what actors cannot say. The music can give to an audience their feelings. It must really convey what the word cannot do. If you're dealing with an emotional subject, this is the complete purpose of a film score.

But if you are dealing with a Hitchcock film, or a film by anyone with enormous skill, the film is only made of segments put together and artificially linked by dissolves, or cuts, or montages (there are many ways a film can be made) it is the function of music to cement these pieces into one design that the audience feels the sequence is inevitable. Now it is one of the paradoxes of cinema music that music correctly used can be music of very poor quality and effective or can be music of magnificent quality and also serve its purpose. But the strange thing about cinema [. . .] is that no one really knows why music is needed. After a lifetime in it, I cannot tell you why. [. . .] If you were to look at a film without music, it would be almost unbearable to look at it.

(Herrmann 1999)

PRODUCTION PRACTICE

Practice Project One: Arrange to provide the sound recording and design contribution to a short film. It might be wise to restrict your first project to a film lasting no more than five or ten minutes. The learning process is more realisable in a college with audio-visual production facilities that can be hired and where there are courses providing teaching and learning for sound, digital video and film production.

Practice Project Two: Select a ten minute sequence of already produced film from any time, digitally strip it down to its visual track only and then post produce a new soundtrack through sound design. It is suggested that you approach the project in two phases. In phase one you utilise sound effects and music already available from libraries and you record your actors in a studio in as near conditions of automatic dialogue replacement (ADR) as you can manage. In phase two you originate and create all of the sound effects yourself through location recording and Foley production sound stage.

Multimedia resources are provided on the companion website to prepare you with skills acquisition guidance. It is hoped you should be able to achieve entry-level operational ability.

It is recommended that you produce sound for film in a team as the technical and creative demands of film operate on an industrial scale of production. In field and location recording, a team of three people can work together to achieve a balance of microphone positioning (whether by boom or lapel), live sound mixing where more than one microphone is being used, and record keeping of the sound log. Well-established professionals in film sound production argue that there can never be enough sound recorded in terms of correct positioning, sound direction angles, ambience and keeping the soundtrack recording going long before the assistant director's shout of 'action' and 'cut'.

Film sound recording and design is effectively broken down into five key phases and the companion website seeks to illustrate these in greater depth:

FIGURE 6.1
Film crew of *Beyond the Forest* on location with the sound recordist holding
microphone suspended from boom, August 2010 (Photo: copyright Tim Crook).

1 Research and study of the script, consultation with the director and
producer

2 Field and location recording

3 Sound effects

4 Building and operating a Foley sound stage

5 Digital postproduction, sound design, multi-track layering and mixing with
musical composition, and final mix-down

The audio postproduction process is normally the most time-consuming, expensive,
sophisticated and complex. In fact audio postproduction usually takes longer than
CGI and visual film editing. Hilary Wyatt in the influential text *Audio Post Production
for Television and Film* sets out an overview of the skills and creative decision
making. She suggests that it can boil down to eight objectives:

• To enhance the storyline or narrative flow by establishing mood, time,
location or period through the use of dialogue, music and sound effects.

• To add pace, excitement and impact using the full dynamic range available
within the viewing medium.

• To complete the illusion of unreality and fantasy through the use of sound
design and effects processing.

- To complete the illusion of continuity through scenes which have been shot discontinuously.

- To create an illusion of spatial depth and width by placing sound elements across the stereo/surround sound field.

- To fix any problems with the location sound by editing, or replacing dialogue in post production, and by using processors in the mix to maximize clarity and reduce unwanted noise.

- To deliver the final soundtrack made to the appropriate broadcast/film specifications and mastered onto the correct format.

(Wyatt and Amyes 2008:3)

THEORY

There is no shortage of high quality books and journal articles academically analysing film sound and some have already been referenced in Chapter 1. Below are some selected recommendations for further reading. I would suggest that the seminal readers *Film Sound: Theory and Practice* (1985) and *Sound Theory, Sound Practice* (1992) are good preliminary reading platforms. The essays suggest that sound in film studies congregates in five streams of enquiry: the cultural history of sound in cinema; the political economy of sound production in the context of film producing institutions; the philosophy and psychology of film sound perception or the psychoacoustics of film sound reception; original, style-setting and unique exponents of sound in film art; and marginalised or neglected film texts and cultures and their associated soundtracks.

It has already been recognised in Chapter 1 that academic analysis of film sound has made as much of a contribution to gestating a critical vocabulary of sound as a cultural phenomenon as any other discipline. Film studies seems open to the multidisciplinary, interdisciplinary and cross-disciplinary symbiosis. Altman's edited volume moves beyond mere textual analysis to acknowledge that:

> Today, political writers learn their trade from cinema scriptwriters; the politicians try to deliver their one-liners with the panache of movie comedians; and now television and cinema have begun to edit dialogue in imitation of political sound bites. Everywhere we turn, we find sound providing a perpetual and highly charged interchange between cinema and its culture.
>
> (Altman 1992:14)

SOME SELECTED RECOMMENDATIONS FOR FURTHER READING

Practice: film sound design

Chion, Michel (1994) *Audio-Vision: Sound on Screen*, Gorbman, Claudia (trans. and ed.) and Murch, Walter (Foreword), New York: Columbia University Press.

Rose, Jay (2008) *Producing Great Sound for Film and Video* (3rd edition), London and New York: Focal Press, an imprint of Elsevier.

Sonnenschein, David (2001) *Sound Design: The Expressive Power of Music, Voice and Sound Effects in Cinema*, Studio City, California: Michael Wiese Productions.

Viers, Ric (2008) *The Sound Effects Bible: How to Create and Record Hollywood Style Sound Effects*, Studio City, California: Michael Wiese Productions.

Wyatt, Hilary and Amyes, Tim (2008) *Audio Post Production for Television and Film: An Introduction to Technology and Techniques* (3rd edition), London and New York: Focal Press, an imprint of Elsevier.

Yewdall, David Lewis (2007) *Practical Art of Motion Picture Sound* (3rd edition), London and New York: Focal Press, an imprint of Elsevier.

Theory: film sound texts

Altman, Rick (ed.) (1992) *Sound Theory, Sound Practice*, London and New York: Routledge.

Dickinson, Kay (ed.) (2002) *Movie Music, the Film Reader*, London and New York: Routledge.

Dickinson, Kay (2008) *Off Key: When Film and Music Won't Work Together*, Oxford: Oxford University Press.

Fairservice, Don (2001) *Film Editing: History, Theory and Practice*, London and New York: Manchester University Press.

Herrmann, Bernard (composer) (1999) *Hitchcock 100 Years: A Bernard Herrmann Film Score Tribute* [audio CD], United States: Milan Entertainment, 73138 35884-2.

Lastra, James (2000) *Sound Technology and the American Cinema*, New York: Columbia University Press.

Sider, Larry, Freeman, Diane and Sider, Jerry (2003) *Soundscape: The School of Sound Lectures 1998–2001*, London and New York: Wallflower Press.

Smith, Steven C. (1991) *A Heart at Fire's Center: The Life and Music of Bernard Herrmann*, Berkeley: University of California Press.

Weis, Elizabeth and Belton, John (eds) (1985) *Film Sound: Theory and Practice*, New York: Columbia University Press.

CHAPTER 7

Sound practice and theory in animation and games

PRACTICE

The combination of games sound with animation sound is somewhat artificial, but as with film the key commonality is that both in theory and practice there is clear bifurcation of production in terms of musical composition and recording, and dialogic, narrative action and drama track through music, ambience and effects. They are also usually communicated with a fusion of sound with vision, though the computer game *Papa Sangre* (www.papasangre.com/) produced by the London-based multimedia company Somethin' Else represents the development of a digital/computer version of the popular South American parlour game Sangre y Patatas, which could be described as a slasher audio movie style Blind Man's Buff. The player is plunged into the sonic immersion field of a castle populated by sound-activating monsters and the folkloric storytelling motifs of Mexico's day of the dead carnival.

The music composer and sound designer of *Papa Sangre*, Nick Ryan, is developing version 2.0, which is going to take the listener into 'big field functionality':

> For me this is the absolute holy grail of this technology. We will enable people to navigate the augmented reality of sound by walking round a big field and we can superimpose things on that space.
>
> (Burrell 2011, 28 March)

GPS activated 'sound spots' in which listeners moving about environmental and geographical space to receive through binaural headphone listening has already been experimented with by BBC Radio Drama and the Hackney Podcast in London.

The companion website sets out some practical suggestions and workshop resources with case histories on practical sound production for multimedia games. Musical composition and editing needs to supply soundtracks for intro, closing, and credit sequences, cinematic sequences, menu screen frames, gameplay ('music occurring during gameplay' Marks 2008:232), plot advancements, cut scenes, tie-ins and what Aaron Marks describes as 'Win' and 'Lose' finale cues:

> When you win, an optimistic flourish of sound rewards your efforts. When you happen to be less successful, the music is either demeaning or mildly encouraging – prodding you to try again.
>
> (233)

Marks notes that the composer also needs to understand the requirement for tracks that can work interactively, provide loops, ambience and what are known as 'stingers':

> stingers are bits of music which are triggered to call attention to a sudden change in the storyline or other significant events. These pieces of music are generally very short in length, beginning and ending within a few seconds; and while noticeable over the other music, they are created to remain within the theme using similar characteristics such as instrumentation and production.
>
> (236)

The production of music for animation, according to Robin Beauchamp, is infusing emotion into the life of an animated character and in particular what he describes as the 'underscore':

> In reality audiences readily accept underscore as a normal part of the cinematic experience, so underscore became the dominant element in the music stem. Underscore is almost always original music tailored in length and character to promote the narrative. Underscore is *thematic* (containing strong melodies) or *ambient* in nature. It is often used as a substitute for ambience, providing a sonic background that promotes fantasy and elicits emotional response.
>
> (Beauchamp 2005:45)

Digital sound production of narration, dialogue, spot and Foley effects and ambiences for games and animation are not in principle any different from the processes and imperatives being driven in film production sound. The scale, of course, is determined by budgets, but it might be argued that games players, so accustomed to high technological application in home cinema, are now expecting high standards of sound immersion and experience in their gaming. Indeed there is evidence that the 3D revolution in digital media is making waves in the palm-top reading applications with Pan Macmillan endeavouring to match high quality soundtracks to sequences of Apple iBook's version of Ken Follett's *Fall of Giants* (Burrell 2011, 28 March).

The key difference in mix-down or sound blending between animation sound and games sound is that a completed linear soundtrack can be synchronised to the animation. In games digital production the sound has to be produced on planes of interactivity, lateral narratology and nonlinearity. Subsequently soundtracks have to be encoded and written into special games production software that could be described as a game writing 'engine'. A sound designer for film selects one track from a range of available sounds that will serve the single dramatic purpose for that moment in the linear film narrative. The games sound designer has to create a world in which 'any permutation, any possibility of sound, any gun, any explosion, etc. is potentially available' (Deutsch 2011:52). As games sound designer Ben Minto explained to Stephen Deutsch in 2011:

> For any given event, say a bullet impact on metal, we will design twenty sounds. We don't decide which one plays at which time; all the engine says to us is, 'a bullet has hit metal. What should I do? We say, pick from one of these twenty sounds.' [. . .] You can tell it to pick randomly between them or to avoid patterning (a bit like iTunes). If I fired twenty bullets you would get a variety of sounds. Obviously, we can apply filters, delays, pitch and such. You could also construct sounds from 'smaller grains' as it were, and can build up the sound 'on the fly'. But to choose something as unimportant as a single bullet sound within a group, we leave that to the engine.

PRODUCTION PRACTICE

Practice Project One: Select an established short sequence of animation and by collaborating with a musical composition student design the soundtrack for it. Your software options are varied. It is possible to synchronise using the free digital video-editing software Windows Moviemaker and Apple Mac iMovie. An ideal collaborative project in a school would be to join a digital animation production team and take responsibility for the soundtrack design.

Practice Project Two: Select a first person shooter game and set about producing a portfolio of sound sequences and tracks for the various lateral, non-linear and interactive video sequences. It will be difficult, without specialised software, to match the sound to the sequences. Hence it would be more advantageous to collaborate with a computer games production course, if it is being run at your school, to volunteer your sound design enthusiasm, skills and aspirations.

THEORY

Video and computer games provide powerful sources for the analysis of media institutions and their intrinsic texts in terms of representations and ideology. The media products marketed as PC, Xbox, playstation, gameboy, mobile phone/PDA and tablet app games are very big business with billions of pounds of investment. The budget for a new game can be equivalent to that of a Hollywood film block-buster. Consequently, as well as being recognised as a significant practical employment area in the emerging cultural industries, the social matrix surrounding their consumption and construction of meaning is enormously significant. Most games engage the player in a narrative state of conflict where there is an opposition with the enemy.

Many games through sonic characterisation, leitmotifs and the dialectical texture of primary, protagonistic and secondary characters can be criticised for constructing 'aliens' and the historical retrieval of prejudices and negative contructions of the present 'Other'. Gender representations are also fruitful lines of academic textual enquiry. Female characters are often created within games narratives as the Proppian helper for the first person shooter protagonist.

The representation of violence has not only triggered media moral panic debates but precipitated calls for regulation and classification. As Stephen Deutsch has said:

> Some of the most popular games, known as 'first person shooters' attempt to create a world which is positioned somewhere between the arcade-like hyper-reality of a Hollywood action film and the simulation experience of the 'real thing'.
>
> (Deutsch 2011:46)

An interesting area for investigation is how and why games audio designers attempt to create 'believable worlds' by matching and aspiring to the virtual reality immersion sound production techniques of contemporary cinema.

In the seminal text *Game Sound: An Introduction to the History, Theory, and Practice of Video Games Music and Sound Design*, Karen Collins discusses games interactivity as being able to physically act with an agency when consuming media. She argues that playing a video game:

> involves both diegetic and extradiegetic activity: the player has a conscious interaction with the interface (the diegetic), as well as a corporeal response to the gaming environment and experience (extradiegetic).
>
> (Collins 2008:3)

In her study of the process of game audio development, she established that rather like film, audio decisions are a series of negotiations with teams of people who have to work together with complex digital computer programming technologies. Mixing is an area where aesthetic output and the functional processes of sound are constantly negotiated. She presciently predicts that new multitouch screens:

> in which images (and potentially sounds) can be moved about on a screen by hand, suggest that a participatory element to audio's consumption will become

a standard in which users may physically manipulate the playback of the audio that they want to hear. Moreover, the rise of dynamic audio in theme parks, museums, educational tools, appliances, toys, art installations, and other areas in our lives suggests that even outside of video games, this cultural form is having a significant impact on the ways in which sound is produced, mediated, and consumed.

(171)

Selected further reading for these subject areas is found below.

PRACTICE AND THEORY TEXTS ON COMPUTER GAMES AND ANIMATION SOUND

Beauchamp, Robin (2005) *Designing Sound for Animation*, London and New York: Focal Press, an imprint of Elsevier.

Childs, G.W., IV (2007) *Creating Music and Sound for Games*, Belmont, California: Thomson.

Collins, Karen (2008) *Game Sound: An Introduction to the History, Theory, and Practice of Video Game Music and Sound Design*, Cambridge, Massachusetts, and London: The MIT Press.

Deutsch, Stephen (2011) 'From *Battlezone* to *Battlefield* Immersion, Sound and Computer Games: An Interview with Ben Minton', *The New Soundtrack*, 1(1): 43–56.

Graber, Sheila (2009) *Animation: A Handy Guide*, London: A&C Black Publishers.

Kuperberg, Marcia (2002) *A Guide to Computer Animation for TV, Games, Multimedia and the Web*, Boston: Focal Press.

Marks, Aaron (2009) *A Complete Guide to Game Audio for Composers, Musicians, Sound Designers, and Game Developers* (2nd edition), London and New York: Focal Press, an imprint of Elsevier.

Winder, Catherine and Dowlatabadi, Zahra (2011) *Producing Animation* (2nd edition), Boston: Focal Press.

Wright, Jean Ann (2005) *Animation Writing and Development*, Boston: Focal Press.

CHAPTER 8

Sound practice and theory in art exhibition and installation

PRACTICE

It could be argued that sound art installation and exhibition has done more than anything else to give the sound dimension of human expression and creativity the dignity, legitimacy, provenance and pervasiveness of a credible art form in its own right. Most critical and historical literature on radio seems to be blighted by an obsession with its 'Cinderella status'. I have always been intrigued by the tendency of visiting sound professionals and artists to Goldsmiths warning my students: 'Well by choosing radio and sound as your medium, you have clearly decided you are not seeking wealth and fame'.

Fortunately, in recent years we have had the great fortune of many outpourings of cultural confidence challenging these attitudes; not least Tony Gibbs in his beautifully designed and written book *The Fundamentals of Sonic Art and Sound Design*:

> times have changed and sound now asserts itself as a viable medium in its own right. It can no longer be relegated to a subordinate role, and now demands to be seen as one amongst equals: as a new and distinct medium and potential art form.

> (Gibbs 2007:8)

One of the glories of sound art practice is there are no limits and everything is possible. The artist can create three-dimensionally and design in exhibition or social and community space, an achievement recognised and already referred to in Chapter 1 in the case of 2010 Turner Prize winner Susan Philipsz whose 'sound sculpture' resonated under bridges in Glasgow as well as in one of the interior spaces of the Tate Modern. Gibbs provides a practical exposition of how sound design now *appears* in everyday life and then features, by way of interview, five contrasting examples of contemporary sound artists: Vicki Bennett, Max Eastley, Janek Schaefer, Simon Emmerson and Knut Aufermann. As Gibbs observes:

> From airports to the marketing of microprocessors, sound that is designed for a purpose is all around us. At a simple level, muzak is used in supermarkets and shopping malls to help mask unwanted noise and create an overall ambience and in a more detailed application, sonic branding is used to identify and reinforce products.
>
> (36)

The companion website contains an interview with the author, academic and sound artist Julian Henriques, which was recorded in stereo in the middle of his installation 'Circle of Sound Sculpture'. The exhibition accompanied a conference at Goldsmiths, University of London, 'Media and the Senses', where sound was debated in the context of the changing nature and definition of senses from an interdisciplinary perspective. Dr Henriques's sound sculpture was described as the exploration of:

> auditory geometry with the spatialisation of sound and sonification of space. Participants experience the sensory qualities of acoustic space (as distinct from the more usual visual space) and within this start to appreciate what an embodied auditory understanding of geometry might be (as distinct from

FIGURE 8.1
'Circle of Sound Sculpture' by Dr Julian Henriques 2011 (Photo: copyright Tim Crook). The sound design is controlled by complex logarithmic and geometrical computer digital design in surround and transmitted through eight different speakers to immerse visitors to the building who wander around for lectures and meetings.

geometry's more usual visual representations). The installation draws a continuous line of sound to describe the edges of an evolving series of geometrical
shapes around the listener, including a cube and the unsettling topological
shape of a möbius strip.

(Department of Media and Communications 2011)

The interview with Dr Henriques reveals a complex and creative collaboration with
sound designers from the discipline of computing and sound design in theatre
and that one of the purposes of the creation was to push the boundaries of digital
sonic exposition and perception. The software and hardware deployed are cutting
edge.

However, the ready access to digital sound editing tools and playback looping
means that sound artists can prepare their work through studio, laboratory,
computer and interactive production. Installation, exhibition and use of community
environment and performance is a matter of negotiation. It should also be
remembered that radio and Internet remain constantly accessible and effective
channels/platforms for sound artistic expression.

PRODUCTION PRACTICE

Practice Project One: Set up an Internet web-space platform on Wordpress to
exhibit a festival of sound art pieces where the options are to playback sound only,
combine sound with video and/or stills photography and paint, drawing or digital
graphics.

Practice Project Two: Organise and set up a sound art exhibition in interior space
that consists of your own work only or a collaboration with others (always more
enjoyable since you can share ideas, experience and skills). The installations should
have three dimensional options with sound operating in interior space with any
combination of additional artistic multimedia materials.

Practice Project Three: Organise and set up a sound art exhibition in community
space. This will require negotiation with the owners and controllers of the space
used. Ideally your work should be intersecting with everyday social behaviour of
people not necessarily specifically seeking to visit your sound art piece.

Guidance, resources and suggestions are provided on the companion website.

THEORY

There has been a veritable explosion of high quality academic writing and discourse
on the subject of sound art that effectively and creatively crosses the disciplines
of art and music. The recommended reading is wholly selective but should also be

juxtaposed with texts suggested in Chapter 5. As a starting point Barry Blesser and Linda-Ruth Salter's *Spaces Speak, Are You Listening? Experiencing Aural Architecture* provides a stimulating journey of thought-provoking chapters on auditory spatial awareness, the history of aural space, the relationship between aural arts and musical spaces, how media technology has invented virtual spaces for music, scientific perspectives on spatial acoustics and auditory spatial awareness as evolutionary artefact. I would argue that the writing is accessible. Even the first chapter steps off from the Winston Churchill quotation: 'We shape our dwellings, and afterwards our dwellings shape us' (Blesser and Salter 2007:1). *Sound Art: Beyond Music, Between Categories* by Alan Licht is another beautifully illustrated book from this genre with rich colour and black and white plates and an accompanying CD. The text is a three-dimensional embodiment of its subject and runs with an intelligent debate on what is sound art, the relationship between environment and soundscapes, sound and the art world and a most informative section on artists' biographies. Licht's view that sound art, like its godfather experimental music, lies between categories because its impact on the listener is in reality between categories, is a sound conclusion if you can forgive the appalling pun:

> Music either stimulates, reinforces, or touches on emotional experiences either directly (through lyrics) or indirectly (through melody and harmony). Even electronic and experimental music, which is often thought of as unemotional or intellectualized, still deals with human thought process, technology, and behavior. Cage's love of nature and all sounds still frames them either as a natural resource to be harnessed by a composer, or as humanist aural spillover from civilization. Music speaks to a listener as a human being, with all of the complexity that entails, but sound art, unless it's employing speech, speaks to the listener as a living denizen of the planet, reacting to sound and environment as any animal would (with all the complexity *that* entails). This sounds dehumanizing, but this appeal to a primal common denominator may, in fact, show human gesture at its most benevolent and least aggrandizing. By taking sound not as a distraction or currency but as something elemental, it can potentially point to the kind of cosmic consciousness that so much art aspires to.
>
> (Licht 2007:216)

A very selective suggestion for further reading is set out below.

SUGGESTIONS FOR FURTHER READING

Radio and sound art texts

Augaitis, Daina and Lander, Dan (1994) *Radio Rethink: Art, Sound and Transmission*, Alberta, Canada: Walter Phillips Gallery, The Banff Centre for the Arts.

Kahn, Douglas and Whitehead, Gregory (eds) (1994) *Wireless, Imagination Sound, Radio, and the Avant-Garde*, London and Cambridge, Massachusetts: The MIT Press.

Niebur, Louis (2010) *Special Sound: The Creation and Legacy of the BBC Radiophonic Workshop*, Oxford and New York: Oxford University Press.

Nyro, Lara (2008) *Sound Media. From Live Journalism to Music Recording*, London and New York: Routledge.

Strauss, Neil (ed.) (1993) *Radiotext(e)*, New York: Columbia University.

Weiss, Allen S. (1995) *Phantasmic Radio*, London and Durham, North Carolina: Duke University Press.

Weiss, Allen S. (2001) *Experimental Sound and Radio*, Cambridge, Massachusetts: The MIT Press.

Sound art

Augoyard, Jean-Francois and Torgue, Henry (eds) (2006) *Sonic Experience: A Guide to Everyday Sounds*, McCartney, Andra and Paquette, David (trans.), London and Montreal: McGill-Queen's University Press.

Blesser, Barry and Salter, Linda-Ruth (2007) *Spaces Speak, Are You Listening? Experiencing Aural Architecture*, Cambridge, Massachusetts, and London: The MIT Press.

Gibbs, Tony (2007) *The Fundamentals of Sonic Art and Sound Design*, Lausanne, Switzerland: AVA Publishing.

LaBelle, Brandon (2008) *Background Noise: Perspectives on Sound Art*, New York and London: Continuum.

Licht, Alan (2007) *Sound Art: Beyond Music, Between Categories*, New York: Rizzoli.

Schafer, R. Murray (1977, 1994) *Our Sonic Environment and the Soundscape: The Tuning of the World*, New York: Alfred Knopf/Random House.

Van Leeuwen, Theo (1999) *Speech, Music, Sound*, London: Macmillan Press.

CHAPTER 9

Sound practice and theory in Internet broadcasting and podcasting

PRACTICE

Exponential and expanding sonic cyberspace and sphere

As at the time of writing, audio broadcasting is now an established practice across cyberspace in the following key forms and genres:

- Internet broadcasting of 'web stations' either as Internet-only operations or the Internet/web dimension of established terrestrial and digital broadcasters

- podcasting in the form of audio productions available as 'audio-streams' and downloadable MP3 files on webpages

- audio slideshow productions offered via video web services such as YouTube or on blogging and multimedia websites

- audio media provision on established multi-platform news, information and entertainment websites either previously established in print, radio, television and film media or uniquely developed in cyberspace.

All of the creative and production skills in terms of audio recording, performance and editing, mixing and production covered in the other chapters in this book and the resources on the companion website are relevant to qualitative and effective communication in web-broadcasting and podcasting. In the early decades of the twenty-first-century practitioners are discovering and appreciating the 'bottom-up' and accessible nature of modest and budget level economies of scale that are available.

The Internet is usually a method of bypassing the state regulated infrastructures for licensing, controlling and approving the right to transmit and indeed the very creation of the content. For example, the UK regulator Ofcom does not 'regulate' the Internet; not even the cyberspace dimensions of terrestrial broadcasters that it does licence and censure in terms of content. Hence, the decision of the *Sun* newspaper to support and promote an Internet radio service built around the controversial talk show host, Jon Gaunt, after he found it difficult to find work on terrestrial radio stations following an Ofcom adjudication that criticised his conduct in an interview with a councillor over adoption policies (Ofcom 2009). The presenter has challenged the reprimand through the British legal system on the grounds that the regulation infringed his freedom of expression human rights (England and Wales High Court 2010).

It would seem that only the voluntary and much criticised UK Press Complaints Commission has decided to apply its ethical code to the Internet dimension of traditional newspaper and magazine publications.

The companion website sets out the case study of Goldsmiths student union radio station, Wired, and how a voluntary audio broadcasting society run and maintained by students, with very low income, can sustain professional level online services with music and speech programming. Live broadcasting is achieved through audio-streaming that requires computer server hosting and licenses in relation to the use of copyright music. In the UK, USA and other countries there are also web station 'hosting' services that provide packages of online facilities for growing numbers of Internet listeners. Obviously the costs increase with concomitant larger scales of potential listening. Streaming technology involves live studio and pre-produced programming being transmitted through an encoder, server, the Internet and then listening player facility on personal computers. The distribution of broadband quality audio-visual transmission means that the compression of audio and visual production, with attendant loss of quality has become less of an issue. For example the Hackney Podcast platform launched in 2008 in an inner city area of East London, has enabled very high quality feature and sound art transmission in the recording of:

> the borough's different faces: one of Britain's poorest places but culturally one of its richest; an area of London profoundly marked by its history but, as the Olympics loom, caught in a frenzied period of change. From its first days, the podcast – available free to download – has provided an eclectic mix of politics, environmental issues and scenes from local life alongside cutting-edge art, literature and music.

> As professional producers working as volunteers, we're eager to broaden our sonic horizons and push our creativity to the limit. We favour montage, allowing the people of Hackney to tell their stories in their own words; create rich

soundscapes, giving listeners an atmospheric sense of the borough; and commission local writers, musicians and poets to create new work.

(Hackney Podcast n.d.)

The provision of podcasting is given significant circulation and distribution boost through RSS feeds and subscriptions. RSS stands for 'Really Simple Syndication' and through RSS aggregators has the effect of widening the notification of updates to online and podcasting services. The connection between website updating and Twitter is another form of information syndication. Apple's iTunes software is an example of a large-scale subscription RSS aggregator. For the purposes of illustration there are two examples of how single-voiced podcasting can enhance entertainment and education. In 2011 the British satirical magazine, *Private Eye*, introduced a digital sound dimension when impressionist Lewis Macleod began submitting audio versions of stories as a sampler for the rest of the content. The *Independent* reported:

Macleod, who does the recordings at home, has also contributed a call for Tony Blair to resign by Tony Ben Ghazi, a correspondent for the Tripoligraph. 'It would be nice to put some Middle Eastern style music behind it and make it sound like a bad satellite signal, we need to get into a studio to do that'.

(Burrell 2011, 14 March)

British philosophy lecturer Nigel Warburton has since 2007 used single voice podcasting to communicate in around five to ten minute podcasts very effective explanations of complex philosophical concepts, ideas, texts and authors on a website called 'Philosophy Bites', and this has intersected with his own blog, appropriately called 'Virtual Philosopher' with the pertinent maxim from John Searle 'If you can't say it clearly, you don't understand it yourself' (Warburton n.d.). 'Philosophy Bites' has expanded out into the interviewing format so that the podcasts have become a regular downloadable audio talk-show on contemporary under-standings, developments and publication about philosophy. Audio equipment companies have begun to provide low-cost audio podcasting kits with high quality USB microphones effectively bypassing the need to use separate digital audio recorders. Single-voiced podcasters are therefore able to record and edit directly onto their computer hard disks.

The companion website provides resources, audio and video demonstrations on developing audio Internet and podcasting skills in terms of setting up a blog with podcasting provision, setting up and running an audio-streamed Internet radio station and producing an audioslide show through the editing of digitised video, digital still photographs and digital sound. As *Multimedia Journalism* author Andy Bull has explained: 'The audio slide show is one of the storytelling forms to have been born out of multimedia journalism. It is a great, hybrid way of telling stories' (Bull 2010:286). Audio slideshow production is realisable through the use of the software programmes

Windows Movie Maker and the Apple iMovie. Mixed down audio slideshows can be uploaded to global digital video publishers such as YouTube and Vimeo and then embedded onto blogging websites hosted by Internet Service providers such as wordpress.com. One of the increasingly popular audio equivalents of YouTube is SoundCloud, which again enables the embedding of sound playback files and downloads.

THEORY

The onset of Internet radio, podcasting and digitisation has stimulated a considerable amount of academic enquiry into the relationship between technological development and its impact on social being. As early as 1998 the edited volume of essays by Peter Kollock and Marc Smith *Communities in Cyberspace* was exploring whether it was possible to define the 'virtual community of cyberspace' and its relationship with 'real communities'. The focus of enquiry, as with most media and cultural studies frameworks, explored issues of representation in terms of race and gender, political economy, and ethics. To what extent do the technical communicative opportunities determine identity, social order and control, community structure and dynamics, and collective action?

As early as in 2000, Dr Martin Spinelli in 'Democratic rhetoric and emergent media: The marketing of participatory community on radio and the Internet' was cautioning at a conference in Cardiff, Wales, on 'Radiocracy':

> Neither the Internet nor radio is a *deus ex machina* of democracy, community or education. The Internet is only an emergent medium, existing in a specific context with and within a real set of material conditions, and certainly with some real potential. But it is a potential that will remain unrealised if we allow the drive to virtualize to obscure its material foundations and the economic realities of the culture in which it exists.
>
> (Spinelli 2000:276–7)

And by 2003, Richard Berry of Sunderland University in a paper entitled 'Speech Radio, The Age' was observing that 'The Internet was proclaimed for many years as the future of radio but while this may be true for music services the same cannot be so confidently said for speech' (Crisell 2006:288). However, he balanced his assessment with the thought that 'in the digital age listeners will be scattered ever more thinly across a myriad of services, which could put speech on a more equal footing' (295). In 2009, Stephen Lax in *Media and Communication Technologies* was concluding that:

> It is often claimed that the rates of technological change are now greater than we have ever known, and this is likely to be true in a quantitative sense on

more-or-less any measure, given that new technological developments depend heavily for their success on previous technologies. In a qualitative judgement, however, the conclusions might not be so straightforward.

(Lax 2009:216)

David Hendy attempted to draw conclusions from an international comparison of the impact of Internet radio and the digitisation of broadcasting as early as 2000 in a journal article entitled 'The Political Economy of Radio in the Digital Age'. He was of the view that 'digitalization's claims to usher in more democracy, more choice, and more interactivity' were 'a little inflated, to say the least' (Hendy 2000b:232). He noted then the warning that convergence in broadcasting regulation in the United Kingdom would bring the price of:

television solutions to be applied to radio problems. This, though, appears to be the likely end game of a decade of steady consolidation in the radio industry- a process in which major players are not just holding greater sway over radio broadcasting, but undergoing wider processes of horizontal and vertical integration, and cross-media ownership-a process, in short, that brings radio's future to a greater extent in line with that of the other mass media.

(233)

Academic analysis of sound communication in new social networks gestated by technological development can scrutinise emotional and political claims made about the aspiration for democracy and communicative freedoms. The role of the youth music station B92 during the Yugoslav civil war and the fall of the authoritarian regime of Slobodan Milosevic in the late 1990s has to some extent been mythologised. The engagement of 'saga discourse' in relation to its history is the subject of the journal article 'Explicating the saga component of symbolic convergence theory: The case of Serbia's radio B92 in cyberspace' by Rita M. Csapó-Sweet and Donald C. Shields. It would seem that these two academics were prepared to conclude that the use of the broadcasters of cyberspace after government takeover and censorship of their terrestrial broadcasting facilities in Serbia played a role in at least the political mythologisation:

Concomitantly, with the creation of the new saga of *Radio B92* in cyberspace and the consciousness-raising concerning its new identity as an independent media engaged in the struggle of a free press for survival, the founding saga's notion of an alternative station got lost. Only time, and the end of the totalitarian government in the new Yugoslavia, will tell what transformations occurred at the station regarding the alternative music, news, and life-style visions. What is known now is that the heroic persona of *Radio B92* as an independent news source, taking its place in the struggle against a totalitarian regime, rose to the fore on the Web-site thanks to the genesis of the new saga of *Radio B92* in cyberspace.

(Csapó-Sweet and Shields 2000:330–1)

Professor Richard Collins of The Open University discussed the social significance of online podcasting in a CD resource produced for the course Understanding Media, which was launched in 2006. He suggested that this media form extended the fluidity between public and private space begun by radio in the twentieth century, and he focused on the home space blog/podcasters 'The Dawn and Drew Show', an American couple who now describe their service as 'two ex gutter punks who fall in love, buy a retired farm in Wisconsin (then move to Costa Rica) and tell the world their dirty secrets . . . always profane, rarely profound,' (Miceli and Domkus 2004–11); 'Dark Compass, the Chronicles of Rowland Cutler, a podcaster', which at the time of writing appears to have developed into a more music-based sound blog; and 'Catholic Insider', produced by Father Roderick, and based at the Vatican:

> It's rather like what pamphleteers must have been like at the end of sixteenth and seventeenth century. Podcasting is like a sound blog. [. . .] Podcasts take you into an extraordinary world.
>
> (*DA204 Understanding Media* Audio CD2 2006: cluster 3, track 3)

Collins' view does support an analysis of Internet podcasting as an interesting evolution of 'pamphleteering' whereby opinion, political, social or entertainment communication, using cabled channels of digitised streaming, can network globally and does not depend on the sponsorship and framing of mainstream media.

The multi-dimensionality and interactivity of narrative direction offered by cyberspace has extended the artistic potential of writing and production in audio drama. A large media institution such as the BBC has certainly provided resources and commissioning space for experimentation. The companion website discusses the transition of interactivity from radio to online participation in plays and dramatisations by Mike Walker (*The Dark House* 2003) and Graham White (*The Unfortunates* by B.S. Johnson 2010).

Recommended reading in terms of practice textbooks and theory publications is set out below.

RECOMMENDED READING

Practice texts

Alten, Stanley R. (2010) *Audio in Media* (9th edition), Belmont, California: Thomson Wadsworth. (Chapter 18, 'Internet Media', recommended.)

Bull, Andy (2010) *Multimedia Journalism: A Practical Guide*, London and New York: Routledge. (Chapters 4, 'Audio and podcasting', and 10, 'Still pictures and audio', recommended.)

Geoghegan, Michael and Klass, Dan (2007) *Podcast Solutions: The Complete Guide to Audio and Video Podcasting* (2nd edition), New York: Friends of Ed, an Apress company.

Lee, Eric (2005) *How Internet Radio Can Change the World: An Activist's Handbook*, New York: iUniverse.
Priestman, Chris (2002) *Web Radio: Radio Production for Internet Streaming*, London and New York: Focal Press, an imprint of Elsevier.
Whittaker, Jason (2009) *Producing for the Web 2.0* (3rd edition), London and New York: Routledge.

Theory texts

Crisell, Andrew (ed.) (2006) *More than a Music Box: Radio Cultures and Communities in a Multi-Media World*, New York, Oxford: Berghahn Books.
Kollock, Peter and Smith, Marc (1998) *Communities in Cyberspace*, London and New York: Routledge.
Lax, Stephen (2009) *Media and Communication Technologies: A Critical Introduction*, Basingstoke, Hampshire: Palgrave Macmillan.
Ledgerwood, Mike (forthcoming) *Cyberspace* (Routledge Introductions to Media and Communications), London and New York: Routledge.

Selected journal articles

Csapó-Sweeta, Rita M. and Shields, Donald C. (2000, September) 'Explicating the Saga Component of Symbolic Convergence Theory: The Case of Serbia's Radio B92 in Cyberspace', *Critical Studies in Media Communication*, 17(3): 316–33.
Hendy, David (2000) 'A Political Economy of Radio in the Digital Age', *Journal of Radio and Audio Media Studies*, 7(1): 213–34.
Spinelli, Martin (2000, August) 'Democratic Rhetoric and Emergent Media: The Marketing of Participatory Community on Radio and the Internet' (Special Issue: Radiocracy), *International Journal of Cultural Studies*, 3(2): 268–78. doi: 10.1177/136787790000300215.

Glossary

This glossary dovetails with a dynamically changing and increasing resource on the book's companion website.

Absorption A critical term that can describe sound as dry, spacious, reverberating and resonant (Van Leeuwen 1999:203). In the physics of sound, absorption is the treatment of surfaces so that they can reflect more or less sound depending on the needs of an auditorium or sound recording studio. Insulation prevents sound from passing into another room so it is a form of sound proofing.

Acousmatic Sound in the cinema or from a film that the audience can hear without seeing its source. Coined by Michel Chion who describes it as an off-screen sound for example emanating from the radio or telephone (Chion 1994:221). The entire soundtrack of Derek Jarman's *Blue* (1993) is acousmatic and in theory so is all of any sequence of audio drama.

Acousmêtre Chion describes his neologism as a 'kind of voice-character specific to cinema that in most instances of cinematic narrative derives mysterious powers from being heard and not seen' (Chion 1994:221).

Acoustics The science of modifying sound in space. The qualities of surfaces have an impact on its quality and the way it is heard. The purpose is to determine how sound can be controlled and changed in enclosed environments through its generation, transmission, reception and the constituent nature of its effects.

A/D converter An electronic device that converts an audio signal into its digital form; hence the abbreviation meaning analogue-to-digital conversion. The analogue waveforms are changed into a series of binary numbers and the standard term 'bits' means that the higher value of the 'bits' the greater the quality of the sampling process. This means that conversion to sound files with 20 or 24-bit resolution will mean they will be of higher quality (White 2003:175).

Algorithm A mathematical formula working in electronics to create and change sound within digital computer processes. It applies a numerical formula to data to change it in a predictable pattern. Algorithms are the building and operational blocks of digital editing sound software.

Alliteration A critical term in literature to denote when two or more words begin with the same consonant sound.

Ambience The background sound in any recording; particularly on location and usually consisting of noise, reverberation and atmosphere. It is sometimes called *atmos* and referred to as presence or room tone. It is also the 'wild-track' that sound producers and engineers are encouraged to record separately when on location for drama and documentary projects (Alten 2008:467).

Amplitude processor (also known as a dynamic or sound processor) A machine that electronically processes a sound signal's loudness and produces effects known as compression, limiting, de-essing, expanding, noise-gating, and pitch shifting (Alten 2008:467).

Analytical listening (also known as critical listening) The concentrated study and analysis of sound content and function. R. Murray Schafer advocated 'ear cleaning' – 'A systematic program for training the ears to listen more discriminatingly to sounds, particularly those of the environment' (Schafer 1994:272 and Alten 2008:467, 469).

Anchorage Fixing and focusing meaning through an emphasised direction of communication and in sound, this is very effectively achieved through voiced-over narration that can have the same impact as a bold caption fused to a photographic image.

Anechoic chamber A special room with highly absorbent sound proofing that halts all sound reflection. It enables studio-based production to record voices as though they were in outside open spaced environments.

Anempathetic sound Michel Chion defined this term as sound that was usually diegetic music and seemed to 'exhibit conspicuous indifference to what is going on in the film's plot, creating a strong sense of the tragic' (Chion 1994:221). He gave the rather evocative example of a radio continuing to play a joyful tune when the character who had switched it on has died.

Ars Acoustica A Latin term for sound art and arising out of the title of a European Broadcasting Union committee that commissioned a series of sound art works by members' companies.

Assonance A critical term in literature recognising the rhyming of vowel sounds within two or more words.

Asynchronous sound A soundtrack in film that is not matching temporally the movements presented in the visual sequence. An example would be lack of synchronisation with the lip movements of the actors.

Attack The beginning of a sound's gestation, for example, through the plucking of a guitar string. It can also be understood as the first part of a sound envelope – often represented in audio-visual graphics in digital sound software programmes (Alten 2008:467). A sound envelope consists of its attack, decay, sustain and release.

Audiogenic In its literal meaning caused by sound or produced by sound. In criticism it could be used to identify a component of multimedia narrative that concentrates or determines meaning by sound alone.

Audio noir Usually a detective or suspense radio/sound thriller with a hard-boiled central male private detective character with a cynical and morally dark attitude about the world and human behaviour who effectively narrates the story that is in time past from a time present perspective.

Auditory imagery A literary term recognising imagery that appeals to the reader and listener's sense of hearing.

Auteur (sound) The producer and director of fiction and non-fiction texts in sound that have a distinctive and recognisable style. The term originated in film criticism and has been used in the context of radio drama to identify an all-round writer/director/producer who takes a much greater authorship of a production than a team of separate writer/screenplay writers, directors and producers.

Back-timing An important method of always knowing how much time is left in live and pre-recorded linear timeframed productions and programmes.

Balanced and unbalanced cabling These sound technical terms enable a sound engineer and producer to understand the risk of electronic interference in the recording and playing back of sound. This can result in a muddy and unpleasant hum or emergency service radio communications undermining the recording and transmission process. Unbalanced lines/cables have two signal carrying conducting wires, one of which is the shield. In balanced lines, the shield, which is earthed, is in addition to the two conducting wires.

Binary oppositions Sound narratives and texts that can be analysed in terms of binary oppositional values, emotions, sounds and representations.

Boom A metal pole used to suspend microphones above the scene on a film set and can be moved to follow the action. Booms are also used in sound documentaries to give the producer and sound recorders more flexibility in capturing sound closer to its source.

Bricolage Collage style borrowing and adoption of fragmented textual components from differing styles and genres to express a new pattern of meaning. Similar to montage editing in sound and film and sometimes described as postmodernist.

The word is also used in historical cultural studies to explain the gradual absorption of transnational cultural influences in a symbiotic osmosis of exchange and negotiated selection rather than the idea of aggressive impact or rapid cultural deluge.

Cause-and-effect structuring This is the method of developing a sound text by moving forward through one scene causing an event leading to the next or a further scene. As a result everything heard and understood needs to be motivated by something heard and understood earlier.

Chronology Ordering narrative in terms of time sequence. A simple method of structuring story telling and usually being met with audience satisfaction. This method also works effectively in investigative, campaigning and expository documentary.

Continuity editing A process of editing sound where the joining together of different sequences (shots in film) recorded at different times and in different locations constructs a narrative.

Contrapuntal sound A technique of sound production in film where the soundtrack does not directly match the image in mood or narrative content and in the process expands the depth of meeting or adds an additional meaning. In music contrapuntal is a technique of counterpoint where two or more voices independent in contour and rhythm are harmonically interdependent and in choral performance join the performance at different times and repeat polyphonically a version of the same melodic element. The concept arises from the Latin expression *punctus contra punctum* meaning 'point against point'.

Convergence (media and sound) A much discussed media and cultural industrial development where the divisions of media institutional production between print, online, television, radio and film are breaking down in a dynamic relationship with the consumption of multimedia. For example, journalists working for the *Guardian* in London or the *New York Times* in New York City could be producing journalistic texts constructed in the print, online, digital sound and video media.

Convolution Recreating the acoustic qualities of a space and the merging of different sounds using computer editing software. In computer sampling the process multiplies the spectrums of two audio files and creates a virtually infinite range of acoustic spaces; hence the fact it is also known as 'convolution reverb' (Gibbs 2007:170 and Alten 2008:469).

Critical autonomy A recognition of intellectual and academic independence of mind and original analysis and thinking in the process of writing essays about the media or analysing media texts.

Cross-fade An equivalent description in sound of the dissolve in picture editing. The first sound is gradually reduced while the second sound gradually increased and for a phase the two sounds blend together in sonic superimposition.

Cultural imperialism In the sound context this is the encoding of sound communication that through the power of dissemination achieves a domination of one culture by another.

Cyberspace (sonic) The use and application of sound communications in the virtual online/Internet environment developed as the result of linking computers. It is a cabled network of communication though in its 'virtual dimension' encoded by signals and imaginative interaction and construction of social community.

Dasein A word used in philosophy, primarily by phenomenologists to contain the idea of existence or presence in the world. It is a state of being there or there being. The word in the context of sound can constitute the idea of being by sonic existence, experience and representation. Martin Heidegger sought to challenge the association of the word as a form of subjective consciousness. *Dasein* should be considered as human entity in the everyday. Philosophers argue that Heidegger's understanding and positing of *dasein* was different to that of Karl Jaspers who articulated a distinction between minimal existence In *dasein* and the authentic being in *existenz*. A somewhat crude or potentially erroneous way of understanding the distinction would be to think in terms of conscious and social existence as an object (*dasein*) and a subject (*existenz*). Heidegger and Jaspers are often discussed in discourse on the social ethics and phenomenology of broadcasting as in Paddy Scannell's monograph *Radio Television and Modern Life: A Phenomenological Approach* (1996).

Delay The insertion of a time lag in sound transmission or processing that can simulate reverberation and echo. It is a time interval between the sound signal and each of its repeats. In digital delay processing, delay time determines how long a sound is held (Gibbs 2007:170 and Alton 2008:470).

Depth of sound field (otherwise referred to as perspective) In recording terms it could be the degree axis of a stereo sound stage or microphone arrangement. In terms of editorial perception it can be distance between action and sound and the position of microphones to ensure a recorded signal that can be understood as having intended meaning for the listener.

Dialect Style of language with features of vocabulary, grammar and intonation that associate the speaker with a specific geographical area.

Dialogue overlap In film and television editing a sequence of sound dialogue or soundtrack that can be heard in the first shot and is also audible under the following visual shot or another perspective and element of the scene.

Diegesis/diegetic and non-diegetic Diegetic sound belongs to the story within the sound or audio-visual programme. It is the sound heard in the fictional world. Most diegetic sound is synthesised and dubbed through sound design multi-tracking. 'Foley' sound artists specialise in creating effects that are realistic to screen scenography and fit aurally into the mise-en-scène. In terms of narrative it is part of the story. Diegesis can also include events, actions and places that are not shown onscreen in the case of film fiction. The words, music and noise have to originate or emanate from a source within the world of the film or audio drama. Non-diegetic sound originates from outside the space of the story/narrative and is usually a term associated with mood music, or narrative linking and commentary.

Diffusion The impact of acoustic and reverberant dynamics on frequencies, particularly in electro-acoustic performance using a matrix of loudspeakers. It is effectively the scattering of sound waves to a uniform intensity (Gibbs 2007:170 and Alton 2008:470).

Direct sound Words, music and noises recorded at the moment of filming on a set or location. It is regarded as the reverse of post-synchronised sound – sound synthesised by studio performance or separate production and post-produced by various techniques to multi-track onto the film.

Dissonance A critical term in literature to represent the sound of words being so different that they clash with each other and create a discordant effect.

Distance of sound recording This is the distance between the position of the microphones and the source of the sound. Consequently in audio production you can have a series of terms to describe the equivalent in camera work of close-up, long shot, medium shot. Studio managers and sound engineers might say 'close-microphone', 'long shot sound' or 'medium position'.

Docudrama A genre of sound/radio programming that interpolates documentary recordings, actuality of live events, and dramatisations of the transcript of factual or fictional events. This mixing of documentary and dramatic material has been described in British radio history as the radio feature.

Documentary A factual genre of media and a key area of sound textual communication. The objective usually is to depict or represent a real rather than imaginary world. There are strands of documentary that intend to record actuality that is unstaged. The genre has generated a significant debate on ethics and power between author/programme maker and subjects. To what extent does the producer simply observe or control? And how genuinely objective is the record of presentation of reality? The most influential theorist on the ethics of documentary is Bill Nichols who discussed in his seminal text *Representing Reality: Issues and Concepts in Documentary* (1991) distinctions that he classified as expository, observational, interactive, reflexive and performative (Crook 1999:2007–9).

Dubbing In sound recording it simply means copying, but in film sound production it describes the process of replacing voices on the soundtrack to correct mistakes or improve the sound design. This is sometimes called lip-synching or postsychronisation.

Dynamics The nature of sound in terms of its volume.

Elektronische Musik Music that is created through the use of electronic musical technology and instruments. Associated with the electronic music studio opened at the German public radio station NWDR in Cologne in 1953 and the composer and musicologist Karlheinz Stockhausen. Werner Meyer-Eppler authored an influential academic thesis in 1949 entitled *Elektronische Klangerzeugung: Electronische Musik und Synthetische Sprache* that focused on the idea of purely produced electronic music based on electronic sources rather than analogue acoustic sources that constituted the French genre of *musique concrète*.

Ellipsis In a production this is a technique of advancing the plot by shortening its duration through the omission of story time. By sound and visual cutting the audience makes a jump of understanding that time has elapsed between consecutive shots.

Emanation speech Antitheatrical and antiliterary speech in film and audio drama where the words are not necessarily heard and understood clearly. It could be described as impressionistic speech sound and Michel Chion decided that as it 'emanates' from the characters rather like a sonic silhouette it deserves its own critical term. The technique is often used by Jacques Tati where human characters can be heard to make vocal kinds of noises but they do not have a clarity of verbal meaning. But they certainly convey a mood and attitude (Chion 1994:177–83).

Empathetic music Michel Chion's term for film music where the mood or rhythm supports and matches the mood and rhythm of the action on the screen. The reverse effect is called anempathetic music (Chion 1994:8 and 222).

Encoding/decoding sound texts The process of charging (encoding) sounds with meaning by sound media producers. The authors of the productions and the media institutions they work for believe that they are capable of manipulating the material to achieve preferred readings that are decoded by the consuming audience. However, empirical research demonstrates that the process of listening or aural decoding is multi-phenomenal and theorists have discussed dominant, negotiated and oppositional modes of interpretation and understanding.

Enlightenment rationality A term arising from the historical period known as the Enlightenment or 'Age of Reason' where there was an intellectual focus on the human individual as Cartesian subjective and conscious self who is committed to the pursuit of knowledge and the notion of human progress. This period is also associated with the pursuit of clear thinking and respect and celebration of empirical and scientific analysis.

Equalisation (EQ) This is the technical 'colouring' of sound by changing the control over specific sound frequencies that transforms the tonal response of sound in bands generally understood as bass (lower), middle (known as presence) and treble (high frequency).

Existenz The German philosopher Karl Jaspers used the word to express and explain the human experience of freedom and possibility, a sense of authentic and social being with positive ethical imperatives that challenged the nature of human contingency, death, guilt, conflict and suffering. *Existenz* is 'the non objective actuality of self-being, true self-hood, existential freedom, undetermined moral decision, or the genuine and authentic self' (Salamun 1999:217).

Expressionism A critical term applied to a study and appreciation of modernist artistic expression where there is a concentration on the emotional and subjective perspective, or a tendency to promote meaning from the point of view and listening of emotional experience rather than material reality. In music Arnold Schoenberg, Anton Webern and Alban Berg composed music devoid of tonality so that the atonality could represent the idea of subconscious interior suffering. Their work is therefore described as *expressionist* music.

External diegetic sound Sound coming from a source within the story that the characters can also hear. Internal diegetic sound represents the sound coming from the mind of a character within the story; equivalent to a soliloquy in Renaissance theatre that is meant to be understood and heard only by the character and the audience.

Fade in and fade out Terms used to describe the increase in volume and brightening of a sound and decrease and diminishing of the sound's clarity.

Film sound crew In large-scale film production the sound crew or team would normally consist of engagement in two processes: location recording and postproduction. On location the sound unit is normally led by somebody called the production recordist or sound mixer. The main purpose is to record dialogue during shooting and the unit will use multi-track portable digital recorders, a variety of microphones, outside broadcast digital mixer and portable computers with processing and editing/mixing capabilities. Usually all the sound of performances and ambience and soundscapes are recorded. In any take sometimes several microphones will record different sonic perspectives on separate digital tracks. The sound unit can include a boom operator to control the position of moving microphones and the supply and equipping of radio or lapel/lavalier microphones on the actors. A third member of the unit is sometimes on hand to support the recording and mixing of multiple sources and microphone positions as well as a complex sound log. In sound postproduction the production recordist can double up as the head of sound design, sound editing and postproduction or these tasks can be taken on by a separate sound production team headed by a sound editor. This process involves the origination of sound and layering on digital multi-tracks all the performance dialogue, location ambiences and perspectives and synthesised atmospheres, effects and Foley tracks to constitute all the elements of the film's soundtrack. The placing of sound sequences is known as spotting and it is quite common for re-recording of dialogue in a process known as dubbing, looping or automated dialogue replacement (ADR). This is done in studios where the actors re-perform their lines by synching their voices to the screen action. Digital sound editing is a highly creative and complex production process and sound post-production can sometimes exceed the timeframe of all the location shooting. The design of sound can be described as an art in itself; hence the use of the term 'sound sculpting' (Bordwell and Thompson 1997:21).

Filter An electronic device that can remove unwanted frequencies or noise from a signal by suppressing different frequency components of the sound (Alten 2008:473 and Gibbs 2007:170).

First person shooter (FPS) A term used in computer gaming to describe the first person shooter where the centre of action and participation on the part of the game-player is around a gun or projectile weapon wielding first person protagonist engaged in combat scenarios. The player sees and hears the action through the point of view and listening of the central and active character who faces a series of hazardous combat journeys.

Fly-on-the-wall documentary The term usually relates to television or film documentary where the camera and boom microphone endeavours to be unobtrusive so that subjects in their natural settings are represented realistically. This is also described as *cinéma-verité*. The equivalent process and practice in sound documentary could be called *audio-vérité* and there was an effective practice culture of this genre at BBC Midlands in the 1990s when the producers Brian King and Sarah Rowlands concentrated on sound networks of experience and communication within social and professional institutions such as schools, hospitals, doctors' practices and airports (Crook 1999:210–1).

Focus (sound) Sharpening and highlighting a sound sometimes with a close microphone position to its source and also in multi-tracking editing by 'equalising' through manipulation of sound frequencies and increasing the sound level in proportion to a decrease in the sound level of the other tracks.

Foley artist A sound effects designer who originates and records sound that can accompany the body movement of film characters and their sonic interaction with mise-en-scène environment. The production takes place in special sound stages where the sound creators often act out in synchrony on-screen action to reproduce the rhythm of the sound that has to be multi-tracked with the visual footage. The specialism is named after Jack Foley who was a pioneer of postproduction sound at Universal Studios. He began by creating the ambient soundtrack for the 1929 musical *Showboat* and Foley's legendary nickname in the cinema business was 'footsteps to the stars'.

Frequency order In film deconstruction and direction/scripting the term relates to the repetition of story events in the plot. Bordwell and Thompson describe it as 'temporal manipulation' (Bordwell and Thompson 1997:479).

Fundamental The lowest frequency that a sound source can produce and also known as the first harmonic or primary frequency (Alten 2008:474).

Gatekeepers Individuals or institutions that determine and give permission on the content of media texts. It is the exercise of cultural, legal and political power over text production and transmission. Gatekeepers are on the axis of determining what shall be communicated and who shall receive it.

Genres Various types and forms of sound programmes usually broadcast on radio station formats. Audiences and programme makers are familiar with narrative and stylistic conventions that define a particular genre. In radio examples of genres include montage, audio-diary, narrative-linked, presenter led discussion, magazine, breakfast news, drive-time, talkback, and night-line phone-in.

Granulation A process critically recognised in sound art as sound manipulation by dissecting an existing noise or sound into very short 'grains' of no more than fifty milliseconds which are then processed, superimposed and copied (Gibbs 2007:170).

Hand-held microphone The term is rather self-explanatory, but it implies that the reporter/producer/sound recordist has direct control of where the microphone can go to ensure a strong direct to indirect sound ratio.

Harmonic A single component frequency to make up a complex sound known as harmonics.

Hauntological A neologism said to have been coined by Jacques Derrida in his book *Spectres of Marx* (1993) and which is being increasingly developed by writers and philosophers as a critical term that analyses the way past and present media forms and representations challenge the idea of human existence into a paradoxical and ambiguous flux of being and non being. Sound recordings of the past can operate as symbolic ghosts that materialise an understanding of present day reality. In a *Sunday Times* review article, published in 2007, 'The Art of Noise Refined: Today's Electronica Has Something Vital to Say' Bethan Cole wrote:

> It's Ghost Box and Mordant Music, with their 'found' sounds, old television themes, soundtracks for public information film, allusions and debt to *musique concrète,* who have really captured the imagination of listeners in search of something new. The critic Simon Reynolds and the blogger Mark Fisher (k-punk) have dubbed the sound 'hauntology'.

Hegemony The operation of a dominant culture in any given society that predominates and perpetuates an ideology of ideas, beliefs and values. Also the exercise of military, political, economic and cultural power transnationally and globally with a distinction between hard (military and economic) and soft (political, diplomatic and cultural) power.

Heimathörspiel A combination of the German words for home and soundplay to suggest the idea of sound defining or being associated with the home environment or location that is more of a private zone of social interaction and existence. The German word *heimspiel* is in use to explain how technology is so embedded in everyday life that there is a social phenomenon of home-play that is discoursed by designers and technologists.

Hermeneutics (sound) Analysing the process of interpreting meaning or studying the theory and practice of interpreting sound as a media text. The exegesis of deriving meaning from the interpretation of sound.

Historicism (sound) This is a term that is frequently contested in terms of a fixed definition. Historicist criticism can be said to focus on the social, political and cultural contexts of events in the process of analysis, explanation and discussion of meaning. New historicism, particularly in literature studies, concentrates on the construction of text, interpretation of meaning relative to the power structures of any given society in any time and period. The US academic Stephen Greenblatt is regarded as a significant exponent of this approach to historical analysis.

Historiography (sound) The discipline of analysing the methodology of studying the history of sound and the way the history of radio/sound narrative has been and is being communicated. It also considers how the successive generations of historians interpret and reinterpret the past through the discovering, retrieval and selection of sound texts.

Hörspiele The literal translation in German is 'sound plays', but it is a term for creative radio programming that originated in Germany in the 1920s. Musicians, poets and writers such as Kurt Weill, Friedrich Bischoff and Alfred Döblin recognised that there was a new art form arising out of mixing noises, music, texts through the superimposition and intertwining of sound waves.

Humanitas **(sound)** The German philosopher Karl Jaspers articulated a liberal ethos of humanity performed in everyday life in terms of moral values and attitudes: courage without self-deception, composure, patience, self-possession and dignity. He also advocated that the individual should avoid ideological bias and dogmatic fanaticism in social, political and economic contexts, accept responsibility for one's actions, and respect the identity and freedoms of the Other. Sound *humanitas* is an ethical ethos for the social sound environment.

Hyperreality and the hyperreal Critical terms used by twentieth- and twenty-first-century philosophers to discuss how the speed and complexities of media matrices distort and undermine the ability of consciousness to mark the boundaries between reality and fantasy. Hence the theory of Jean Baudrillard's simulacrum and Paul Virilio's discourse on the impact of speed and scale of communication streams on social being. Hyperreality is a phenomenon that has the capacity to generate false consciousness, distort and propagandise meaning, and exercise social, political and cultural power.

Icon and iconography (sound) It could be argued that sound is capable of referring to and describing a person or object that is substantially invested with cultural, religious and political power, particularly if it can trigger visual representation in the imagination of the listener.

Ideology A system of values, beliefs and ideas shared by a social or political group or propagandised by a state, corporate or social or private institution and where the members take them for granted as natural truth.

Idiolect A literary term defining the way language identifies a particular individual.

Imagery Any aspect of a text that appeals to a reader or listener's senses and constructed into literary schemes of similes and metaphors. As the framework of senses includes sound, and in psychology and philosophy it is often accepted that sensory perception is a connected matrix controlled and experienced by the mind, auditory imagery can often be aligned with touch, taste, smell and vision.

Imaginative spectacle The listening imagination is indicated as an important fourth dimension of analysing sound texts and this is recognised by many leading theorists. Michael Chion talked about magnetisation that he synonymously described as mental spatialization: 'the psychological process (in monaural film viewing) of locating a sound's source in the space of the image, no matter what the real point of origin of the sound in the viewing space is' (Chion 1994:223). Chion also referred to phantom sounds, which were false perceptions based on psychological rather than physical stimulus. Theo Van Leeuwen deploys the critical term 'abstract-sensory modality' to engage the role of a listening perception that is more mind-based (Van Leeuwen 1999:203):

A criterion for judging the modality of sound events which rests both on the presence of abstract representation (representation concentrating on certain essential or generalized aspects of what is represented) and on emotive effect. The more a sound event fulfils these criteria, the higher its abstract-sensory modality. A musical representation of a steam train will have high abstract-sensory modality if it represents, for instance, only the rhythm and pitch contour of the locomotive, but not its 'mechanical' sound: the use of a musical instrument rather than a sound effect would achieve the 'sensory' dimension.

Informal language Speech and language that is familiar, casual, conversational and obviously the opposite of formal or heightened speech.

Intellectual montage Juxtaposing sound sequences to generate an abstract idea that is not inherently present in one sound sequence alone. Emotional montage conveys abstract ideas by juxtaposing sound sequences to move the feelings of the listener.

Intertextuality Derived from postmodernist discourse and a critical term applied to the understanding of postmodern texts by linking and relating its meaning to other texts. When examining sound texts the objective should be to evaluate how much of it has been constructed with overt and covert sequences and allusions to previously produced sound artefacts or multimedia sources. It might be argued that an example of intertextual sound production would be an independently produced series for BBC Radio Two in 2011 called *Sounds of the Twentieth Century* where montage-style one hour documentaries drew on archive soundtrack from newsreel, television, film and music, and off air radio broadcasts. The repetitive recycling of sound symbolism and archive from the past generates a cultural currency of ideological exchange. These documentaries are the sites of texts intersecting with other texts and thus producing a postmodernist intertextuality.

Intonation The use of the tone of the voice to convey meaning and represent identity.

Inversion (inverted syntax) A technique of writing whereby the normal order of words in a phrase or sentence is reversed for dramatic effect. This technique can apply to sound editing and mixing in order to create an emphasis of meaning.

Irony A sound or sequence of language that expresses the opposite of what is meant. There can also be a reference to an event having reverse consequences of those intended or expected. In dramatic irony meaning is held by the audience – that is, the listeners who possess knowledge and understanding beyond that held by the character or characters in the diegesis of the constructed narrative.

Jump cut In sound this is a jagged edit that interrupts the cohesion between narrative voice and/or dialogue and the background ambience. This can create a style of sound ellipsis.

Leitmotiv A recurring musical theme represented usually in operas but also in symphonic poems. The device highlights dramatic action and can offer psychological insight into characterisation. Another function enables listeners to recognise musical phrases and themes that are relevant to a dramatic event.

Linearity The pattern of cause and effect that represents the onward progress of a plot in a film's screenplay 'without significant digressions, delays, or irrelevant actions' (Bordwell and Thompson 1997:479). Linearity can also be applied to the ruthless application of the time frame in sound production and transmission. Time is by its very nature linear and the manipulation of content can only be achieved within its frame.

Long take/long scenes/one take/long shot A style of narrative, direction and production where the story unfolds in one sound location and for long periods in the style of stage/theatre drama. In French film this is sometimes referred to as the *plan-séquence*. The internal dynamic and flow of the performance can be contained and sustained in an aesthetic unity with a long successful 'take' and limited editing between takes. This is a feature of studio-based television, radio and film drama that could be argued to be counterintuitive to the contemporary fashion for action/location film narrative. Studio-based television drama production is very rare now. There are also former and current film-makers that favour the direction, performance and recording of radio/audio drama always on location and outside the studio.

Mainstream sound/radio media Media institutions generating sound productions and texts for large audiences. The BBC, NPR and the Guardian Media group would be examples of mainstream media, whereas the Hackney Podcast or the community arts station in London, Resonance FM, could be described as niche or minority media publishers.

Meaning The construction of meaning is generally regarded as the prerogative of the listening audience though in the construction of sound it would be fair to recognise the intentions of sound artists, scriptwriters and directors/producers. This can be achieved through the manipulation of referential meaning, the references to shared prior knowledge outside the story of the audio or film narrative. These could be described as cultural allusions. Explicit meaning is understood through obvious and clearly stated language and action/drama. Implicit meanings tend to be something of a contingency. They can be the space for ironic resonance where there is covert meaning intended by the authors of a text and recognised by the audience as knowledge and understanding not shared by the diegetic characters and sections of the audience; usually elite and power groups in society. An open sound text is said to lack clarity in preferred meaning thereby open to multiple and different listening and a closed text has a preferred meaning heavily and overtly anchored usually through voice-over commentary. Symptomatic meaning provides understanding against the aesthetic, political and cultural ideological frame of a media narrative's purpose and intentions. This process occurs catalytically in relation to historical or social context (Bordwell and Thompson 1997:480).

Media effects theory Theories that discuss the impact of sound media communication and consumption on individuals, society and culture. The theories debate how the process of communication and reception changes attitudes, values, precipitates social action and materialises reality. The Frankfurt School of social scientists initially exiled to American universities as a result of the persecution of Jews and left-wing intellectuals by the German-Austrian Nazi regime discussed the mass audience as homogenously passive and capable of being manipulated, indoctrinated and propagandised by media institutions overtly and covertly controlled by ruling class ideologies. Many of their early qualitative and quantitative surveys and studies were based on sound communication as they focused on the impact of radio, the first electronic mass means of media communication. The hypodermic needle model metaphorically envisages the injection of ideology into passive audiences. Media effects theorists argue that media texts can condition audiences and desensitise them in a process of cultivation and consequently media communicators have a responsibility for anti-social behaviour and in the context of hate media communication (*Les Médias de la Haine*) can even be held culpable for crimes against humanity such as genocide.

Media events and media rituals These are events or occasions reported by the media that have been precipitated, cued or prefigured by media communication in the context of individual, group or government actions.

Metanarratives Overarching explanations and theories explaining the nature of existence and society that provide a coherent explanation and accounting for knowledge and understanding. They are also referred to as grand narratives and in the age of structuralism, post-structuralism and counter-enlightenment are regarded as philosophical tropes and ideologies based on false consciousness.

Metaphor (sonic) A comparative effect in words, music or noise that is not literally true because it refers to something as if it were something else.

Method performance In film acting and radio drama performance it is a style of acting where the actor fathoms the motivation and personality of the character in order to express realism and naturalistic truth of identity and existential being. It is closely associated with the aesthetic of social realism and in the result it will match scripting that endeavours to reproduce the reality of human speech in terms of human utterance, noises and verbal interactions though such performances and scripts will be strongly scored and directed in terms of heightened dramatic values.

Micro-controller An extremely small computer operated by a one chip circuit board microprocessor that conduits input and output for interactive digital systems (Gibbs 2007:170).

Microphone angle/position This concerns the position of the microphone in order to produce a sound texture and impact from the point of recording. Obviously close-microphone tends to be associated with intimate speech that very often represents internal thoughts, the mind and consciousness of characterisation. The term is also dependent on the kind of microphone(s) since this will determine the nature of the recording, such as unidirectional or omnidirectional. Positioning the microphone behind a speaker creates a kind of back sound or the equivalent of the point of listening replicating the hearing of somebody who has their head and back turned away from the face-to-face position. Michel Chion called this kind of sound 'back voice', 'If his or her back is turned, the listener perceives less treble in the voice' (Chion 1994:222).

Mise-en-scène (sound) In film and visual media deconstruction the phrase encompasses everything seen in the picture/screen frame such as movement, set, location settings, lighting, costumes and props, but it can also be applied to a sound design in terms of the constituent elements of sound – that is, words from characters in action and drama, words in narrative, sound effects, location ambience or 'soundscape', music, and sound processing. In analysis the student asks 'what is actually put into the scene' and what are the elements and streams of sound that combine to create the overall audio-montage?

Mixer An electronic system either virtual digital or physical for combining multiple sound signals, both pre-recorded and live from microphones, and applying some processing functions. Also known as a mixing desk, console or control panel (Gibbs 2007:170 and Alten 2008:478).

Mixing A common term in sound production for combining and/or cross fading two or more soundtracks in multi-track digital editing software programmes.

Mockumentary An increasingly popular genre of programme in what is sometimes described as a cynical postmodernist age whereby the documentary form parodies itself or fiction satirises documentary. The conceit or trick is to either deceive an audience that they are watching 'true' documentary or entertain the audience with a mocking pastiche.

Modernism This is the identification of a creative and artistic renaissance at the end of the nineteenth century that lasted well into the post-Second World War years. In essence it was an opposition and challenge to traditional forms of expression and aesthetic perceptions with a creative experimentation of form and content. The phenomenon has been subdivided into artistic movements such as futurism, imagism, symbolism and expressionism. In addition to the turning over of traditions and retrieval of past forms and concerns, it could be argued that modernism also breaks up and disrupts the coherence and internal continuity of form and content.

Modes of listening Michael Chion set out a system of defining the listening process for cinematic sound in terms of the semantic, reduced and causal. Causal listening has the purpose of gaining information about the source of any sound (Chion 1994:222); reduced listening happens when a member of the film's audience wants or needs to focus on the qualities of the sound itself (223) and semantic listening concentrates on gaining information about what the sound is communicating (224). Chion discusses this framework of listening analysis with reference to the writing of Pierre Schaeffer (25–34), and he concedes that these modes are neither discrete nor theoretically and psychologically comprehensive (33):

The question of listening with the ear is inseparable from that of listening with the mind, just as looking is with seeing. In other words, in order to describe perceptual phenomena, we must take into account that conscious and active perception is only one part of a wider perceptual field in operation. In the cinema to look is to explore, at once spatially and temporally, in a 'given-to-see' (field of vision) that has a limited perspective contained by the screen. But listening, for its part, explores in a field of audition that is given or even imposed on the ear; this aural field is much less limited or confined, its contours uncertain and changing.

Sonnenschein advocates a fourth mode of listening which he describes as the referential:

being aware of or affected by the context of the sound, linking not only to the source but principally to the emotional and dramatic meaning. This can be an instinctual or universal level for all humans (e.g., a lion's roar), culturally specific to a certain society or period (e.g., a horse and buggy on cobblestone), or within the confines of the sound coding of a specific film (e.g., *Jaws*' famous *dah-Dah . . . dah Dah*). (Sonnenschein 2001:78)

Monologue (interior) An extended speech by a character that is spoken with interiority as though the expression of the thoughts of the character's mind are not heard by any of the diegetic characters of the story. It tends to be produced with mouth close to microphone.

Montage This is a style of editing and sound narrative that has similar and different meanings in the visual medium. Soviet filmmakers of the 1920s applied the term to define narrative that created meaning through the juxtaposition of images despite that meaning not being present in the constituent shots themselves. The relationship between the joined sequences was dynamic and frequently discontinuous. The dynamism was related to the idea and impact of shots colliding together. In sound/audio documentary montage, particularly in the Scandinavian and continental tradition of programme making, the word relates to programme narrative where the interviewees and actuality itself unfolds, discloses and generates meaning rather than being explicitly directed by a narrative and linking voice.

Montage sequence A device in film and sound storytelling where the plot and/or story is compressed by an edited summary of symbolic, referential, explicit and/or implicit sequences. The representation of the passage of time is accelerated through cross-fades or sonic superimpositions.

Moral panic A social reaction to a media (sound) broadcast or communication where a group of individuals is demonised or problematised because their behaviour subverts the social order or threatens a dominant cultural hegemony. The term was gestated in the title of the book *Folk Devils and Moral Panics* (1972) and its developing discourse by the sociologist Stanley Cohen. Media institutions and their texts are criticised for fabricating or exaggerating a perceived threat to social norms and in the process minority groups are made scapegoats and demonised. The reported panic of radio listeners in the USA on Halloween night 1938 during and after the broadcast by CBS of the Mercury Theatre of the Art dramatisation of *War of the Worlds* led to the first academic analysis of a socio-psychological response to a media broadcast. Moral panic theory has been developed into a more complex understanding of how media texts generate fear, anxiety and prejudice about social and racial groups beyond single media events or transmissions.

Motif (sound) An element of sound that could be imagistic, a phrase or representation of action that occurs repeatedly. The sound motif takes on a special meaning through its repetition. An example could be a popular tune used in an advertising campaign or is sonically iconic of a popular film that then transfers mood and ideological feeling when used in other texts or repeated in the same text. The music becomes a social, personal, cultural and political characterisation and is capable through its association to invoke the power of media celebrity.

Multimodal The increasing mixing and interpolation of multimedia codes.

Multi-tracking A sophisticated recording and sound production system whereby sound can be designed by the parallel layering of soundtracks and then varying their relationships by changing their respective levels.

Musique concrète Electro-acoustic music that is made up of sounds from beyond traditional analogue acoustic instrumentation and human voices to include the noises of nature. The aesthetic was pioneered by Pierre Schaeffer and other engineers and artists at the French state broadcasting institution Radiodiffusion-Télévision Française in Paris where in 1951 he convened the *Groupe de Recherche de Musique Concrète*. The research and composition was assisted by the acquisition of magnetic tape recorders and splice editing.

Musique concrète renforceé A phrase playfully created in a BBC Third Programme satirical broadcast in 1956 of Henry Reed's *Hilda Tablet* and discussed by Louis Niebur where the eponymous character sets about creating her own brand of *musique concrète* for her new production of *Anthony and Cleopatra*. 'To realise this, Cleverdon [the BBC director/producer] used his knowledge and experience of *musique concrète*, now increasingly known in Britain as "radiophonic techniques," to collaborate with composer Donald Swann to create "some examples . . . based on comb and paper, Marjorie Westbury's zip fastener, etc"' (Niebur 2010:19).

Naturalistic dialogue Dialogue that sounds like ordinary everyday natural conversation.

Neo-realism Arising out of the Italian fascist documentary movement, coined by screenwriter Antonio Pietrangeli in his criticism of Visconti's film *Ossessione* and influenced by the French filmmaker Jean Renoir's genre of *poetic realism*. It is the deployment of documentary style in fictional film. It is characterised by location shooting rather than studio stage sets, a simulation of everyday life, limiting the role of narrative voice, representing social reality and a naturalistic style of dialogue so that the actors sound non-professional. There is an example of this in the 'actuality' sequences of Olive Shapley's 1939 BBC drama-documentary *The Classic Soil* where it is unclear whether a sequence of dialogue between a rent collector seeking the repayment of a debt from an impoverished householder in Manchester is real documentary or dramatised performance. The programme itself is overwhelmingly didactic in its use of narrative and Shapley later reflected in her memoirs *Broadcasting A Life* the feature 'was probably the most unfair and biased programme ever put out by the BBC' (Shapley 1994:56). She relished the artifice in framing the programme with Engels's *The Classic Soil*, the metaphorical land where capitalism flourished:

By recording much of the programme in Salford flea market among an odd little group of families who lived in a condemned warehouse in Pollard Street, we proved to our satisfaction and everyone else's intense annoyance that basically Manchester was unchanged since Engels wrote his famous denunciation of the city in 1844.

New feminism A form of feminism that advocates the belief that men and women have different strengths and roles and supporting equality for both genders. In essence the complementarity of men and women rather than privileging one sex over the other.

Noise-gate An electronic device that reduces or eliminates unwanted interferences of low-level sounds such as rumble, and room ambience. It operates by only passing a signal when its volume exceeds a predetermined level (Gibbs 2007:170 and Alten 2008:479).

Non-diegetic insert A sequence or sequences of sound originating from a source beyond the story frame of the narrative that is cut into the overall programme sequence.

Non-simultaneous sound Diegetic sound belonging to the story world of a film or audio drama but originating from a different time point when associated with the images or superimposed on the sound it is joined with.

Octave This word has a critical application in poetry and music. In the former it refers to the first eight lines of a Petrarchan sonnet. In music an octave covers the eight notes of any scale; a scale being a series of notes in alphabetical order, starting with the key note after which the scale is named.

Off-screen sound In film a sound originating from the diegesis but located outside the visible frame of the screen. Chion described this as the acousmatic.

Omniscient narrator/voice An all seeing, all knowing narrator who can be a character within a fictional story, but might also be a neutral 'voice of god', or a linking presenter for a documentary.

Onomatopoeia Language in poetry, drama or prose that resembles and imitates the sounds that it describes.

Opening exposition The beginnings of audio dramas are said to be more demanding in terms of capturing the interest and commitment of a listening audience because of the wallpaper nature of radio and sound entertainment consumption. There is always the challenge of the visual paradigm. Hence the tendency for many audio dramaturges to emphasise the importance of beginning the narrative in crisis location and temporality where urgent, enigmatic and intriguing questions are asked. It is the equivalent of *in medias re* in screenplay conventions where the narrative begins in the middle of things. Intensive expectations, possibilities are raised, interesting locations, exciting ideas and powerful characterisations are introduced.

Overdubbing A process used in multi-track editing to layer soundtracks to an existing recording and increase the intensity and texture of sound (Gibbs 2007:171).

Paradoxical sound An expression of sound in terms of communication that is contradictory, but nonetheless expresses a truth; seemingly absurd, but true.

Parallelism or parallel sound A technique where the sound structure has a similar structure or pattern and is used to frame a sequence of communication usually for dramatic purposes. In parallel editing narrative is moved back and forth between two or more lines of action that are meant to be occurring at the same time.

Pathetic fallacy A term of literary criticism where the expression of natural elements such as the weather represents human attitudes, moods and emotions. Sound design can equally be used in this way.

Personification (sonic) When an object, animal or non-human being or concept is articulated or treated with human characteristics, speech and behaviour.

Phantasmagoria Originally a genre of theatre where magic lanterns and light illusions were used to create the projection of gothic and supernatural images onto the set of semi-transparent screens. In modernist media texts the concept has developed into ghostly representations of sound and imagery in horror style and fantastic stories. It is an understanding that depends on the engagement of the human imagination in sound though it can obviously be triggered by the store of cultural memory of film and theatre presentations.

Phantasmic radio A term coined by the creative and much respected cultural critic Allen S. Weiss to present a new theoretical perspective on avant-garde radio experiments by Antonin Artaud and John Cage and others. Weiss argued in the book with this expression as its title published in 1995, that there is a *phantasmic* realm of radio that embraces artistic representations of the alienation of the self, the annihilation of the body, the fracturing, dispersal and the reconstruction of the disembodied voice, modernism and modern consciousness.

Playback singing A production process, usually in film, whereby songs are pre-recorded by specialist singers so that the actor lip-synchs the lyrics. It is sometimes applied in live theatre where it is referred to as miming. It is a conventional motif and production device in the Indian film industry – known as Bollywood (Benyahia 2009:431).

Pleasure sound The concept of how sound provides physical and psychological pleasure for listeners. The frame of consideration can bridge musical harmony and melody, spoken poetry, plainsong, choral chanting, meditative mantras, and horror suspense in terms of audio drama. In Freudian psychoanalytical theory it could be argued that the love of looking, scopophilia, must have its equivalent in love of listening or hearing that could be represented in the word audiophilia, which was adopted and applied in a journal article in *Screen* entitled 'Audiophilia: audiovisual pleasure and narrative cinema in *Jackie Brown*' by Robert Miklitsch. He argued (Miklitsch 2004:287) that audiophilia:

> is a manifest, constitutive aspect of the film's 'musical imaginary'. My close reading of Tarantino's film will also endeavour to show how what I call the 'acoustic signifier' – in the form of, in particular, non-diegetic as opposed to diegetic music – not only provides a pointed perspective on the agency or perceived mastery of the various main characters but reflects the dynamic relation that obtains between the look and the gaze or between, in the sonic register, 'listening' and 'being audited'.

Plot All the events directly presented in the fiction and non-fiction narrative frame of the programme in terms of chronological order, duration, cause and effect, frequency, and locations as opposed to the over-arching story that can be imagined, discovered by further research, assumed or known by the listening audience. The audience can have a separate understanding of where characters originated and arrived from, and events that could have happened before, parallel and after the narrative frame so communicated. This could be the difference between *syuzhet* and *fabula* in narratological Russian formalism. In brief the plot is the way that a story is organised and is the employment of the devices of narrative, whereas *fabula* is raw material of the story and the chronological order of narrated or retold events. *Syuzhet* would be represented in a story's narrative frame of flashbacks and flash-forwards and ellipses, but *fabula* would be the actual historical timeline. There is a parallel understanding of this distinction in the use of the critical terms of discourse and real time in narrative. The former relates to the timeline represented in the action of the narrative as opposed to actual historical chronological time.

Point of listening (POL) This is an equivalent of the concept of POV in film and was first critically applied by the British radio drama theorist Alan Beck. It is the perspective of communication from the point of understanding and constructed focus of a character, ideological position or even the listener. It is easier to anchor point of listening through narrative words or voice-over. However, the point of listener could be a character who never speaks as in Andrew Sachs's experimental radio play *Revenge*. The point of listening as in point of view is very often determined by the type of microphone and its positioning in the recording process.

Polyphonic In music an instrument that can play multiple notes at the same time. Synthesisers and electronic musical technology means that polyphonic sound is more realisable. Polyphonic music developed from plainchant and is a method of composition that combines two or more melodies so that they make musical sense (Dimond 1982:5).

Polysemic In linguistics the capacity of single signs in language to have multiple meanings.

Post-Marxism Development of Karl Marx's ethical, politico-economic and political philosophical ideas to engage modern and postmodern societies.

Postmodernity The social and cultural environment after the age of twentieth-century modernity and focusing on the nature of living in an information age with global and accelerating networks of media and communications systems. The concept is also associated with ideological insecurity about truth, progress, history and identity along with a breaking up and fusion through pastiche and collage of form and style with a debunking of sincerity by celebrating irony, parody and satire. The term is contested in its meaning and complex in its application. It is sometimes suggested that postmodernity refers to a selfconscious belief that human identity is constructed by media style and presence.

Poststructuralism Another term that is complex and difficult to tie down in terms of a simple phrase. An uncontroversial explanation would be the theoretical and intellectual response to structuralism, the argument that culture is a construction and interpretation of language and that the close analysis of media texts and how they are interpreted is the proper site for determining the nature of culture.

Postsynchronisation Adding sounds to film/image sequence after they have been recorded and edited through dubbing and lip-synching. It is often part of the complex and usually expensive and time-consuming stage of postproduction. It is the synthesis of sound as opposed to the recording of ambient and location direct sound.

Preamplifier An electrical boosting circuit that amplifies a lesser signal to higher amplitude so that the sound playback can be effectively heard and processed. Microphone signals often need pre-amplifying when connected to mixers (Gibbs 2007:171).

Prefiguring (sonic) A literary critical term that can be applied to sound narrative when the programme or sequence anticipates a future development. This is also known as foreshadowing.

Propaganda (sound) Persuasive communication aimed at manipulating listener's values, beliefs and behaviour and to indoctrinate with an ideology. The art of sound propaganda has a history that extends back to the pressing of 78rpm discs in the early years of the phonograph industry by political campaigners such as the Suffragettes in Britain. Radio propaganda was developed during the Italian invasion of Abyssinia in 1935 and the Spanish Civil War between 1936 and 1939. The global conflict of the Second World War led to large-scale sound/radio propaganda strategies represented typically in Sefton Delmer's autobiographical text *Black Boomerang* (1962) in which he described his leading role in establishing fake German dissident radio stations that were broadcast to Germany. Theodor Adorno wrote a detailed academic study of sound propaganda techniques in *The Psychological Technique of Martin Luther Radio Addresses* (2000) by analysing the radio broadcasts of the now-forgotten Martin Luther Thomas, an American fascist-style demagogue of the Christian right in the 1930s. Adorno did his analysis while he was living in the United States and working with Paul Lazarsfeld on the social significance of radio.

Radiophonic As a neologism of radio and phonic, it can be simply understood as a preoccupation with the production of creative sound for radio programmes. It is a word strongly associated with a production laboratory at the BBC that was set up to provide creative sound effects and new electronic style music for radio and television productions.

Rendering Michel Chion's term for utilising sound to communicate feelings associated with the situation on the screen. It is a sound enhancement or dramatisation, sometimes with hyperbole processing, to agglomerate the sensations. The sound is counter-realistic though has the effect of reinforcing a naturalistic or realistic perception. It is a longstanding paradox known by sound designers that real sound of an event lacks dramatic content and impact. In production the sound has to be made more representational through a dramatic intensifying of the sound.

Reverberation The dying away of sound in real or virtual environments, which involves multiple blended and random reflections against surface after the sonic source has stopped vibrating. Reverberation time is simply the duration of a sound's journey to silence or more precisely how long it takes to reach one-millionth of its original intensity (Gibbs 2007:171 and Alten 2008:482).

Rhetorical sound Production and communication devices in sound that are used to make the message more powerful and persuasive. The technique can be word based, but it could also be a style of production and editing. In its most clumsy form it is prone to being criticised for being over-didactic, unsubtle, a form of preaching. The Nazi propaganda film *Der Ewige Jude* is often cited as being one of the most ineffective and repugnant texts of propaganda history.

Rhythm A critical notion rooted in sound in terms of the narrative paradigm determining the series of film shots, and movements within the shots. Rhythm as a critical concept is often broken down in terms of beat or pulse, accent or stress and tempo or pace. In the early days of animation, the sound would be produced first and the drawing and graphics were then created to match the rhythm of the soundtrack.

Sampler An electronic machine consisting of hardware and software that records short sound events such as noise, a note or musical phrase into computer memory that can then be triggered by Musical Instrument Digital Interface (MIDI) sequencing. It is also used in electro-acoustica to process and synthesise real-world sounds (Gibbs 2007:170 and Alten 2008:483).

Sensorium (media) A major interest of the Canadian cultural theorist Marshall McLuhan who focused on the impact of individual and multiple media on the human senses and the process of overall perception in the social and cultural context.

Sequencer A combination of digital software and hardware that is used for recording, editing, mixing and playing back music in digital audio or MIDI, a signal system that allows electronic instruments to communicate with each other (Gibbs 2007:170–1).

Serialism A term used in music to describe the alternative to traditional chord structures and tonality. The process involves structuring music according to time, dynamics and timbre without orchestral composition or arrangement. It is a genre that is counter-intuitive to the style of music characterised by melody, rhythm and harmony. The genre is associated with Schoenberg, Stravinsky, Babbit and Boulez (Gibbs 2007:171).

Sibilance A style of language where there is a repletion of the 's', 'z', 'sh' and soft 'c' sounds.

Simulacrum and simulacra The substitution of concrete reality and authenticity with copies and representations. In a postmodern and postindustrial age complex multimedia streams of digital social networking confuse and blur the delineation of what is truth and originality. In media studies the concept is associated with the French philosopher Jean Baudrillard who argues that reality has become hyperreality and vocabulary such as imitation, duplication and parody has lost value and significance because reality has been replaced by a contingent flux and fluidity of virally replicating signs. The cultural and social environment has been derealized by the media and over-saturation and immersion of the social environment with simulation.

Simultaneous sound Sound occurring parallel to the story represented by the image that is also diegetic.

Sine wave A single pitch known as pure tone and consequently lacking any harmonics (Gibbs 2007:171).

Sound bridge The sound from the previous scene that overlaps for a short period before the sound connected with the new scene begins. In the alternative shortly before the end of a scene, the sound from the next scene provides the direction of narrative into that scene.

Sound perspective The perception by the audience of a sound's position in the spatiality of the film or audio drama. This can be achieved by the application of volume, pitch, timbre and panning dynamic in the context of stereo, binaural or surround sound.

Sound symbolism Using sound to represent something concrete or abstract. The idea of 'sound image' indicates that sounds can be analysed for their meaning in the same way as visual pictures.

Sound zoom A sonic equivalent of the idea of the focal length zoom shortening or lengthening to give a closer or wider view. A sound zoom is achieved by the selection of narrow field uni-directional microphones. A closer or distant recording is achieved by pointing directly at the source of a sound or moving it away (off-mic). The effect can also be produced by moving towards or retreating from a sound source with microphones selected for their pick-up dynamics and sensitivity. This creates a moving dynamic in location recording between foreground and background.

Square wave A sound very rich in harmonics as a result of its complex pitch (Gibbs 2007:171).

Stream-of-consciousness A style of sound communication and production that expresses a flow of thoughts through characterisation or story telling without any introduction, linking presentation and narrative. It is sometimes synonymous with the word 'montage'.

Structuralism Focusing on the form of a sound text and also appreciating the meaning of the sequence of ideas within it.

Synchresis Michel Chion describes the term as a meaningful fusion of the relationship between what is seen and heard at the same time (Chion 1996:22).

Synchretic *acousmêtre* A phrase gestated by Louis Niebur to describe a sound that is referential and at the same time unknowable. In his analysis of sound effects used in the 1950 BBC science fiction series *Journey Into Space* he writes: 'The ability to combine the synchretic nature of a rock launch with the mysterious acousmatic "unknowableness" of the futuristic technology renders the rocket a virtual synchretic acousmêtre' (Niebur 2010:13).

Synchronous sound A technical term for matching sound to the movements on the screen, for example, dialogue sound corresponding to visible lip movements.

Synergy Linked to the debate about convergence, this word describes how media institutions harness the relations between multimedia modes of production, distribution and publication. This can result in rationalisation of resources and content creation and/or creative and cross-media symbiosis in terms of the scale of communicating fiction and factual texts. Media agglomerates acquire production and publication synergies through ownership of radio, online, traditional print, music and film production operations. Even state and taxation funded public sector broadcasting (PSBs) institutions such as the BBC engage in cross media and public/commercial/privatised synergies. For example radio dramas produced and transmitted free to air are merchandised as audio drama through MP3 downloads online in a commercial market of sound entertainment downloads. Furthermore, it is also possible for the same sound recording for television or film to be used in CD, online or radio products. The word synergy, as a combined or correlated academic and practice production focus on sound, has been used in this book through the expression *praxis* synergy. *Praxis* is a Greek word meaning the practice of a technical subject or art and in Marxism is understood to mean the willed action by which a theory or philosophy becomes a practical social activity.

Synthesiser A device combining digital hardware and software that enables a flexible creation of sound from electronic sources such as oscillators through filtering and enveloping (Gibbs 2007:171).

Technological determinism A tendency to overemphasise the importance and role of sound and radio media technologies in explaining and analysing social, political, cultural change. This could be a charge laid against the medium is the message and massage theorist Marshall McLuhan.

Territory sounds Michel Chion coined the term to describe the presence of sounds that provided a special perspective and defined the nature of the ambience. He gave as examples the sound of birdsong or ringing church bells since these could identify a particular location through the continuation and pervasiveness of the sounds (Chion 1994:75, 79, 85 and 87).

Textual speech A term defined by Michel Chion to explain speech in a film that cues and generates the images that it evokes. This is generally voice-over commentary and it controls the film's narration and Chion eloquently observes: 'Textual speech is inseparable from an archaic power: the pure and original pleasure of transforming the world through language, and of ruling over one's creation by naming it' (Chion 1994:173).

Theatre of the absurd A term coined by a former Editor of BBC Radio Drama, Martin Esslin, to describe a creative movement in drama emerging from the continent during the 1950s that disrupted and subverted conventional approaches to plot and dialogue in prose, poetry and drama to stress the absurdity of existence; a form of existentialism.

Theatrical speech The dialogue of characters in a film that is simultaneously heard by the audience. This dialogic sound term can also be applied to the vocal interaction of characters in an audio/radio drama (Chion 1994:171–2 and 224).

Transducer An electronic machine that converts one form of energy into another but for the purposes of sound production is useful in enabling a microphone to turn sound as vibrations in air into an electrical signal that can power sound transmission from speakers.

Uses and gratifications theory An understanding that the audience plays an active role in determining the meaning of media texts, makes independent choices, and is not a passive recipient of messages as though being injected with hypodermic syringes. J.G. Blumler and E. Katz in *The Uses of Mass Communication* (1974) argued that listener reception can involve the use of media texts to be diverted from everyday problems and routine, the construction of identity by bricolaging characters, values and behaviour represented in the media texts, surveillance information gathering and deriving emotional inspiration and support as an imaginative personal relationship with the text.

Virtual reality Cyberspace and computer-simulated networks of communication, sometimes described as 'virtual communities' generate notions of a cyber-world where social interaction is digitally computer-mediated in and around websites, social networking and bulletin boards. Sound performs a significant communicative function through Skype, podcasting, Internet radio and sonic conferencing and online computer gaming.

Virtual synchresis Louis Niebur argues that the conventional nature of sound effects in radio involves the audience's assumptions of the source of sound being proved correct:

If a character in a radio play announces, 'Hark! A horse approaches!' and the sound of galloping hooves (be they real horses or coconut shells) follows and gets louder, listeners do not need a visual picture of a horse to believe that a character has just ridden up on a horse.

Here synchretic sound combines synthesis – the actual sound effect – with sychronisation (a function of dialogue, other sound effects and context) (Niebur 2010:12–13).

Virtually acousmatic Louis Niebur uses the term to describe radio sounds that simulate the filmic technique of *acousmêtre* (Niebur 2010).

Vocoder An electronic machine that generates synthesised speech. Gibbs describes its technical specification as a system that 'imposes the energy distribution of one sound (the modulator) on to another (the carrier)' (Gibbs 2007:171). White (2003:196) defines it as a signal processor that:

imposes a changing spectral filter on a sound based on the frequency characteristics of the second sound. By taking the spectral content of a human voice and imposing it on a musical instrument, talking-instrument effects can be created.

Consequently Coryat describes it as a 'cool, retro sound [. . .] Think "Mr. Roboto" by Styx' (Coryat 2008:153).

White noise A sound made up of a frequency distribution of one with all elements of equal intensity and was originally used for audio testing purposes. Tony Gibbs argues that it is a 'very rich potential sound source' (Gibbs 2007:171).

White space A term in sound art where a gallery space is devoid of decorative features and there is tendency to whitewash the walls and ceilings so that the 'set' minimises qualification and impact on the work being exhibited. The convention equates to white and black box theatre stage sets (Gibbs 2007:171).

Bibliography

BOOKS

Adorno, Theodor (2000) *The Psychological Technique of Martin Luther Thomas' Radio Addresses*, Stanford, California: Stanford University Press.

Alburger, James R. (1999) *The Art of Voice Acting: The Craft and Business Performing for Voice-Over*, Boston and Oxford: Focal Press.

Alten, Stanley R. (2008) *Audio in Media* (8th edition), London and New York: Thomson, Wadsworth.

Altman, Rick (ed.) (1992) *Sound Theory, Sound Practice*, London and New York: Routledge.

Andersen, Earl (1994) *Hard Place To Do Time: The Story of Oakalla Prison 1912–1991*, New Westminster, British Columbia: Hillpoint Publishing.

Andrews, Graham J. (1995) *You're On Air: A Guide to Writing, Preparing and Presenting Programs for Community Radio*, Sydney, Australia: Currency Press.

Arnheim, Rudolf (1936) *Radio*, Ludwig, Margaret and Read, Herbert (trans.), London: Faber & Faber.

Attali, Jacques and Massumi, Brian (1985) *Noise: The Political Economy of Music*, Minneapolis, Minnesota: University of Minnosota Press.

Augaitis, Daina and Lander, Dan (1994) *Radio Rethink: Art, Sound and Transmission*, Alberta, Canada: Walter Phillips Gallery, The Banff Centre for the Arts.

Augoyard, Jean-Francois and Torgue, Henry (eds) (2006) *Sonic Experience: A Guide to Everyday Sounds*, McCartney, Andra and Paquette, David (trans.), London and Montreal: McGill-Queen's University Press.

Avery, Todd (2006) *Radio Modernism: Literature, Ethics, and the BBC, 1922–1938*, Aldershot, Hampshire: Ashgate.

Bakhtin, M.M. (1981) *The Dialogic Imagination: Four Essays*, Austin, Texas: University of Texas Press.

Bannerman, R. Leroy (1986) *Norman Corwin and Radio – The Golden Years*, Tuscaloosa, Alabama: University of Alabama Press.

Barnard, Stephen (2000) *Studying Radio*, New York and London: Arnold, Hodder Headline Group.

Barthes, Roland (1977) *Image Music Text*, Heath, Stephen (trans.), London: Fontana Press/HarperCollins.

—— (1990) *S/Z*, Oxford: Wiley-Blackwell.

Beauchamp, Robin (2005) *Designing Sound for Animation*, London and New York: Focal Press, an imprint of Elsevier.

Beck, Alan (1997) *Radio Acting*, London: A&C Black.

Bennett, Andy (2000) *Popular Music and Youth Culture*, London: Macmillan Press; New York: St Martin's Press.

—— (2001) *Cultures of Popular Music*, Buckingham and Philadelphia, Pennsylvania: Open University Press.

Benyahia, Sarah Casey, Gaffney, Freddie and White, John (2008) *Film Studies AS: The Essential Introduction* (2nd edition), London and New York: Routledge.

—— (2009) *Film Studies A2: The Essential Introduction* (2nd edition), London and New York: Routledge.

Berry, Cicely (1992) *The Actor and His Text*, London: Virgin.

Biewen, John and Dilworth, Alexa (eds) (2010) *Reality Radio: Telling True Stories in Sound*, Chapel Hill, North Carolina: The University of North Carolina Press.

Birch, Dinah, Martin, Graham and Walder, Dennis (2001) *A319 Block 2 – The Impact of Modernism, Literature in the Modern World*, Milton Keynes: The Open University.

Birdsall, Carolyn and Enns, Anthony (2008) *Sonic Mediations: Body, Sound, Technology*, Newcastle-upon-Tyne: Cambridge Scholars Publishing.

Blesser, Barry and Salter, Linda-Ruth (2007) *Spaces Speak, Are You Listening? Experiencing Aural Architecture*, Cambridge, Massachusetts, and London: The MIT Press.

Bordwell, David and Thompson, Kristin (1993) *Film History: An Introduction*, New York: McGraw-Hill.

—— (1997) *Film Art: An Introduction* (5th edition), New York: McGraw-Hill.

Borwick, John (ed.) (1996) *Recording Studio Practice* (3rd edition), Oxford: Oxford University Press.

Bracewell, John L. (1993) *Sound Design in the Theatre*, Englewood Cliffs, New Jersey: Prentice Hall College Division.

Brewster, Bill and Broughton, Frank (1999) *Last Night a DJ Saved My Life: The History of the Disc Jockey*, London: Headline Book Publishing.

Briscoe, Desmond and Curtis-Bramwell, Roy (1983) *The BBC Radiophonic Workshop*, London: BBC Books.

Brown, R.D. (2000) 'From Burckhardt to Greenblatt: New Historicisms and Old', in Whitlock, K. (ed.) *The Renaissance in Europe – A Reader*, New Haven and London: Yale University Press.

Brown, Ross (2009) *Sound. A Reader in Theatre Practice*, London: Palgrave Macmillan.

Buckland, Warren (1998) *Film Studies*, London: Hodder & Stoughton.

Bull, Andy (2010) *Multimedia Journalism: A Practical Guide*, London and New York: Routledge.

Bull, Michael (2000) *Sounding Out the City: Personal Stereos and the Management of Everyday Life*, Oxford and New York: Berg.

Bull, Michael and Back, Les (eds) (2003) *The Auditory Culture Reader*, Oxford and New York: Berg.

Bunn, Rex (1993) *Practical Stage Lighting*, Sydney, Australia: Currency Press.

Burke, Peter and Briggs, Asa (2002) *A Social History of the Media – From Gutenberg to the Internet*, Cambridge: Polity.

Burris-Meyer, Harold (1959, 1979) *Sound in the Theatre* (revised edition), New York: Theatre Arts Books.

Cage, John (1973) *Silence: Lectures and Writings*, London: Marion Boyars.

Cantril, Hadley and Allport, Gordon W. (1935) *The Psychology of Radio*, New York and London: Harper & Brothers Publishers.

Chadabe, Joel (1997) *Electric Sound: The Past and Promise of Electronic Music*, Englewood Cliffs, New Jersey: Prentice Hall; London: Pearson Education.

Chanan, Michael (1994) *Musica Practica – The Social Practice of Western Music from Gregorian Chant to Postmodernism*, London: Verso.

—— (1995) *Repeated Takes: A Short History of Recording and Its Effects on Music*, London and New York: Verso.

Chantler, Paul and Stewart, Peter (2003) *Basic Radio Journalism*, London and New York: Focal Press, an imprint of Elsevier.

—— (2009) *Essential Radio Journalism: How to Produce and Present Radio News*, London: A&C Black.

Chaplin, Elizabeth (2006) *DA204 Understanding Media, Study Guide 4*, Milton Keynes: The Open University.

Chapman, Robert (1992) *Selling the Sixties: The Pirates and Pop Music Radio*, London and New York: Routledge.

Chignell, Hugh (2009) *Key Concepts in Radio Studies*, London: Sage Publications.

Childs, G.W., IV (2007) *Creating Music and Sound for Games*, Boston: Thomson Course Technology.

Chion, Michel (1994) *Audio-Vision: Sound on Screen*, Gorbman, Claudia (trans. and ed.) and Murch, Walter (Foreword), New York: Columbia University Press.

Collins, Karen (2008) *Game Sound: An Introduction to the History, Theory, and Practice of Video Game Music and Sound Design*, Cambridge, Massachusetts, and London: The MIT Press.

Collins, Richard and Evans, Jessica (eds) (2006) *Media Technologies, Markets and Regulation*, Maidenhead: Open University Press.

Collison, David (1976, 1982) *Stage Sound* (2nd edition), London: Cassell Illustrated.

Corwin, Norman (1947) *Untitled and Other Radio Dramas*, New York: Henry Holt and Company.

Cory, Mark Ensign (1974) *The Emergence of an Acoustical Art Form*, Lincoln, Nebraska: University of Nebraska Press.

Coryat, Karl (2008) *Guerrilla Home Recording: How To Get Great Sound From Any Studio* (2nd edition), New York: Hal Leonard.

Couldry, Nick (2003) *Media Rituals: A Critical Approach*, London and New York: Routledge.

Cox, Christoph and Warner, Daniel (eds) (2008) *Audio Culture: Readings in Modern Music*, New York: Continuum.

Crisell, Andrew (1994) *Understanding Radio* (2nd edition), London and New York: Routledge.

—— (ed.) (2006) *More than a Music Box: Radio Cultures and Communities in a Multi-Media World*, New York, Oxford: Berghahn Books.

Crook, Tim (1999) *Radio Drama: Theory and Practice*, London and New York: Routledge.

—— (2007) 'The Sociology of Radio', in Ritzer, George (ed.) *Blackwell Encyclopedia of Sociology* (Volume VIII), Oxford: Blackwell, pp. 3777–81.

Curran, James (2002) *Media and Power*, London and New York: Routledge.

Curran, James and Seaton, Jean (2009) *Power with Responsibility* (7th edition), London and New York: Routledge.

Curran, James, Smith, Anthony and Wingate, Pauline (1987) *Impacts and Influences*, London and New York: Methuen.

Dancyger, Ken (1991) *Broadcast Writing: Dramas, Comedies, and Documentaries*, Boston and London: Focal Press.

Dastbaz, Mohammad (2002) *Designing Interactive Multimedia Systems*, Maidenhead, Berkshire: McGraw-Hill Education.

De Fossard, Esta (2005) *Writing and Producing Radio Drama*, London and Thousand Oaks: Sage Publications.

Delmer, Sefton (1962) *Black Boomerang: The Story of His Secret 'Black Radio' Operation in World War 2 – and How It Has Boomeranged Today*, London: Secker & Warburg.

De Oliveira, Nicolas, Oxley, Nicola and Petry, Michael (2003) *Installation Art in the New Millenium: The Empire of the Senses*, London: Thames & Hudson.

Derrida, Jacques (2006) *Spectres of Marx: The State of the Debt, the Work of Mourning and the New International*, London and New York: Taylor & Francis.

Devereux, Paul and Richardson, Tony (2001) *Stone Age Soundtracks: The Acoustic Archaeology of Ancient Sites*, London: Vega, an imprint of Chrysalis books.

Dimond, Peter (1982) *Music*, London: Heinemann.

Dolar, Mladen (2006) *A Voice And Nothing More*, Cambridge, Massachusetts: The MIT Press.

Douglas, Susan J. (1999) *Listening In: Radio and the American Imagination, from Amos 'n' Andy and Edward R. Murrow to Wolfman Jack and Howard Stern*, New York: Times Books, Random House.

Downie, Alan (1981) 'The Growth of Government Tolerance of the Press to 1790', in *Development of the English Book Trade 1700–1899*, Oxford: Oxford Polytechnic Press.

—— (1994) *To Settle the Succession of the State – 1678–1750*, London: Palgrave-Macmillan.

Doyle, Peter (2006) *Echo and Reverb: Fabricating Space in Popular Music Recording, 1900–1960*, Middleton, Connecticut: Wesleyan University Press.

Drakakis, John (ed.) (1981) *British Radio Drama*, Cambridge: Cambridge University Press.

Drever, John Levack (2010) 'Sound Effect – Object – Event', in Brown, Ross (ed.) *Sound: A Reader in Theatre Practice*, Basingstoke, Hampshire: Palgrave Macmillan.

Durham Peters, John (1999) *Speaking into the Air: A History of the Idea of Communication*, Chicago: The University of Chicago Press.

Eliot, T.S. (1955) *Selected Prose*, Haywood, John (ed.), Harmondsworth, England: Penguin.

—— (1975) *Collected Poems, 1909–1962*, London: Faber and Faber.

Elmes, Simon (2007) *And Now On Radio 4: A 40th Birthday Celebration of the World's Best Radio Station*, London: Random House Books.

—— (2010, 27 January) 'Stories From Life', handout to students for seminar provided to Department of Media and Communications, Goldsmiths, University of London.

Emmerson, Simon (2000) *Music, Electronic Media and Culture*, Aldershot, Hampshire: Ashgate.

Esslin, Martin (1980) *Theatre of the Absurd* (3rd edition), Harmondsworth: Penguin.

—— (1987) *The Field of Drama: How the Signs of Drama Create Meaning on Stage and Screen*, London: Methuen.

Evans, Jessica and Hesmondhalgh, David (eds) (2006) *Understanding Media: Inside Celebrity*, Maidenhead: Open University Press.

Evans, Roger (1987) *How to Read Music*, London: Guild Publishing.

Everest, Alton (1975) *Handbook of Multichannel Recording*, Blue Ridge Summit, Pennsylvania: Tab Books.

Fairchild, Charles (2001) *Community Radio and Public Culture*, Cresskill, New Jersey: Hampton Press.

Fairservice, Don (2001) *Film Editing: History, Theory and Practice*, London and New York: Manchester University Press.

Findlay, Polly (2009) *War Horse Educational Workpack*, London: National Theatre.

Fisher, Margaret (2002) *Ezra Pound's Radio Operas: The BBC Experiments, 1931–1933*, Cambridge, Massachusetts, and London: The MIT Press.

Fleming, Carole (2010) *The Radio Handbook* (3rd edition), London and New York: Routledge.

Foucault, Michel (1991) *Discipline and Punish: The Birth of the Prison*, Alan Sheriden (trans.), Harmondsworth: Penguin.

Frith, Simon and Goodwin, Andrew (eds) (1990) *On Record, Rock, Pop, and the Written Word*, London and New York: Routledge.

Gardner, Sebastian (1995) 'Aesthetics', in Grayling, A.C. (ed.) *Philosophy 1: A Guide Through the Subject*, Oxford: Oxford University Press.

Garnett, David (2002) *The Secret History of PWE – The Political Warfare Executive 1939–1945*, London: St Ermin's Press.

Geller, Valerie (2009) *Creating Powerful Radio: Getting, Keeping and Growing Audiences, News Talk, Information, Personality*, London and New York: Focal Press, an imprint of Elsevier.

Gibbs, Tony (2007) *The Fundamentals of Sonic Art and Sound Design*, Lausanne, Switzerland: AVA Publishing.

Gibson, Bill (2007) *The Ultimate Live Sound Operator's Handbook*, New York: Hal Leonard Books.

Gilette, J. Michael (2008) *Theatrical Design and Production: An Introduction to Scenic Design and Construction, Lighting, Sound, Costume, and Makeup* (6th edition), London and New York: McGraw-Hill Higher Education.

Gilfillan, Daniel (2009) *German Experimental Radio*, Minneapolis, Minnesota, and London: University of Minnesota Press.

Gillespie, Marie (ed.) (2006) *Media Audiences*, Maidenhead, Berkshire: Open University Press.

Gillespie, Marie and Toynbee, Jason (eds) (2006) *Analysing Media Texts*, Maidenhead: Open University Press.

Goldberg, RoseLee (2001) *Performance Art: From Futurism to the Present World*, London: Thames & Hudson.

Gombrich, E.H. (2000) *Art and Illusion: A Study in the Psychology of Pictorial Representation* (5th edition), London: The Folio Society by arrangement with Phaidon Press.

Gondin, William R. and Mammen, Edward W. (1970) *The Art of Speaking*, London: Made Simple Books, W.H. Allen.

Goodman, Steve (2010) *Sonic Warfare: Sound, Affect, and the Ecology of Fear*, Cambridge, Massachusetts, and London: The MIT Press.

Grayling, A.C. (ed.) (1995) *Philosophy 1: A Guide Through the Subject*, Oxford: Oxford University Press.

—— (ed.) (1998) *Philosophy 2: Further Through the Subject*, Oxford: Oxford University Press.

Green, Michael (1958) *Stage Noises and Effects*, London: Herbert Jenkins, Practical Stage Handbooks.

Harrison, Charles and Wood, Paul J. (eds) (1992) *Arts in Theory 1900–2000: An Anthology of Changing Ideas*, Oxford: Wiley/Blackwell.

Hart, Anne (1997) *Cyberscribes. I: The New Journalists*, San Diego, California: Ellipsys International.

Hartley, John (2011) *Communication, Cultural and Media Studies: The Key Concepts* (4th edition), London and New York: Routledge.

Hausman, Carl, Benoit, Philip and O'Donnell, Lewis B. (2000) *Modern Radio Production: Production, Programming and Performance* (5th edition), New York and London: Wadsworth, Thomson Learning.

Hegarty, Paul (2009) *Noise/Music: A History*, New York and London: Continuum.

Hendy, David (2000a) *Radio in the Global Age*, Cambridge: Polity Press.

—— (2007) *Life on Air: A History of Radio Four*, Oxford: Oxford University Press.

Henriques, Julian (2009) 'Multi Senses & Multi Media' paper abstract, *Future of Sound Future of Light, Synaesthesia Symposium*, Goldsmiths, University of London, 24 March 2009.

—— (2011) *Sonic Bodies: Reggae Sound Systems, Performance Techniques, and Ways of Knowing*, New York: Continuum.

Hesmondhalgh, David (2006) *Media Production*, Maidenhead, Berkshire: Open University Press.

Hewston, Miles, Stroebe, Wolfgang and Stephenson, Geoffrey M. (1999) *Introduction to Social Psychology* (2nd edition), Oxford: Blackwell Publishers.

Hilmes, Michele (1990) *Hollywood and Broadcasting: From Radio to Cable*, Urbana, Illinois, and Chicago: University of Illinois Press.

—— (1997) *Radio Voices: American Broadcasting, 1922–1952*, Minneapolis, Minnesota: University of Minnesota Press.

—— (2002) *Only Connect: A Cultural History of Broadcasting in the United States*, London and New York: Wadsworth, Thomson Learning.

Hilmes, Michele and Loviglio, Jason (2002) *Radio Reader: Essays in the Cultural History of Radio*, London and New York: Routledge.

Holman, Tomlinson (2008) *Surround Sound: Up and Running* (2nd edition), London and New York: Focal Press, an imprint of Elsevier.

Holmes, Thom (2008) *Electronic and Experimental Music: Technology, Music and Culture* (3rd edition), London and New York: Routledge.

Horace (2000) *Art of Poetry: Classical Literary Criticism*, London and New York: Penguin Classics.

Hughes, Robert (1991) *The Shock of the New: Art and the Century of Change*, London: Thames & Hudson.

Hyde, Stuart W. (1971) *Television and Radio Announcing* (2nd edition), Boston: Houghton Mifflin Company.

Ihde, Don (2007) *Listening and Voice: Phenomenologies of Sound* (2nd edition), Albany, New York: State University of New York Press.

Jarman, Derek (1994) *Blue: Text of a Film*, Woodstock, New York: Overlook Press.

—— (2nd edition 1995) *Chroma*, London: Vintage Classics; USA: University of Minnesota Press.

Jaspers, Karl (1986) *Karl Jaspers: Basic Philosophical Writings*, Atlantic Highlands, New Jersey: Humanities Press.

Jay, Martin (1996) *The Dialectical Imagination: A History of the Frankfurt School and the Institute of Social Research 1923–1950*, Berkeley and London: University of California Press.

Johansen, T.K. (2007) *Aristotle on the Sense Organs*, Cambridge and New York: Cambridge University Press.

Kahn, Douglas (2001) *Noise, Water, Meat: A History of Sound in the Arts*, Cambridge, Massachusetts: The MIT Press.

Kahn, Douglas and Whitehead, Gregory (eds) (1994) *Wireless, Imagination Sound, Radio, and the Avant-Garde*, London and Cambridge, Massachusetts: The MIT Press.

Karpf, Anne (2006) *The Human Voice: The Story of a Remarkable Talent*, London: Bloomsbury.

Katz, Bob (2007) *Mastering Audio: The Art and the Science* (2nd edition), London and New York: Focal Press, an imprint of Elsevier.

Katz, Mark (2004) *Capturing Sound: How Technology Has Changed Music*, Berkeley and London: University of California Press.

Kay, Deena and LeBrecht, James (2000) *Sound and Music for the Theatre: The Art and Technique of Design* (2nd edition), London and New York: Focal Press, an imprint of Elsevier.

Kay, Michael and Popperwell, Andrew (1992) *Making Radio: A Guide to Basic Broadcasting Production and Techniques*, London: Broadside Books.

Keith, Michael C. (2007) *The Radio Station: Broadcast, Satellite and Internet* (7th edition), London and New York: Focal Press, an imprint of Elsevier.

Kittler, Friedrich A. (1999) *Gramophone, Film, Typewriter*, Winthrop-Young, Geoffrey and Wutz, Michael (trans.), Stanford, California: Stanford University Press.

LaBelle, Brandon (2008) *Background Noise: Perspectives on Sound Art*, New York, London: Continuum.

Lacey, Nick (2000) *Narrative and Genre: Key Concepts in Media Studies*, London: Macmillan Press.

Lansley, Andrew (2011) *Sound Production: A Guide to Using Audio within Media Production*, London and New York: Routledge.

Lastra, James (2000) *Sound Technology and the American Cinema*, New York: Columbia University Press.

Lax, Stephen (2009) *Media and Communication Technologies: A Critical Introduction*, Basingstoke, Hampshire: Palgrave Macmillan.

Lazarsfeld, Paul F. (ed.) (1940) *Radio and the Printed Page: An Introduction to the Study of Radio and Its Role in the Communication of Ideas*, New York: Duell, Sloan and Pearce.

—— (ed.) (1946) *The People Look at Radio*, Chapel Hill, North Carolina: The University of North Carolina Press.

Lazarsfeld, Paul F., Berelson, Bernard and Gaudet, Hazel (eds) (1944) *The People's Choice: How the Voter Makes Up His Mind in a Presidential Campaign*, New York: Duell, Sloan and Pearce.

Lazarsfeld, Paul F. and Kendall, Patricia L. (eds) (1948) *Radio Listening in America*, New York: Prentice-Hall.

Lazarsfeld, Paul F. and Stanton, Frank N. (eds) (1941) *Radio Research 1941*, New York: Duell, Sloan and Pearce.

—— (eds) (1944) *Radio Research 1942–1943*, New York: Duell, Sloan and Pearce.

Lee, Eric (2005) *How Internet Radio Can Change the World: An Activist's Handbook*, New York: iUniverse.

Leonard, John A. (2001) *Theatre Sound*, New York: Routledge.

Levin, David Mitchell (1989) *The Listening Self: Personal Growth, Social Change and the Closure of Metaphysics*, London and New York: Routledge.

Lewis, C.A. (1924) *Broadcasting from Within*, London: George Newnes.

Lewis, Cecil (1936, 1993, 2000) *Sagittarius Rising*, London: Folio Society.

Lewis, Peter (ed.) (1981) *Radio Drama*, Harlow, Essex: Longman.

Lewis, Peter M. and Booth, Jerry (1989) *The Invisible Medium: Public, Commercial and Community Radio*, London: Macmillan.

Leyshon, Andrew, Matless, David and Revill, George (eds) (1998) *The Place of Music*, New York and London: Guilford Press.

Licht, Alan (2007) *Sound Art: Beyond Music, Between Categories*, New York: Rizzoli.

Local Radio Workshop (1983) *Capital: Local Radio and Private Profit*, London: Comedia Publishing Group.

—— (1983) *Nothing Local About It: London's Local Radio*, London: Comedia Publishing Group.

Loviglio, Jason (2005) *Radio's Intimate Public: Network Broadcasting and Mass-Mediated Democracy*, Minneapolis, Minnesota: University of Minnesota Press.

Lynch, Joanna R. and Gillispie, Greg (1998) *Process and Practice of Radio Programming*, Lanham, Maryland: University Press of America.

Maltby, Richard (2003) *Hollywood Cinema* (2nd edition), Oxford: Blackwell Publishing.

Marks, Aaron (2009) *A Complete Guide to Game Audio for Composers, Musicians, Sound Designers, and Game Developers* (2nd edition), London and New York: Focal Press, an imprint of Elsevier.

Martin, Graham (1991) 'What was Modernism?' in *The Impact of Modernism, Literature in the Modern World*, Milton Keynes: The Open University.

Martin, Peter J. (1995) *Sounds and Society: Themes in the Sociology of Music*, Manchester and New York: Manchester University Press.

Matheson, Hilda (1933) *Broadcasting*, London: Thornton Butterworth.

Mattern, Joanne (2002) *From Radio to the Wireless Web*, Berkeley Heights, New Jersey: Enslow Publishers.

McLeish, Robert (1994) *Radio Production* (3rd edition), London and New York: Focal Press, an imprint of Elsevier.

McLuhan, Marshall and Fiore, Quentin (1967) *The Medium is the Massage: An Inventory of Effects*, Harmondsworth: Penguin.

McWhinnie, Donald (1959) *The Art of Radio*, London: Faber and Faber.

Merleau-Ponty, Maurice (2002) *Phenomenology of Perception*, Smith, Colin (trans.), London and New York: Routledge.

Milam, Lorenzo Wilson (1988) *Sex and Broadcasting: A Handbook on Starting a Radio Station for the Community*, San Diego, California: MHO & MHO Works.

Mills, Jenni (2004) *The Broadcast Voice*, London and New York: Focal Press, an imprint of Elsevier.

Milner, Greg (2009) *Perfecting Sound Forever: The Story of Recorded Music*, London: Granta Books.

Mitchell, Caroline (ed.) (2000) *Women and Radio: Airing Differences*, London and New York: Routledge.

Mithen, Steven (2006) *The Singing Neanderthals: The Origins of Music, Language, Mind and Body*, London: Weidenfeld & Nicholson.

Moran, Dermot (2000) *Introduction to Phenomenology*, London and New York: Routledge.

Morley, David (1992) *Television, Audiences and Cultural Studies*, London and New York: Routledge.

Mundy, John (1999) *Popular Music On Screen: From the Hollywood Musical to Music Video*, Manchester and New York: Manchester University Press.

Munson, Wayne (1993) *All Talk: The Talkshow in Media Culture*, Philadelphia, Pennsylvania: Temple University Press.

Murray, P. (2000) *Classical Literary Criticism*, London and New York: Penguin Classics.

Nancy, Jean-Luc (2007) *Listening*, Mandell, Charlotte (trans.), New York: Fordham University Press.

Napier, Frank (1948) *Noises Off: A Handbook of Sound Effects* (3rd edition), London: Frederick Muller.

Nelmes, Jill (ed.) (1996) *An Introduction to Film Studies*, London and New York: Routledge.

Nichols, Bill (1991) *Representing Reality: Issues and Concepts in Documentary*, London: John Wiley & Sons.

—— (1995) *Blurred Boundaries: Questions of Meaning in Contemporary Culture*, London: John Wiley & Sons.

Nichols, David (ed.) (2002) *The Cambridge Companion to John Cage*, Cambridge: Cambridge University Press.

Niebur, Louis (2010) *Special Sound: The Creation and Legacy of the BBC Radiophonic Workshop*, Oxford and New York: Oxford University Press.

Nyre, Lars (2008) *Sound Media: From Live Journalism to Music Recording*, London and New York: Routledge.

O'Sullivan, Dan and Igoe, Tom (2004) *Physical Computing: Sensing and Controlling the Physical World with Computers*, Cheltenham: Premier Press.

Partridge, Simon (1982) *Not the BBC/IBA: The Case for Community Radio*, London: Comedia Publishing Group.

Paul, Christiane (2008) *Digital Art*, London: Thames & Hudson.

Pear, T.H. (1931) *Voice and Personality*, London: Chapman and Hall.

Piotrowski, T. (1998) *Poland's Holocaust*, Jefferson, North Carolina, and London: McFarland.

Popkin, Richard H. and Stroll, Avrum (1956, 1969, 1993) *Philosophy* (2nd edition), Oxford: Butterworth-Heinemann, Made Simple Books.

Priestman, Chris (2002) *Web Radio: Radio Production for Internet Streaming*, London, New York: Focal Press, an imprint of Elsevier.

Propp, Vladimir (1968) *Morphology of the Russian Folktale* (2nd revised edition), Austin, Texas: University of Texas Press.

Rattigan, Dermot (2002) *Theatre of Sound: Radio and the Dramatic Imagination*, Dublin: Carysfort Press.

Reese, David E. and Gross, Lynne S. (2002) *Radio Production Worktext: Studio and Equipment* (4th edition), London and New York: Focal Press, an imprint of Elsevier.

Reith, John (1924) *Broadcast Over Britain*, London: Hodder & Stoughton.

Richter, J.P. (1939) *The Literary Works of Leonardo da Vinci*, Oxford: Oxford University Press.

Riegler, Thomas (2004) *Digital-Radio: Alles über DAB, DRM und Web-Radio*, Baden-Baden, Germany: Siebel-Verlag.

Riley, Richard (2008) *Audio Editing Adobe Audition* (2nd edition), Thetford, Norfolk: PC Publishing.

Rodger, Ian (1982) *Radio Drama*, London: Macmillan Press.

Roscoe, Jane and Hight, Craig (2001) *Faking It: Mock-documentary and the Subversion of Factuality*, Manchester: Manchester University Press.

Rose, Jay (2008) *Producing Great Sound for Film and Video* (3rd edition), London, New York: Focal Press, an imprint of Elsevier.

Rosenbaum, Marcus D. and Dinges, John (eds) (1992) *Sound Reporting: The National Public Guide to Radio Journalism and Production*, Dubuque, Iowa: Kendall/Hunt.

Rudin, Richard (2011) *Broadcasting in the 21st Century*, London: Palgrave Macmillan.

Rush, Michael (2005) *New Media in Art*, London: Thames & Hudson.

Russolo, Luigi (1987) *The Art of Noises*, Hillsdale, New York: Pendragon Press.

Salamun, Kurt (1999) 'Jaspers', in Critchley, Simon and Schroeder, William R. (eds) *A Companion To Continental Philosophy*, Oxford: Blackwell Publishers.

Scannell, Paddy (ed.) (1991) *Broadcast Talk*, London and Newbury Park, California: Sage Publications.

—— (1996) *Radio, Television and Modern Life*, Oxford: Blackwell Publishers.

Schafer, R. Murray (1977, 1994) *Our Sonic Environment and the Soundscape: The Tuning of the World*, New York: Alfred Knopf/Random House.

Schwarz, David (1997) *Listening Subjects: Music, Psychoanalysis, Culture*, Durham, North Carolina: Duke University Press.

Seib, Philip (1993) *Rush Hour: Talk Radio, Politics, and the Rise of Rush Limbaugh*, Fort Worth, Texas: The Summit Group.

Serres, Michel (2008) *The Five Senses: A Philosophy of Mingled Bodies (1)*, Sankey, Margaret and Cowley, Peter (trans.), New York: Continuum.

Shapley, Olive (1996) *Broadcasting a Life*, Chipping Norton: Scarlet Press.

Shaw, Bernard Graham (2000) *Voice-Overs: A Practical Guide*, London: A&C Black.

Shingler, Martin and Wieringa, Cindy (1998) *On Air: Methods and Meanings of Radio*, London and New York: Arnold, Hodder Headline Group.

Sider, Larry, Freeman, Diane and Sider, Jerry (2003) *Soundscape: The School of Sound Lectures 1998–2001*, London and New York: Wallflower Press.

Siegel, Bruce H. (1992) *Creative Radio Production*, Boston, London: Focal Press.

Siepmann, Charles (1950) *Radio, Television and Society*, New York: Oxford University Press.

Sieveking, Lance (1934) *The Stuff of Radio*, London: Cassell and Company.

Smith, Steven C. (1991) *A Heart at Fire's Center: The Life and Music of Bernard Herrmann*, Berkeley: University of California Press.

Smulyan, Susan (1994) *Selling Radio: The Commercialization of American Broadcasting 1920–1934*, Washington and London: Smithsonian Institution Press.

Soley, Lawrence C. and Nichols, John S. (1987) *Clandestine Radio Broadcasting: A Study of Revolutionary and Counterrevolutionary Electronic Communication*, Westport, Connecticut: Praeger.

Sonnenschein, David (2001) *Sound Design: The Expressive Power of Music, Voice and Sound Effects in Cinema*, Studio City, California: Michael Wiese Productions.

Squier, Susan Merrill (2003) *Communities of the Air: Radio, Century, Radio Culture*, Durham, North Carolina: Duke University Press.

Starkey, Guy (2004) *Radio in Context*, Basingstoke, Hampshire: Palgrave, Macmillan.

Starkey, Guy and Crisell, Andrew (2009) *Radio Journalism*, London: Sage Publications.

Stern, Jonathan (2003) *The Audible Past: Cultural Origins of Sound Reproduction*, London and Durham, North Carolina: Duke University Press.

—— (ed.) (2011) *The Sound Studies Reader*, London and New York: Routledge.

Stewart, Peter (2006) *Essential Radio Skills: How to Present and Produce a Radio Show*, London: A&C Black.

Strauss, Neil (ed.) (1993) *Radiotext(e)*, New York: Columbia University.

Street, Seán (2002) *A Concise History of British Radio: 1922–2002*, Tiverton, Devon: Kelly Publications.

—— (2006) *Crossing the Ether: British Public Service Radio and Commercial Competition, 1922–1945*, Eastleigh, Southampton: John Libbey Publishing.

—— (2006) *Historical Dictionary of British Radio*, Lanham, Maryland, and Oxford: The Scarecrow Press.

—— (2012) *Radio and the Poetic Imagination: The Colour of Sound*, London and New York: Routledge.

Szendy, Peter (2008) *Listen: A History of Our Ears*, Mandell, Charlotte (trans.), New York: Fordham University Press.

Tisdall, Caroline and Bozzola, Angela (1978) *Futurism*, London: Thames & Hudson.

Todorov, Tsvetan (1975) *The Fantastic: A Structural Approach to a Literary Genre*, Howard, Richard and Scholes, Robert (trans.), Ithaca, New York: Cornell University Press.

—— (1988) 'The Typology of Detective Fiction', in *Modern Criticism and Theory: A Reader*, Lodge, David and Wood, Nigel (eds), London and New York: Longman White Plains.

Toop, David (1999) *Exotica: Fabricated Soundscapes in a Real World*, London: Serpent's Tail.

—— (2001) *Ocean of Sound: Aether Talk, Ambient Sound and Imaginary Worlds*, London: Serpent's Tail.

—— (2005) *Haunted Weather: Music, Silence and Memory*, London: Serpent's Tail.

—— (2010) *Sinister Resonance: The Mediumship of the Listener*, New York: Continuum.

Trewin, Janet (2003) *Presenting on TV and Radio*, London and New York: Focal Press, an imprint of Elsevier.

Turner, J. Clifford (1993) *Voice and Speech in the Theatre* (2nd edition), Morrison, Malcolm (ed.), London: A&C Black.

Van Leeuwen, Theo (1999) *Speech, Music, Sound*, London: Macmillan Press.

Viers, Ric (2008) *The Sound Effects Bible: How to Create and Record Hollywood Style Sound Effects*, Studio City, California: Michael Wiese Productions.

Vitruvius, Pollio (1960) *Vitruvius: The Ten Books on Architecture*, New York: Dover Publications.

Voegelin, Salomé (2010) *Listening to Noise and Silence*, New York and London: Continuum.

Walcutt, David (ed.) (1998) *Passport to Web Radio: Really Cool Wired Sounds From All Over the World*, Penn's Park, Pennsylvania: Lawrence Magne.

Walker, Jesse (2001) *Rebels on the Air: An Alternative History of Radio in America*, New York and London: New York University Press.

Walne, Graham (1990) *Sound for Theatre (Stage and Costume)*, London: A&C Black.

Warburton, Nigel (1999) *Philosophy: The Basics* (3rd edition), London and New York: Routledge.

—— (2006) *Philosophy: The Classics* (3rd edition), London and New York: Routledge.

Ward, Jamie (2008) *The Frog Who Croaked Blue: Synaesthesia and the Mixing of the Senses*, Hove and New York: Routledge. (See also www.thefrogwhocroakedblue.com)

Weis, Elizabeth and Belton, John (eds) (1985) *Film Sound: Theory and Practice*, New York: Columbia University Press.

Weiss, Allen S. (1995) *Phantasmic Radio*, London and Durham, North Carolina: Duke University Press.

—— (2001) *Experimental Sound and Radio*, Cambridge, Massachusetts: The MIT Press.

White, Paul (2003) *Recording and Production Techniques*, London: Sanctuary Publishing.

Whittaker, Jason (2002) *Producing for Web 2.0: A Student Guide* (2nd edition), London and New York: Routledge.

—— (2009) *Producing for Web 2.0: A Student Guide* (3rd edition), London and New York: Routledge.

Wilson, Stephen (2003) *Information Arts: Intersections of Art, Science and Technology*, Cambridge, Massachusetts: The MIT Press.

Winston, Brian (2000) *Lies, Damn Lies and Documentaries*, London: BFI Publishing.

Wishart, Trevor (1994) *Audible Design: A Plain and Easy Introduction to Sound Composition*, York: Orpheus the Pantomime.

Wishart, Trevor and Emmerson, Simon (1997) *On Sonic Art*, London and New York: Routledge.

Wood, Michael (2007) *The Story of India*, London: BBC Books, Random House.

Woolf, Virginia (1925, annotated 1992) *Mrs Dalloway*, Showalter, Elaine (introduction) and McNichol, Stella (ed.), Harmondsworth: Penguin.

Wyatt, Hilary and Amyes, Tim (2008) *Audio Post Production for Television and Film: An Introduction to Technology and Techniques* (3rd edition), London and New York: Focal Press, an imprint of Elsevier.

Yewdall, David Lewis (2007) *Practical Art of Motion Picture Sound* (3rd edition), London, New York: Focal Press, an imprint of Elsevier.

JOURNAL ARTICLES

Beck, Alan (1998) 'Point of Listening in Radio Plays', *Sound Journal* [online], www.kent.ac.uk/arts/sound-journal/beck981.html, accessed 30 March 2011.

Becker, Howard (1949, April) 'The Nature and Consequences of Black Propaganda', *American Sociological Review* 14(2): 221–35.

Crook, Tim (2001) Book Review—Theodor Adorno, the Psychological Technique of Martin Luther Thomas' Radio Addresses, *Journal of Radio Studies*, 8(1): 238–41.

Csapó-Sweeta, Rita M. and Shields, Donald C. (2000, September) 'Explicating the Saga Component of Symbolic Convergence Theory: The Case of Serbia's Radio B92 in Cyberspace', *Critical Studies in Media Communication*, 17(3): 316–33.

Cubitt, Sean (2010) 'The Sound of Sunlight', *Screen*, 51(2): 118–28. doi: 10.1093/screen/hjq005.

Gottlieb, William P. (1947) 'Picture Views of Music World Personalities', *Down Beat*, 14(21). Repository: Library of Congress Prints and Photographs Division, William P. Gottlieb Collection (DLC) 99-401005.

Hendy, David (2000b) 'A Political Economy of Radio in the Digital Age', *Journal of Radio and Audio Media Studies*, 7(1): 213–34.

Hopkinson, Amanda and Tacchi, Jo (2000, August) 'Special Issue: Radiocracy – Radio, Democracy and Development', *International Journal of Cultural Studies*, 3(2).

Huwiler, Elke (2010) 'Radio Drama Adaptations: An Approach Towards an Analytical Methodology', *Journal of Adaptation in Film and Performance*, 3(2): 129–40. doi: 10.1386/jafp.3.2.129_1.

Klein, Georg (2009) 'Site-Sounds: On Strategies of Sound Art in Public Space', *Organised Sound*, 14(1): 101–8.

Miklitsch, Robert (2004) 'Audiophilia: Audiovisual Pleasure and Narrative Cinema in *Jackie Brown*', *Screen*, 45(4): 287–304. doi: 10.1093/screen/45.4.287.

Mortola, Peter (1999) 'Narrative Formation and Gestalt Closure: Helping Clients Make Sense of "Disequilibrium" Through Stories in the Therapeutic Setting', *Gestalt Review*, 3(4): 308–20.

Sonnenschein, David (2011) 'Sound Spheres: A Model of Psychoacoustic Space in Cinema', *The New Soundtrack*, 1(1): 13–27. doi: 10.3366/sound.2011.0003.

Spinelli, Martin (2000, August) 'Democratic Rhetoric and Emergent Media: The Marketing of Participatory Community on Radio and the Internet' (Special Issue: Radiocracy), *International Journal of Cultural Studies*, 3(2): 268–78. doi: 10.1177/136787790000 300215.

Stedman, J.W. (1976) 'Enter a Phonograph', in *Theatre Notebook: A Journal of the History and Technique of the British Theatre*, XXX, 1.

Street, Seán (2004) 'Programme-Makers on Parker: Occupational Reflections on the Radio Production Legacy of Charles Parker', *The Radio Journal: International Studies in Broadcast and Audio Media*, 2(3): 187–94.

Varney, Denise (2008) 'Scenographies of the Everyday in Contemporary German Theatre – Anna Langhoff and Sasha Waltz Restage the Family Drama', *Contemporary Theatre Review*, 18(1): 56–68.

ACADEMIC THESES

Knight, Paula (2007) *Radio Drama: Sound, Text, Word; Bakhtin and the Aural Dialogue of Radio Drama* (doctoral thesis), Goldsmiths, University of London.

Nyre, Lars (2003) *Fidelity Matters: Sound Media and Realism in the 20th Century* (doctoral thesis), Department of Media Studies, University of Bergen, Faculty of Media and Journalism, Volda University College, Norway.

AUDIO AND MEDIA

BBC Music (2008) *BBC Radiophonic Workshop: A Retrospective.* Released on the Grey Area of Mute, Phonic3cd, 5099923698826, LC05834, BBC Worldwide, under exclusive license to Mute Records.

BBC Music (2005 and 2008) *BBC Radiophonic Music.* Released on the Grey Area of Mute. Original mono recordings digitally remastered. Original album produced at the BBC Radiophonic Workshop. Produced and remastered for compact disc by Mark Ayres. Executive Producer Lois Pryce, BBC Worldwide.

BBC Television Four (2004) *The Alchemists of Sound: The BBC Radiophonic Workshop,* transmitted 28 May 2005, www.bbc.co.uk/bbcfour/music/features/alchemists. shtml.

British Library (2011) *Evolving English: One Language, Many Voices* [exhibition], November 2010–April 2011, www.bl.uk/evolvingenglish/maplisten.html, accessed 28 July 2011.

Britton, David (writer) (2003, 9 November) *Chelsea Dreaming,* BBC Radio Three. Directed by Alison Hindell. Licensed for educational study in track 2 of DVD 00031 *DA204 Understanding Media*, Milton Keynes: The Open University. Also see 'Dave Britton Radio Plays', at www.suttonelms.org.uk.

Burgess, Marya (producer) (2010, 25 August) 'Case Study: SB – The Man Who Was Disappointed with What He Saw', *All in the Mind*, BBC Radio Four, presenter Gloria Hammond, www.bbc.co.uk/programmes/b00tgd1g, accessed 28 July 2011.

—— (producer) (2011, 19 and 23 April) *Ghost Music*, BBC Radio Four, www.bbc.co.uk/ programmes/b010dp0s, accessed 28 July 2011.

The Charles Parker Archive Trust (n.d.) The Charles Parker Archive, Birmingham Central Library, www.cpatrust.org.uk/, accessed 28 July 2011.

Cheny, Roz, Curran, Alvin, Amirkhanian, Charles, Saariaho, Kaja, Knizak, Milan, Belles, R. and Iges, J. (1991) *Ars Acoustica: EBU Selection* [audio CD], Geneva: European Broadcasting Union and Euroradio.

Cooper, Giles (1984) *Under the Loofah Tree and The Disagreeable Oyster* [audio cassette], BBC Plays On Tape, ASIN: B00412OA2W. Two comedies written by Giles Cooper and performed by the BBC Radiophonic Workshop. Cassette contains both original BBC broadcasts in full.

DA204 Understanding Media Audio CD1 (2006) Audio cluster 1 'Sounds and meaning' (study weeks 17, 19 and 23), tracks 14, 15 and 16, CDA5316, Milton Keynes: The Open University.

DA204 Understanding Media Audio CD2 (2006) Audio cluster 3 'Radio on: understanding radio' (study week 25), tracks 1–3, CDA5317, Milton Keynes: The Open University.

Goudie, John (producer) (2011, 23 April) 'The Chekhov Challenge: The Sound of a Breaking String' (first broadcast January 2010), *Between the Ears*, BBC Radio Three, www.bbc.co.uk/programmes/b010m03t#synopsis, accessed 28 July 2011.

Herrmann, Bernard (composer) (1999) *Hitchcock 100 Years: A Bernard Herrmann Film Score Tribute* [audio CD], United States: Milan Entertainment, 73138 35884-2.

Hill, Fiona (producer) (2008, 17 June) 'Synaesthesia', *All In The Mind,* BBC Radio Four, presenter Gloria Hammond, www.bbc.co.uk/radio4/science/allinthemind_ 20080617.shtml, accessed 28 July 2011.

Hörspiele, Jeux pour L'oreille (1995) Harold Brandt et Chantal Dumas, Rémy Carré, Philippe Le Goff, Tom Mays, Christian Rosset, Christian Sébille, Paris: France Culture.

The John Baker Tapes, Volume 1, BBC Radiophonics, Rare and Unreleased Workshop Recordings 1963–1974 (2008) Trunk Records, JBH028CD.

The John Baker Tapes, Volume 2, Soundtracks, Library Home Recordings, Electro Ads, Rare and Unreleased Recordings 1954–1985 (2008) Trunk Records, JBH029CD.

McColl, Ewan, Parker, Charles and Seeger, Peggy (1958, 2 July) 'The Ballad of John Axon', *Radio Ballads*, BBC. Available on CD at www.topicrecords.co.uk/, accessed 28 July 2011.

—— (1959, 5 November) 'Song of a Road', *Radio Ballads*, BBC. Available on CD at www.topicrecords.co.uk/, accessed 28 July 2011.

—— (1960, 16 August) 'Singing the Fishing', *Radio Ballads*, BBC. Available on CD at www.topicrecords.co.uk/, accessed 28 July 2011.

—— (1961, 18 August) 'The Big Hewer', *Radio Ballads*, BBC. Available on CD at www. topicrecords.co.uk/, accessed 28 July 2011.

—— (1962, 27 March) 'The Body Blow', *Radio Ballads*, BBC. Available on CD at www. topicrecords.co.uk/, accessed 28 July 2011.

—— (1963, 13 February) 'On the Edge', *Radio Ballads*, BBC. Available on CD at www. topicrecords.co.uk/, accessed 28 July 2011.

—— (1963, 3 July) 'The Fight Game', *Radio Ballads*, BBC. Available on CD at www.topic records.co.uk/, accessed 28 July 2011.

—— (1964, 17 April) 'The Travelling People', *Radio Ballads*, BBC. Available on CD at www.topicrecords.co.uk/, accessed 28 July 2011.

May, Julian (producer) (2011, 26 and 28 March) *Walls of Sound*, BBC Radio Four, presenter Professor Seán Street, www.bbc.co.uk/programmes/b00zq9mz, accessed 28 July 2011.

Milligan, Spike and Stephens, Larry (writers) (1956, 20 December) Episode 12, Series 7, *The Goon Show*, BBC Light Programme. Performers: Peter Sellers, Spike Milligan and Harry Secombe; producer: Pat Dixon.

Pour En Finir Avec Le Jugement De Dieu/Artaud Remix (2001) Artaud/Chalosse, France: Signature and Radio France, SIG 12008/9. HM 63x2.

Sachs, Andrew (1978) *Revenge*, BBC Radio Four, 'Pioneering Thriller Featuring Sound Effects and Eleven Actors, But No Written Dialogue,' recently rebroadcast on BBC 7 and BBC Radio 4 Extra. Produced and directed by Glyn Dearman.

Sieghart, Mary Ann (2010, 24 October) 'Glenn Beck', *Profile*, www.bbc.co.uk/programmes/b00vg905, accessed 28 July 2011.

Spinelli, Martin (2005) Radio Radio, http://writing.upenn.edu/pennsound/x/RadioRadio.html, accessed 23 July 2011.

Series of programmes on experimentation in radio. Program 11: Piers Plowright and Program 14: Jane Draycott and Elizabeth James.

Thall, Nelson and Newfeld, David (producers) (1994) *The Medium Is the Message: McLuhan*, Canada, Thall Time Again Productions, CD2218.

Thomas, Dylan (writer) (1999) *Under Milk Wood* (BBC Radio Collection) [audio CD], BBC Audiobooks. The 1963 radio dramatisation, with Richard Burton as the narrator, of Dylan Thomas's 'play for voices', about the inhabitants of a small Welsh village.

—— (2008) *Under Milk Wood* (BBC Audio, 2003 production) [audio CD], BBC Audiobooks.

Warburton, John (producer) (2004) *Here's a Piano I Prepared Earlier: Experimental Music in the 1960s*, BBC Television Four, executive producers Victor Lewis-Smith and Graham Pass, transmitted 3 December 2005, www.bbc.co.uk/bbcfour/music/features/experimental-music.shtml.

Wilson, Paul (2011, 29 March) 'Walls of Sound', *Sound Recordings Blog*, British Library, http://britishlibrary.typepad.co.uk/archival_sounds/2011/03/walls-of-sound.html?cid=6a00d8341c464853ef014e60646dbf970c, accessed 28 July 2011.

Woolf, Virginia (1937) 'Virginia Woolf's Broadcasts and Her Recorded Voice', www.virginiawoolfsociety.co.uk/vw_res.broadcast.htm, accessed 28 July 2011.

Ziegler, Thomas and Gross, Jason (producers) (2000) *OHM+: The Early Gurus of Electronic Music: 1948–1980*, Special edition 3CD, Ellipsis Arts, CD3690.

National Sound Archive – The British Library

Classical Music: sound recordings
    www.bl.uk/reshelp/findhelprestype/sound/classmusic/classical.html
Drama: audio and video collections
    www.bl.uk/reshelp/findhelprestype/sound/drama/dramasound.html
Home page
    www.bl.uk/reshelp/bldept/soundarch/about/soundarchive.html
Literature: audio and video collections
    www.bl.uk/reshelp/findhelprestype/sound/literature/literaturesound.html
Moving image collections
    www.bl.uk/reshelp/findhelprestype/movingimage/movingimagecoll/index.html
Oral history
    www.bl.uk/reshelp/findhelprestype/sound/ohist/oralhistory.html
Page for researchers
    www.bl.uk/nsa

Popular music: audio and video collections
www.bl.uk/reshelp/findhelprestype/sound/popular/popmusic.html
Radio recordings
www.bl.uk/reshelp/findhelprestype/sound/radio/radio.html
Wildlife sounds
www.bl.uk/reshelp/findhelprestype/sound/wildsounds/wildlife.html
World and traditional music: sound recordings
www.bl.uk/reshelp/findhelprestype/sound/wtmusic/worldmusic.html

BBC College of Production

Clear Sound best practice tips
www.bbc.co.uk/academy/collegeofproduction/tv/best_practice_tips
Clear Sound planning ahead
www.bbc.co.uk/academy/collegeofproduction/tv/clear_sound_planning_ahead
Clear Sound recording drama
www.bbc.co.uk/academy/collegeofproduction/tv/clear_sound_recording_drama_tv
Clear Sound recording factual
www.bbc.co.uk/academy/collegeofproduction/tv/clear_sound_recording_factual_tv
Clear Sound self shooting
www.bbc.co.uk/academy/collegeofproduction/tv/clear_sound_self_shooting_tv
Sound matters
www.bbc.co.uk/academy/collegeofproduction/tv/sound_matters_cohen

Companion website for *The Sound Handbook*

www.routledge.com/textbooks/crook

War Horse online video and sound

Educational resource pack
http://warhorselondon.nationaltheatre.org.uk/education/
Sights and sounds
http://warhorselondon.nationaltheatre.org.uk/sights-sounds/

FILMOGRAPHY

Darabont, Frank (writer and director) (1994) *Shawshank Redemption*, United States:
Castle Rock Entertainment. Based on the short novel *Rita Hayworth and Shawshank Redemption* by Stephen King.
Frears, Stephen (director) (2000) *High Fidelity*, United States: Touchstone Pictures.
Screenplay by D.V. De Vincentis, Steve Pink and John Cusack.
Jarman, Derek (writer and director) (1992) *Blue*, United Kingdom: a Basilisk
Communications/Uplink production for Channel Four Films in association with the
Arts Council of Great Britain, Opal and BBC Radio Three. Produced by James
Mackay and Takashi Asai; composer: Simon Fisher Turner; associate director:
David Lewis; sound design: Marvin Black.
Lumet, Sidney (director) (1982) *The Verdict*, United States: Twentieth Century Fox.
Screenplay by David Mamet.

Welles, Orson (director) (1941) *Citizen Kane*, United States: RKO Radio Pictures. Screenplay by Herman J. Mankiewicz and Orson Welles.

Wyler, William (director) (1961) *The Children's Hour*, United States: The Mirisch Corporation. Screenplay by John Michael Hayes.

CITATIONS AND REFERENCES FROM ONLINE/ WEBSITE RESOURCES

BBC (2001, 31 May) 'The Portsmouth Sinfonia', Edited Guide Entry, www.bbc.co.uk/dna/h2g2/A546491, accessed 2 October 2009.

BBC News (2008, 8 May) 'Why are TV adverts so loud?', http://news.bbc.co.uk/1/hi/magazine/7388473.stm, accessed 2 January 2011.

BBC Press Office (2011, 15 March) 'BBC Vision announces results of TV audibility research', www.bbc.co.uk/pressoffice/pressreleases/stories/2011/03_march/15/audibility.shtml, accessed 18 March 2011.

Burrell, Ian (2011, 14 March) 'Ian Burrell: Lord Gnome may scoff at new media but the 'Eye player' is a hit', *Independent*, Media on Monday, www.independent.co.uk/news/media/online/ian-burrell-lord-gnome-may-scoff-at-new-media-but-the-eye-player-is-a-hit-2241211.html, accessed 1 April 2011.

—— (2011, 28 March) 'Fall of giants: That book sounds good', *Independent*, www.independent.co.uk/life-style/gadgets-and-tech/features/fall-of-giants-that-book-sounds-good-2254631.html, accessed 28 July 2011.

Cole, Bethan (2007, 25 March) 'The Art of noise refined: Today's electronica has something vital to say', *The Sunday Times*, http://entertainment.timesonline.co.uk/tol/arts_and_entertainment/music/article1554704.ece, accessed 28 July 2011.

Collingwood, Faith (2010, 16 September) 'Auricular Live Staged Audio Drama', email to the author.

'Commercial Advertisement Loudness Mitigation Act' (2008) Bill Summary and Status 110th Congress (2007–8) H.R. 6209, http://thomas.loc.gov/cgi-bin/bdquery/z?d110:h.r.06209:, accessed 20 March 2011.

Crook, Tim (2000) *Val Gielgud and the BBC: Going Beyond Praxis Contemporary to 1929*, IRDP (Independent Radio Drama Productions), www.irdp.co.uk/GIELGUD/valbbc14.htm, accessed 2 May 2010.

Cutler, Rowland (n.d.) 'Dark Compass, The Chronicles of Rowland Cutler, a podcaster', http://network.fatbuzz.com/profile/RowlandCutler, accessed 28 July 2011.

Department of Media and Communications (2011) 'Media and the Senses' conference website, Goldsmiths, University of London, www.gold.ac.uk/media-communications/calendar/?id=4336,, accessed 10 May 2011.

Deutches Rundfunkarchiv (DRA) (2004, October) *Document des Monats Oktober 2004* [Document of the Month October 2004], www.dra.de/online/document/2004/oktober.html, accessed 2 November 2010.

Dowell, Ben (2009, July 6) 'Radio 4 reaches out to younger listeners', *Guardian*, www.guardian.co.uk/media/2009/jul/06/radio-4-reaches-out-to-youth, accessed 28 July 2011.

Dowell, Ben (2011, 20 March) 'BBC World Service to sign funding deal with US State Department', *Guardian*, www.guardian/media/2011/mar/20/bbc-world-service-us-funding, accessed 2 April 2011.

Dvorkin, Jeffrey A. (2004, 4 February) *BBC Reports: 'Sentence First. Verdict Afterwards?'*, NPR Ombudsman, http:www.npr.org/yourturn/ombudsman/2004/040204.html, accessed 20 November 2010.

England and Wales High Court (2010) 'Gaunt v OFCOM', EWHC 1756 (QB), www.bailii.
org/ew/cases/EWHC/QB/2010/1756.html, accessed 20 November 2010.

Hackney Podcast (n.d.) 'About us', http://hackneypodcast.co.uk/about-us/, accessed
1 January 2011.

Higgins, Charlotte (2010, 6 December) 'Turner prize won by Susan Philipsz for a sound
installation', *Guardian*, www.guardian.co.uk/artanddesign/2010/dec/06/turner-
prize-winner-susan-pilipsz, accessed 4 March 2011.

The Hutton Enquiry (2004) *Investigation into the Circumstances Surrounding the Death of
Dr David Kelly*, www.the-hutton-inquiry.org.uk/, accessed 1 April 2011.

Miceli, Dawn, and Domkus, Drew (2004–11) 'The Dawn and Drew Show', podcasting site,
http://thedawnanddrewshow.com/, accessed 28 July 2011.

NPR (National Public Radio) (1993, 24 May) 'Noam Chomsky interviewed', *Morning
Edition*, www.chomsky.info/interviews/19930524.htm, accessed 24 December 2010.

Ofcom (n.d.) 'FAQs', UK Television Reception Advice, www.ofcom.org.uk/static/
reception_advice/faqs/index.asp.html#1, accessed 1 April 2011.

Ofcom Adjudication (2009) 'BBC Brand/Ross fine' (adjudication on Russell Brand
Show, BBC Radio Two, 18 October 2008), http://consumers.ofcom.org.uk/2009/04/
bbc-brandross-fine/, accessed 28 July 2011.

Ofcom Broadcast Bulletin (2009, 11 May) 'Broadcast Bulletin Issue number 133 –
11/05/09', http://stakeholders.ofcom.org.uk/enforcement/broadcast-bulletins/
obb133/, accessed 28 July 2011.

QAA (Quality Assurance Agency) for UK Higher Education's benchmark statement
on Communication, media, film and cultural studies for 2008, www.qaa.ac.uk/
Publications/InformationAndGuidance/Documents/CMF08.pdf, accessed 28 July
2011.

Reynolds, Gillian (2009, 24 August) 'Radio review: Radio 2 does more than its rivals for
older listeners, Gillian Reynolds reviews The Reunion, An Interior Life, The Atheist
and the Bishop and The Hybernaculum', *Daily Telegraph*, www.telegraph.co.uk/
culture/culturecritics/gillianreynolds/6082727/Radio-review-Radio-2-does-more-than-
its-rivals-for-older-listeners.html, accessed 28 July 2011.

Somethin' Else Productions (2010, 22 December) 'Papa Sangre on sale now', www.some
thinelse.com/2010/12/22/papa-sangre-on-sale-now/, accessed 1 April 2011.

Vonhögen, Father Roderick (n.d.) 'Catholic Insider', http://catholicinsider.sqpn.com/,
accessed 28 July 2011.

Warburton, Nigel (n.d.) 'Virtual Philosopher' and 'Philosophy Bites', http://nigelwarburton.
typepad.com/, accessed 2 March 2011.

Index

2001: A Space Odyssey 77
39 Steps, The 15

absorption 26, 97, 114–15, 193
Abumrad, Jad 126
accent 9, 30–1, 40
acousmatic 57, 76, 193, 211, 216
acousmêtre 7–8, 57, 76, 193, 216, 218
acoustics 2–3, 12–13, 52, 92–7, 113, 162, 174, 184, 193
A/D converter 193
Adobe Audition 110, 119
Adorno, Theodor 52, 135, 138–45, 214
Adult Contemporary Rock (AOR) 156
African National Congress 37
Alchemists of Sound 55–6
algorithm 53, 194
Allee der Kosmonauten 163
All In The Mind 26–7
alliteration 68, 194
Allport, Gordon W. 81
All That Fall 7, 55, 161
Alten, Stanley R. 89, 93–5, 112–15, 118–19, 191, 194–6, 200–1, 207, 210, 214–15
alternating current 95
Althusser, Louis 35
Altman, Rick 174–5
ambience 96–7, 108, 111, 113, 160, 171–2, 176–7, 182, 194, 200, 205, 207, 210, 217

American Audio Pocket Record 99–100
American Public Radio 36–7
American Sociological Review 144
Amos 'n' Andy 32, 135
amplitude (processor) 93–6, 110, 194, 213
Analysing Media Texts 137–8
analytical listening 194
anchorage 141, 194
And Now on Radio 4: A Celebration of the World's Best Radio Station 148
anechoic chamber 97, 194
anempathetic sound 194, 199
animation 26, 53, 82–3, 176–8, 180, 215
An Interior Life 131, 237
anti-Semitism 60, 125–6, 139, 140–3
Apple iBook 177
Apple Mac iMovie 178
Archive Hour 47
Arendt, Hannah 59
Aristotle 41–4
Arnheim, Rudolf 13, 84–5, 159, 162
ars acoustica 194
art deco vii, 78, 80
Art and Illusion: A Study in the Psychology of Pictorial Representation 62–3
Art of Poetry 42–3
assonance 68, 195
asynchronous sound 194
attack (sound) 94, 106, 167, 195
audibility 9–10, 92, 102, 160

AudioBoo 40
Audio Culture: Readings in Modern Music
   86, 167, 169
audiogenic 57, 67, 117, 120, 195
Audio in Media 89, 119, 191
audio noir 51, 195
*Audio Post Production for Television and
   Film* 173, 175
audio-vérité 100, 154, 201
Audio-Vision 7, 175
audience 20, 51, 57–8, 82; animation and
   games 177; Bakhtin theory 24;
   constructing sound meaning 30–34;
   film and sound 72–4, 160–3; glossary
   terms 193–218; key concept 5–6;
   media language impact 11–14; music
   166; noise level limits 9; radio studies
   122–57; relation to institution 36; relation
   to narrative 42–7; response to sound
   reproduction 113–18; role in sound
   analysis 16–17; sound in *Shawshank
   Redemption* 1–2
Auditory Culture Reader, The 86, 169
auditory fatigue 95
auditory imagery 195, 204
Aufermann, Knut 182
Augoyard, Jean-Francois 168, 185
Auld, Georgie vi, 13
aurality 22
auricular theatre 82, 163
auteur (sound) xiii, 58, 67, 120, 152,
   195

B92 (Belgrade radio station) 190, 192
Back, Les 86, 167
*Background Noise: Perspectives on Sound
   Art* 14, 185
back-timing 195
Bacon, Francis 54
Bakhtin, Mikhail 24, 44
Balance, John 75
balanced and unbalanced cabling 104,
   108, 195
Bannerman, R. Leroy 59
Barnouw, Erik 140
Barthes, Roland 45–6, 133
Basinski, Michael 130
batch conversion 109, 112
Battle of the Somme 78
Baudrillard, Jean 51, 203, 215
BBC 2LO *(first radio station)* 77
BBC 4 (Television digital channel) 56
BBC Light Programme 234
BBC Radio Drama 74

BBC Radio Four 26–7, 31, 37, 39, 47,
   131, 133
BBC Radio Two 133–4
BBC Radio Three 7, 18, 33, 73, 122
BBC Third Programme 56, 209
BBC Vision 9, 236
Beauchamp, Robin 177, 180
Becker, Howard 144
Beckett, Samuel 7, 55, 70, 161
Bell Laboratories 94
Benchley, Robert 59–61
Bennett, Andy 170, 221
Bennett, Vicki 182
Berendt, Joachim-Ernst 14
Berkeley, Reginald 67
Berlin viii, 144, 162
Bernstein, Charles 130
Bentham, Jeremy 2
Berg, Alan 139
Berry, Cecily 166, 169
Berry, Richard 189
Between the Ears 47, 73, 121–2
Beyer microphones dynamic M58 and
   MCE72 104
bidirectional 105–7
Biewen, John 120–1, 126–8, 137
binary oppositions 46, 152–4, 195
binaural 90, 97, 100, 107, 116, 176,
   216
Blair, Tony 188
Blesser, Barry 184–5
Bloomsbury Group 67
Blue (film by Derek Jarman) xiii, 74–7, 161,
   193
Blue Cockatoo (pub/restaurant in Chelsea
   in 1920s) 79
Blue Veils and Golden Sounds 56
Boaden, Helen 148
Bogosian, Eric 139
boom (sound equipment) vii–viii, 98, 100,
   104, 107, 116, 172–3, 195, 200–1
Bordwell, David 12, 15, 17, 29, 200–1,
   205–6
Bournemouth University 37
Boyle, James 148
Bracewell, John L. 91–2, 96, 158–60,
   164
Bradford, Sidney 26
Bradnum, Frederick 55
Bragg, Melvyn 131
Brand, Russell 133, 155–6
Brecht, Bertolt 45
bricolage 195
Briscoe, Desmond 54–5, 137

British Broadcasting Company (BBC) viii, 3, 18, 39–40, 62, 84, 122, 124, 185, 201; Cage, John 166; dramatic control panel 109; early microphone play 64; feature makers 129–31; first London station 2LO 77–8; genre of radio programme 47; glossary terms 204–17; hearing survey 9–10; institutional key concept 36–7, 145–6; man cured of blindness programme 26–7; Mosley, Oswald 140; online experiments 191; radio drama pioneers in 1920s 67; Radio Four 148; radio monitoring in WW2 65; radiophonic workshop and the Goons Show 55–7; radio plays with non-speaking parts 51; Radio Two 155–6; regulation issues 137–8; Reith, John C.W. 146–7; representation in programmes 31–3; research of David Hendy 6–7; Savoy Hill HQ 80; sound spot experimentation 176; studios in 1920s 97

British Columbia 2
British Library 37–9, 80
Britton, David 18, 25, 232
Broadcasting House viii, 129, 147
Broadcast Over Britain 147
Broadcast Talk 85
Brookes, Chris 123, 125
Brown, Ross 163
Bruce, Ken 156
Buchan, John 15
Bull, Andy 188, 191
Bull, Michael 86, 167, 169
Buggins, The 32

cadence 30
Cage, John 166, 184, 212
Cantril, Hadley 81
cardioid 104, 107–8, 113, 116
cause and effect structuring 196, 205, 212
CBS, Columbia Broadcasting System 2, 58, 209
Center for Documentary Studies (Duke University) 121
Centre de recharge sur l'espace sonore et l'environnement urbain 168
Champlain, Barry 139
Channel Four (UK Television) 74
Chekhov, Anton 73–4
Chekhov Challenge: The Sound of a Breaking String, The 73
Chelsea Dreaming 18, 24, 29

Cherry Orchard, The 73–4
Chignell, Hugh 5, 22–3, 135
Children's Hour, The 14, 235
Childs, G.W. IV 109–10, 112, 119, 180
Chion, Michel 7, 16, 76, 175, 193–4, 199, 204, 207–8, 211, 214, 216–7
Chomsky, Noam 35
chorus 112
Christopherson, Peter 75
chronology 196
chronos 44
Cigarettes and Chocolate 51
Citizen Kane 2, 12
Classic FM 33, 36
Cleverdon, Douglas 57, 210
Close Up 148
Club d'Essai 55
Cobbing, Bob 130
Collingwood, Faith 163
Collins, Karen 179–80
Collins, Richard, Professor 191
Commercial Advertisement Loudness Mitigation Act 9
Communities in Cyberspace 189, 192
community radio 36
compression 9, 70, 93, 99, 112, 153, 187, 194
Constanduros, Mabel 32
continuity editing 196
contrapuntal sound 196
control rooms vii, 13, 97, 113–15
convergence 190, 192, 196, 217
convolution 196
Cooper, Giles 51, 55
Corporation for Public Broadcasting 36
Correll, Charles 32
Corwin, Norman 58–62
Coryat, Karl 109, 112, 119, 219
Coughlan, Charles Father 139
Cox, Professor Brian 9
Cox, Christoph 86, 167, 169
Creating Music and Sound for Games 109, 119, 180
Cresson 168
Cripps, Sir Stafford 142
Crisell, Andrew 5–7, 18, 21–2, 30, 135, 189, 192
critical autonomy 196
Crossing the Ether: British Public Service Radio and Commercial Competition 1922–1945 84, 136
cross-fade 112, 196, 209
Csapó-Sweet, Rita M. 190
Cubitt, Sean 87

cultural imperialism 196
Curious Ear, The 123
Curtis-Bramwell, Roy 55, 137
cyberspace (sonic) 197

Daily Express 140
Daily Mail 156
Dallas, Texas 139
Danger (radio play) 64
Danson Brown, Richard 141
Darabont, Frank 1–2
Dark House, The 191
Dasein 59, 197
Davis, Beryl vi, 13
Davis, Katie 127
DAW (digital audio workstation) 108, 113
decibels 94–5, 105, 112
delay (sound) 98, 112, 178, 197
Delmer, Sefton 135, 140, 142–3, 145,
    214, 223
Denver, Colorado 139
depth of sound field 196
Derbyshire, Delia 55–6, 131
Der Chef 138, 143–5
Derrida, Jacques 38, 202
destructive (sound) editing 110
Deutsch, Stephen 178–80
Deutsches Rundfunkarchiv 38
dialect 31, 40, 197
Dialogic Imagination: Four Essays, The 24,
    44
dialogue overlap 197
dictabelt 37, 40
Diderot, Denis 121
diegesis, diegetic and non-diegetic 1–2, 8,
    12, 17, 46, 51, 76, 154, 179, 194, 197,
    200, 205–6, 208, 210–12, 215
diffraction 97
diffusion 97, 198
Dilworth, Alexa 120–1, 126–8, 137
direct sound 198
Disagreeable Oyster, The 55
Discipline and Punish 2–3
Disc World 43
dissonance 198
distance of sound recording 198
distortion 10, 57, 92, 100, 102, 104, 108,
    112–13, 160
Dobie, Marthe 14
Doctor Who 56
docudrama 154, 198
documentary xi, 25–6, 28, 73, 82;
    aesthetics 152; Corwin, Norman 58;
    glossary terms 194–211; ideology
and institution 34–7; Michael Wood
and *Story of India* 3; montage 30;
Nyre, Lars and realism 10; Parker,
Charles and Plowright, Piers 129;
radiophonic workshop 56; recording
technique 100, 103; representing reality
debates 132–7; sounding ancient
instruments 39; story action 43; styles
of content 51; 'true stories' 120–3
Dolby 115, 117–18
Dorsey, Tommy vi, 13
Douglas, Lesley 156
Douglas, Susan 22–3, 135
Downie, Alan 121, 223
Down the Line 133
dramatic control panel 79
Draycott, Jane 130
Drever, John Levack 160–1
Dr Faustus 56
dubbing 108, 111, 198, 200, 211, 213
Dufresne, Andrew 1
Duke of York (theatre in Brighton) 74
Dunn, John 156
dynamics 114, 150–1, 155, 189, 198,
    215–16

Eastley, Max 182
Eckersley, Peter P. 78
Eco, Umberto 24
Edinburgh International Festival 76
Edirol R-OH9 vii, 103
Edison, Thomas 38, 160–1
Eins, Gustav Siegfried 142–4
Eisenstein, Sergei 15
elektronische musik 55, 57, 198
Eliot, T.S. 69–70
ellipsis 43, 199, 205
Elmes, Simon 130–2, 148
emanation speech 160, 199
EMI 36
Emmerson, Simon 170, 182
empathetic music 194, 199; *see also*
    anempathetic
encoding/decoding sound texts 11, 62,
    95, 105, 199
Encyclopédie 121, 124–5
enigma code 44–5, 51, 211
Enlightenment rationality 199
envelope (sound) 66, 92, 94, 160, 195
equalisation/equaliser EQ 199
Erickson, Stephen 130
Essay 7
Esslin, Martin 7, 21–2, 57, 217
Evans, Chris 156

Evolving English: One Language Many Voices 39–40
exhibition 40, 53, 66, 74, 82–3, 96–7, 114, 117, 181–5
existenz 59, 127, 197, 199
expressionism 24, 47, 57–8, 199, 208
external diegetic sound 200
Ezra Pound's Radio Operas: The BBC Experiments, 1931–1933 84, 137

fabula 17, 43, 45, 212
fade in and fade out 12, 112–13, 196, 200, 209
Fagandini, Maddalena 55
fairness doctrine 139
Falling Tree Productions 124
Fall of Giants 177
Fanny and the Plaster Saints 130
Fantastic, The 44
Federal Communications Commission (FCC) 36, 139
Field of Drama: How the Signs of Drama Create Meaning on Stage and Screen, The 21
film 1–2, 11–12, 14, 29, 44, 51, 73–9, 82–4, 87, 111, 132–4, 137–9, 171–5, 193–219
Film als Kunst 84
Film Sound: Theory and Practice 174
film sound crew 200
filter 20, 104, 108, 113, 178, 201, 217–18
Findlay, Polly 71
First 25 Years: The BBC Radiophonic Workshop, The 55
First Person Shooter (FPS) computer game 51, 82, 178–9, 201
Fisher, Margaret 84, 137
Fletcher-Munson Curve 94
fly-on-the-wall documentary 201
focalisation 44, 51
focus (sound) vii, 13, 43, 67, 74, 77, 83, 107–8, 194, 201, 213, 217
Foley artist 201
Follett, Ken 177
Foreign Office (UK) 39, 142
Foucault, Michel 2, 51, 155
France Musique 33
Frears, Stephen 12, 236
Freeman, Morgan 1, 32
frequency 9, 60, 63, 81, 92–4, 96, 105–8, 110, 112, 114–15, 117–18, 160–1, 199–202, 212, 218–19
frequency order (film) 201
Frieden Frieden 163

Friedlander, Max J. 63
Frog Who Croaked Blue, The 27
fundamental (sound) 93, 201
Fundamentals of Sonic Art and Sound Design, The 181
futurists 8

gain change 102, 112–13
Galvin, Frank (character in *The Verdict*) 14
games, computer 82–3, 109, 119, 176–80
Game Sound: An Introduction to the History, Theory, and Practice of Video Games Music and Sound Design 179
Garden of Allah, The 87
Garnett, David 138
Garrick Theatre 71
gatekeepers 201
General Strike of 1926 (UK) 147
genre(s) 5, 7, 82, 88, 170, 184; audio-deception 140; audio-documentary 120; glossary terms 195–215; key concept discussion 47–51; media sound language 11; narrative 42–3; non-genre texts 45; Radio Four 148; radio studies issues 150–6; representation 32; representing reality 132–5; sound art 66–7; talk radio 138; theatre in the dark 161
Gestalt theory and psychology 42
Ghost Music 39
Ghost Train, The (Arnold Ridley play) 71
Gibbs, Tony 181–2, 185, 196–8, 200, 202, 207, 210–11, 213–19
Gielgud, Val 79
Gillette, Michael 158
Gilligan, Andrew 133
Glass, Ira 127
Goffman, Erving 10
Golden Web – A History of Broadcasting in the United States II – 1933 to 1953, The 140
Goldsmiths, University of London xiii, 28, 53, 60, 62, 66, 130, 181–2, 187
Gombrich, E.H. 63–6
Goon Show, The 56–7
Gordon, Rob 12
Gosden, Freeman 32
Goudie, John 73–4
Gramsci, Antonio 34
grand opera vi, 3
granulation 202
Green, Michael 72
Greenblatt, Stephen 141

Gregory, Richard 26
Grissell, Laurence 130
Guggenheim Museum 33
Guthrie, Tyrone 73, 79

Habermas, Jürgen 52
Hackney Podcast 176
Hamilton, David 'Diddy' 156
hand-held microphone 202
Handspring Puppet Company 70
Hannay, Richard 17
harmonic 93–4, 196, 201–2, 215–16
Harry Potter 43
hauntology, hauntological 202
Hayes, John Michael 14
Hearing Voices 121
Heart (radio UK) 36
hegemony 34, 52, 153, 202, 209
Heidegger, Martin 126, 197
heimathörspiel 40, 202
Hendy, David 5–7, 135, 190, 192
Henriques, Julian viii, 28, 54, 182–3
Henry, Pierre 55
Hepburn, Audrey 14
Herbert Jenkins 72
Herman, Edward S. 35
hermeneutic(s) 45, 58, 154, 202
Herrmann, Bernard 171–2, 175
Herzog, Herta 141
High Fidelity 12
Hight, Craig 133–4
Hilmes, Michele 84–5, 135–6
*Historical Journal of Film, Radio and
     Television* 86
historicism (sound) 10, 40, 141, 202–3
historiography (sound) 10, 40, 203
Hitchcock, Alfred 15, 171–2, 175
Hitler, Adolf 38, 85, 140, 142, 147
Holman, Tomlinson 117, 119
Honess-Martin, Jacqui 163
Horace 43, 225
Hörspiele 57, 203
*How to Get Great Sound from Any Studio
     (No Matter How Weird or Cheap Your
     Gear Is)* 109, 119
Hubbard, Andrew 18, 25
Hughes, Richard 64
humanitas (sound) 59, 203
Hutton enquiry (into BBC) 146, 148
Huwiler, Elke 88, 231
hyperreality, the hyperreal 52, 203, 215

icon and iconography (sound) 6, 30, 56,
     154–7, 203, 209

ideology 5, 29–35, 125, 141–2, 146, 153,
     178, 202–3, 206, 214
idiolect 203
imagery 30, 69, 84, 140, 195, 203–4, 213
imaginative spectacle 16, 22, 42, 45, 77,
     204
informal language 204
installation 32, 53, 55, 66, 80, 82, 87, 114,
     117, 180–5
institution 19, 85, 124; academic study
     80–1; animation and games 178;
     audience 33; BBC Radio 146–50;
     documentary issues 133; film theory
     174; genre 47; glossary terms 196–217;
     ideology 35; Internet broadcasting 191;
     Internet sources 89; key concept 5–6;
     media language 11; media studies topic
     36–41, 153–7; narrative 43; radiophonic
     workshop 55; representation 31
intellectual montage 204
International Journal of Cultural Studies
     88
Internet 55, 82–3, 89, 102, 122–5, 130,
     136, 148, 153, 183, 186–92, 197,
     218
intertextuality 45, 75, 154, 204
In the Dark: theatre movement 82, 161;
     arts project 123
intonation 111, 197, 204
inversion 205
irony 24, 32, 40, 59, 141, 205, 213
ISL (inverse square law) 118

James, Elizabeth 130
Jameson, Derek 156
Jarman, Derek xiii, 74–7, 161, 193
Jaspers, Karl 59, 126–8, 131, 197, 199,
     203
*Journal of Adaptation in Film and
     Performance* 88
Journal of Radio and Audio Media 86
Judge, The 160
jump cut 205
Jung, Karl 40

Kabaka of Buganda 39
kairos 44
Kampala University 39
Kant, Immanuel 63
Kauai O'o A'a 40
Kavanagh, Peter 74
Keith, Michael C. 139, 226
Kelly, Dr David 146
Kelly, Ronan 123, 130

Kennedy, Sarah 156
Kentucky Minstrels, The 32
Kermode, Frank 44
key concepts (media studies) 5, 135
Kingdom of Heaven 87
Kitchen Sisters (Davia Nelson and Nikki Silva), *The* 126
Klein, Georg 87–8, 231
Knight, Paula 24
Kollock, Peter 189, 192
Königsberg 13
Kubrick, Stanley 77

LaBelle, Brandon 14, 166, 185
Lacan, Jacques 51
Langhoff, Anna 163
language register 31
lapel/lavalier vii, 98–101, 104, 106–7, 172, 200
Larkin, Philip 130
Law, Arthur 160
Lawrence of Arabia 87
Lazarsfeld, Paul 141, 214
Lax, Stephen 189–90, 192
LBC Radio 36
leitmotiv(f) 205
Leonard, John A. 72, 161, 164
Les Aveugles 73
Levi-Strauss, Claude 46
Lewis, Cecil viii, 67, 78, 146
Lewis, Peter M. 85–6
LFE (low frequency enhancement) 115, 118
Library of Congress vi–vii, 80
Licht, Alan 184–5
Life On Air: A History of Radio Four 148
Limbaugh, Rush 139, 229
linearity 178, 205
Lingard, Joseph 131
Liotard, Jean Etienne 63
Long, Janice 156
Longinus 43
long take/long scenes/long shot 205
Lost Sounds Orchestra 39
loudspeakers 12, 97, 114–18, 198
Loviglio, Jason 85
Lowlands 2008/2010 66
Lubiri Palace 39
Ludwig, Margaret 84
Lux Hollywood Radio Theatre 2
Lyotard, Jean-François 52

Macbeth 74, 159
McCoy, Jennifer and Kevin 130

Mackenzie, Compton 67
McKinley, Ray vi, 13
MacLaine, Shirley 14
Macleod, Lewis 188
Maconie, Stuart 156
McWhinnie, Donald 55–7
Maida Vale studios 55
mainstream sound/radio media 149, 155, 191, 205
Mamet, David 14, 235
Mandela, Nelson 37–8, 40
Mannerheim, General Carl Gustav 38
Manufacturing Consent: The Political Economy of the Mass Media 35
Marantz 60, 104
Marinetti, Filippo Tommaso Emilio 67
Marks, Aaron 177
Marriage of Figaro 1
Martin, Graham 70
Martin, Maria 128
Marx, Groucho 59
masking 45, 96, 138
Matheson, Hilda 7
Maugham, W. Somerset 161
May, Mike 26
Mayo, Simon 156
meaning 82, 136, 146, 163; animation and games 179; audiogenic literature 67–9; early human sound 3–4; glossary terms 193–218; Gombrich, E.H. 63–5; immersion 8; media sound language 11–21; media studies 149–51, 154–5; microphones 105–6; modern critical tradition 52; narrative 41, 44–5; radio semiotics 6; radio play analysis 24–5; representation 29–33; sound technology 95, 97; stage sounds 73–4; *The Goon Show* 57
media effects theory 206
media events and media rituals 38, 108, 206, 209, 222
media sound language 11–29
Media Student's Handbook, The 30
media studies 5, 10, 14, 32, 36–7, 83, 192, 215, 225–6, 231–2
metanarratives 52, 206
metaphor (sonic) 2, 12, 41, 56, 69, 91, 93, 129, 203, 206, 210
method performance 206
Media and Communication Technologies 189, 192, 226
Mercury Theatre on the Air 2
Merleau-Ponty, Maurice 52, 227
micro-controller 207

microphones vii, 30, 37, 95, 98–101, 104–8, 113–14, 116, 118, 159, 167, 188, 195, 197–8, 200, 207, 216
Migone, Christof 130
Miller, Paul D. (aka DJ Spooky) 130
Milosevic, Slobodan 190
Minghella, Anthony 51
mini-disc 91, 110
Minto, Ben 178
Miroo 130
mise-en-scène 11–12, 16, 30, 47, 153, 197, 201, 207
mixer/mixing 105–6, 109, 113, 200, 207, 213
mockumentary 120, 133, 207
modality 8, 25–6, 204
modernism 58, 67, 207–8, 212, 220–1
modernity 6–7, 51, 213
modes of listening 86, 208
monitoring 109, 113, 115–18
monologue 16, 131, 208
montage 19, 30, 51, 69, 90, 100, 111, 123, 134, 152, 172, 187, 195, 202, 204, 207–9, 216
montage sequence 209
moral panic 31, 134, 153, 156, 179, 209
Morphology of the Russian Folktale 44, 47
Morpurgo, Michael 70
Morris, Tom 71, 161
Morrissey, Mickey 14
Mosley, Sir Oswald 140
motif (sound) 12, 16, 59, 74, 87, 154, 176, 209, 212
Mozart, Wolfgang Amadeus 1, 126, 168
MP3 sound files 99–102, 124, 186, 217
Mr Fletcher the Poet 130
Mrs Dale's Diary 156
Mrs Dalloway 67, 69, 231
Multimedia Journalism 188, 191
multimodal 209
Museum of Modern Art 33
music 51, 73, 82–4, 102, 123, 126, 131, 158, 163; aesthetic analysis 152; analysis in radio 22–6; art and exhibition 183–5; audience and ideology 32–6; *Blue* 74–7; critical concept and traditions 16–19, 51–66, 70; folk 128; function in media 6–13; glossary terms 196–218; Internet broadcasting 187–92; Mozart in *Shawshank Redemption* 1–2; narrative 44; Radio Two music policy 155–6; representation 39–40; stage theatre 160–1; synaesthesia 28–30; technological production 91–4, 104, 107

111–15, 119; theory and culture 86–8; theory and practice 165–80
musique concrète (renforceé) 51, 55, 57, 168, 199, 209–10

NAACP, National Association for the Advancement of Coloured People 32
Nahokobani 64
Napier, Frank 71, 73, 164
Nathan The Wise 125
National Audit Office (UK) 148
National Public Radio (USA) 36, 124
National Sound Archive (NSA) 37, 80
National Theatre (UK) 71
naturalistic dialogue 201
Nambudiri *Brahmins* 3
neo-realism 210
New Atlantis, The 54
new feminism 210
Newman, Paul 14
Newman, Thomas 2
News of the World 156
New Soundtrack, The 86, 180
New York Film Festival 76
New York Times 36, 196
Nicholas, John 143
Nichols, Bill 124, 132–3, 137, 198
Niebur, Louis 7–8, 55–7, 185, 209–10, 216, 218
Nightingale, Florence 38
noise-gate 210
Noises Off 71
non-diegetic insert 210
non-simultaneous sound 210
Norddeutscher Rundfunk 55
Nostradamus 75
Nuendo 110
Nyre, Lars 10–11, 185

Oakalla Prison Farm 2
Ocean of Sound: Aether Talk, Ambient Sound and Imaginary Worlds 84, 169
Octave 211
Ofcom 9, 36, 155–6, 187
off-screen sound 211
Old Vic (theatre) 73
omnidirectional 98–100, 104–5, 107, 167, 207
omniscient narrator/voice 211
onomatopoeia 68, 211
opening exposition 211
Open University, The 17–18, 69, 191
Optics 66
Oram, Daphne 28, 55

Organised Sound: International Journal of Music and Technology 86
Our Betters 161
Our Sonic Environment and the Soundscape: The Tuning of the World 19, 185
overdubbing 211
Ovid 64

Pacifica (US public radio network) 36
Panetta, Francesca 130
Pan Macmillan 177
Papa Sangre 176
paradoxical sound 211
parallelism or parallel sound 211
Parker, Charles 128–9, 232–3
pathetic fallacy 211
PE (protective earth) 119
Pear, T.H. 80
Personification (sonic) 211
Peter and the Wolf 168
phantasmagoria 211
phantasmic radio 212
phantom power 106
phase 93–4, 96, 107, 111, 196
Phenomenology of Perception 52
Philipsz, Susan 66, 181
philosophes 121, 124–6
philosophy 5, 35, 45, 52, 54, 58, 84, 112, 124, 127, 152, 167, 169, 174, 188, 197, 204, 217
phonographs (Edison) 160
Picker, Lester 15
Pierce, C.S. 30, 160
pitch (bending and shifting) 12, 16–17, 19, 26, 29–30, 36, 61, 74, 93, 96, 112, 166, 178, 194, 204, 215–16
Plato 43, 64, 147
playback singing 212
pleasure sound 212
plot 12, 16–17, 32, 41–3, 45, 47–8, 56, 92, 139, 145, 161, 177, 194, 199, 201, 205, 209, 212, 217
Plowright, Piers 129–30
podcasting xi, 55, 82–3, 102, 186–92, 218
Poetics 41–2
point of listening (POL) 11, 17, 44, 51, 108, 153, 207, 213
Political Warfare Executive (PWE) 135, 138, 140, 142
polyphonic 23, 30, 196, 213
polysemic 25, 30, 213
portable listening/recorders/recording 23, 90, 98–105, 113, 120, 167, 200

Portsmouth Sinfonia 166–7
postmarxism 213
postmodernity 213
poststructuralism 213
postsynchronisation 213
PPM 113
Pratchett, Terry 43
preamplifier 213
prefiguring 214
Press Complaints Commission (PCC) 187
Price, Vincent 60
Private Dreams and Public Nightmares 55
Private Eye 188
Prix Italia 24, 51, 124
proairetic code 46
propaganda (sound) 35, 82, 138–45, 152, 214
Propp, Vladimir 43–50, 179
Protools 110
PRX 121–2
Psychoacoustics 52, 97, 174
Psychological Technique of Martin Luther Thomas's Radio Addresses, The 138, 139–45
Psychology of Radio, The 81
Ptolemy 66
Public Radio International (PRI) 36, 122

qualitative and quantitative survey 81
Quentin, John 74–5

Radcliffe, Mark 156
radio 2–3, 15–16, 18, 51–3, 73–5, 94, 102, 116, 119, 159, 164, 166, 169–70; academic analysis 20–40; analysis of artistic expression 60–7; Berlin studio 162; early BBC programming culture 77–80; genre 47; glossary terms 193–219; Internet broadcasting and podcasting 186–92; key concepts and media studies 5–10; Norman Corwin's audio drama 58; radiophonic literature of T.S. Eliot 69–70; sound spots activated 176; sound standard for transmission 102–3; studio production 113; studying in context of sound 81–8; surreal sound effects 55–7; theory and practice 120–57
Radio Ballads 128
Radiocracy 88
Radio Drama: Sound, Text, Word; Bakhtin and the Aural Dialogue of Radio Drama 24

Radio Journal: International Studies in Broadcast and Audio Media, The 86
Radiolab 121–2
Radio Luxembourg 155
radiophonic 55–8, 120, 137, 185, 210, 214
Radiophonic Workshop 55–6, 137, 185
Radio Reader: Essays in the Cultural History of Radio 85
Radio, Television and Modern Life: A Phenomenological Approach 84
Radio: The Art of Sound 84
Radio Times, The 80
Rampling, Charlotte 14
Read, Herbert 84
Reality Radio: Telling True Stories in Sound 120, 137
Redding, Ellis 'Red' 1
reel to reel tape 91, 98
referential (cultural) code 46, 132, 205, 208–9, 216
Reinholz, Johannes 144
Reith, John (later Sir and Lord) 146–7
rendering 7, 77, 101, 153, 214
representation 17, 26, 74, 116; animation and games 178–9; art exhibition 183; fictional technology 7; glossary terms 195–215; hauntology 38–9; key concept in media studies 29–32; media sound language 11; media studies curriculum 146–54; narrative codes 43–7; propaganda 138–9; reality and truth in documentary 132–4; sonic literature 67–71; sound editing 110–11; studio production 113; sunlight in film 87; *Undecided Molecule* 62–4
Representing Reality 132, 137, 198
Resonance FM 33, 205
Revenge 51, 213
reverb(eration) 19–20, 74, 97, 113, 115–16, 118, 167, 194, 197, 214
reverse (time) 17, 74, 112, 114, 153, 198–9, 205
Reynolds, Gillian 6, 131
rhetorical sound 214
rhythm 8, 15–16, 29–30, 69–72, 111–12, 165, 196, 199, 201, 204, 215
Ridley, Arnold 71
Rivonia Trial 37
Roscoe, Jane 132–3
Ross, Jonathan 133
Royal Flying Corps 78
Royal Shakespeare Company 166
Rowling, J.K. 43

Rush Hour: Talk Radio, Politics and the Rise of Rush Limbaugh 138, 140
Russolo, Luigi 67
Ryan, Nick 176

Sachs, Andrew 133
Sadie 110
Sagittarius Rising 78
Salamun, Kurt 127
Salter, Linda-Ruth 184
sampler/sampling 215
Sanders, Paul 144
Sarrasine 45
Satie, Erik 75
Savoy Hill 79
Scannell, Paddy 84–6, 197
Schaefer, Janek 182
Schaeffer, Pierre 55, 208–9
Schafer, R. Murray 4, 19, 28, 53, 185, 194
Screen 21, 86, 88, 212
SD cards 91, 99–102, 104
Searle, John 188
Seib, Philip 138, 140
semic code 45
semiotics 6, 18, 35, 65, 88, 154
sensorium (media) 215
sequencer 215
serialism 215
Shakespeare, William 58, 64–5, 141, 159, 166
shape 28, 30, 47, 65, 94, 97, 107, 160, 183
Shawshank Redemption 1–2
Shields, Donald C. 190
Shklovsky, Viktor 43
Shock Jock 139–40
Showalter, Elaine 69
sibilance 215
Sidney, Sylvia 61
Sieveking, Lance 7, 57, 67, 78–80
Sifichi, Black 74
silence 2–3, 6, 13, 16, 30, 85–6, 112, 144, 166, 169, 214
simulacrum and simulacra 52, 203, 215
simultaneous sound 215
sine wave 215
Sinister Resonance: The Mediumship of the Listener 41, 169
Skinner, Paul 39
Smith, Helen, inquest of 40
Smith, Marc 189
Soley, Lawrence C. 136, 143–4
Somethin' Else Productions 176

Sonic Experience: A Guide to Everyday Sounds 168, 185
Sonnenschein, David 14, 20, 42, 76–7, 89, 119, 175, 208
Sony Walkman and ECM909 microphone 105
Sorcerer's Apprentice, The 168
Sound: A Reader in Theatre Practice 163–4
sound art xi, 14, 83, 97; academic study 80; alchemists of sound 55; glossary terms 194–219; Internet broadcasting 187; microphone applications 103–4; music 165; publication sources 86–8; radio platform 120, 124, 130; relevance of E.H. Gombrich 63; surround sound 117; theorists 52–3; theory and practice 181–5; Turner Prize and Susan Philipsz 66–7
Sound Art: Beyond Music, Between Categories 184–5
sound bridge 216
Soundcloud 189
Sound Design: The Expressive Power of Music, Voice and Sound Effects in Cinema 89, 119, 175
Soundfield 104, 118
sound houses 54–5
Sound Media: From Live Journalism to Music Recording 10, 185
sound perspective 8, 22, 66, 118, 216
Soundprint 121
Sound Recordings Blog 38
sound studios 92, 97, 108
sound symbolism 204, 216
Sound Theory, Sound Practice 174
Soundtrack, The 86
sound zoom 216
Spaces Speak, Are You Listening: Experiencing Aural Architecture 184
Speech, Music, Sound 8, 25, 185
Spinelli, Martin 129–30, 189, 192
Spragg, Frank 38–9
square wave 216
stage 2–3, 54, 67, 82–3, 137, 139, 170, 183; academic sources 88; film sound link 172–3; glossary terms 197–219; media studies benchmark 153; narrative theory 44; Shakespearean 65; sound projection in theatre spaces 113–16; sound technologies 92, 104–5, 107, 110; theatre of the absurd 57; theatre sound 70–74; theory of Martin Esslin 21; theory and practice of sound 158–64; voice training 166

Stage Noises and Effects 72
Stanford University Press 139
Starkey, Guy 5, 7, 136
Stedman, J.W. 160
Stone, Oliver 139
Story of India, The 3
stream of consciousness 216
Street, Seàn i, xiii, 5, 37–40, 84, 136–7
structuralism 41, 206, 213, 216
Stuff of Radio, The 79
Sunderland University 189
Supreme Court (UK) 37
surround sound 9, 72, 83, 90, 96, 103–5, 107–8, 115–19, 161–2, 174, 216
Surround Sound: Up and Running 117, 119
Sweeney Agonistes: Fragments of an Aristophanic Melodrama 69–70
Swinton, Tilda 74–5
symbolic code 46
synaesthesia 27–8, 87
synchresis 7–8, 57, 76, 216, 218
synchretic acousmêtre 216
synchronous sound 216
synergy 28, 80, 217
synthesiser 28, 103, 167, 213, 217
syuzhet 17, 24, 43, 212
S/Z 45
Szymanowski, Karol 75

tablet (editing technology) 90, 101, 108, 179
Talked to Death: The Life and Murder of Alan Berg 139
Talk Radio (film) 139–40
Tappern, James 39
Tate Modern 182
technological determinism 216
territory sounds 217
Terry, Nigel 74–5
textual speech 217
theatre *see* stage
Theatre 503 (London) 163
Theatre Journal 88
Theatre Notebook: A Journal of the History and Technique of the British Theatre 160
theatre of the absurd 57, 217
Theatre Sound 72, 164
theatrical speech 217
Third Coast International Audio Festival 120, 122, 124
This American Life 121–2
Thomas, Dylan 24–5

Thompson, Kristin 11–12, 15, 17, 29, 200–1, 205–6
time-compression/stretching 112
Times (London) 36
Today 31, 133, 146, 148
Todorov, Tzvetan 44, 46–8
Too Much Information 124
Toop, David 41, 84, 169
Torgue, Henry 168
Traité des principes et des règles de la peinture 63
transducer 114, 218
Turner Prize 66, 181
Turner, Simon Fisher 74–5
Tutankhamen 39

Ubuweb 124
Uher tape recorder 98, 101
Undecided Molecule, The 58–66
Under Milk Wood 24
Understanding Media 191
Understanding Radio 17–20, 23, 191
Under the Loofah Tree 55
Unfortunates, The 191
unidirectional 105, 107, 207
Upton, Lawrence 130
USB 99, 101, 108, 188
uses and gratifications theory 218

van Leeuwen, Theo 8, 10, 18–20, 22–6, 185, 193, 204
Varney, Denise 163
Verdict, The 14
Vimeo 189
virtually acousmatic 218
virtual reality 218
virtual synchresis 218
Vitruvius, Pollio 54
VLV, Voice of the Listener and Viewer 9
vocoder 218
Voice and Personality 80
Voices of the Powerless 131
volume (sound) 12, 16, 22, 30, 60, 94, 101, 106, 109, 112, 166, 198, 200, 210, 216
Von Kunst und Kennerschaft 63
VU meter 112–13

Waggoners' Walk 156
Wagner's Method 44
Walker, Johnnie 156
Walker, Mike 191
Walls of Sound 37–40, 47
Walsh, Peter, character in *Mrs Dalloway* 68
Waltz, Sasha 163
Warburton, Nigel 188
Ward, Jamie 27–8
War Horse 70, 72
War of the Worlds 133
Wavelab 110–11
wavelength 93, 120
WAV sound file 99–100, 102
We Hold These Truths 58
Welles, Orson 2, 12, 133, 171
White, Graham 191
White, Josh vi, 13
Whitehead, Gregory 130, 185
white noise 219
white space 219
Whitsun Weddings, The 130
Williams, Mary Lou vi, 13
Wilson, Paul 38
Windows Moviemaker 178
Winston, Brian 133, 137
WMCA (US radio station) vi, 13
Wogan, Terry 156
Wonders of the Universe 9
Wood, Michael 3–4
Woolf, Virginia 67–9
Wright, Jean Ann 180
Wright, Karen 14
Wright, Steve 156
Wyatt, Hilary 173–5
Wynn, Keenan 60

XLR (connections) 104–5, 108

Young, Jimmy 156
YouTube 101, 148, 186, 189

'Zang Tumb Tumb Tuumb Tuuuum Tuuuum Tuuuum' 67
'Ziwzeh Ziwzeh Oooh Oooh Oooh' 56
Zoom H1 vii, 102